Voices of Russian Literature

Voices of Russian Literature

Interviews with Ten Contemporary Writers

Sally Laird

OXFORD
UNIVERSITY PRESS

OXFORD

UNIVERSITY PRESS

Great Clarendon Street, Oxford OX2 6DP

Oxford University Press is a department of the University of Oxford.
It furthers the University's objective of excellence in research, scholarship,
and education by publishing worldwide in

Oxford New York

Athens Auckland Bangkok Bogotá Buenos Aires Calcutta
Cape Town Chennai Dar es Salaam Delhi Florence Hong Kong Istanbul
Karachi Kuala Lumpur Madrid Melbourne Mexico City Mumbai
Nairobi Paris São Paulo Singapore Taipei Tokyo Toronto Warsaw

with associated companies in Berlin Ibadan

Oxford is a registered trade mark of Oxford University Press
in the UK and in certain other countries

Published in the United States
by Oxford University Press Inc., New York

British Library Cataloguing in Publication Data

Data available

Library of Congress Cataloging in Publication Data

Data available

ISBN 0–19–815181–0

10 9 8 7 6 5 4 3 2 1

Typeset in Utopia
by Jayvee, Trivandrum, India
Printed in Great Britain
on acid-free paper by
Biddles Ltd.,
Guildford and King's Lynn

ACKNOWLEDGEMENTS

Many people have inspired and helped me to put this book together, and I would like to thank them. The late George Theiner, then editor of *Index on Censorship*, gave me the initial idea for the project when he sent me to explore the literary scene in Russia in 1987. Several *émigré* writers and critics whom I got to know at that time, among them Zinovy Zinik, Natasha Rubinshtein, and Sergei Yurenen, gave me the benefit of their knowledge and friendship. I owe a special debt to Igor and Lina Pomerantsev, who made me welcome in their world, and influenced mine in all sorts of ways.

My work on this book involved many visits to Moscow, and I am grateful to Natasha Perova for being such a generous host to me there, putting herself, her apartment, and her address book at my disposal. She also kindly obtained for me most of the photographs in this collection. Catherine Shepherd has been a very entertaining and tolerant host on my visits to London to do research. My mother Shirley Laird helped to make the research possible by looking after her granddaughter on numerous occasions.

Inge Larsen, Helle Dalgaard, and Tanja Koleva made me feel at home in Denmark by including me in their Russian corner of Aarhus, and have been very helpful in finding Russian books and journals for me there. In England, I have enjoyed many stimulating conversations on Russian themes with Svetlana Carsten from the University of Bradford. Robert Porter, at the University of Bristol, has given me useful bibliographic help.

I would like especially to thank Martin Dewhirst from Glasgow University, who at very short notice undertook to read painstakingly through the typescript. His comments, suggestions, help with references, and not least his friendly encouragement have been invaluable to me, and his eagle eye has saved me from all manner of infelicities and errors (any errors that remain are of course my responsibility alone).

My editors at the Oxford University Press have been patient during my slow production of this book. I am grateful to Andrew Lockett for his helpful comments on the first chapters, to Sophie Goldsworthy, Frances Whistler, and Janet Moth for supervising the preparation of the book, and to Mary Worthington for her careful reading of the text and her many useful suggestions and corrections.

All the writers whom I interviewed for this book (including several whose interviews, to my regret, could not be included here for reasons of space) have been generous in giving me their time. It has been a pleasure to get to know them.

My husband Mark Le Fanu and daughter Sylvia have cheerfully tolerated my many absences while I have worked on this project. They have also given me all sorts of things to enjoy and care about besides Russian literature, and I dedicate this book to them.

Sally Laird

August 1998

CONTENTS

LIST OF ILLUSTRATIONS

A NOTE ON STYLE

In this book I have used a modified version of the standard British transliteration system. My aim has been to make Russian words both recognizable to speakers of Russian, and reasonably pronounceable and familiar to non-Russian speakers. Thus I have used 'Ye' for 'e' at the beginnings of words, and after other vowels (e.g. 'Yevgeny', 'Chapayev'); 'yo' or 'o' for ё (e.g. Pyotr), except in names where the spelling 'e' is commonly used (e.g. Khrushchev, Gorbachev); 'y' for name and adjectival endings in both ый and ий, to conform to the common British practice with names such as Dostoyevsky; 'ii' for nominative and genitive plural endings in ии and ий; 'ei' for ей, to conform with the common practice with Germanic names such as Norshtein; 'oi' for ой, except with names such as Tolstoy where the 'oy' ending is commonly used; and 'ai' for ай. The soft and hard signs have been indicated only in the bibliography and in the titles of literary works or publications given in the main text.

Except where otherwise stated, dates given in brackets after the titles of works are dates of publication.

CHRONOLOGY OF EVENTS

1932   (April) Party decree 'On the Restructuring of Literary and Artistic Organizations', involving systematic unification of cultural life under Party leadership and creation of single Union of Writers of the USSR (and analogous unions for other arts).

(May) The term 'socialist realism' is first used by I. Gronsky, Chairman of the Organizing Committee of the Union of Writers.

1934   (August) First Congress of the Union of Writers. Socialist realism adopted as the approved method for all Soviet writers.

(December) Assassination of Leningrad Party leader Sergei Kirov signals start of the Great Terror.

1935   (January) Start of mass deportations to the White Sea and Kolyma to 'avenge' Kirov's death.

1936   First of the 'show trials' of Stalin's enemies in the Party (Kamenev and Zinovev).

1937–9   Height of the Great Terror, involving 'show trials' of top members of the Party and military and mass arrests of innocent people. Over 2,000 writers are arrested, of whom half eventually perish in the camps.

1941   Germany invades USSR (June). Evacuation from Moscow and Leningrad of certain writers, artists etc. to safety in cities further east. During the war ideological control over writers is partially relaxed.

1941–4   Siege of Leningrad.

1945   (9 May) Germans surrender.

1946   (August) Andrei Zhdanov, the Party's ideological watchdog, issues a decree on literature, vilifying Anna Akhmatova and Mikhail Zoshchenko. Start of the period of 'zhdanovshchina': ideological clamp-down on the arts and xenophobic attack on 'cosmopolitans' which continues until Stalin's death.

1953   (5 March) Death of Stalin.

(September) Nikita Khrushchev becomes First Secretary of the Communist Party of the Soviet Union (CPSU).

1954   Ilya Ehrenburg publishes his novel *The Thaw*, signalling new direction in literature and giving name to the period that follows.

(December) Second Congress of the Union of Writers takes place (with only 20 per cent of original members alive to participate), becoming occasion for first denunciation of Stalin's repressions.

1955   Founding of the journal *Yunost'* (Youth) in which many young writers of the Thaw period make their name.

1956   (February) Twentieth Congress of the CPSU. Khrushchev makes his 'Secret Speech' denouncing Stalin's crimes. Start of 'rehabilitation' of writers and others repressed under Stalin.

Publication of liberal anthology *Literaturnaya Moskva* (Literary Moscow), edited by Konstantin Paustovsky.

1957   Boris Pasternak's novel *Doctor Zhivago* is published in Italy.

1958   Pasternak awarded the Nobel Prize for Literature but forced to renounce it after being attacked by the Union of Writers for his 'betrayal'.

The conservatively orientated Union of Writers of the Russian Republic (RSFSR) is founded.

1959   Andrei Sinyavsky (alias Abram Terts) publishes his essay 'What is Socialist Realism?', together with other works, in France.

1962   (November) *Novy mir* publishes *One Day in the Life of Ivan Denisovich*, by Aleksandr Solzhenitsyn.

1964   (February) Iosif Brodsky is arrested.

(October) Khrushchev is deposed. Leonid Brezhnev succeeds him as General Secretary of the CPSU.

1966   (February) Trial of Andrei Sinyavsky and Yuly Daniel.

1967   (May) Fourth Congress of the Union of Writers takes place. Solzhenitsyn writes letter to delegates calling for abolition of censorship.

1969   (November) Solzhenitsyn expelled from Union of Writers.

1970   Aleksandr Tvardovsky removed as editor of *Novy mir*.

(October) Solzhenitsyn awarded Nobel Prize.

1974   (February) Solzhenitsyn expelled from USSR.

1979   Publication of uncensored anthology *Metropol'*, edited by Vasily Aksyonov *et al.* Expulsion of Yevgeny Popov and Viktor Yerofeyev from Union of Writers.

Brezhnev awarded Lenin Prize for literature.

1982   (November) Death of Brezhnev. Yury Andropov succeeds him as General Secretary of the CPSU.

1984   (February) Andropov dies. Konstantin Chernenko succeeds him.

1985   (March) Mikhail Gorbachev comes to power following Chernenko's death.

1986   Gorbachev summons leaders of Writers' Union in advance of their Eighth Congress (June) to urge idea of *glasnost* (openness).

New editors appointed to run leading journals.

Vladimir Nabokov published for first time in Soviet Union.

1987   Publication of many formerly banned works includes Anna Akhmatova's *Requiem* and Mikhail Bulgakov's *Heart of a Dog*. Fazil Iskander and Andrei Bitov publish previously censored works.

Yevgeny Popov reappears in print.

Poems by Iosif Brodsky published in *Novy mir* (December) after he is awarded Nobel Prize.

1988   Pasternak's *Doctor Zhivago* published in *Novy mir*. Among many others, previously banned works by Boris Pilnyak, Andrei Platonov, Varlam Shalamov, Yevgeny Zamyatin, and Vasily Grossman appear.

Yury Bondarev, head of conservative RSFSR Union of Writers, attacks *glasnost* for destroying fine Soviet writers.

New Congress of People's Deputies created, including some non-Communists.

1989 (March) New statutes written for Union of Writers. No mention made of socialist realism.

Liberal writers form Committee to Support *Perestroika* ('Aprel').

1990 New law 'On the Press and Other Mass Media' puts end to censorship.

The weekly *Literaturnaya gazeta* and certain literary journals disaffiliate themselves from Union of Writers.

74 leading conservatives protest to Party leadership against new liberalism. Reactionary newspaper *Den'* is founded.

Viktor Yerofeyev publishes 'Wake for Soviet Literature'.

Solzhenitsyn's works published in *Novy mir, Nash sovremennik, Neva, Zvezda,* and *Druzhba narodov.*

1991 (June) Boris Yeltsin elected President of the Russian Republic (RSFSR)

(July) Reactionary writers sign an open letter, 'A Word to the People', saying the country must be 'saved from destroyers'.

(19–21 August) Attempted coup against Gorbachev. Yeltsin successfully leads movement to take power both from Gorbachev and the organizers of the coup.

(23 August) Yeltsin suspends Communist Party in Russia.

Gorbachev resigns as General Secretary of the CPSU.

New liberal leadership elected for Union of Writers.

(December) Commonwealth of Independent States (CIS) replaces USSR. Gorbachev resigns as overall leader.

1992 (January) Removal of price controls on 90 per cent of goods and privatization of state assets.

Commonwealth of Writers' Unions created.

(June) Rival International Association of Writers' Unions established by conservatives from RSFSR Union.

(December) First 'Booker Prize for the best Russian novel of the year' awarded to Mark Kharitonov.

1992–3 Yeltsin battles with reactionary Russian parliament over economic reforms. Battle reaches climax in September 1993 after Yeltsin suspends parliament. Attempted 'White House' coup by anti-reformists crushed by government troops on 4 October.

1993 (December) Ultra-nationalist 'Liberal Democrats' led by Vladimir Zhirinovsky win unexpectedly large vote in new elections to Russian Duma (parliament).

1995 (December) New elections to Duma reduce power of right-wingers and Communists.

Ratification of new Constitution of Russia.

1996 (June–July) Yeltsin re-elected President in run-off with Communist leader Zyuganov.

INTRODUCTION

The ten writers presented in this collection are among the finest writing in Russian today. They range from Fazil Iskander, who began his career in the 1950s, to Viktor Pelevin, who published his first work when the Soviet Union was on the brink of collapse. Together, they offer an insiders' account of the fate of Russian literature over the last four decades, from the post-Stalin Thaw, through the repressions of the Brezhnev years, to the heady revival of literature under *glasnost* and the radical recasting of the writer's role in the post-communist market-place.

Since the war, news of Russian literature has come to the West primarily by way of political scandal. The humiliation of Boris Pasternak, the trial and exile of Iosif Brodsky, the arrest of Sinyavsky and Daniel, and the persecution of Aleksandr Solzhenitsyn for his monumental exposé of the Soviet regime all propelled these writers to international fame. In the late 1970s and early 1980s the suffocating atmosphere of censorship and repression forced a host of other talented writers, musicians, ballet-dancers, artists, and film-makers into protest and exile. Never, perhaps, has a country scored such a spectacular series of own goals as did Russia in the twilight of the Brezhnev era.

Yet if the persecution of writers, and the expulsion or departure of many to the West, brought a bitter celebrity to those involved, in some ways it distorted our understanding of Russian literature as such. Russian writers were read less for their contribution to art, more for the political message they embodied. Attention was naturally focused on those whose criticism of the regime was most direct and outspoken, and who had suffered most dramatically in consequence. To take one example, the name of the poet Irina Ratushinskaya, imprisoned and exiled in the 1980s for her anti-Soviet beliefs, is perhaps more familiar to readers in Britain—where an active campaign for her release was conducted—than that of Aleksandr Kushner, one of the finest Russian poets of the century, who has lived all his life in St Petersburg. There has been a tendency to assume a stark polarity between 'dissident' writers who fetched up in the West and 'conformists' who toed the Party line at home. Yet among those forced or pressured into exile, by no means all were political crusaders; in many cases their 'dissidence' lay simply in the assumption that art should be free from ideological directives of any kind. Meanwhile, despite the fact that much of their work remained unpublished until the late 1980s, many of the most innovative and artistically subversive writers remained in the Soviet Union. Alongside the didactic realism espoused by many among both the regime's defenders and its detractors, other traditions were developed and pursued, both in Russia and in emigration.

One purpose of this book, then, is to present this more complex picture, and to give voice to writers whose contribution may have been eclipsed, in the West, by too great an emphasis on what Vladimir Makanin calls the 'beautiful', or heroic, biography. In actual fact, as these interviews show, history by itself has afforded fairly spectacular biographies to most Russians, at least above a certain age. But the reflection of their experience in literature has been subtle and varied. The present collection, it is hoped, may give the reader some sense of how rich and multi-faceted the Russian literature of the past forty years has been, and how complex the path of those who have sought, against the odds, to express their own individual vision as artists.

It should be said at the outset that the writers included here are not intended to be 'representative'. A writer, in the end, can represent only himself. All of the writers presented here have been included because I admire their work and because I believe they have interesting things to say about their experience. But it goes without saying that they are not the only contemporary writers worthy of attention.

Some of those included are—at least in Russia—well-established figures; others are relatively new to the literary scene. In most cases I made their acquaintance in the late 1980s, when I was doing research on the impact of *glasnost* for the magazine *Index on Censorship*. It was during this period that many of the writers here first made their name or achieved new popularity. Lyudmila Petrushevskaya and Yevgeny Popov had been able, for the first time, to publish collections of their prose, while Tatyana Tolstaya, a newcomer, had just made her début to much controversy and acclaim. Andrei Bitov and Fazil Iskander were enjoying a renaissance of popularity after almost a decade in the shade, while Vladimir Makanin had finally emerged from critical obscurity as one of the most interesting writers of his generation. Vladimir Sorokin, though still unpublished in Russia, had achieved a certain notoriety as a key figure in the literary underground, while Zufar Gareyev and Viktor Pelevin were just embarking on their careers. It would be a couple of years before the *émigré* Igor Pomerantsev, a subtle commentator on the scene from afar, would find a home for his own work in Russia, but his name was already known through radio broadcasts. It was partly with his help that I embarked on exploring the Russian literary scene in 1987. Two of the interviews included here date from that time; the others were conducted between 1991 and 1994.

None of the writers presented here would at any time have called himself or herself a dissident. To the extent that they have concerned themselves with politics, they belong, to be sure, to the 'liberal' camp: their anti-Stalinism can be taken for granted, as can their belief in human values and complexities that lie beyond the narrow confines of ideology. But with the exception of Fazil Iskander, who served a brief term as a member of the Russian parliament, none of them has been actively engaged in politics; as writers their concerns—moral, literary, aesthetic—have lain elsewhere. Nor have most of them suffered any direct persecution in the form, at least, of imprisonment or exile. Igor Pomerantsev, the one exception, was briefly arrested in the late 1970s and subsequently forced to emigrate; but in his work he wears this martyrdom lightly, making virtually no reference to his own treatment at the hands of the KGB. Apart from Tatyana Tolstaya, who now teaches in the United States, all the other writers in this collection have lived and worked for most of their lives in Russia.

But that is not to say that their careers have been straightforward. A brief survey of political and literary developments over the past four decades may help to set both their work, and their words in the interviews that follow, in clearer context.

The oldest of the writers in this collection belong to the generation that grew up under Stalin and came of age in the Thaw. Fazil Iskander, born in 1929, celebrated his twenty-fourth birthday the day after Stalin died. Andrei Bitov, Vladimir Makanin, and Lyudmila Petrushevskaya, all born in the late 1930s, were then in their teens. All of them had lived through war and famine. But quite what else they—or their families—had survived would become apparent only later, when the horror of Stalin's rule began slowly and partially to be revealed in the late 1950s and early 1960s. The job of uncovering the truth belonged, in the first place, to older men and women—to writers such as Vladimir Dudintsev* and Aleksandr Solzhenitsyn,† both born just after the Revolution; Aleksandr Tvardovsky,‡ 40 when he first became editor of the journal *Novy mir*, and the veteran Ilya Ehrenburg.§

The Thaw was thus experienced at different levels, by its principal agents on the one hand and by its younger beneficiaries on the other. Its key features were, of course, the revelation of Stalin's crimes, first set in motion by Khrushchev's 'secret' speech to the Twentieth Party Congress (1956); the partial relaxation of ideological control over literature, to make way for a more elastic interpretation of 'socialist realism';¶ the recovery of part, at least, of the suppressed literary heritage of the

---

* Vladimir Dudintsev (1918–98) served as an officer in the Second World War and worked in the military procuracy before becoming a correspondent of the newspaper *Komsomol'skaya pravda* (Komsomol Truth) in the late 1940s. He made his name in 1956 with the publication of his controversial novel *Not by Bread Alone*, about the conflict between an inventor and the Stalinist bureaucracy that represses him. A second novel, *White Robes*, written in the 1960s, was published only twenty years later in 1987.

† Aleksandr Solzhenitsyn, b. 1918, educated as a mathematician, historian, and philosopher, was arrested in 1945 for alleged 'anti-Soviet agitation' while serving as a soldier on the front, and sentenced to eight years in the camps and a further three in exile in Central Asia. This experience became the basis for his novella *One Day in the Life of Ivan Denisovich* (1962) and his subsequent novels *Cancer Ward* and *The First Circle* (both published abroad in 1968 but not until 1990 in the Soviet Union). His courageous opposition to censorship and repression, and especially the publication abroad of *The Gulag Archipelago* (1973–5; first published in Russia in 1990), in which he documented the history of repression in the Soviet Union from 1918, led to his forced exile in 1974.

‡ Aleksandr Tvardovsky (1910–71) first made his name in the 1930s with 'orthodox' narrative poems such as *The Country of Muraviya* (1936), awarded the Stalin Prize in 1941 for its depiction of collectivization. A Party member since 1940, he was entrusted in 1950 with the editorship of the journal *Novy mir*, turning it during his stewardship (1950–4, 1958–70) into the principal platform for liberal opposition to Stalinism (see below). His poem *By Right of Memory* (written in 1967–8), which depicted the true impact of collectivization in describing the fate of his own father, a persecuted 'kulak' ('rich peasant'), was published in Russia only posthumously in 1987.

§ Ilya Ehrenburg (1891–1967), best known for his novel *The Thaw* (1954), became a revolutionary in his teens, emigrating to Paris in 1908 and returning to Russia after the Revolution. He spent much of the period 1921–41 abroad on official assignments, including a stint in German-occupied Paris, an experience which led to his Stalin Prize-winning novel *The Fall of Paris* (1942). Although much of his earlier work had reflected the official Party line, after Stalin's death Ehrenburg became one of the prime movers in helping to 'rehabilitate' the repressed writers of the 1920s, especially Isaak Babel and Marina Tsvetaeva. His most important work in this respect was his memoir *People, Years, Life* (1961–6).

¶ 'Socialist realism' was adopted as the approved method for Soviet writers at the First Congress of the Union of Writers in 1934. The method required that writers give a 'truthful (*pravdivoye*), historically concrete depiction of reality', not necessarily as it was now, but 'in its revolutionary development', and that literature should serve 'the tasks of ideational transformation (*ideinaya peredelka*) and education in the spirit of socialism'. Later, the untranslatable terms 'partiinost' and 'narodnost' (implying 'faithfulness to the Party' and 'accessibility to the people') were added to the definition. The imposition of this 'method', and the creation of the Union of Writers itself, were the means by

1920s and 1930s; and the reopening of channels to and from the West, which enabled Soviet citizens for the first time to read Faulkner and Hemingway, Sartre and Camus, to admire Audrey Hepburn and experience Fellini, to listen to jazz, and even dance to rock'n'roll.

For writers of the older generation, these luxurious imports meant little compared with the freedom at last to tell (part of) their own story. Only they could fully appreciate what that freedom meant. They had witnessed at first hand not only the impact of Stalin's Terror on the population at large, but the gradual suffocation of literature since the 1930s and the decimation of their own ranks: it has been estimated that some 2,000 writers were arrested during the Stalin period, of whom at least half perished in the camps. In the extreme, xenophobic closure of Soviet society just after the war, when Andrei Zhdanov—the original champion of 'socialist realism' at the First Writers' Congress in 1934—presided over the vilification of some of the country's best writers and the vicious campaign to rid Soviet culture of 'cosmopolitan' (i.e. Jewish) elements, Soviet literature had reached the nadir of its fortunes. Urged to depict a life of ease and joy in a society supposedly freed of all conflict, hack writers such as Semyon Babayevsky had become almost surreally removed from the grief and trauma that surrounded them.

It was against this background that Soviet readers turned so eagerly to works such as Ehrenburg's *The Thaw* (1954), the novel that was to lend its name to the era, to Vladimir Dudintsev's *Not by Bread Alone* (1956), and to numerous other memoirs and fictional evocations of the period. Taking the lead in publishing these works was the journal *Novy mir*, which reached the height of its critical reputation with the publication, in 1962, of Solzhenitsyn's *One Day in the Life of Ivan Denisovich*, the first work published in the Soviet Union to deal with the experience of Stalin's camps.

These works played a crucial role in the 'de-Stalinization' campaign; for millions of ordinary people they represented the first truthful expression of their own experience. Yet their authors were also, in important respects, creatures of their time. Men such as Ehrenburg, Dudintsev, and Tvardovsky believed that Stalinism had corrupted the Party and profoundly distorted its cause; yet they did not reject the cause itself or ultimately dispute the Party's right to leadership. They saw that Soviet literature under Stalin had become an instrument of deception; yet they believed in the use of literature for 'good' propaganda, and in the responsibility of the writer to impart a clear moral message. Solzhenitsyn's sphere of criticism, of course, would eventually encompass the entire Soviet enterprise. Yet, as he freely admitted, he himself had been a fervent Marxist-Leninist in his youth; and like many a convert, he carried into opposition some of the ardour and intolerance of his original beliefs. Self-irony or ambivalence were foreign to his work.

For the new generation, the works of these writers were important in revealing, at

which Stalin sought to make literature an instrument of Party policy and bring writers to heel on pain of exclusion from cultural life, arrest, torture, and ultimately death. (For an account of the fate of Russia's suppressed writers, see Vitaly Shentalinsky, *The KGB's Literary Archive*.) While the methods employed to enforce it became much less draconian after Stalin's death, and especially after *glasnost* (see below), 'loyalty to the Party' officially remained a requirement right up to the demise of the Soviet Union. 'Socialist realism' was not dropped from the statutes of the Writers' Union until 1989.

least partially, the forces that had dominated their own childhood and youth. Yet their attitude towards the past was necessarily different. They themselves were not implicated, thus far, in their country's fate; there was a natural impulse to draw a line between themselves and their parents' generation and to establish a distinct, 'post-Stalinist' identity. The most popular young poet of the era, Yevgeny Yevtushenko (b. 1933), summed up their demands—and their accusations—in the loud proclamation 'Lying to the young is wrong!' But works such as Vasily Aksyonov's *Ticket to the Stars* (1961) described not just the desire for truth, but a more deep-seated restlessness and scepticism in a generation that had from afar glimpsed freedom in the culture of the West.

As important as the revival of links with the rest of Europe was the search among this generation for roots and connections in pre-Stalinist Russia. The recovery of (selected) works by the repressed writers of the 1920s and 1930s—Akhmatova, Tsvetayeva, Mandelshtam, Platonov, Olesha, and Bulgakov—gave impetus to renewed experiments in form and style. There was a move away from the grand, omniscient narratives of the 1930s and 1940s towards smaller-scale works which reflected both a distrust of the overbearing statement and a search for sincerity at the more personal, subjective level. When writers such as Yury Trifonov and Andrei Bitov turned to explore the past, it was with questions rather than answers. Doubt, complexity, irony, and ambivalence would become part and parcel of their artistic style.

The Thaw thus spawned not only a youth movement but a new breed of Soviet intelligentsia—or, perhaps more accurately, it allowed the intelligentsia at least partially to recover its identity. At an institutional level these developments were sanctioned through the revival of the Writers' Union as a quasi-independent body; the creation of several new journals, including *Yunost'* (Youth), where writers such as Iskander, Aksyonov, Yury Nagibin, Bella Akhmadulina, Yevgeny Yevtushenko, and Andrei Voznesensky first made their name; and the establishment of 'Poetry Days', on which the new poets would publicly declaim their verse. At their height, in the late 1950s, these readings could fill an entire football stadium with young people high on a sense of recovered freedom. Enthusiasm soon spilled over into unofficial activities too. Young Muscovites took to gathering in Mayakovsky Square, round the newly erected monument to the poet, for impromptu readings of their own poetry. Under the inspiration of Konstantin Paustovsky,* two virtually uncensored collections of writing, introducing a number of new names and reviving others that had been suppressed, were published independently of the authorized channels.

Meanwhile, however, the Stalinist old guard was still in place. At the long-postponed Second Congress of the Writers' Union, held seventeen years behind schedule in 1954, speaker after speaker had denounced the false literature of the Stalin years. But the bureaucrats who had presided over the suppression of their

---

* Konstantin Paustovsky (1892–1968), best known for his lyrical autobiography *Story of a Life*, begun just after the war but published only in 1966. Like Ilya Ehrenburg, Paustovsky worked actively after Stalin's death to help rehabilitate repressed writers such as Bulgakov, Babel, and Olesha. He was the principal editor of two 'liberal' anthologies, *Literaturnaya Moskva* (Literary Moscow, 1956) and *Tarusskiye stranitsy* (Tarusa Pages, 1961).

fellow writers, and in some cases signed the warrants for their arrest, were almost all reappointed to their positions. Aleksandr Fadeyev, General Secretary of the Union since 1946, committed suicide in the wake of the Twentieth Party Congress. But many of his accomplices weathered the Thaw to recover their power under Brezhnev.

Writers such as Aleksei Surkov, who took over from Fadeyev as General Secretary of the Union, watched with anger and alarm both the growing power of *Novy mir*, which was becoming increasingly outspoken, and the rise of a 'decadent' youth culture strongly influenced by the West. At the Third Congress of the Writers' Union in 1958, the conservative establishment rallied its forces. A new organization, the Writers' Union of the Russian Republic (RSFSR), was established with its own weekly newspaper, *Literaturnaya Rossiya* (Literary Russia) and two new journals: *Moskva* (Moscow) and *Nash sovremennik* (Our Contemporary). Together with the established journal *Oktyabr'* (October) and the new, conformist youth journal *Molodaya gvardiya* (Young Guard), these new publications became the vehicles of reaction to the new liberalism of *Novy mir* and *Yunost'*. For the first time since the early 1930s, in other words, there was open disagreement within the 'official' literary world itself.*

Throughout this time, Khrushchev performed a balancing act. His wavering commitment to the 'liberal' cause was reflected in the changing fortunes of Aleksandr Tvardovsky, temporarily ousted from the editorship of *Novy mir* in 1954 but reinstated in 1958. Alarmed by the uprisings in Poland and Hungary in 1956, in which writers and intellectuals had played a key role, Khrushchev personally reminded a group of leading writers of their duty to submit to 'Leninist guidance' in matters of literature and art. In 1958 the need for 'vigilance' was clearly demonstrated, to those at the top, by the scandal that erupted over the award of the Nobel Prize to Pasternak,[†] following the publication abroad of his novel *Doctor Zhivago*. At this point even *Novy mir* joined in the general condemnation of Pasternak's 'betrayal'. Yet the campaign for de-Stalinization continued, not least under pressure from the writers grouped around *Novy mir*. In 1962 Solzhenitsyn's *One Day in the Life of Ivan Denisovich* was published with Khrushchev's personal authorization.

There was a certain logic in these apparent reversals. Like Gorbachev thirty years later, Khrushchev saw no contradiction in the concept of 'sanctioned freedom'. To the extent that it enabled them to function more effectively, writers and artists were

---

* As Vladimir Makanin remarks on p. 58, the 'thick' literary journals, which include both original literature, criticism, and social and political commentary, have since the 19th cent. played a key role in Russia's literary and social development (one reason why, as Makanin points out, publication in the leading journals has often carried greater prestige than publication in book form).

† Boris Pasternak (1890–1960) published his first collections of verse before the Revolution, but established his reputation as one of the finest lyrical poets of the new century with *My Sister, Life* (1922) and *Themes and Variations* (1923). Unable to adapt to the requirements of Stalinist literature, Pasternak restricted himself after 1936 principally to translations (including distinguished Russian versions of Shakespeare's tragedies). During the war he was able to publish two further collections of poetry, and in 1954 the journal *Znamya* published ten poems from his novel *Doctor Zhivago*. But the novel itself, which depicted the spiritual impact on the eponymous poet-hero of the Revolution and the years that followed, was rejected with fierce criticism by *Novy mir*. After the novel was published abroad in 1957, helping to earn the author the Nobel Prize in 1958, Pasternak was condemned as a traitor, publicly vilified, and forced to renounce the prize. He remained an outcast until his death. *Doctor Zhivago* was eventually published by *Novy mir* in 1988.

to be put on a longer leash. But they were still bound ultimately to serve the interests of the Party. The Party's programme had changed, but the writer's duty in relation to it had not. Any attempts to circumvent the official channels—by publishing one's work independently or abroad—were frowned upon. Nor did Khrushchev, a man of simple tastes, have time for anything remotely avant-garde. His limits in this respect were plainly demonstrated in his vulgar attack on modernist painting at the Manezh exhibition in 1962, an attack which gave comfort to the conformists and sparked a fresh offensive against 'formalism', 'negativism', and 'bourgeois influence'.

With the removal of Khrushchev in 1964, the conservatives could draw a sigh of relief. Under Mikhail Suslov, the leading ideologue of the Brezhnev era, there was a clamp-down on anti-Stalinist criticism and a renewal of hostility towards the West. The carnival of youth was over, and so was the heyday of *Novy mir*, from which Aleksandr Tvardovsky was permanently removed as editor in 1970.

For many, the event which marked the end of the Thaw was the arrest in 1965 of Andrei Sinyavsky and Yuly Daniel, both of whom had published their work abroad under pseudonyms. In 1956 Sinyavsky, a young literary scholar and specialist on Pasternak and Gorky, had written a brilliant article, 'What is Socialist Realism?', in which he exposed the contradiction at the core of that doctrine, arguing that the classical, dispassionate, analytical style, adopted from nineteenth-century realism as the 'correct' approach for Soviet literature, was inherently incompatible with its ideological message. He advocated, instead, the practice of a 'phantasmagorical' art which would more accurately capture the grotesque realities of the era, and made his own excursion into that genre in a series of fantastic, satirical tales.

Sinyavsky's sophisticated analysis put him at odds not only with the Stalinist old guard but with many members of the liberal establishment grouped around *Novy mir*. Hence his decision to send his work to France, where it was published from 1959 onwards under the pseudonym Abram Terts. The young satirist Yuly Daniel ('Nikolai Arzhak') had followed a similar trajectory. Their work, in particular Sinyavsky's essay, provoked a flurry of speculation abroad and a frenzied search for the perpetrators at home. Discovered in 1965, they were brought to court the following year in a surreal trial at which, for the first time, works of fiction became the central *corpus delicti*. Both were condemned to several years' hard labour; Sinyavsky eventually emigrated to France in 1973.

But this spectacular trial was not quite the victory for the authorities, nor the return to Stalinism, that it appeared to be. The defendants' calm—almost mocking—rebuttal of the charges against them served to break for good the spell of the Stalinist show trials, and inspired vociferous protests at home and abroad. Indeed, the birth of the human rights movement, conducted through the medium of *samizdat* (the circulation of unpublished material, usually in typescript) and the growing use of foreign radio stations, which broadcast back to the Soviet Union documents smuggled abroad, can be dated from this trial.

The extent of this movement should not, of course, be exaggerated. The penalties for anything construed as 'slander' or 'anti-Soviet agitation and propaganda' (imprisonment, exile, or hard labour for up to ten years, sometimes more) were sufficiently severe to ensure that most people kept their heads down and their mouths shut in public. Beneath the surface, however, there was growing disillusionment, cynicism, and contempt. The hope and idealism that had briefly flared in the Thaw had been effectively put out. Each new incident of repressed protest, news of which was often passed along the grapevine, served further to alienate the liberal intelligentsia.

For the next twenty years, the Soviet authorities could do little more than operate a policy of 'containment'. The fear and the sense of isolation engendered by the Terror were greatly diminished. The Thaw had served to identify the anti-Stalinists as a distinct group, and in some cases lent them an authority which made them invulnerable, at least to arrest. The Fourth Congress of the Writers' Union in 1967, planned as a celebration of writers' solidarity on the fiftieth anniversary of the Revolution, was thrown into disarray by Solzhenitsyn's letter to the delegates, calling for a proper discussion of censorship and the role played by the Union in the repression of writers. The authorities reacted to Solzhenitsyn's insubordination by expelling him from the Union (1969) and eventually from the USSR (1974). But by that time the damage had been done. Solzhenitsyn's works, including *The Gulag Archipelago*, had been published abroad to international acclaim, and through smuggled copies and radio broadcasts their contents were soon well known to thousands of Soviet citizens.

Privately, the authorities must have known that their battle to win the hearts of the intelligentsia was lost. Under the leadership of Brezhnev and Kosygin, their policies were directed rather at making life safe, stable, and comfortable for themselves. The Writers' Union played its part in this scheme by operating its own system of pressures and incentives. Through membership of the Union, 'loyal' writers reaped substantial rewards not only in the form of massive print-runs, huge royalties, and prizes, but in free apartments, medical care, holidays, and privileged access to a whole range of scarce goods and services. The system was arranged hierarchically, and the men* who benefited most were, of course, the top functionaries of the Union themselves: men such as Georgy Markov, First Secretary of the Union from 1971 to 1986, and Sergei Mikhalkov, one of the principal agents in the campaign against Solzhenitsyn, who was elected Chairman of the RSFSR Union in 1970. In most cases their contribution to literature as such was negligible; sometimes, indeed, the works of these functionaries (dubbed 'secretarial literature') went straight from printers to pulpers, for lack of interest in between. Yet it was they who determined the 'tasks' of the writer in the light of successive Party congresses; they who ensured that socialist realism (once succinctly defined by Vladimir Voinovich as 'praise of the leaders in terms they can understand') remained Union doctrine; they who had the power to 'legitimate' some writers while leaving others, such as Iosif Brodsky, vulnerable to charges of 'parasitism' through exclusion from—or non-membership of—the Union. As members of the boards of all the principal publishing houses and journals, moreover, it was they who ultimately determined what could and could not be published.

But this great edifice was not quite as monolithic as it appeared. As these interviews show, a number of good writers and editors found a niche in its nooks and crannies and were able to give each other a helping hand. Throughout the late 1960s

---

* There was hardly ever a token woman among these functionaries.

and 1970s, a surprising amount of good literature continued to be published. Yury Trifonov reached the height of his reputation in the mid-1970s with the publication, in the journal *Druzhba narodov* (Friendship of the Peoples), of *The House on the Embankment*, his subtle study of the fate of the intelligentsia during Stalin's time and after. Yury Kazakov achieved great popularity as a fine writer of lyrical short stories in the tradition of Chekhov and Bunin. Iskander, Bitov, Aksyonov, and Voinovich all continued, until the mid-1970s, to find an outlet for some of their work in *Novy mir*, though they subsequently fell foul of the authorities by sending their 'unpublishable' work abroad. Alongside Yevtushenko and Voznesensky, many more interesting poets continued to publish, among them Aleksandr Kushner, David Samoilov, Bella Akhmadulina, and Yunna Morits. Nor were serious literary criticism and scholarship entirely suppressed. Yury Lotman's school at the University of Tartu achieved international renown for its development of semiotic and structuralist analysis. Elsewhere, many critics succeeded in maintaining a sophisticated dialogue with their readers by developing a coded, 'Aesopian' form of language, planting objective and original commentaries between their routine obeisances to Marxism-Leninism.

This period also saw the consolidation of two particular schools of writing. The first consisted of a loose grouping of writers who would later be known as the 'Moscow school', as writers of 'urban prose', or just as 'the forty-year-olds' (by their approximate age at the end of the 1970s). Among them were Vladimir Makanin, Anatoly Kim, and Ruslan Kireyev, all of whom began writing and publishing in the 1960s or 1970s though they achieved critical recognition only later. Widely divergent in theme and style, they were nevertheless linked by their investigative, non-didactic approach and their interest in the subtleties and ambiguities of human motivation. Many of their heroes were men like themselves, individuals from an urban, middle-class milieu whose inner doubts, adjustments, and compromises reflected the mood and dilemmas of the intelligentsia under Brezhnev.

More immediately distinct was the movement dubbed 'village prose', the principal vehicle for which was the journal *Nash sovremennik*. In marked contrast to the work of Westernized, liberal writers such as Aksyonov and Bitov, its orientation was Slavophile and conservative. Depicting the traditional life-style and values of the Russian peasantry, writers such as Vladimir Tendryakov, Fyodor Abramov, Viktor Astafev, Vasily Belov, and Valentin Rasputin became increasingly outspoken in their critique of Soviet modernity and the destruction wrought to village, church, and countryside by collectivization and industrialization. Less tendentious, but similarly concerned with the (often comic) contrast between rural and city life was the brilliant short-story writer Vasily Shukshin, who also pursued a successful career, during this period, as an actor and film-maker.

The anti-Western nationalism implicit in the work of many of these writers evidently struck a chord with elements within the Party leadership, sanctioning a degree of criticism that would not have been permitted their more liberal colleagues. This underlying sympathy became evident in the realignment of forces that began to take place shortly before the collapse of communism, when some of these writers—notably Belov and Rasputin—were to join forces with communist die-hards in condemning the reforms and promoting an openly anti-Semitic, chauvinistic ideology of Russian nationalism. But this turnabout should not obscure the genuine contribution made by this movement to the literature of the 1960s and 1970s.

Parallel to this official culture, meanwhile, an 'alternative', or 'second' culture was gradually taking shape. At its most elementary, it consisted in the myriad, off-the-record conversations of disaffected intellectuals in their private homes. By day they went through the motions of conformity; by night they gathered at their kitchen tables to exchange the latest political jokes, pass on news gleaned from foreign radio stations (attempts at jamming were never entirely effective), and listen to 'magnitizdat': copied tapes of music by the new bards of the age: Aleksandr Galich, Bulat Okudzhava, and Vladimir Vysotsky, whose ballads, sung to a guitar, captured their own mood of melancholy irony. Some were in contact with foreign visitors, and were able to pass on smuggled literature published by the growing number of *émigré* publishing houses and journals; others took the risk of retyping and circulating *samizdat* typescripts. Writers who despaired of publication read their work aloud to select gatherings or, like Lyudmila Petrushevskaya, found an outlet through the 'amateur' performance of their plays in makeshift theatres and private apartments.

The growing disparity between official culture and private consciousness engendered a revival of the kind of literature that Sinyavsky had advocated twenty years before: estranged, satirical works that found ready-made forms of the fantastic and grotesque in the sham, hyperbole and double-think of everyday Soviet life. Aleksandr Zinovev (b. 1922), whose satirical novel *The Yawning Heights* was published in Switzerland in 1976, and Vladimir Voinovich, whose Russian Švejk, *The Life and Adventures of Private Chonkin*, appeared in France in 1975, were both eventually forced to emigrate. But others, like Venedikt Yerofeyev (1938–1990), remained at home. Indeed, Yerofeyev's existence outside the Soviet Union is somehow unthinkable, even as his survival within it, for just over fifty years, was little short of miraculous. His novel *Moscow-Petushki* (written in 1969), which became an underground classic of the Brezhnev era, is a tragi-comic hymn to the hallucinatory powers of alcohol in all its forms. By the time he died of throat cancer, Yerofeyev had sampled most of them, along with an extraordinary range of books, jobs, philosophies, and habitats, which together formed the combustible fuel of his art.

Unlike Zinovev and Voinovich, Yerofeyev had never been part of the 'official' intelligentsia, but had lived on the margins of Soviet life and assumed from the start that his work was unpublishable. In this he resembled many of the writers who, from the late 1960s onwards, began to form a self-conscious underground movement in Moscow and Leningrad. Too young, for the most part, to have been touched by the Thaw, they had dismissed from the outset both the possibility of political reform and of personal salvation from the effects of Soviet culture. In this sense, they were immune to the kinds of despair—and hope—that would drive many of their colleagues abroad. For writers such as Viktor Yerofeyev (not to be confused with Venedikt) and Yevgeny Popov, or the poets Dmitry Prigov and Lev Rubinshtein, Soviet society—its language, its aesthetics, its mores, its madnesses—was an object of phenomenological interest, not of political speculation. At the same time they saw themselves, absurdly and inescapably, as part of the phenomenon, and entered their own works in this capacity.

True, Popov and Viktor Yerofeyev—unlike the latter's namesake—had started their careers as published authors, and even, briefly, been members of the Writers' Union. The watershed for them, as for several of their older colleagues, was the appearance in 1979 of the almanac *Metropol'*, an uncensored (and therefore unsanctioned) collection of writing which they had compiled and published with the help of Vasily Aksyonov, Andrei Bitov, and Fazil Iskander. The collection, which also included work by Voznesensky, Akhmadulina, Vladimir Vysotsky, Yuz Aleshkovsky, and a host of other, less well-known names, was above all an expression of protest against censorship and bureaucracy. Like *Literary Moscow* and *Tarusa Pages*, the unofficial collections which Paustovsky had helped to publish two decades earlier, it contained nothing that could be construed as directly 'anti-Soviet'. But its appearance alone outraged the authorities. Popov and Viktor Yerofeyev were expelled from the Union; Bitov and Iskander were effectively blacklisted and denied publication, while Aksyonov finally emigrated in 1980.

With the Soviet Union in the depths of 'stagnation', *émigré* literary circles had by now assumed an importance not seen since before the war. Older *émigrés* such as Solzhenitsyn and Sinyavsky, Vladimir Maksimov and Viktor Nekrasov had been joined in the 1970s by a number of younger writers who effectively made their careers abroad, and for whom, in many cases, life in emigration became as important to their work as life 'back home'. They included Sasha Sokolov in North America, Yury Miloslavsky in Israel, Sergei Yuryenen in France, and Zinovy Zinik and Igor Pomerantsev in Britain. They found outlets for their work in the wide range of literary journals published abroad, among them *Kontinent* (Continent), *Sintaksis* (Syntax), *Ekho* (Echo), *Kovcheg* (The Ark), and *Tret'ya volna* (Third Wave) in Paris, and *Vremya i my* (The Time and Us) and *22* in Israel. Publishing houses such as Ardis in Michigan and YMCA press in Paris likewise served as focal points for *émigré* literary activity, as well as providing a crucial facility for *tamizdat*, the uncensored publication abroad of works by writers still based in Russia. Many of the new *émigrés* found employment in Radio Liberty or the BBC Russian Service, both of which served as vital cultural links and sources of uncensored news for listeners in the Soviet Union.

By the mid-1980s, then, many fine writers had either left the country or had 'emigrated internally', forming underground groups such as the 'conceptualist' circle in Moscow, where Vladimir Sorokin first made his name, or 'Club 81' in Leningrad, a group which included the poets Viktor Krivulin and Yelena Shvarts, and which—albeit under the watchful eye of the KGB—had achieved semi-official status as a literary association. The growing interest which these groups attracted abroad added to the pressure on the authorities. Crucially, however, there continued to be a powerful, if suppressed constituency for change within the Writers' Union itself. Neither *tamizdat* nor *samizdat* could satisfy the natural demand of most writers to meet their readers in their own language and country and on their own terms. Some writers, such as Lyudmila Petrushevskaya, had succeeded in publishing only a fraction of their work; others, such as Iskander, had seen their best work mauled by censorship. Even those who had continued to publish successfully, such as Vladimir Makanin, chafed at the constant supervision by and interference of the authorities. The *Metropol'* incident had heightened awareness, even among those not directly involved, of the irksome restrictions under which they all laboured, and the dispiriting exodus of many of their colleagues added to their frustration and impatience for change.

With the advent of Mikhail Gorbachev in 1985, the pressure finally erupted. *Glasnost* (openness), originally conceived only as a necessary adjunct to 'rebuilding' (*perestroika*), rapidly acquired a momentum of its own, unleashing the pent-up energies of the previous thirty years. The residual reverence for the ideals of the Revolution which had tempered the Thaw three decades earlier had withered in the interim. In a sense, the forebodings of reactionaries in the 1950s and 1960s were proved quite justified, for this time the demand for 'openness' would lead within five years to the collapse of the entire Soviet edifice.

The process began with the publication of 'delayed' literature, a euphemism for all the works that had been banned or censored during the past fifty years or more. Between 1986 and 1990 the circulation of the 'thick' journals soared as they competed to publish a backlog that included Akhmatova's *Requiem* and Bulgakov's *Heart of a Dog*, Vasily Grossman's *Life and Fate* and Pasternak's *Doctor Zhivago*, as well as works by Zamyatin, Pilnyak, Gumilyov, Mandelshtam, and Platonov that had never before appeared in the Soviet Union. The work of early *émigrés* such as Vladimir Nabokov, Mark Aldanov, and Vladislav Khodasevich was admitted at long last to the official pantheon, while Orwell's *Nineteen Eighty-Four* and Joyce's *Ulysses* were among the foreign works published in full for the first time for Soviet readers. There was a revival of interest in the Russian religious philosophers, such as Nikolai Berdyaev and Vladimir Solovyov, who had been central figures in the 'Silver Age' before the Revolution but whose work, until the late 1980s, was virtually unknown to Soviet readers.

Meanwhile a number of contemporary or more recently deceased writers achieved new prominence through the publication of previously suppressed works. They included Yury Dombrovsky and Varlam Shalamov, eloquent witnesses of Stalin's Terror; Aleksandr Tvardovsky, Anatoly Rybakov, and Vladimir Dudintsev, figures from the Thaw who had kept part of their *œuvre* buried until more propitious times; and—in a quite different key—Venedikt Yerofeyev, whose *Moscow-Petushki* was finally published in 1989, ironically in a journal entitled *Sobriety and Culture*. It was during this period, as noted earlier, that several of the writers presented in this collection returned—or emerged—into the limelight. Thus in the late 1980s Andrei Bitov was finally able to publish a complete version of his *Pushkin House*, and Fazil Iskander the full text of *Sandro of Chegem*, while Lyudmila Petrushevskaya, who had waited twenty years to publish her first collection of short stories, became one of the most controversial 'new' writers of the period. Yevgeny Popov, whose official career had been nipped in the bud a decade earlier, likewise became a popular and prolific contributor to the new literary scene.

It took a little longer for the more recent *émigrés* to be readmitted to the mainstream, but from 1989 onwards they too began to appear on the pages of the Soviet literary journals. In 1990 no fewer than five such journals competed to publish the works of Aleksandr Solzhenitsyn. Aksyonov and Voinovich were among the many *émigrés* who 'returned' in print during this period, while younger writers who had made their careers abroad—among them Igor Pomerantsev from this collection—effectively made a fresh début in Russia during the early 1990s.

Ironically, the sheer size of the literary backlog which the journals and publishing houses were now seeking to overcome meant that there was relatively little room at first for the emergence of younger writers. Initially, moreover, interest had again been focused—as it had been during the Thaw—on politically motivated works such as Anatoly Rybakov's *Children of the Arbat* or Vladimir Dudintsev's *White Robes* which resumed, in more explicit terms, the anti-Stalinist crusade embarked on thirty years before. Less attention was paid to thematically innovative or artistically experimental works. Gradually, however, a number of new names began to emerge, and with them a variety of new approaches.

Many of the new authors, it is true, continued to write in a broadly realist vein, but they investigated topics that had hitherto been taboo. Sergei Kaledin (b. 1949) set his first novella among down-and-outs and alcoholics making a corrupt living at a city cemetery (*The Humble Cemetery*, 1987), while his later *Stroibat* (1989) looks at the grim, violent life of a military construction battalion in Siberia. Both works were seen as essays in a genre that came to be known as 'tough' or 'harsh' prose—works that offered an unvarnished picture of the often brutal realities of Soviet life. Two younger authors who were also identified with this genre were Oleg Yermakov (b. 1961) and Aleksandr Terekhov (b. 1966), who likewise made their débuts in the late 1980s with works depicting the grim experience of soldiers in the Afghan war (Yermakov) and the abuse of young conscripts in the Soviet army (Terekhov). Marina Palei meanwhile offered a perspective on women's sufferings in works such as 'The Ward of the Ruined' (1991), a story set in the obstetrics ward of a backward provincial hospital.

But by no means all the new writing was in this documentary vein. Tatyana Tolstaya's stories were striking above all for their linguistic vitality and lushness; with their exquisite prose and aristocratic freedom from conventional Soviet concerns they emitted an unmistakable aroma of pre-revolutionary Russia. Zufar Gareyev and Nina Sadur, both of whom were noted for their fine craftsmanship and highly individual styles, combined elements of the surreal and fantastic in exploring the lives of loners, misfits, and the inhabitants of the Soviet 'lower depths'. Vyacheslav Petsukh brought an ironical modern eye and gamesmanship to his reworking of age-old Russian arguments in a contemporary Soviet context; while, from an older generation, Mikhail Kurayev (b. 1937) caught public attention in 1987 with the publication of his experimental work *Captain Dickstein*, a fantastic narrative set against the historical background of the 1921 Kronstadt rebellion. Andrei Sinyavsky was among the work's admirers, reading in it proof that socialist realism—some thirty years after he had rung its death knell—was now officially dead. A few years later, sitting on the jury of the first Russian Booker Prize in 1992, Sinyavsky would similarly commend Mark Kharitonov's *Lines of Fate*, the winner of the prize, for its experimental narrative and sophisticated interweaving of fact, fiction, and philosophy.

A more direct assault on the moral and aesthetic precepts of socialist realism came from a group of writers who were dubbed 'postmodernists', and who included Viktor Yerofeyev, Valeriya Narbikova, Vladimir Sorokin, and Igor Yarkevich. Their hallmarks were a general iconoclasm, a flouting of Soviet taboos on sex and other bodily functions, a scorn for the conventions of realist narrative and—especially in Sorokin's case—the parodic use of Soviet style to expose its inherent hypocrisies. The high priest of this movement was Viktor Yerofeyev, who in 1990 published a controversial article entitled 'Wake for Soviet literature', in which he argued that the liberal writers of an older generation, no less than their reactionary opponents, had exhausted their role. Many of them, he argued, had adapted so successfully to the restrictions of censorship, cultivating a sly, allusive style to express their covert dissent, that they were unable to cope aesthetically with freedom. What was needed, Yerofeyev proclaimed, was a new kind of literature, freed from the sense of social responsibility and excessive didacticism that had burdened Russian literature in the past.

Yerofeyev's article provoked a flurry of indignation, both on the grounds that it was unjust to many fine writers of the older generation, and that the kind of 'irresponsible' literature it advocated failed to meet the continuing need of Russian readers for serious reflection on their history and society. Nevertheless, it successfully captured the sense of crisis that had hit the official literary community. The Writers' Union had by now become the scene of open warfare, with the conservative, chauvinist establishment—represented by such figures as Yury Bondarev and Aleksandr Prokhanov—fighting a rearguard action to stymie political reform, while the liberals had joined forces in 1989 to condemn the Union leadership and form their own Committee in Support of Perestroika, dubbed 'Aprel' or 'April'.

In 1990 the Supreme Soviet dealt a final blow to the power of the old Union by adopting a law on 'Mass Media' that officially put an end to censorship and proclaimed the freedom of the press. As a result, leading weeklies and monthlies such as *Literaturnaya gazeta*, *Znamya*, and *Oktyabr'* disaffiliated themselves from the Union and became independent publications. The conservatives in turn retaliated by establishing their own organ, *Den'* (Day), which became the mouthpiece for Russian nationalist and anti-liberal sentiment, openly attacking Gorbachev and ideologically preparing the ground for the coup against him in August 1991.

In the wake of the failed coup, with several top officials of the Writers' Union discredited by their support for the *putsch*—and alleged involvement in its preparation—the liberals successfully elected a new leadership, including several prominent figures from their own camp. But their power was short-lived, for with the final dissolution of the Soviet Union in December 1991 the Writers' Union itself collapsed, to be replaced in due course by a 'Commonwealth of Writers' Unions', representing the more liberal organizations within the old structure, and a rival 'International Association', which included the arch-conservatives from the Writers Union of the Russian Republic (RSFSR).

Throughout the early 1990s the battle for succession, which centred on these organizations' rival claims to the considerable property of the Writers' Union of the USSR, continued to dominate the literary press, to the detriment of any genuine discussion of literature. Indeed, many of the writers at the centre of the quarrel, such as the ultra-nationalist Valentin Rasputin, had temporarily given up even the semblance of literary activity. Outsiders to the debate, including younger writers who had never been involved in Union politics, tended to call a plague on both 'liberals' and 'reactionaries'. They rightly perceived that the demise of the old order had irreversibly changed the position for all writers, regardless of their political colours. Henceforth, no single organization could afford the kinds of material and professional protection that the old, Party-backed Union had once offered its loyal members. As ordinary citizens struggled to make ends meet in the brave new world of rampant inflation and growing unemployment, readership of the literary journals had plummeted. Many readers had neither time nor money to invest in serious literature, which now, moreover, competed for attention with populist genres such as crime fiction, romance, pornography, or business 'How to' manuals. From now on Russian authors, like writers everywhere else, would have to struggle individually for a place in the sun, supplementing their literary earnings with other work and aspiring to print-runs of thousands rather than millions of copies.

With the removal of censorship, moreover, the role of writers has necessarily changed. For two centuries or more Russian readers, deprived of open debate, had looked to their writers to supply a coded commentary on social and political issues. Now that such issues are the domain of a free press, writers have lost some of their cachet as a social force—or, to put it positively, they are free to concentrate on literature for literature's sake. As Vladimir Makanin argues in the interview here, the writers who have come to the fore over the past decade are those for whom literature is an essential means of expression, not a substitute for polemical journalism or political debate.

But despite the difficulties of adjustment to which several of the writers in this collection testify, the literary scene in the 1990s has proved lively and resilient. Alongside the mainstream Moscow journals, which have so far weathered their economic crises to retain a reasonably stable, if much smaller readership than hitherto, a host of new publications has sprung up over the past few years, among them *Soglasiye* (Concord), *Solo*, *Vestnik novoi literatury* (Herald of New Literature), *Moskovsky vestnik* (Moscow Herald), and *Idiot* (Vitebsk). Older provincial journals such as *Volga*, published in Saratov, and *Ural* (Yekaterinburg), have achieved new prominence in recent years by cultivating lively circles of talented younger writers, including Aleksandr Ivanchenko and Andrei Matveyev in Yekaterinburg and the Saratov-based writer Aleksei Slapovsky, whose novel *The First Second Coming* was a runner-up for the Russian Booker Prize in 1994. While the big publishing houses of the Soviet era, such as Sovetsky pisatel (Soviet writer) and Khudozhestvennaya literatura (Artistic literature), have been forced to reduce drastically their output of contemporary literature in favour of more commercially viable 'products', their role in this respect has been partially taken over by independent new publishers such as Terra, AST, Knizhny sad, and Vagrius.

One champion of contemporary literature in the 1990s has been *Glas*, a Moscow-based magazine of Russian literature in English translation produced by the redoubtable Natalya Perova, a translator and former editor on the magazine *Soviet Literature*, together with Arch Tait of Birmingham University. Perova, now in her fifties, has also published a number of new authors in the original, including Vladimir Sorokin, whose stories—deemed untouchable by other Russian publishers—first appeared under her imprint Russlit. Zufar Gareyev, Igor Pomerantsev, and Viktor Pelevin have been among the other avant-garde authors to appear in *Glas*.

Pelevin (b. 1962), the youngest author in this collection, has proved that serious literature can still command a sizeable readership in Russia: his first collection of stories, *The Blue Lantern*, sold 100,000 copies when it came out in 1991. He has been among the beneficiaries of another institution that has given succour to Russian literature in the 1990s: the Russian Booker Prize, mentioned earlier. Awarded each December since 1992 for the best Russian novel of the previous year, it has been supplemented by an anonymously donated subsidiary prize, 'The Little Booker', variously offered, for example, for the best new literary journal, the best début in fiction, and the best collection of stories (Pelevin won the latter in 1993). Many of those presented in this collection have been associated with the Prize, either as judges (Iskander and Popov), runners-up (Petrushevskaya and Sorokin), or outright winners (Pelevin and Makanin).

Indeed the Prize has offered, each year, an excellent cross-section of current literary trends. Presenting in one forum both new names and established figures, *émigré* writers and former members of the 'underground', it has served both to reunite the disparate strands of Russian literature and to highlight—often through heated controversy—their differences of approach. Not surprisingly, many of the works considered focus on uniquely Russian themes. In 1996 the short-listed works ranged from Viktor Astafev's *I Want to Live So Much*, the realistically told story of a gifted individual whose life is shattered by the experience of war and labour camp, to Andrei Sergeyev's prize-winning *Stamp Album*, which chronicles sixty years of Russian history through a sequence of notes, documents, diaries, and snatches of verse. Other works interweave historical and documentary episodes from the eighteenth century (Pyotr Aleshkovsky's *Vladimir Chegrintsev*) and from Soviet Russia (Dmitry Dobrodeyev's *Return to the Union*) in fictional investigations of the Russian soul and experience.

As they contemplate their troubled past, writers at the end of the century may be less inclined than their predecessors to preach, condemn, or extol. Their narratives—often fragmentary and disjoined—frequently suggest the difficulty of distilling truth from subjective experience and historical distortions. But their voices are by no means always grim. Sentiment and lyricism have miraculously survived, along with an age-old Russian hilarity at the fantastic and absurd, for which life in the new Russia continues to supply all too plentiful material.

1

Fazil Iskander

(b. 1929)

Fazil Iskander is among the best-loved contemporary writers in Russia, his books regularly featuring among the 'top ten' bought by readers each year. An Abkhazi* by birth (though he writes in Russian), he has created a unique literary realm from the people, landscapes, and traditions of his native land, and drawn on its culture of toasting and story-telling to create an authorial persona of immense charm.

Iskander is a leisurely raconteur, meandering, lyrical, and humorous. The world he celebrates is one whose tastes and values are directly antithetic to those of modern, urban, northern Russia—a slower, sunnier place in which the rewards of hard labour, and the pleasures of feasting, conviviality, and neighbourliness, have not been lost. To be sure, his characters—including the children who feature prominently in his work—are far from perfect beings: they can be shrewd, selfish, and deceitful, and Iskander is funny and unsentimental about them. Still, they have not forgotten the value of friendship and kindness, and in that sense make poor material for conversion to a political ideology that respects neither.

Beneath Iskander's benevolence lies an uncompromising ethical judgement that was not lost on the Soviet authorities. It emerges explicitly in openly satirical works, like the political fable *Rabbits and Boa Constrictors*, but is implicit in all his writing. He knows that the idyll he evokes is fragile and doomed; from beyond the safe court-yards and sunny verandahs the shadows constantly obtrude. The forces that menace his world are powerful and hypnotic. But Iskander also knows that 'the thing the public hypnotist fears most is laughter in the hall'. It is through laughter rather than preaching that Iskander has tried to help his readers recover their better selves.

Fazil Iskander was born in Sukhumi and grew up there, spending his summers with cousins in a mountain village in Abkhazia. Both locations are immortalized in his

---

* From Abkhazia, on the Black Sea. See note, p. 6.

work, respectively as 'Mukhus' and 'Chegem'. Sukhumi was a bustling port in which a multitude of different nationalities—Abkhazis, Georgians, Armenians, Russians, Jews, Turks, and Persians—lived side by side and spoke each others' languages. Iskander's father, an office worker, was Persian by origin and carried an Iranian passport. In 1938 he was deported as an 'alien' from the USSR, and Iskander never saw him again: he was arrested in Iran and died in exile on an island in the Persian Gulf. Iskander was brought up by relatives on his mother's side.

After completing school, Iskander went to Moscow and enrolled as a student at the State Library Institute. In 1951 he began writing poetry, and was accepted at the Gorky Literary Institute,* where he studied alongside the poets Bella Akhmadulina, Yunna Morits, and Yevgeny Yevtushenko. After graduating, he was sent to the central Russian towns of Bryansk and Kursk, south-west of Moscow, where he worked as a reporter on local newspapers, covering, among other things, developments in agriculture. He thus witnessed at first hand the sorry effects of Soviet agricultural policy—an experience later put to comic use in his satirical novel *The Goatibex Constellation* (1966), in which a journalist sets out to explore the miraculous benefits of a new, experimental species of goat. The novel became a satire not only on the fanciful 'campaigns' of the Khrushchev era,† but on the general Soviet propensity to base policy on ideology rather than on sound science.

In 1956 Iskander returned briefly to Sukhumi, where he worked at the Abkhazi State Publishing House, and the following year he published there his first collection of poems, *Mountain Paths*. In the late 1950s, however, he returned to Moscow and became a regular contributor to the recently founded journal *Yunost'* (Youth), where several prominent writers of his generation—the novelists Vasily Aksyonov and Anatoly Gladilin, the poets Andrei Voznesensky and Robert Rozhdestvensky—were making their name.

Until the early 1960s Iskander had concentrated almost exclusively on poetry, but in 1962 he published two stories in *Yunost'*, and from then onwards turned increasingly to prose. His first collections of stories, *Forbidden Fruit* and *The Thirteenth Labour of Hercules*, were published in 1966, the same year that *The Goatibex Constellation* appeared in *Novy mir*.

Though his poetry had been admired by critics, it was through prose that Iskander won popularity and found his distinctive voice. While it was apparent to any discerning reader that he shared the moral concerns of the 'Thaw generation'—the implicit rejection of Stalinism, the concentration on individual experience and emotion—his work differed strikingly in tone and theme from the restless, sceptical, urban sophistication of contemporaries such as Aksyonov. Iskander anchored himself in tradition, not modernity, and his irony was tempered by a strong element of lyricism. He looked to the natural world for models of grace, innocence, and honour, and sought truth and sanity in the naïve vision of children. His first published stories took him back to the world of his childhood, and he remained constant to that world in almost all his subsequent prose.

Natalya Ivanova,‡ in her study of Iskander, notes his affinity with the naïve artist

---

* The Gorky Institute for Literature in Moscow was founded in 1933. It offers a four-year course of training for aspiring writers.

† See note, p. 12.   ‡ Natalya Ivanova, *Smekh protiv strakha, ili Fazil' Iskander*.

Pirosmani, and writes: 'Childishness for Iskander is a synonym for the first discovery of the world, for fresh, new vision . . . It was in childhood that Iskander found, undissipated, that store of goodness and energy which is necessary for artistic creation . . . For Iskander, the joy and happiness of childhood are the normal emotional condition of man . . .'.

This tone was the more striking because Iskander's point of reference was the terrible decade of the 1930s—a period that would try to the limits what he called the child's 'touching, profound, unconscious faith in the necessity of common sense'. But for Iskander, it was precisely the child's experience that provided the necessary measure of cruelty and horror. On the surface, his boy heroes may go along with the mania for discovering spies and saboteurs round every corner, and accept the sudden alterations to history meted out in school. Below the surface, however, they register acutely the fear and disquiet around them.

In *The Tree of Childhood* (1970) the child hero and his family listen helplessly to the sound of a cow being mauled by a bear at night; in the morning, they watch with horror and pity as the rest of the herd, incomprehending, wander up to the mutilated corpse of their fellow creature. Such scenes, with all the force of unstated analogy, enter the child's soul. Without fully knowing why, the boy in *The Old House under the Cypress Tree* (1987) is angered by the sight of a poster depicting a laughing, dancing man and proclaiming, in Stalin's words: 'Life has got better, life has got jollier.' As it happens, the boy has ample opportunity to study the poster while his father stands in a long queue for bread. 'I sensed a sort of shameful inappropriateness in [the dancer's] jolliness alongside the queue. I had nothing against his being jolly, but I felt it might have been better if he'd been jolly somewhere else, near the cinema or in the park, where music was played of an evening, or as a last resort in the privacy of his own home.'

In a recent work, *A Man and his Surroundings* (1992), Iskander describes how he pictured his autobiographical hero 'always running . . . permanently on the lookout for something funny, as if collecting arguments against grief'. The most sustained record of these 'arguments' are Iskander's stories of the boy Chik and his friends, begun in the 1970s and continuing to the present day.

In a sense, Chik is interchangeable with the 'I' of Iskander's more overtly autobiographical stories. But in the Chik stories, Iskander keeps firmly at bay the hindsight and explanations of an older self—reserving for his hero, as he says in the interview here, the on the whole 'brighter passages of life'. Chik nevertheless 'knows more than he knows he knows'. Keen-eyed and mischievous, though not unkind, he registers, and sometimes exploits, the comic hypocrisies and inconsistencies of adults. But he also discovers—slowly—the sources of their confusion. Judging one's fellow men turns out to be a complicated business. Honour consists sometimes in keeping one's mouth shut, and the urge to wreak vengeance can be tempered, at the last minute, by pity for the wrongdoer. The consequences of missing one's step morally were, in those days, peculiarly terrible. But Iskander for the most part leaves this eloquently unsaid. Growing up—without entirely losing one's capacity for laughter and happiness—is, he suggests, a complex enough business as it is.

Iskander was writing these stories at a time when his own life as a writer was becoming increasingly difficult. The days of the Thaw were long over. The trial of

Sinyavsky and Daniel in 1966, the persecution of Solzhenitsyn, and the clamp-down on the liberal journal *Novy mir* had made clear the consequences of any form of literary dissent. Iskander, though not an active dissident, felt bound to lend his signature to protests against these developments, and became a marked man in the eyes of the authorities. In 1972 he himself was to experience the direct impact of censorship in the mutilation, in print, of his *magnum opus, Sandro of Chegem*.

Iskander's most celebrated hero, the charming and unreliable Sandro—dancer, toast-master, and ne'er-do-well, trickster and raconteur—belongs to the same world as the boy Chik, and made his first appearance in a single story, published (under the title 'Sandro of Chegem') in the weekly newspaper *Nedelya* in 1966. Gradually Iskander added new episodes to the life of Sandro and his numerous relatives, conceiving the collection as a single, loosely woven work, 'a gentle parody', as he said, 'on the picaresque novel'.

As always with Iskander, the prevailing narrative tone of *Sandro* is ironic and humorous; the stories move in relaxed manner from digression to anecdote to further digression, accumulating ever more characters and details on the way. Iskander's disregard for chronological sequence, his emphasis on the natural rhythms of the day and the season, and his concern with 'universal' themes— love, sorrow, death—lend the work a mythological, timeless, cyclical quality: a quality reinforced by the work's open-endedness, for, with new episodes constantly added, it is clear that the novel (like the stories of Chik) will never strictly be 'finished'.

But as the novel expanded, ranging freely from pre-revolutionary times to the modern day, Iskander realized that here, in effect, he was painting a portrait of an entire society and culture. *Sandro* became a vehicle through which, more or less directly, Iskander would comment on the central historical events of his time—the Civil War, collectivization, the Terror, and the destruction of patriarchal tradition in his beloved Abkhazia.

The censors' treatment of *Sandro* was a bitter tribute to the seriousness of the work. More than half of the novel was cut from the version that appeared in *Novy mir* in 1972. In despair, as Iskander relates here, he eventually allowed the novel to be published in full abroad, knowing full well the likely consequences. As it happened, the appearance of *Sandro* in the United States in 1979 coincided with the publication of the uncensored literary almanac *Metropol'*, to which Iskander was one of the contributors. For the next eight years, until the arrival of *glasnost*, Iskander was effectively banned from publishing his work.

The immediate impact of the 1972 *Novy mir* publication was twofold. On the one hand, Iskander seems to have found consolation in devoting himself to the continued stories of Chik and his friends. At the same time, a new note of sarcasm was to appear in his work, notably in the philosophical fable *Rabbits and Boa Constrictors*, written at the time that *Sandro* was being put through its tortures at *Novy mir*. In this bitter, witty analysis of the nature of Soviet power, Iskander portrays a society of rabbits, ruled by their own corrupt king and his courtiers, but ultimately subject to— in fact regularly eaten by—the boa constrictors who live alongside them under the leadership of the Great Python. It never occurs to the rabbits to question the boas' rights, until one fine day an impertinent rabbit speaks up from inside a boa's belly.

Why do the rabbits connive in the boas' power? Partly because they are content with their allotted share in the order of things—lesser creatures keep them well supplied with vegetables; partly because they are enthralled by the promise of even greater prosperity—a diet of cauliflower—in the future; generally because they appear to have been hypnotized and deprived of the capacity for reason.

Iskander develops a labyrinthine plot around this theme and unleashes the full force of his comic imagination to elaborate its details. But for all its humour, *Rabbits and Boa Constrictors* is a punishing attack on the pusillanimity and corruption of the Soviet intelligentsia. And its venom, perhaps, was partly self-directed. Iskander had indeed protested 'from inside the boa's belly', but he knew that he had allowed himself—and his masterpiece—to be swallowed in the first place.

Not surprisingly, *Rabbits and Boa Constrictors* remained unpublished in the Soviet Union until 1987, the same year that the banned chapters of *Sandro* finally appeared. After *glasnost*, Iskander experienced a new wave of popularity and was even elected a deputy to parliament—an experience comically described in his most recent novel, *A Man and his Surroundings*. Confessing there his difficulty in staying awake during parliamentary sessions, Iskander reflects that the very air of parliament had been poisoned by its history. It would take a good hundred years, he suggests, to air the building and dismiss its ghosts.

Though he calls it a novel, *A Man and his Surroundings* is really a collection of philosophical and autobiographical reflections on Iskander's life and times, connected by the simple device of keeping the narrator anchored in the seaside restaurant 'Amra'. 'In order to be wise', the narrator says at one point, 'You have to think a great deal, but lazily.' As he stays nursing his drinks at the table, thoughts, memories, and people come and go. Among them is a man who, having spent years researching the life of Lenin, suffers periodically from the delusion that he *is* Lenin himself. The encounter prompts the narrator to reflect on the nature of Lenin and the kind of mind-set he bequeathed to his country. These reflections, far from pompous, shock precisely by their simplicity. Just as some people are tone deaf in music, Iskander suggests, so others lack what he calls 'ethical hearing'. Lenin was one of these. 'Lenin's low level of human understanding cannot, I think, be explained by the fact that his great revolutionary work distracted his thoughts from such things. On the contrary, his great revolutionary work was itself the consequence of his low level of human understanding. It unleashed in his soul an unbelievable, joyous energy of destruction.'

A Man and his Surroundings was published in 1992, when the final demise of the Soviet Union made it possible, for the first time, to say such things in public—although it was still a shock to see the emperor so plainly divested of his clothes. By that time, however—just after this interview took place—a different kind of destruction had taken over. A tide of ethnic unrest had swept throughout the periphery of the old Soviet Union; and Abkhazia, at war with Georgia for its independence, was among the victims and the perpetrators. The old, mixed culture of 'Mukhus' and 'Chegem' had finally gone for good.

◆   ◆   ◆

SL As an Abkhazi* by birth who's always written in Russian—and never seen any contradiction in that position—I imagine you must feel very ambivalent about the breakup of the old Soviet Union and the rise of nationalist forces.

FI I have to say that for me it's extremely sad. In various essays and articles I've tried to express my fears. The problem from the outset was that our central government lagged behind the various centrifugal forces on the periphery—and now its failure to take action in time has led to the victory of those forces. Our despotic government gave up being despotic, but without setting up the necessary democratic structures—and nationalist forces have rushed to fill in the vacuum. Pogroms are so much easier than progress. The material for ethnic conflict is always there—nations have always insulted and offended one another—but of course it's madness, vanity, to turn these grudges into outright enmity and bloodshed. I've tried in what I've written to appeal to people's better nature. Perhaps I'm a bit naïve, but maybe writers have to have a certain *naïveté*.

SL Do you feel that what has happened in Abkhazia complicates your own task as a writer—in some sense cutting off your natural relationship with your subject?

FI Of course what's happened in Abkhazia worries me especially. It's a very complex position. The Abkhazis want their independence from Georgia—there are very strong anti-Georgian sentiments there with deep historical roots. But if a new Karabakh[†] should get going in Abkhazia it will all end in tragedy. That makes me terribly afraid. It isn't just that I fear for my own particular friends or relatives—the point is that the whole place is being transformed before one's eyes, and transformed for the worse. I would hate to find Abkhazia torn apart ethnically, because precisely what inspired me about it was its multiple voices, the sense that it was a little Babylon with its own music, its own orchestra. I would hate to see that orchestra dispersed. Let's hope that the orchestra itself will come to its senses, despite all the awful conductors it's had.

But as regards my purely literary relationship to the country—to my own

Interview recorded in December 1991.

* The Abkhazis are an ethnically and linguistically distinct nation who since the 6th cent. have inhabited a region on the Black Sea to the north-west of Georgia. Declared a full republic of the Soviet Union after the Revolution, Abkhazia was demoted in 1931 to an autonomous republic within Georgia. Between 1989 and 1991, when Georgia moved to establish its own independence from the Soviet Union, unrest broke out among its ethnic minorities, including the Abkhazis. After the breakup of the Soviet Union in December 1991—when this interview was recorded—the conflict escalated, with the Abkhazis demanding restoration of their independent status. A bloody civil war broke out in August 1992, when Georgian forces attacked and occupied the Abkhazi capital Sukhumi (Iskander's birthplace). The Abkhazis retaliated with the support of the hill peoples of the northern Caucasus and heavy weapons supplied by Russia in the latter's bid to regain hegemony over the area. By September 1993 the Abkhazis had regained control of their territory. But Abkhazia's status as an independent country (unilaterally declared in 1992) has not been recognized by any other party. The war led to atrocities and heavy casualties on both sides, as well as to the destruction of Sukhumi, and created hundreds of thousands of refugees. Under a 1994 UN-mediated agreement, Georgia and Abkhazia committed themselves to a cease-fire and to the repatriation of refugees, but as of 1998 some 300,000 ethnic Georgians were still displaced, while conflicts between Abkhazi militiamen and Georgian guerrillas continued and a Russian-drafted peace protocol remained unsigned.

† A reference to the conflict between secessionist ethnic Armenians living in the Nagorno-Karabakh enclave of Azerbaijan, and the Azeri government. The conflict, which began in 1988, has led to tens of thousands of dead on both sides.

literary realm—I carry that in my heart, and no one can take it away from me. I can't change my direction as a writer. The literary tree which I keep on cultivating was planted long ago, it's sunk deep roots, and it can only grow in the direction it's started off—I can't alter its course.

SL The world you evoke in your work is in any case a vanished world, isn't it?—both objectively, in the sense that the old patriarchal world you describe has long since gone, and 'subjectively' in the sense that this was the world of your childhood—you left it for good in your twenties—and in much of your work it's seen through a child's eyes.

Childhood experience is a natural resource for many writers, but it seems to occupy a special place for you. Much of your humour is inextricably linked with the child's-eye view. Chik wants to believe in the good sense of adults, but his innocent commentaries on their doings make their behaviour absurd. In a way he's slyer and brighter than they are. But his innocence is also protective—he doesn't yet know how bad and mad the world can be, and his experience is still filled with elementary pleasures: stolen fruit, the sea, the sun, the thrill of overcoming danger and outwitting grown-ups.

Were you conscious in returning to these experiences of seeking a kind of 'refuge' from your adult knowledge of the world?

FI When I began writing those stories I didn't think about the reasons: they emerged of their own accord; I couldn't have explained why rationally. Perhaps it's true that they did constitute a certain refuge. But maybe they were also an attempt in some way to correct my own childhood. Of course I have happy recollections and these emerge in the stories. But it so happened that in my childhood the person I loved most in the world, my beloved uncle, was arrested. And then another uncle was arrested, and my father was exiled—I never saw him again. So maybe—it's very difficult to say exactly—but maybe these stories were a sort of attempt to take revenge for the fact that my childhood didn't work out too well.

In recent years I've been working on some more stories about Chik, and I've found myself reluctant to write directly about the tragic pages of my own childhood. For the time being I've come to the conclusion that I should leave Chik only the brighter passages of life—as if all this had bypassed him more or less.

SL Will you ever regard Chik's story as being 'finished'?

FI I don't know ... Once a critic asked me: what are you going to write about when your childhood is over? I said that everything depended on one's poetic relationship to a subject—and that may never be exhausted. When certain material inspires you poetically, you'll use any means to write about it. I once wrote that there's a certain principle in art—I can make an elephant out of a fly but the fly must be alive to start with. I always take as my starting-point something that really did happen—and then I let my fantasy work around it.

SL At the time when you began writing the Chik stories, in the early seventies, it would of course have been impossible to publish anything that dealt directly with the blacker sides of your childhood ...

FI Well, impossible to publish, yes, but not impossible to write about these episodes in principle. I didn't choose to write as I did about Chik just because of censorship—it was an artistic decision.

sL In fact your novella *School Waltz** does relate the story of your uncle and father. Unlike the Chik stories it's written in the first person, but it clearly belongs to the same genre, and the tone in much of the story isn't fundamentally different—it's full of humour and gaiety. It's only at the end that we feel directly the narrator's acute 'hot pain' at the news of his father's death.

FI Yes. Of course I had to wait a long time to publish that story. It was first published in *Znamya* in 1987, and even then it had to be cut. The story originally ended with two 'political' dreams—a dream about Stalin and a dream about Lenin—and when I published it in *Znamya* the part about Lenin had to be cut: you could tell the truth about Stalin then but Lenin was still taboo.

Now of course everything has changed. Recently I've written a story about Lenin[†]—an ironic, philosophical piece—about a mad professor who's spent his whole life studying Lenin and has gone mad doing it. He has this sort of flickering consciousness: at certain times he knows that he's just a researcher on Lenin, at other times he feels that he is Lenin himself.

Just the other day I read this piece at a theatre institute, and afterwards a woman came up to me, a psychiatrist, who said that I'd actually given a very precise description of a certain kind of psychological state. That was a nice compliment! Though when I was reading it people found plenty to laugh about...

sL Once—in your story 'The Beginning'[‡]—you reproached your readers for the fact that they always expect laughter from you.

FI That was meant as a joke, although there's a certain truth in it. When people get used to a certain image of a writer, it's quite difficult to change it. But I hope all the same that one can write about even the most tragic things without losing one's sense of humour.

Strangely enough, the source of my love for humour in literature was Shakespeare. Once as a child, at my cousin's home, I found a little book of Shakespeare—and since I felt like reading and there was nothing else to read I sat down to it. I couldn't make very much sense of the tragedies, but I got great pleasure out of the comedies—*Much Ado about Nothing* and lots of other things. And even as a child, without understanding much, I somehow penetrated that particular mentality of Shakespeare's fools. I must have felt that something in them corresponded to our particular relationship to reality. I saw how the jester's position gave him the possibility of speaking the truth in the guise of a joke.

sL I remember you describe your first encounter with Shakespeare in your story 'The Cock':[§] 'I realized that it was not the jesters who depended on the royal courts but the royal courts that depended on the jesters,' you wrote there. That was one of your very first stories, yet it's striking how its theme and tone are already completely distinctive, and characteristic of your later work.

FI Yes ... I began writing prose comparatively late. In the fifties I concentrated on

---

* First published in *Znamya* (1987) as *Stary dom pod kiparisom* (The Old House under the Cypress Tree).

† 'Lenin na "Amre"' (Lenin at the 'Amra'), published as the first part of *Chelovek i yego okrestnosti* (A Man and his Surroundings), 1992.

‡ 'Nachalo', in *Derevo detstva*, 1970.

§ 'Petukh', 1962.

poetry and never really thought of going over to prose. I wrote just one story—
'First Task'* at the request of some friends who were working on the journal
Pioneer, but I hadn't really thought of it as a story, it was just a sort of sketch about
a boy going to the country. I only really got going with prose in my thirties: and
'The Cock' was my first story as a conscious prose writer.

But now when I return to it I see that it's very much in tune with my later work.
It seems to me that it sometimes happens with writers that the very first thing they
write contains all the particular characteristics of their later work. The hero of the
story, a boy, has this comical relationship with the cock in the yard; they loathe
one another and get into ridiculous fights. The boy gets so hurt in the final scrap
that the grown-ups decide enough's enough, and the cock gets killed and eaten.
And then all of a sudden the boy feels very sorry for his old adversary. He realizes
how unequal the fight has been. Animals can never win against human beings.

SL Animals show up the less admirable side of humans, just as children show up the
less admirable sides of grown-ups. I see a kind of hierarchy of innocence there—
children at least understand the language your animals talk, and they're usually
on their side. Though, as I recall, the boy's sorrow at the end of 'The Cock' isn't
undiluted. He can't help enjoying the tasty meal they make of the poor bird.

FI Well, that's right. Most of the story is comic, but it ends if you like on a tragic note.

SL The 'turn' in that story is especially typical of your work: suddenly the enemy—
in this case the cock—turns into the victim and becomes pathetic. In 'The
Revenge'† you see the same thing. Chik tries to get revenge for the actions of one
bully by setting a more powerful bully on him, but he's horrified and ashamed at
the result.

FI Yes, and that's an important turning-point for him—he no longer sees anything
romantic in the powerful Motya, the big bully with steely eyes. Motya of course
ends up in gaol. But I give a clear hint at the end of that story that bullies aren't to
be found only among criminals, but also among people who are perfectly 'strait-
laced'—who enjoy power officially, in other words.

SL You began writing during the Thaw, in what we tend to think of as a period of
unprecedented freedom. In fact it was obviously a mixed time: on the one hand
there were a bunch of young writers, you among them, being given space in
Yunost' and *Novy mir* to express a different view of the world; Russia was opening
its doors to Western music and literature; Solzhenitsyn published his *One Day in
the Life of Ivan Denisovich* and so on ... On the other hand there was Pasternak
being hounded for publishing *Doctor Zhivago* abroad, Khrushchev scolding the
intelligentsia and haranguing avant-garde artists. I wonder how this period looks
to you now, in retrospect?

FI Well of course it all ended very sadly. But I have to say that the foretaste of
freedom then was sweeter than the taste of freedom itself. I remember the time
when the first signs appeared. Of course the principal sign was the Twentieth
Party Congress when Khrushchev read out his report on Stalin: at first it was
concealed from us, non-Party people, but gradually the rumours seeped out

---

* 'Pervoye delo', first published in *Pioner* in 1956, was republished in *Pervoye delo: Rasskazy i
povest'* (1972).

† 'Vozmezdiye', in *Detstvo Chika: rasskazy* (1994).

everywhere—and it seemed to us something unbelievable. The sweetness of that time is unrepeatable. It was as if a little sunbeam had suddenly peeped over the prison wall: the sensation one had was of the undreamed-of happiness of freedom.

At that time we didn't fully understand how many sorrowful events accompanied this freedom—and the freedom itself departed very quickly. Khrushchev's time was cut short and the dead season of Brezhnev set in. It was extremely sad. But despite everything there was a new sense, a real sense that one wasn't completely cowed or helpless, even after the arrest of Sinyavsky and Daniel and the persecution of dissidents started. Appeals and protests were made, some action was taken, even if the only real effect was to provoke further persecutions. I was never an active dissident myself, but I put my name to some of these appeals.

SL You say that you weren't conscious of all the 'sorrowful' events in the fifties, but the hounding of Pasternak surely made its impact on you?

FI Yes, of course I felt it very keenly, but I was still very young in a literary sense at the time, and there wouldn't have been any point in my making a move of protest even if I'd dared to do so. I suffered for Pasternak because I loved him very much as a poet; indeed, the Zhivago affair occurred at the crest, so to speak, of my love for him. Though I have to say that I was quite disappointed when I read *Doctor Zhivago*. It seemed to me that he'd somehow betrayed himself, taken a false turning. I still feel that. Here and there in the novel, in the descriptions of nature, in certain spiritual passages, one can recognize Pasternak, his special world—but it seems to me that he wanted to write a novel like everyone else and in doing so he somehow lost himself.

I don't mean that he betrayed himself in the highest spiritual sense, of course not. He just wanted to write something in a more accessible form. But I think he somehow cheapened his extraordinarily rich world, and—well, it's too late to speak of it now, but I think it would have been better for him simply to write something like his 'past and thoughts'—reminiscences about his life. Considering the spiritual energy he put into *Doctor Zhivago*, he could so easily have done it. I suspect that we lost a great book there.

But as regards my participation in any kind of protest, that came a great deal later. I think the first letter of that kind that I signed was in connection with Solzhenitsyn's letter to the Fourth Writers' Congress in 1967, protesting against censorship. Later I was presented with other such petitions: the same buttons tended to get pressed all the time. And this had its effect as far as my ability to get published was concerned.

SL In what sense?

FI Well, once for instance I was summoned to the Central Committee apropos of my story *The Tree of Childhood*, which was eventually published in 1970 by the publishing house Soviet Writer. But before that it sat waiting for a decision for a long time. There had been a whole heap of internal reviews about it, all of them positive, yet no one made a move to publish it. In the end for the first and last time in my life I appealed on my own behalf to the Central Committee. I lived on my literary work and I needed to get published. So I wrote a letter saying that I felt I'd been treated unjustly.

The director of the publishing house was a certain [Nikolai] Lesyuchevsky. I had had the misfortune to go on an official tour with him to the Baltic Republics, some time in the mid-1960s, in the course of which we were invited to the home of a certain Estonian writer, and, as often happens on such occasions, everyone had far too much to drink and our tongues were loosened. Various bigwigs from the Union of Writers were present, along with this Lesyuchevsky, and of course they were all delighted about the removal of Khrushchev, which they read as a green light for the return of Stalinism—even though nothing officially had been said to that effect. But they felt that their time had come, and, having drunk a bit too much, they all started reminiscing about Stalin's time and praising him, and I felt I couldn't keep my mouth shut, though it was interesting how the Estonian writers kept silent, didn't say a thing. Anyway I started arguing with them, and this Lesyuchevsky just turned on me and attacked me. That was the last time I was included on such a delegation! The point was that I was a completely unknown quantity to them at the time. They thought of me primarily as a humorous writer, which they found 'acceptable', but on the other hand they saw that there was this dangerous 'social' element in my writing.

These literary bureaucrats always had the illusion that they could 'use' certain elements in your writing—like your talent for making people laugh—and turn them in a direction that was advantageous to them. Maybe that was the reason they'd taken me along on that trip, to coax me into staying on their side. But it became clear that I didn't belong there, and the whole thing ended in a terrific row, though I'd done no more than to support what had been said at the Twentieth Party Congress, which, as far as I knew, hadn't yet been repudiated.

Anyway, all this time my *Tree of Childhood* had been sitting there waiting to be published, and it turned out that it hadn't got a single negative review, so there was no excuse. This Lesyuchevsky had a rather dark reputation; it was said that he'd been involved in the persecution of writers such as Zabolotsky under Stalin, and had only just escaped a Party trial after the Twentieth Party Congress. He'd escaped unscathed, but perhaps he'd been schooled by bitter experience to keep his head down a bit more. So although he could doubtless have ordered someone to write a bad review, or simply sent the story to writers known for their 'anti-liberalism', he was probably wary of being accused of partiality, and just hoped that it would happen of its own accord. He was a very sly fellow. And good reviews or no, he had the power just to sit on my manuscript. Which was why in the end I was reduced to making my appeal.

So I was summoned by some official at the Central Committee of the Party and had this long conversation, in which he said: 'Imagine what a difficult position you're putting the head of this publishing house in ... if they publish your book now, other "rejected" writers will start saying they did it only because you'd been to the top of the Party. It would look very corrupt.' It was all just sheer demagogy, of course, but he'd got a cunning argument up his sleeve. 'How come', he said, 'all these appeals you write somehow end up in the Western press and on foreign radio stations?' I got very upset at this, because I'd never sent anything abroad. Intuitively I knew that almost certainly they themselves were sending these appeals to the West, just in order to add to their arsenal of accusations against me.

I made various other 'appeals'. For instance I sent Kosygin, then the Prime Minister* of the country, a very sharp telegram protesting against the attacks on *Novy mir* and its editor Tvardovsky, and that resulted in a summons to the Central Committee as well. On that occasion I was told: if you knew what kinds of articles *Novy mir* had been planning to publish, particularly about the state of agriculture, you wouldn't be defending this journal. I replied that agriculture in our country was in such a catastrophic state that precisely such articles were needed. It was a question that concerned me very much at the time.

SL Obviously that was the starting-point for *The Goatibex Constellation.*

FI Yes, and the reason why *The Goatibex* got published was that Tvardovsky himself was very concerned about the situation of agriculture and our peasantry. He liked the novel a lot. Formally speaking it could be taken as an attack on Khrushchev's so-called 'voluntarism', although in fact the story was a satire not just on Khrushchev's mad, catastrophic campaign to make the whole country grow maize,[†] but on all such Soviet campaigns, on the whole nature of Soviet society. But Khrushchev's removal in 1964 naturally made it easier for Tvardovsky to print the thing.

SL How was it received in the press at the time?

FI On the whole the critics in Moscow were rather restrained, although there was a lot of publicity about the novel in Abkhazia. But much later I learned from a critic on *Pravda* that the novel had provoked a great internal debate there, with several people wanting to 'blast' it. But there were a few liberals in *Pravda* who argued that it wasn't worth making an enemy of a promising young writer, and in the end they gave it a neutral review, neither good nor bad. But it was salutory to realize that my fate as a writer hung by a hair then. *Pravda* could have destroyed me.

SL Presumably the public at that stage was quite unused—had got unused—to satire in general?

FI Well the public received it with great warmth; they understood its meaning very well. I got a lot of letters about it. And of course the novel isn't just satirical. It has a lot of lyrical moments in it. In general I'm not a great lover of harsh satire. I think the combination of seriousness or lyricism with irony and satire is much more interesting—more human.

SL I remember your saying once that satire was the expression of wounded love—towards an individual or one's country or humankind in general. The love and the sorrow are somehow there, along with the sarcasm.

One senses in you a desire, too, not to make things too bitter for your readers, to 'take care' of them, give them pleasure even while making an oblique moral point.

FI A German critic once wrote something like that about me—that I was a sort of hedgehog without spines! I do think about my readers more or less consciously

---

* i.e. Chairman of the Council of Ministers.

† In 1959 Khrushchev had visited the United States and been impressed there by the benefits of maize-growing. Against the advice of agronomists, he subsequently inaugurated a campaign in the Soviet Union to turn vast areas of fertile country over to the cultivation of maize. The campaign turned into a fiasco: production of other essential crops fell drastically, while in 1962 less than a fifth of the maize crop ripened and much of it proved unusable even as silage. It was because of such rash campaigns that Khrushchev was accused by the Party of 'voluntarism', the wilful imposition of experimental and often ill-thought-out new policies.

when I write, and I've had the reward of many readers writing to me and saying that my work helped to lift them out of some kind of spiritual depression.

Maybe my writing is also a way of pulling myself out of a bad mood, and this somehow affects the reader as well. But in so far as I use irony or satire it's perhaps been the result of knowing, more or less subconsciously, that you have to say the truth but you can't do so directly, you have to do it obliquely. Irony gives you that possibility—making certain twists and turns through which the reader recognizes the contours of the truth.

In that sense, however paradoxical it may seem, the existence of censorship—not of course Stalin's censorship, but the milder forms of censorship such as we had under Khrushchev or Brezhnev—perhaps gave you the possibility of refining your style. It required you not to go in a straight line but to take a more interesting artistic approach. Though what I say is controversial, and perhaps it's true only for certain writers.

SL It's a view I've heard quite often recently—as if many older writers felt disorientated by the 'loss' of censorship.

FI It's a very complex process. The picture was certainly much clearer before. The first task, for everyone, was somehow or other to fight dictatorship. Dictatorship presented a kind of wall which every honest writer was duty bound to hack away at with any instrument he possessed. And at the same time the deeper you plunged into this work, the better you carved yourself out a sort of peaceful, harmonious niche within the wall.

When the wall collapsed, everything turned out to be much more complicated. Because on the one hand there was freedom, but on the other the wall had somehow collapsed on top of us. And the country had no strength left to clear up all the resulting mess.

In the old days we felt so sure that if you could only take away censorship and the rule of the Party, a 'normal' government would result. Now it's evident how very much more complicated it is. Writers and artists have to come to terms with the fact that they found a certain harmony in those caves they'd dug themselves, a certain shelter.

The truth in those days seemed so much more obvious. Now it's much harder to seize hold of anything, to construct a certain world of artistic truth. That's why I haven't written fiction for a long time—only essays, journalism. Though now it's beginning to work again.

SL From the late fifties onwards you were a regular contributor to *Novy mir*, and you mentioned Tvardovsky's[*] particular support for *The Goatibex Constellation*. What were your relations with him personally?

FI I knew how busy he was and I didn't want to impose myself on him, so at first I shrank even from meeting him. But after *The Goatibex* was published I was invited to go and see him, and eventually I was taken up to his office on the first floor at *Novy mir* and for the first time I met him face to face. I remember how he sat there looking at me with his very small, piercing blue eyes. I immediately sensed his intelligence, his shrewdness, and later, when I met him again,

---

[*] Aleksandr Tvardovsky, then editor of *Novy mir*. See Introduction, p. xv.

I learned how attentively he read and worked on everything that went into the journal.

The journal was to publish my story 'Trout-Fishing in the Upper Kodor'*—a rather innocent story, on the whole, but there was a moment in it when the narrator gets offered, for his fishing trip in the mountains, some special caviar as bait for the trout, and he goes into a great ode over this caviar. Well it would be completely obvious to any Soviet reader that the man who offers the narrator the caviar must be from some élite, privileged circle, for only the highest officials in the land could get hold of such stuff. And Tvardovsky had picked out this point—when the story was already in proof—and asked me to remove it. Which I did, feeling slightly ashamed of myself.

SL Why ashamed?

FI Because this was just a little piece of literary hooliganism on my part, it wasn't really essential to the story, but it could have threatened the journal. I realized that Tvardovsky was in a very delicate position, constantly under attack from the Party. I didn't want to risk the life of the journal for the sake of two or three phrases which the Central Committee could have seized on—'Look, they're laughing at us,' they could have said, 'and Tvardovsky approves of their laughter and lets them go ahead.' Of course he did take risks, a lot of risks, where he thought it essential, but these few phrases weren't so important.

Anyway the point of all this is that I realized that Tvardovsky really did read everything very carefully. Many people thought he didn't bother himself with the details of the journal, and only set the general direction, but that clearly wasn't true. And he was prepared to take risks for something he thought important, but not just for the sake of having a laugh.

Novy mir also published my story 'Summer Day',† about a German who meets the narrator by chance and tells the story of how he was recruited by the Gestapo. Essentially it was a story about what a totalitarian regime does to a person, and all my friends were sure that it would never be published in our lifetime. The poet David Samoilov said to me: this is a straightforward set of instructions for how to conduct yourself in the KGB! But I believed that no one would dare to say to me: you're writing about us, not about the Gestapo—and that proved to be the case.

SL *Sandro of Chegem* was of course published by *Novy mir* too, after Tvardovsky's removal—but in a very truncated form.

FI Yes, it's the saddest story, what happened to *Sandro*. I tried to get it published in Russia at the very worst time, in the early 1970s, when Tvardovsky, as you say, had been removed from *Novy mir* and there were completely different people in charge. They tried to pretend that it was still the same journal, but in fact only a bare skeleton remained. However, there was nowhere else to go, and I decided to take *Sandro* to them.

The truth was that when I started writing *Sandro* I thought at first that it was just a humorous thing, a kind of parody of a picaresque novel. But gradually I realized that I'd been overtaken by the poetry of folk life, the life of patriarchal Abkhazia, that I was *singing* that life. And that's the direction I went in—celebrating that life

---

*   'Lov foreli v verkhov'yakh Kodora' (1969).   † 'Letnim dnyom' (1969).

on the one hand, and on the other looking satirically at everything that was happening to the country, at what had become of our little mountain village in Abkhazia, and to Abkhazia in general. Gradually a certain image of the book became clear to me. I realized that here I would write, in a sense, about everything—that I would relate through the prism of this small world all the main events of our country.

And at the same time I gradually perceived the structure of the novel—that it would all be in the form of stories, novellas. I felt that maybe I had a certain natural gift as a story-teller and that this structure would work best. I very much doubted that the whole thing could be published in my lifetime, but I thought that at least, this way, certain stories could be published, even if others got chucked out.

So I took it along to *Novy mir*. As I'd expected, the stories concerning Stalin or collectivization flew straight out of the window—I was prepared for that. But what I wasn't prepared for was that out of the remaining chapters they'd throw out all the strongest things, all the things that were most important. The whole process was sheer torture for me, and at the end of it I wrote to the editors and said I wanted to take the work back. But then they tried to compromise—they'd taken out perhaps 80 per cent of the novel, and they gave me back, let's say, 10 per cent. I gave in, and the work came out horribly mutilated. The experience for me was like handing over my beloved child and watching it being hacked to pieces.

It was at that time that Carl Proffer, who ran Ardis publishers in America, started coming here, and a friend of mine gave him *Sandro* to read. The novel had been circulating quite widely in manuscript, especially the chapter about Stalin—it was easy to retype that one chapter, and I was amazed to realize later how many people had read it. Anyway, Proffer offered to publish it. For a long time I kept prevaricating, and he kept repeating his offer. But in the end I felt that I had to rehabilitate myself, and I agreed to let him go ahead. So the novel was published in unabridged form by Ardis in 1979.

I had foreseen all sorts of unpleasant consequences, but then a strange thing happened which in a way points to the absurdity of our whole situation at that time. It was just around then that Aksyonov[*] had proposed publishing an uncensored almanac, *Metropol'*. The point was not to publish outspoken political works but just to refuse to let the censors touch our texts. So I gave him a couple of stories for the journal. As the Russians say, if you've had your head chopped off you don't weep for your hair...

In comparison with *Sandro*, which really did contain some reflections on the realities of our life, *Metropol'* was really a rather harmless, toothless thing, there was nothing too terrible in it.

So it happened that these two events occurred more or less simultaneously: *Metropol'* came out, and *Sandro* was published in America. *Metropol'* hadn't yet been sent abroad, but it had been presented at the Union of Writers and caused

---

[*] Vasily Aksyonov, b. 1932, novelist and short-story writer, was one of the editors of *Metropol'* (see Introduction, p. xxiii). In 1980 he left the USSR and emigrated to the United States, where he successfully continued his literary career. Since *glasnost* Aksyonov has again become a respected literary figure in Russia and a regular visitor to his former homeland.

an absolute uproar—not really because of its contents, which even then, as I say, seemed rather inoffensive, but just because we'd dared to break the rules, we'd refused to submit it to the censors. The whole affair was discussed at the highest level, more or less in the Politburo. They examined the whole train of events and came to ridiculous conclusions, comparing our little group with the Petöfi circle in Hungary, and the writers in Czechoslovakia who'd supposedly been responsible for 1968, and deciding that we'd have to be dealt with severely, or else ... In general an absurd amount of attention was devoted to this almanac. It was as if their entire, repressed, evil energy had been unleashed on it.

But the result was that when *Sandro* came out in America they had no psychological energy left for it. They'd already used up all their swear words and said everything damaging they could about me. And perhaps by then they realized, too, that they'd damaged themselves by overreacting to *Metropol'*, they'd actually inflated people's interest in it and given themselves terrible publicity abroad. So the direct persecution that I'd expected in connection with the publication of *Sandro* didn't materialize.

Short of arresting me there was nothing much more they could do about me anyway. I'd already been under close scrutiny because of various letters I'd signed in defence of imprisoned writers and so forth, and *Metropol'* put the finishing touches—I was effectively blacklisted. These blacklists were circulated internally—editorial boards were told that such-and-such writers were not to be published—and editors adhered to these rules.

Of course the youngest contributors to *Metropol'* were dealt with even more severely, and expelled from the Writers' Union. Obviously they decided it would have caused a further scandal to do that in the case of the better-known writers. But in any case they appeared to be politically exhausted. They simply asked me how *Sandro* had come to be published, and I pretended to be ignorant of the whole affair—the novel had been circulating in manuscript, I said, and it was out of my control.

So that was how the first major text of *Sandro* appeared.

SL But the novel wasn't complete at that stage—you added more chapters later?

FI That's right. I gave Proffer everything I had written up to that time. But later I added more chapters. The complete two-volume text has been published only this year [1991] by Soviet Writer—although earlier, from 1987 onwards, various journals had started publishing the previously banned chapters.*

SL What do you think happens when a work isn't published 'on time'—at the time it was written? What effect has it had on you, as a writer, and on the way in which your work has been received later?

FI A lot depends on the personality of the writer. *The Goatibex Constellation* was the only one of my obviously controversial works to appear on time, and it was very lucky that it did. At the time the censors 'corrected' only one phrase in the book, inadvertently making it much funnier than the original. There's a moment, if you remember, when the hero is walking round with the chairman of the collective farm, looking at the maize that's been planted on the peasants' private

---

* The publishing house Moskovsky rabochy also published a 3-vol. edition of *Sandro* in 1989.

plots, and he notices that it looks different from the maize on the collective farm. So he asks the Chairman why this should be, and the Chairman replies that it's because the peasant goes to a lot of trouble over his own plot, he fences it round carefully and stops the cows from trampling on it, whereas on the collective farms they don't bother so much. The journalist conscientiously takes notes, and when the Chairman asks him why he's writing it all down the journalist says 'It's the truth, isn't it?' To which, in my original version, the Chairman replies 'You can't write the truth, surely?' But they changed that phrase to: 'You can't write *just any* truth, surely?'—which of course is much funnier! They simply revealed their own stupidity. But this was the only change they made, so the social impact of the work was quite strong.

In general of course it's ideal that a writer should get his work published as he writes. If you have an unpublished work lying around it's like having an unborn child. The writer remains connected to the work by his blood vessels, and this gives him the illusion that the work's unfinished, there's something still to come. In order to move on to new things a writer needs to publish his work, to separate himself from it, not feel bound to it any more.

So publication is psychologically very important to a writer. There's another factor, too: a writer who doesn't get published can harbour the illusion that he has immense riches tucked away in the desk drawer, when this isn't in fact the case. Or else out of desperation he may start to make compromises and censor himself, or even add in special passages to prove his loyalty—and the problem with that is that then even the things he's written well and sincerely and honestly will start to lose their meaning. Art in general is a very capricious process, elusive, difficult, and absolute sincerity is essential to it.

SL Meanwhile the fact that so many works—not just yours but those of others—were left unpublished for so long must have made a profound difference to the overall course of Russian literature. One imagines how different it might have looked if Platonov, Bulgakov, Nabokov, all Akhmatova's works—to name just a few—had never been suppressed.

FI Yes, our social consciousness would have been completely different. Even if, let's say, there'd been an undemocratic government but literature had been comparatively free, which is conceivable in principle—it's happened elsewhere, in Franco's Spain, for example.

SL I think it's difficult to conceive of in Russia, where literature has always assumed such importance.

FI Yes—I remember the reply given by one of Franco's ministers when asked why a certain outspoken poet hadn't been arrested in Spain. He said: 'Why should we arrest him? Everyone knows that poets are mad.' It would have been much better for us if our government had taken that view. But in Russia a certain tradition and mythology have grown up around literature. On the one hand it's given writers what Tolstoy called the energy of illusion—the illusion that they can play some very significant role in society. In some ways that belief has been justified and it's helped literature to develop. But on the other hand it may have weakened literature, deprived it of that sense of pure artistry which I think is much stronger, for example, in English literature. Precisely because our governments have paid such attention to writers, they've perhaps tended to take themselves too seriously, become a bit pompous—writers can exaggerate the significance of what they write and spoil it a little.

Of course one thinks endlessly about the fate of writers earlier in the century who fell under the wheel—one imagines what might have been.

The cases of Olesha* and Babel[†] show what a dictatorial regime can do to writers who are naturally very gifted. Babel's *Red Cavalry* is still in my view the greatest book about the Civil War. For all that he in some sense poeticized the Revolution, gave it a certain pathos, as a genuine artist he saw within this poeticization the emerging face of death. He knew what was completely unacceptable. There's a moment of genius in the book when a Red Army soldier writes a letter to his newspaper, full of worry: what are we battling for, he writes, what have we been fighting for? The whole thing is incomprehensible to him.

And of course there's the Jewish theme which is very important. You see this man sitting in this little Jewish village, watching first the Reds come, and then the Whites, and both of them stealing and looting—there's a very clear sense of the absolute mindlessness of the thing, the sheer madness of it. Babel romanticized that madness, but he said a great deal of truth about it too. That's why the book was so unacceptable to the Bolsheviks: it showed this multi-coloured revolution where there was blackness and cruelty on both sides. In fact of course there was more cruelty on the side of the Reds—though it's immoral even to start making such judgements. But later fiction painted a completely false picture, with only the Whites portrayed as cruel. The truth is that any murderous war leads to bestiality on both sides.

And Olesha in his enchanting novel *Envy* saw and understood a great deal too, though when I read it now I feel how it already contains the seeds of his future defeat—or partial defeat. *Envy*, as you remember, is about the conflict between two men—one of them a big, prosperous *chinovnik*[‡] who sings in the lavatory every morning; he's a happy, useful worker for the new Soviet regime, the inventor of a special type of sausage—while the narrator, an idle bohemian, envies

---

* Yury Olesha (1899–1960), best known for his novel *Envy* (1927), retreated into silence during the Stalin years, admitting at the First Congress of the Union of Writers in 1934 that he would have had to 'lie and invent' to meet the requirements of socialist realism: the approved themes were 'not in his bloodstream'. Although he worked as a journalist during the war, his name as a writer was banned from mention until 1956, when some of his works were reprinted. An autobiographical work, *Not a Day without a Line*, appeared posthumously in 1965.

† Isaak Babel (1894–1940), the son of a Jewish merchant in Odessa, achieved literary fame with the publication in 1926 of *Red Cavalry*, a series of short stories and vignettes based on his experience as a correspondent riding with Budyonny's Cossack regiment during the Civil War. Subsequently he published two plays and a further collection of stories, *Odessa Tales* (1931). During the 1930s Babel came under heavy criticism for having treated the Civil War 'too subjectively', and in 1939 he was arrested on a series of preposterous charges, including that of having accepted an offer from André Malraux to spy against the Soviet Union for the French. All his manuscripts were confiscated, and under torture Babel denounced his own writing. He was 'tried' and executed in 1940. Babel was partially 'rehabilitated' in 1954, but it was not until the 1990s that the full details of his fate came to light (see Vitaly Shentalinsky, *The KGB's Literary Archive*).

‡ *Chinovnik*, derived from the word *chin*, meaning grade or rank in an official hierarchy of ranks, was originally used neutrally to mean 'civil servant', but acquired a derogatory meaning as 'functionary' or 'bureaucrat': in this case a functionary of the new Bolshevik state.

him his place in the world. But what's interesting is that Olesha drew an aesthetic rather than a moral contrast between the two, although the aesthetic side is just a surface symptom of what was happening underneath. He somehow created a picture in which right is on the side of this unpleasant sausage-maker; the future and the truth belong to him, and only good taste is on the side of the degenerate narrator. That's what we're supposed to believe.

Of course this was untrue at root, because in fact there was no rightness and justice in the whole adventure of Bolshevism at all; there was only coercion, maybe attended by some element of genuine illusion that this violence would bear fruit. But in Olesha's novel the force is left to one side and softened.

The point is that there was this masochistic element in our intelligentsia, an attempt to recognize their own wrongness, to blame themselves for the revulsion they felt at what looked so unattractive, but was 'in essence'—in its supposed 'future essence' at least—great and heroic.

It's striking how Bulgakov* in his early work *Heart of a Dog* understood the falsity of all this so clearly. You have the feeling with Bulgakov that he never doubted the correctness of his own vision, his intuition that these people were just barbarians who had nothing good to offer at all, now or in the future. But there were extremely talented people who gave in to this illusion: Mayakovsky,† an absolutely tragic figure, and to a certain extent both Babel and Olesha.

SL Your philosophical fable *Rabbits and Boa Constrictors* examines the way in which the 'rabbit-intelligentsia' connive in their own fate and allow themselves to be hynotized by the prospect of a blessed future full of cauliflower while the boas, their masters and murderers, happily go on consuming them. It's the most sarcastic and bitter of your works—written, I assume, in reaction to everything that had happened with you over *Sandro*, your depression at the powerlessness of the intelligentsia and the whole atmosphere of the 1970s ...

FI Maybe, although the work seems to have struck a chord even now among young people today—it was published here for the first time only a few years back [1987]. I think younger critics have looked at it on a more aesthetic level, enjoying the cartoon comedy of the work. Of course it's had its political opponents too. It was attacked very acidly in the [conservative] journal *Our Contemporary*:‡ the critic there decided that the rabbits in the work represented the Russians, and

---

* Mikhail Bulgakov (1891–1940), son of a Professor at the Kiev Theological Academy, trained as a doctor in Kiev. During the 1920s he published a series of short stories, including the satirical *Diaboliad* (1926), but much of his work, including the novella *The Heart of a Dog* (written in 1926) and his masterpiece *The Master and Margarita* (written 1928–40) remained unpublished during his lifetime. *The Heart of a Dog* (*Sobach'e serdtse*) was first published in Russia in 1987.

† Vladimir Mayakovsky (1893–1930), who joined the revolutionary movement in his teens and published his first verses in 1912, was one of the leading figures in the avant-garde Futurist movement. He established his reputation with four wartime narrative poems, including *A Cloud in Trousers* (1915), and after the Revolution devoted himself to propaganda pieces such as *150,000,000* (1920) and *Vladimir Il'ich Lenin* (1924). Gradually, however, he became disillusioned with the development of the new regime, a scepticism expressed in satirical plays such as *The Bedbug* (1928). Despair at the Stalinist clamp-down on literary experiment, compounded by personal difficulties, led to his suicide at the age of 37. Ironically, Mayakovsky was canonized after his death by the Soviet regime, earning great praise from Stalin himself.

‡ Reference to an article by Aleksandr Kazintsev, 'Ochishcheniye ili zlosloviye?', in *Nash sovremennik*, 2 (1988).

that I'd done the Russians an injustice, failing to feel properly sorry for them! This is the kind of mad thinking you get among these patriots. You might just as well have accused Krylov of attacking the Russian people in his fables. I didn't have any particular nation in mind in *Rabbits*. I was trying to analyse the way that power works in general, and the way that those subject to it—whatever nation they belong to—connive in their powerlessness.

SL But he was wrong, anyway—you surely *did* feel sorry for the rabbits in the novel, however deluded they may be?

FI If I hadn't felt sorry for the rabbits I wouldn't have written the work!

But, of course, I feel that they have to bear a great part of the blame themselves. That's what the book's about. They've adapted to their situation and don't want to change.

SL Just as you said earlier that writers in the Brezhnev era made a kind of cosy niche for themselves ... the whole system operated on a mixture of bribery and fear, didn't it? Part of the bribery was delusive—the era of communism or cauliflower was always just over the horizon—but part of it was real: there was a reasonable supply of the good things of life if you stuck to the rules.

FI That's right, and of course that sense of security has disappeared now. And the old political fear has been replaced by something different. The fear we have in the country now is of a different order—it's the more basic fear of catastrophe and the possibility of hunger.

SL It seems to me not a simple fear—it's as if some people interpret what's happening to them now as a kind of punishment for the past.

FI Yes, yes, that's true. But listen to them down in the street! [the interview is interrupted by sounds of shouting in the street below] They're queueing for milk. There are scuffles and fights in these queues now every morning, and you can sense the panic behind their anger.

SL The dream of communism may have been an illusion, but—in the beginning, at least, among those who believed in it—it did give people a sense of hope and purpose. What's the equivalent of the rabbits' longed-for 'cauliflower' now? What do people live in hope of?

FI For the time being, I'm afraid to say, cauliflower has become part of the past! One wouldn't dream of such things at the moment. That's why, you see, people lapse into thinking that everything was fine under Brezhnev—it was easy to buy vodka and there were two different sorts of sausage to be had. In actual fact life was pretty hard, there were endless queues then as well, but it was predictable, and in retrospect it looks quite decent.

SL Is it more healthy to believe in the future, however illusory, than to believe in the past?

FI Well that's a complex question, and of course it depends on what past you're speaking about. It would have been quite 'healthy' for a German, for example, in Hitler's day to feel nostalgic about the Weimar republic. What we see in this country is a completely illusory view of what the past was. I can understand that Party bureaucrats look back on the good old days and miss the privileges they used to have—that's only natural. But when our poor unfortunate ordinary people start thinking about the immediate past as a happier time, it's extremely sad.

The point is that the old order created elements of comfort and harmony, however false. It certainly gave the man in the street a miserly but stable minimum. It was difficult in those days to throw a man out of work, so long as there was no political element involved. So long as you kept your mouth shut politically, you could be an extremely bad worker, indeed salaried professional, and feel quite secure in your job. There was very little unemployment in the old days.

So our society offered security to people who didn't demand too much, and the point was that people don't demand much if everyone around them has more or less the same, and there's the promise that you'll get a bit more sooner or later. Awful though it is to say it—and of course we're ironical about it now—this did make a difference to us, somewhere in the depths of our souls.

sl And this applied to the intelligentsia too?

fi Yes, though it's a very complex question. Recently I was visited by a writer and we got talking about the upheavals of the last year, and I could see that in certain ways he regretted what had happened—he regretted that the dream was finished. You see, communism was a kind of religious, drunk illusion produced by a sober atheistic head. And people made great efforts to reconcile this conundrum in themselves, because somewhere in the depths of their souls—in Russia at least—there's always been this religious dream about brotherhood and justice, and, however imperfect, indeed terrible the reality may have been, this idea of communism touched people's hearts. Among many good people there was always this distorted religious feeling about the Revolution. I'm not speaking here of those people who simply robbed or murdered or wanted to take other people's places as bosses, though there were plenty of those too. But there was this illusion among good people that you could accomplish a heavenly mission by earthly means.

So there is something negative about seeing this dream destroyed, however necessary the whole process may be. People now are very disorientated and afraid. They watch the crude market process of accumulation that the West went through long ago—and which Russia herself had embarked on before the Revolution, but was then forced to forget—and the whole thing is incomprehensible and makes them feel helpless. And, of course, there's been no proper experience of democratic government either, and there's no confidence that even the so-called democratic forces in this country are freed from the old habits and passions of the past.

sl How do you feel that literature has responded to all this?

fi It's hard to say. So far there haven't been any major works about this period. And I don't think it will be simple to create a serious convincing work within this present chaos. We will need more time.

sl You said earlier that you've embarked on a new work yourself this year.

fi Yes ... It's a work that I've provisionally called *A Man and his Surroundings*. It's an attempt on a larger scale to see the human soul and its passions in our time, and it deals in a sense with our whole epoch. As I said, it's partly an attempt to understand or conceive of Lenin himself. I was working on this part of the novel just before the attempted coup against Gorbachev, and this madman who thinks he's Lenin keeps saying the whole time that there's going to be a great upheaval any time now, that he's in charge of it and that everything will be different from now on! He believes that everything that happened was just the result of Stalin's counter-revolutionary policies. I wanted to try and look at Lenin in a literary way, to say something about his personality and teachings and the type of psychology that led to everything we've experienced here.

I had a plan, by the way, to make Sandro meet finally with this false Lenin—Sandro who saw the real Trotsky and the real Stalin. But I haven't got there yet.[*]

sl So *Sandro* is still being written?

fl I think it's more or less finished, though I wanted to complete the story of the girl Tali in the novel; I've had it for a long time in a rough draft. Tali gets exiled with her husband, who's half-Turkish, spends a long time in Siberia, and generally has a terribly hard fate. And I'd like to write about the death of old Khabug, Sandro's father, who represents, in a way, the essence of that vanished patriarchal life in Abkhazia. It's seemed to me that this is necessary for the final truthfulness of the general picture. But at the moment Sandro doesn't trouble me. Whereas the story of Chik is still going on in my head. I haven't finished with my childhood yet.[†]

---

[*] Sandro's encounter with the false Lenin indeed takes place in the last part of *A Man and his Surroundings* (*Chelovek i yego okrestnosti*, 1992), completed after this interview was recorded.

[†] Since this interview was recorded, Iskander has published further stories about Chik in *Kontinent* (1994) and *Znamya* (1994 and 1996) as well as a new book of Chik stories (*Detstvo Chika*, 1994). Other recent works include the novella *Sofichka*, the tragic story of its eponymous heroine, a great-niece of Old Khabug. Khabug does indeed die in the course of the story, which also reacquaints us with Sofichka's cousin Tali, daughter of Sandro. *Sofichka* is the title-work in a recent collection of Iskander's prose (1997) which includes, alongside essays on literature and short stories with a contemporary setting, the novella *Pshada* (first published 1993), about the death of a Russian general whose thoughts in old age revolve around his murder of two German prisoners during the war, and the lost world of his childhood in Abkhazia. In 1993 Iskander was awarded the prestigious German Pushkin Prize for his lifetime's work.

2

Lyudmila Petrushevskaya

(b. 1938)

Lyudmila Petrushevskaya was born in Moscow shortly before the outbreak of the Second World War, and, like all her generation, was marked for life by the events of her childhood: war, evacuation, the post-war hunger and deprivation, as well as the intangible, universal fear generated by Stalin's Terror.

After leaving school in 1956 Petrushevskaya studied journalism at Moscow University, and in the 1960s worked as a reporter and reviewer in radio and television and on the magazine *Krugozor*. Married and widowed in her twenties, she spent several years struggling to fend for herself and her first child. Later she remarried, and in the early 1970s became a full-time writer, earning her living with reviews, screenplays, and translations from Polish. She now lives with her family in Moscow.

Petrushevskaya made her début as a writer in 1972, publishing two short stories in the Leningrad magazine *Avrora*. Over the next fifteen years, a handful of other stories appeared, at long intervals, in *Avrora*, *Druzhba narodov*, and the Estonian-based journal *Raduga* (Rainbow). But it soon became clear that few editors would risk publishing her prose. In 1969 she had taken her first stories to the then editor of *Novy mir*, Aleksandr Tvardovsky, who decreed: 'Withhold publication, but don't lose track of the author.' As far as *Novy mir* was concerned, that decision was to stand for almost two decades, and as late as 1987, when we first met, Petrushevskaya was doubtful that her collected stories would ever see the light of day.

In the mid-1970s, however, Petrushevskaya turned instead to writing plays, encouraged by the playwright Aleksei Arbuzov whose workshop she attended. It was these early plays, performed in back rooms, makeshift theatres, and factory clubs, that first established Petrushevskaya's name among a limited circle of Moscow *cognoscenti*. Today many of those who sat or stood in those cramped rooms recall the extraordinary emotional impact of the plays: the shocked laughter and tears of people who seemed for the first time to have seen and heard a true account of themselves. Reflecting on the more immediate success of her plays,

Petrushevskaya points both to their humour and to the opportunity they gave for a kind of social catharsis: the chance 'to create a common humanity in the face of suffering'.*

Petrushevskaya's reputation was further enhanced, in 1979, by the success of Yury Norshtein's award-winning animated film *Tale of Tales*, for which she had written the screenplay (in 1984 an international jury voted it the best animated film ever made). In the same year the journal *Teatr* published her one-act play *Love*, staged two years later at the Taganka Theatre under director Yury Lyubimov, and in 1983 two further plays (*Music Lessons* and *The Stairwell*) appeared in print, side by side with the work of her friend and fellow playwright Viktor Slavkin, in a volume officially designed to promote 'amateur artistic initiatives'. By the mid-1980s her work was reaching a wider audience, with performances of *Three Girls in Blue* and *Columbine's Apartment* in mainstream Moscow theatres, and in 1988 Petrushevskaya was finally able to publish her *Songs of the Twentieth Century*—collected plays and 'monologues'—and *Immortal Love*, a collection of stories written over the previous twenty years. Several individual collections have since followed, as well as her *Collected Works* in five volumes, and Petrushevskaya has recently become a prolific contributor to journals such as *Znamya* and *Oktyabr'*. Her novel *The Time: Night* (1992) was short-listed for the first Russian Booker Prize.

In 1983, in a brief introduction to Petrushevskaya's work, Aleksei Arbuzov wrote that 'the magic of her talent, on the face of it, lies just in her precise vision and acute ear. But no—her genius consists in her ability to seize on the disparate details of everyday life and render them as a finished, perfect whole, in which even the most unpalatable reality is made beautiful by the perfection of her art.'

The surface realities that Petrushevskaya deals in are often, indeed, 'unpalatable'. Poverty, sickness, old age, abortion, broken families, alcoholism, prostitution—all are countenanced in her work. She finds her stories in the discarded out-takes of life, the bits that will never make the news. Her settings are cramped offices, shared flats, shabby hospitals, places where gossip swarms, quarrels flare, and people rub together in a forced, chafing intimacy. Money, food, time, and living space are all in short supply. So, too, catastrophically, is love. In the midst of their crowded lives many of Petrushevskaya's characters live in a state of irremediable loneliness. Almost all of them are women: naïve young girls, single mothers, battling wives, middle-aged women panicking at the approach of old age, bewhiskered old dames still racked by desire. Few find direct expression for their needs and longings. Their lives are muddled and anxious, their minds colonized by detail. Rather than ask what became of their hopes and ambitions, they rail at the person who ate the last eggs from the fridge or pocketed the roubles stashed behind the skirting board.

On the surface, indeed, many of Petrushevskaya's heroines appear to live their lives ineptly. The girls, for the most part, seem lacking in even the rudiments of pride or strategy. The hapless girl in 'The Adventures of Vera',† setting her sights at each male colleague in turn, becomes the predictable laughing stock of the office, as

---

* See p. 47.   † 'Priklyucheniya Very', in *Bessmertnaya lyubov'* (1988).

does the heroine of 'The Story-Teller',* guilelessly relating the most intimate details of her life to an audience that couldn't have cared less. Elsewhere we see the inevitable consequences of girlish ardour in a string of single mothers or mothers-to-be: the narrator of 'Nets and Snares',† abandoned to give birth in the most perilous circumstances; the penniless pregnant heroine of 'The Violin',‡ fabricating a fiancé to rescue her self-esteem; Alyona, the fatherless daughter in *The Time: Night*, spawning a second generation of fatherless children while clinging, against the odds, to some original vision of love. The evident truth—that men are not to be trusted—appears to escape most of these young women.

Nor does age necessarily bring wisdom. Alyona's mother, heroine of *The Time: Night*, scorns her daughter's ineptitude but displays just as great a susceptibility to the charms of disreputable men; even her own mother, by now old and deranged, appears to harbour senile hopes of romance. The middle-aged heroine of 'A Dark Fate'§ is under no illusion about the quality of the man she has finally brought home: he's ugly, greedy, self-centred, and childish, and 'does his thing' without a vestige of grace. But such is her longing that she knows she'll go on pursuing him, vainly repeating the pattern of countless other lonely women.

Family life, meanwhile, offers little by way of relief. Indeed, it's perhaps here—in the relationship between mothers and children, husbands and wives—that we see Petrushevskaya's characters at their most self-defeating, repelling the very people they most seek to hold. In 'A Case of Virgin Birth',¶ a mother and son take turns to deflect each other's needs: the infant who once clung to his distracted young mother becomes, in adolescence, the would-be escapee from an intimacy that now crushes and repels him. Here, the outward expression of need is checked, at least, by a kind of stifling courtesy. Elsewhere, more typically, such niceties are dispensed with. In *The Time: Night*, in *Music Lessons*,‖ or again in *Three Girls in Blue*** we see love turned to naked manipulation as mothers, wrapped in self-pity, openly bully and harangue their grown-up children. In 'Father and Mother'†† a wife runs screaming down the street to retrieve the husband she despises and loathes, while in 'Elegy'‡‡ precipitous death proves the only issue from unbearable wedlock. All manner of emotional horrors precede these ends: threats, insults, staged humiliations. Stephen Mulrine, translator of Petrushevskaya's plays, aptly remarks that her characters 'lack a sense of scale, of decorum', of elementary tact. Even by Russian standards of emotional straightforwardness, they quarrel at an astonishing pitch of anger and abuse.

The outward picture, in short, is bleak: the conditions miserable, the behaviour often dreadful. Yet it is a rule with Petrushevskaya that things are not what they seem. For a start, her work is often very funny. It is only rarely—in 'Xenia's Daughter', for instance, or 'Another Land'§§—that she falls into a single cadence of lament,

---

* 'Rasskazchitsa', ibid.; first published in *Avrora*, 7 (1972).
† 'Seti i lovushki', in *Bessmertnaya lyubov'*, first published in *Avrora*, 4 (1974).
‡ 'Skripka', in *Bessmertnaya lyubov'*, first published in *Druzhba narodov*, 10 (1976).
§ 'Tyomnaya sud'ba', in *Bessmertnaya lyubov'*.   ¶ 'Sluchai Bogoroditsy', ibid.
‖ *Uroki muzyki*, in *P'esy* (1983).   ** *Tri devushki v golubom*, in *Pesny XX veka: p'esy* (1988).
†† 'Otets i mat'', in *Bessmertnaya lyubov'*.
‡‡ 'Elegiya', ibid.; first published in *Chistyye prudy* (1987).
§§ 'Doch' Kseni' and 'Strana', in *Bessmertnaya lyubov'* (1988).

as if not trusting her subjects (in these stories two prostitutes and an alcoholic mother) to unkind laughter. For the most part her humour is unsentimentally robust. Her plays are full of comic grotesquerie. Even *The Time: Night*, which tells a tale of apparently unremitting misery, can be read as black comedy almost to the end.

The laws which govern human behaviour are seen, in Petrushevskaya's work, to be infinitely subtle and mysterious. Curses turn into blessings; the weak prove resilient; the strong unexpectedly helpless. Tanya, daughter of the warring parents in 'Father and Mother', turns into a wonderfully blithe spirit, immunized to misery for ever after by the wretchedness of her childhood. The apparently luckless heroines of 'The Wall',* of 'Klarissa's Story',† or of 'Nets and Snares' prove to be possessed of an unexpected determination and gift for survival. The 'Story-Teller', in the tale of that name, proves less impervious than first appears to the mockery of her colleagues—but weathers it to acquire, by the end, a sudden dignity. Even the giddy Vera, 'victim' of numerous failed romances, turns out at the end of her story to have one loyal boyfriend after all.

To read Petrushevskaya, in short, is a discomfiting experience, for one's initial judgements repeatedly prove misplaced. Nowhere more so, perhaps, than in *The Time: Night*, where our sympathies are torn between the heroine-narrator and the ramshackle family whom she loves, vilifies, and seeks to control. The narrator is Anna Andrianovna, an ageing, unsuccessful poetess who struggles, on her meagre income, to support a son just out of prison, an unmarried daughter, three accidental grandchildren and her own senile mother, now confined to a mental hospital. Casting herself by turns as martyr and warrior, skilled strategist, ironist, and victim of fate, Anna alternately arouses our admiration and deflects our sympathy. Her account—a collection of night-time jottings, subtitled 'Notes from the Edge of the Table'—is hurried and chaotic, fraught with fury, resentment, and worry. It is only at the end, when Anna is forced to acknowledge herself as redundant and bereft, that she achieves a final grace and commands our full pity. As in many of Petrushevskaya's stories, the end compels us to back-track through the narrative and discover, beneath the clamour of self-pity and argument, the submerged voice of the heroine's real fears and regrets.

The Time: Night is Petrushevskaya's only novel and represents her art at its most intense. But it belongs in form with several earlier works, telling a complex story through the voice of a single narrator. Petrushevskaya indeed gave the term 'monologues' to several of the stories in her first collection, among them 'Nets and Snares', 'This Little Girl'‡ and 'Our Circle'.§ Like *The Time: Night*, these stories typically embark *in media res*, fastening on a few, initially baffling details before spiralling outwards to reveal, by degrees, their real meaning and motive. In each case the narrator tells her story in passionate detail, with every show of candour. Yet certain crucial secrets are withheld or obscured. In 'Our Circle', for instance, we realize only gradually that the narrator is terminally ill. Her gossipy tone and clownish behaviour obscure the central preoccupation of her life: how to ensure a future for her young son once she is dead.

* 'Stena', ibid.   † 'Istoriya Klarissy', ibid.; first published in *Avrora* (1972).
‡ 'Takaya devochka', in *Bessmertnaya lyubov'*.
§ 'Svoi krug', ibid.; first published in *Novy mir* (1988).

These stories reveal Petrushevskaya's fascination with the nature of story-telling itself. All narratives, she shows, are in some sense fiction—attempts, on the part of the narrator, to make arrangements of chaos, to find a meaning, to reassert control. Such assertions frequently backfire: in the 'monologues' we see how the narrators contradict themselves—deny an admission only just made, or betray, between the lines, some quite other motive they will not admit to at all. But their shifting stories also convey a truth. For if biography is fiction, so, to a certain extent, is personality. People are mutable and full of surprises.

This is one moral of Petrushevskaya's stories. In her third-person narratives—what she calls the 'histories'—we see people change, grow, discard their old selves. The heroine of 'Klarissa's Story' undergoes half a dozen transformations before settling, warily, into happy marriage; Nina, the heroine of 'Youth',* is likewise unrecognizable by the end of her story. Such transformations are here a source of hope. But other lives, Petrushevskaya suggests, remain essentially closed, undeveloped. For every garrulous heroine in Petrushevskaya's work, bent on conveying the 'truth' of her life, there's a silent character who won't give up his secret: Uncle Grisha,† in the story of that name, shuffling about his summerhouse and garden until fate, in the form of some nameless hoodlums, randomly disposes of him at the garden gate; or Pavel, the game, tolerant husband in 'Elegy', who abandons his clinging family in the subtlest fashion, slipping off his roof while fixing a TV aerial. Standing at the junction of others' stories—the objects of rumour, judgement, and gossip—such people stay to the end unfathomable, their lives failing to yield any singular meaning.

Petrushevskaya's stance within these stories is at once passionate and detached. Plunging us pell-mell into her characters' lives, she involves us willy-nilly in their fears, furies, anxieties. But she offers no tidy solution or summary. Who can know, she suggests, who was really to blame, who suffered most, whose story was truest? Who, in any case, are we to judge?

This determined agnosticism accounts for much of the misunderstanding of Petrushevskaya's work. Accustomed to the didactic traditions of Soviet literature, many readers have been puzzled by her refusal to sort out villains from heroes, or construed as casual condonement her failure to condemn. Others, on the contrary, have pointed to a moral that was not there, interpreting her work as a straightforward indictment of the social ills—drink, divorce, poverty, moral decline—that Soviet society in its braver moments could admit to. Petrushevskaya's plays were at first compared with those of her short-lived contemporary, the dramatist Aleksandr Vampilov, whose tragi-comedies about individual human failings and the problems of Soviet society were popular in the period after the Thaw.

The comparison is in some ways apt. Like Vampilov, Petrushevskaya uses comedy as a principal 'weapon'. But her wit, her criticism—her pity—strike further. Here, albeit at its grimmest or most forlorn, is not just the Soviet comedy but the human one—no less so for the fact that her characters themselves often fail so lamentably to address the broader, universal issues, beyond the leaking roof and the lack of eggs. Indeed, that is part of what makes them so funny, and so sad.

---

* 'Yunost'', in *Bessmertnaya lyubov'*; first published in *Avrora* (1987).
† 'Dyadya Grisha', in *Bessmertnaya lyubov'*.

Petrushevskaya's works were for years deemed unprintable not just because they presented a true picture of Soviet living conditions, but because they pointed to problems of the human heart—how to love and be loved and make sense of your life—that were beyond the help of ideology or sound economy or government fiat. To be sure, Soviet ideology, with its false optimism and black-and-white morality, failed glaringly to deal with such existential *angst*. But so, in the end, do shopping malls and designer clothes. Petrushevskaya, as she makes plain in the interviews here, has no illusions that life is fundamentally easier elsewhere, or was ever easier in human history, even if the margins for courtesy and social grace have sometimes been greater than they are in the kitchen of a Moscow apartment.

The reader, she makes clear, should have no illusions either. Petrushevskaya puts at our service a penetrating knowledge of the human heart and a ruthless eye and ear for its pretences. Her wit is superbly tuned to all the nuances of bravado, self-pity, self-deceiving hope, or plain Russian *vranyo* (fibbing developed to the plane of art) with which people present their stories. Orchestrating and amplifying the voices of her characters, she makes audible, to those listening, their tragic undertones. But she counts on her readers to be listening hard—to catch the pathos behind the bravado, and supply to these lives a transforming gesture of pity.

◆   ◆   ◆

SL The family and family relationships are at the heart of your work. What can you tell me about your own family and upbringing?

LP My mother was the daughter of a very well-known professor of linguistics, Nikolai Yakovlev, while my father came from a peasant family, so I have a mixed heritage. But my father didn't spend long with our family: he abandoned us after just one year. So he had no influence on me at all, except perhaps that I've inherited from him a kind of peasant fortitude and practicality, an ability to survive, which in itself of course is very important.

Just about all my mother's relatives—my great aunts and uncles—were arrested or shot around the time I was born: 1937, 1938. They were Old Bolsheviks, members of the Party since the 1890s, the people who had made the Revolution—and they were first in line for repression under Stalin.

But my great-grandfather survived and during the War—he was already 80 years old—he managed to get the whole family out of Moscow and take us to Kuibyshev:* my grandmother, my mother, my aunt, and me, his great-granddaughter. The hardest years were from 1943 to 1947: there was no work or food to be had, and the family simply starved. Eventually my mother placed me in a children's home, a kind of sanatorium for starving children. I was 9 years old and so skinny that even among those waifs and strays I earned the name *moskvichka spichka*, the Moscow matchstick. There I was fed and clothed and for the first time in my life I remember

Interview recorded in December 1992 and May 1993.

* Kuibyshev, now called by its pre-Stalinist name Samara, is an industrial city on the Volga, southeast of Moscow. During the war it became the temporary capital of the USSR when Moscow was threatened by the German advance. Many Muscovites were evacuated there and to other cities east of Moscow.

I took part in a kind of show: we were dressed up in all sorts of beads and finery and performed a sort of gypsy song and dance! The teachers there were marvellous, wonderful women.

My mother meanwhile established herself back in Moscow and eventually brought me home, and so began the torment of life in a communal city apartment. By the time I was 10 I felt I'd been through all the circles of hell. For eight years my grandfather, mother, and I shared a single, twelve-square-metre room: it was all that was left to us of my grandfather's apartment, and it also housed his library of 5,000 books. My grandfather had been sacked from his post and deprived of his pension in 1951, supposedly for some political misdemeanour. He was one of the most distinguished professors in his field, a pioneer of the Jakobson* school of linguistics, spoke twenty-three languages, worked incredibly hard, and had always been surrounded by students who loved him. But after he lost his job not a single person came to his aid, and in the following years he slowly went mad. He suffered from insomnia and would cry out at night in the darkness, but sharing the room with us he was deprived even of the insomniac's right to turn on the light and read. So our home was like a mini-Gulag, with no privacy at all for him and not a single peaceful night for us. In 1956 he was finally 'rehabilitated', but he spent the next fifteen years in a mental hospital.

SL What were the escape routes for you as a child?

LP My mother did her best for me, and every summer I'd be sent to a sanatorium where I'd put on weight, study, dance, sing, enjoy myself. But at home there was simply nowhere to be, so virtually every evening after school I simply went to the library and stayed there until it closed. When I finally left school and said goodbye to the children's library the librarian told me I was their champion reader—I'd read more books than anyone else!

But there were thousands of children in my position. The choice was very stark: either you went to the library or you went out on the street. So that was where the split between the intelligentsia and the working class began: the children of the intelligentsia grew up in libraries, while the rest learned the life of the street—stealing, drinking, fighting. There was virtually no contact between the two. I remember feeling a complete outcast in the yard outside our house where the other kids played. And I think that's precisely where my love of ordinary people comes from—from this feeling both of exclusion and of guilt before them. As a writer I've always sought to get inside this world that was inaccessible to me as a child, to discover the beauty of its language, to show its suffering.

SL It's a striking feature of your work, though, that these social or political issues are never touched upon directly. The 'macro' scale is absent from the scene; everything takes place on the 'micro' scale of home, family, the office. Do you see yourself as an 'apolitical' writer?

LP I've never concerned myself with politics—it doesn't interest me at all, for all sorts of reasons. Don't you see—I was born in the belly of the beast, the very

---

* Roman Jakobson (1896–1982), founder of the Moscow and Prague schools of linguistics, subsequently Professor at Harvard and the Massachusetts Institute of Technology, and author of numerous influential works on linguistics, semiotics, and the relation between language and meaning.

womb, and from earliest childhood I rejected it completely—like almost all my generation. As our poet Aleksandr Kushner—our greatest living poet—said:

> People do not choose the times
> When they begin and end their lives*

You live your life under the roof you've been allotted, not knowing how high or low it is. Our generation lived despite the times—in a way, we didn't even notice them. Of course we came into collision with the system, but we were so skilled at living, at just surviving. We'd been born in the belly of the beast and it was quite an art to stay whole, not to be dissolved completely.

SL   You mentioned that several members of your mother's family were arrested in the late thirties. Did you learn about Stalin's 'repressions' in your childhood?

LP   No—not until 1956. My mother hid it all from me. She was a member of the Party and she had to hide the fact that she was a relative of 'enemies of the people' or she would have lost her job—and her work was our sole means of survival.

Very little has been written about all this but probably some 80 per cent of the population at that time were some sort of partisans, underground people. Everyone hid very carefully what they really thought, even within the family. Because if the children started babbling the game would soon be up. In those terrible times everyone had to learn this.

That's why I've never had any desire whatsoever to get involved in politics or enter public life in any way. All my life the only task I've set myself was to survive as a writer and as the mother of my children. It was only when I started writing that I came into direct conflict with the system—as a system which rejected what I wrote absolutely. Or rather, they simply didn't like what I wrote, my whole way of writing. I understood this as just a law of life. And like every other writer I tried to find ways out.

SL   What were the options?

LP   We looked for ways round. It was very funny. Some people would get themselves jobs in publishing houses or on editorial boards. Others would try to make friends with editors-in-chief or do ghost-writing for them. Others just gave in and tried to write what was required of them. Women of course had their own methods which were quite understandable! I won't name names, but there were some who took that route.

We all knew these hundred prescriptions by heart. But I didn't take any of them. As far as finding a protector went, every instinct in me rejected that solution, although I did get a few proposals of that kind. One editor, at Sovremennik publishing house, advised me that if I were just to change the endings of all my stories and make them more positive—have everyone get married, for instance—everything would be just fine!

After I'd been turned down by *Novy mir*—the most liberal of the big journals in the 1960s—I adopted the simple method of just going to the library and copying down the addresses of all the other literary journals I knew, then making copies of my works and sending them off one by one.

---

* 'Vremena ne vybirayut | V nikh zhivut i umirayut . . .', from *Kanva iz shesti knig* (Sovetsky pisatel', 1981).

As it happened the second envelope I sent went to the journal *Avrora* in Leningrad. The editor at that time was Aleksandr Volodin, whom I already knew and liked—so I thought it might be worth a try.

Six months later I got a reply. I remember clearly I was washing the floor at the time. I heard something drop into the letterbox and went to have a look. And there was the letter. I tore open the envelope and read: 'Dear L. Petrushevskaya, you are a real writer . . .'. At which point I fell to my knees on the newly washed floor and burst into tears! And about six months later they published me there—in the summer of 1972. My first stories. I was 34 years old.

SL But *Avrora* turned out to be an exception, didn't it? As I recall, you had only a handful of stories published over the next fifteen years. Why do you think it was so obvious to everyone that your stories were 'impossible'?

LP You know, people had an amazing instinct for spotting anything that was alive and truthful and crushing it on the spot—because it was too threatening. Even if they published a text they'd unfailingly get rid of the best thing in it.

Of course everyone understood that it was a great compliment to have your work singled out for banning—it was a sign of quality. Public praise of any kind was the mark of the devil, we all knew that instinctively. If a play was widely advertised it meant it wasn't worth seeing, no one went. Whereas crowds and crowds would turn up for something that hadn't been advertised at all; everyone would hear about it by word of mouth and by the time you turned up at the appointed place you could hardly get in, there'd be rioting round the entrance.

To be banned was the opposite of being stigmatized, they banned you out of sheer enthusiasm for your work!

SL You can laugh now about the ruses people took to get published in the old days. But it must have been terribly depressing effectively to be deprived of an audience.

LP Well of course if it hadn't been for the theatre—yes, it would have been very bad. Around the mid-seventies I felt I had reached an absolute dead end, there seemed to be no hope at all. But in 1973, 1974 I started writing plays: *Music Lessons, Cinzano, Meetings of Friends*,* and others—and just as I seemed to have reached a dead end with the stories, an underground theatre took up the plays and started performing them, more or less in private apartments. It would be announced as a 'creative evening' or 'a meeting with young actors', without mentioning the author or the name of the work.

SL Your real breakthrough came though, didn't it, with Mark Zakharov's production of your play *Three Girls in Blue* in the Lenkom [Leninsky Komsomolets] theatre?

LP Yes, *Three Girls in Blue* was one of the first plays to be 'unbanned' under *glasnost* and the theatre was absolutely packed. I arrived late for the first performance—I'd been in a traffic jam—and found a whole crowd wringing their hands outside the door, unable to get in. Eventually they opened the back entrance for us and I rushed in there with the whole crowd following behind—I shouted 'they're all my relatives!' and somehow they managed to pack us in.

---

* *Uroki muzyki, Chinzano, Vstrechi druzei*, in *Pesni XX veka: p'esy* (1988).

The atmosphere in the hall was quite incredible. It was 1985—just after Gorbachev had come to power—and everything was just beginning, all the arrests and bannings and restrictions were still fresh in our minds. The emotional charge was extraordinary. When I went backstage afterwards I was in pieces, I just cried my eyes out, I barely made it onto the stage to take a bow.

At the time I still hadn't had a single book published—all I had in print were those few stories, plus one or two bits and pieces. *Three Girls in Blue* itself had been published in 1983 thanks to the courage of a few people who'd simply taken the responsibility on themselves. A woman in the Ministry of Culture had said— this play is about me! And then Vasily Chichkov, who was then Chief Editor of the journal *Sovremennaya dramaturgiya* (Contemporary Dramaturgy), took it on himself to publish it.

Behind the publication of every banned work of literature there was a tale of fantastic heroism, selflessness. People forget so quickly the conditions we lived in then. *That* was a time of civil war, *that* was a time of real devastation.

SL How did the public react to the play when they saw it?

LP They roared with laughter virtually throughout—right up to the crucial scene when the heroine Ira, who's been having a hopeless affair with a married man, is desperately trying to get back home to the child she's abandoned, and you see her on her knees in the airport shouting 'I'm not going to make it! I'm not going to make it!' There was a girl sitting in front of me who was so distraught she was lit- erally tearing her hair out!

I've never been able to bear watching this scene myself, I always start crying.

SL You've said before how important it is that your plays should reach a proper catharsis—that people should go away with a sense of relief. Was that achieved in this performance?

LP Yes, they did the finale in a very interesting way. As you remember, there's an aristocratic old lady in the play, Leokardiya, who doesn't say a word until the very end, when she suddenly points out in an unexpectedly clear, ringing voice that the rain is coming in through the roof of the dacha where most of the play takes place—and then everything freezes in a tableau.

Now Mark Zakharov had introduced some additional, silent characters into the play: they were all dressed in clothes from the turn of the century and wan- dered round like the shades of people who had lived in this same house long ago. And at the end of the play they sat down and began playing a Schumann quartet, with Fyodorovna playing the cello. At which point Ira comes onto the stage carry- ing the little child—and the two of them simply stare out at the audience! *Every- one* was crying! There was such an extraordinary atmosphere—this wonderful, heavenly music and these figures set deep back on the stage.

They had removed the first six rows of seats to bring the stage forward so that it seemed absolutely grandiose, the depth was incredible. And there right at the back of the stage in the shadows you could see illuminated all these tattered old photographs of an old military family—the men with whiskers and sideboards, dressed in military greatcoats, and the women and children in white dresses. The stage was bounded by glass at the back so that one had the sense of looking through to a terrace or verandah with a garden and shrubs beyond, and from time to time these shades in their long dresses and bearing torches would emerge from behind the glass—as if searching for their future.

It was a clear allusion to Chekhov's *Three Sisters* ...

SL Mark Zakharov's idea was presumably to make an ironic allusion to the three sisters' hopes for a radiant future a hundred years hence?

LP Yes of course—there were Chekhov's characters saying 'in a hundred years life will be beautiful'—and now a hundred years have passed and look what's happened!

SL It's clear from what you've said that Mark Zakharov and the company that staged *Three Girls in Blue* gave you a kind of creative home, a spiritual refuge in the 1980s. Have there been other groups or circles that have played that role for you at other stages in your life?

LP My first real refuge was the journal *Novy mir*—I took my earliest work there in 1969 when Tvardovsky was still Editor-in-Chief.

SL But for years *Novy mir* wouldn't publish you!

LP Yes, but as you remember they wouldn't 'lose track' of me either. That was their decision: 'withhold publication, but don't lose track of the author'.

SL So you kept taking them things?

LP Of course! For twenty-three years! It's been the most serious friendship of my life. *Novy mir* fed me, gave me work, all through the most difficult and hungry times they gave me reviews and book reports to do. They couldn't publish me but they fed me and read me and gave me their opinion—always. Above all my first editor there, Nina Petrovna Borisova, literary godmother to me and to many other writers—Yevgeny Popov, Fridrikh Gorenshtein. She said to me once: 'You're in such good company, Lyusya, you've no idea what heaps of excellent books and stories I've got stashed in there.'

And when the time came, they did publish me. It was *Novy mir* that first published my story 'Our Circle'.

SL One of the reasons why you've been misunderstood by critics—and presumably why it took so long for your work to be published—is that you give the reader only the obliquest clues to your own moral attitude towards your characters. 'Our Circle' is a typical example: one's first reaction to the woman narrator is one of horror at her apparent callousness in abandoning her child while she parties with friends. It's only at the end that you realize she's desperate, she knows she's dying, and her act is a way of forcing her friends to grow up, take responsibility— in effect replace her as a mother. But it takes a second reading to get over one's squeamishness and feel sympathy for her.

LP Of course! But the right people understood 'Our Circle'. The thing is that my work is of no use to stupid or evil people—they hate it, reject it, see only the bare facts I present and not what surrounds them. They don't understand the game I'm playing.

SL Some critics, I remember, saw 'Our Circle' as an indictment of your whole society, of the moral decay and corruption of the Brezhnev period. Is there any truth in that reading?

LP 'Our Circle' is about a group of friends who've known each other from student days and whose lives are transformed in the face of death. It would be too easy to say that their story was somehow the prerogative of Soviet society. Anywhere in the world you could find a group of people like this, a group in which each person develops a particular role in the company of the others and always sticks to this one role—so that after a while they cease to have the right to play any other. And yet every one of those people is mortal—this actor and that actor, the villain and the clown—all of them are going to die. And when the shadow of death falls over them, when they are suddenly faced with this clear threat, everything changes, everything. That's what the story's about.

In Russian we have a word, *tusovka*, which describes the circle of your closest friends or companions, your gang, the people who surround you at a particular stage in your life. The moment of parting from it, saying farewell, is always a landmark; to move from one *tusovka* to another is like shedding one life and starting all over again.

'Our Circle' isn't just about Russia or just about the 1970s. It's a story about the end of a *tusovka*—which means a story about the end of love. No one at first realizes that the heroine—the narrator—adores her friends: this charismatic couple, Marina and Serge, and all the people who surround them. They're all she has in life, they're her whole world. And yet she consciously sets about losing them, losing their love and respect, in order to save her own child.

But of course the story was misread by many people—they thought it was a story somehow condoning the selfishness of adults who neglected their own children. You can't imagine the indignation it aroused. I got two whole sackfuls of letters cursing me! In the end I decided to stop reading it in public. Wherever I went there were sure to be at least two or three crazed people in the audience who were convinced—they simply knew!—that what I had written was pure autobiography.

SL In many of your stories—including 'Our Circle'—the first-person narrator at first escapes our sympathy by assuming an air of toughness or bravado, or by lying transparently about her real situation and motives: like the girl in 'The Violin', who pretends to her fellow patients in a maternity ward that she's a student at the music conservatoire and has a respectable fiancé who'll turn up at any moment. In fact she's quite alone in the world and her 'illness' is a transparent ruse just to get herself fed and survive. But she puts on all kinds of airs to conceal her own desperation.

LP Yes, she's an inveterate liar, she lies constantly, contradicts herself. But you have to see how the theme of her lying and boasting is mixed with the theme of her hunger—the empty bedside table, the empty glass—and with the theme of her solitude: she's constantly writing, constantly talking, but nobody ever comes to see her. And then there's the role played by the colour yellow in the story, the colour of doom—her yellow comb, her yellow raincoat ... And you have to hear the second voice in the story, the voice of her companions in the ward—who try to persuade the doctor not to discharge her ...

SL Precisely because they know she's lying.

LP Of course! But this second voice provides the counterpoint, it makes the *fugue* of the story. There's one voice, the voice of the crowd, the voice of gossip and disdain and squeamishness—the voice of the crowd that will later find the story itself unacceptable, and which listens only to itself. And then there's this second voice, the voice of kindness and pity—see the way the other women in the ward start slipping her food, and how she eats and eats! Hunger. And then there's the third strand that joins these two: the mind of the reader. I know many readers have wept over this story—women, naturally, who understand everthing! My best readers have always been women.

SL Some of your characters give such bewilderingly conflicting accounts of themselves that one can only guess at the truth behind them.

LP That's always the case to some extent—in real life too. In my play *A Glass of Water** one of the two characters tells at least three different stories of her life—all of them incompatible! Some might say that she was simply mad—that would be one possible interpretation. And others might say that the author is just playing with her readers—giving them various versions to play with, to reflect on. Any work of art is a kind of game played between the author and the reader. I've always considered my real heroes to be not the characters in my books but my readers who reflect on those characters' lives.

SL In a way that your characters themselves so rarely do! Some of your stories and plays trace a journey to a kind of understanding—we see Ira, for instance, shocked into a proper recognition of what's important in her life in *Three Girls in Blue*. But a defining feature of almost all your characters to begin with is their complete *lack* of self-awareness. It can be comical or endearing or deeply pathetic in the case of a naïve young girl, like the over-talkative heroine of 'The Story-Teller'. With your manipulative and self-righteous characters—mothers, very often—their lack of self-knowledge is almost grotesque.

LP But the reader or the audience must always know more than the hero, that's a basic principle of art. My ideal hero is the person sitting in the theatre or reading the book, reading about a hero who, as you say, isn't ideal at all—maybe the very opposite. But by reading or watching, that person comes to reflect on his own life too.

I've always wanted my work to shock, to strike, to wound the *spiritual users* of my work—to set in motion the process of forming the pearl inside them. A pearl's life can only begin with a trauma, a blow.

I know someone who was so affected by reading one of my plays, *Music Lessons*, that it really did change his life. In that play I start off with the bare fact that a girl, a poor waif, gets taken in off the street by a domineering couple who attempt to instal her as a 'wife' for their young son, in place of the boy's own fiancée. The girl is only too glad to be given shelter, but when the son rejects her she's tossed out of the house as casually as she was taken in. Anyway, there was one young man I knew who, like Nikolai in the play, insisted on marrying the girl he loved. His parents were dead against it and he had to struggle to defend his choice. In the end it all worked out all right and they've been married fifteen years now. But just recently his mother told me 'You know, Lyusya, he said a very strange thing to us all those years ago—he said, "I'm not having any music lessons in my house"!' It must have been just around that time, 1973, that I gave that family the text of my play to read.

---

* *Stakan vody*, in *Pesni XX veka: p'esy* (1988).

When a person is *touched* by something he's read, and later finds himself in some analogous situation, it's bound to affect the path he takes.

SL It's clear that children are at the centre of your moral universe: in *Music Lessons* a baby wails in the background, and elsewhere we see children abandoned or torn apart in tugs-of-love. In these 'grown-up' stories we can only guess at their feelings—they are the helpless witnesses or victims of adult strife. But there's a parallel strand to your work—your *skazki* or fairy-tales—where you give rein to a more tender, child's-eye vision of the world. Your screenplay for the film *Tale of Tales* seems to me to be part of that strand—it's a film that can be enjoyed at different levels by both children and adults. How did it come about—was it your idea or Yury Norshtein's, the director's?

LP I worked on that film with Yury Norshtein over a long period of time. Norshtein is a simply fantastic director, probably the greatest director of animated films in the world—he showed that animation was a genre for adults as well as children, that it was one of the highest forms of art, just as serious as music or painting.

But in order to get a film started you had to have a screenplay and Yury simply can't bear writing, he's organically incapable of it. So I undertook to write it and it was a long process. For four or five months Yury and I discussed it virtually every day. He told me that he wanted to make a film about his wartime childhood that would somehow bring together various disparate strands or images—a drawing by Picasso and a poem by Nizametdin Akhmetov, 'Tale of Tales', and a traditional Russian lullaby—all these elements had to be woven together.

So we would sit there and tell each other stories and together we tried to find the right approach. I invented the figure of the poet who would go through the whole film, writing and writing, and his pages would simply fly away in the breeze and no one would read his verse. And then a little wolf by chance picks up one of the pages and runs away with it—and as he runs with the page it turns into a baby.

Later on the figure of the poet more or less disappeared and it was the little wolf that drew everything together. The poet appears only as one of the figures in the tableau that reappears from time to time in the film.

SL But does the film represent Norshtein's vision of childhood or yours—or both?

LP Visually it was Yury's—it's his house that you see, his back yard, the barracks nearby where lots of families live. But the song in the film, the tango*—that came from my childhood. And in fact that song turned out to be the starting-point of the whole film. It was a wartime song, everyone knew it. I was 3 years old already when the war began and by the time I was 4 or 5 I could sing all those songs myself—whereas Yury was that bit younger and never knew that song. So the leit-motif of the dance, where one by one the women's partners vanish from their arms against the background of that song—that came from my childhood.

SL The sense I took away from the film was above all of the timelessness of childhood, with the circular recurrence of certain tableaux—the dance, the idyll of the garden in summertime, the wintry park where a lonely child munches an apple in

---

* The song in question is the famous 'Utomlyonnoye solntse' (The Weary Sun), which is also, incidentally, used in—and gives its title to—a recent film by Nikita Mikhalkov, *Burnt by the Sun* (*Utomlyonnyye solntsem*). The song in fact dates from the 1930s, though it was evidently still popular during the war years. (Thanks to Martin Dewhirst for his information on this point.)

a tree and watches snowflakes fall—and all these images periodically crushed in sudden flashforwards by modernity, cars, the highway.

LP In fact time does exist in the film—you see the war from beginning to end, you see the soldiers go off and the letters come back, reporting death and injury—and then the victory fireworks at the end.

But of course the central tableau in the film—the one we've got the drawing of here, over there above the piano—is an image of timelessness: the 'Picasso' scene with the poet, and the girl skipping, the baby in the pram, the fish, the bull, and the poet happily writing away and the little girl teasing him. That's eternity of course—eternity, bright, sparkling, full of sunshine. It represents family life—the eternal life of the family that has gone on just the same under Ivan the Terrible or Stalin, that goes on, I suppose, all over the world.

So there's the theme of the family, of happiness, and the theme of the war and the story of the little wolf who draws everything together.

SL Your account of your own childhood is so dark, and the scenes of family life in your work are so fraught with anger and anxiety and misunderstanding that it comes as a surprise to hear you talk of 'family life' and 'happiness' as almost axiomatically conjoined.

LP Happiness is ... the lullabies sung to the child in his cradle—and cabbage soup—and catching the light of a wave in the sea—and seeing the light that streams out from an open doorway in the darkness, and some kind person passing whose name you can call out.

All that belongs to childhood but that doesn't mean that childhood as such is happiness. In general writers who pretend their childhood was radiant and perfect are awful liars, like Aleksei Tolstoy—a fine writer but a dreadful liar. Life has been so hard in this country, I don't think I know anyone who had a truly happy childhood.

SL How much of your sense of childhood do you think comes from your own memory and how much from being a mother? The childless woman in your work—like the sad, enigmatic, literally brittle character in your story 'Weak Bones'*—tends to be seen as a pathetic, even tragic, figure, but at the same time the *pain* of motherhood—the fear of some crucial failure, the foreboding of loss—is very strong in your writing.

LP The truth is that I started writing only after I'd had my first child—in fact I wrote my first story, 'This Little Girl', when my son was 3 years old. I was nearly 30 by then. Everything I'd written before that was rubbish, virtually unreadable. I started writing properly only when I discovered about suffering—not suffering on my own account, but *fear* for a beloved being. Until that moment, until the birth of your first child, you know only fear for yourself—but when a child is born a completely different world opens up.

SL So having a child is for you a crucial step in growing up?

LP It should be, but unfortunately it so often isn't! There are plenty of people—mothers, grandmothers—who go through life without ever growing up—without ever understanding anything!

---

* 'Slabyye kosti', in *Bessmertnaya lyubov'* (1988).

SL   One of your early stories is simply called 'Youth', and it expresses as vivid a sense as I've read anywhere of what it means to be young. Indeed 'youth' and 'life' are at one point equated in the story—momentarily it seems to the heroine that 'life simply *is* youth'.

LP   Momentarily, yes—but 'Youth' is actually a story about *loss* of youth—about bewilderment and disillusionment and then, paradoxically, about the gains they bring, or can bring to the wise.

Disillusionment is an essential part of human existence; without it there's no movement forward. Success weakens the muscles—whereas disappointment, the tragic perception of how one can fail or not get there in time—is the most powerful motivator to action.

The most repellant feature in any person is complacency, it's the sign of the thief or the murderer. Only completely immoral people are satisfied with themselves—whereas disappointment and yearning and a concern with the ultimate questions are the features of someone who's moving, developing, regardless of age. 'Youth' is concerned with the biological, physical squeezing out of life. But that's a necessary process too. When a pearl forms it squeezes the oyster inside the shell, makes life uncomfortable for it, and the older the oyster is the more pearls form and the more uncomfortable it gets.

All one can do, all one can leave in life are these pearls—one's spiritual life, one's creativity. A person's creations, his thoughts—in whatever form they take, be it machines or roads or books or painting or music—are all that gets left, while the life of the body, yes, it belongs only to youth, it's doomed to fade and be pushed out and die.

It's true that many of my stories are in some way about life in that physical sense—I love the life of the flesh, it's very precious to me, but as a writer, a reader, what matters to me is everything that happens around and on top of the simple facts of life. The life of the flesh *per se*—birth, the trials of love, and so on—is bound to end in tragedy, but what matters is the way we reflect on that tragedy.

SL   But it would certainly be true to say that a central preoccupation of your characters—however we may reflect on them philosophically ourselves—is precisely the process of ageing in that physical sense. Your work is informed by a very strong sense not just of the charm of youth but of the real horrors of old age. That seems to me one of the central elements in *The Time: Night*.

LP   It's true that *The Time: Night* is a novel about old age, that's one of the reasons it took so long to write. I wanted to get to the age of my heroine myself—or more or less! I haven't quite got there yet—Anna is about 60 years old.

Old age is a very mysterious thing; many people are afraid of it. I was still relatively young when I started writing *The Time: Night*, still the mother of a small child. But already the thought of old age worried me dreadfully. I suppose I wrote the novel as a kind of warning to myself—so that I would approach old age forewarned, forearmed. In writing it I lived through experiences I hoped never to live through in real life. But on the way, as my own old age grew closer, I learned a lot—and in particular that old age doesn't really exist.

A person never really feels that he is old—never. It's the people around you that 'make' old age, as a retinue makes a king. But the person himself doesn't feel it—ill or unwell, yes, but not old as such. Once I asked a woman of 84—a friend—what it felt like to be old. She'd had a very hard life—seventeen years altogether in the camps—but she was an unusually beautiful woman, physically beautiful still and in quite good health. Recently though she'd undergone an eye operation to restore her sight and she had to wear rather thick glasses which limited her field of vision.

'So, Vera Aleksandrovna,' I asked, 'how does it feel to be old?' And she said, 'Well, you know, Lyusya, I sometimes trip up when I'm trying to step over a puddle in the street—I haven't got used to these glasses yet.' And that was it! And suddenly I understood—old age doesn't exist! Here was the solution to the riddle!

SL What was the starting-point of the novel for you?

LP As I say, I wrote it over a very long period—about seven years altogether. I had written various versions of it to begin with, and then one day I met a woman who told me the story of her life—and all of a sudden this story magnetized all the themes I'd been working on, drew them together from all sides.

It was the story of a woman whose son had been in prison and come out again and found himself unable to live, spiritually annihilated. And he abused his mother's enormous love for him—just used her. Then all sorts of other stories I'd heard from other people attached themselves to this tragedy—especially the story of a poetess, a terribly poor, comical, touching figure: she told me the story of her life as well.

Russia is a land of women Homers—women who tell their stories orally, just like that, without inventing anything. They're extraordinarily talented story-tellers. I'm just a listener among them. But I dare to hope that *The Time: Night* is a kind of encyclopaedia of all their lives. However terrible these narratives may be, people's lives, it turns out, are infinitely rich, rich in humour as well as tragedy.

SL You say the mainspring for the novel was the story of a woman whose son had been imprisoned—and of course that remains in the story. Yet the central relationship is surely that between Anna, the poet-narrator, and her daughter Alyona—which mirrors Anna's relationship with her own mother. It's a novel above all about mothers and daughters, isn't it?

LP Perhaps that seems the most striking thing because the relationship between mothers and daughters is virtually taboo in literature. Or at least, how can one put it—there has been a certain legend, a dream, an ideal that probably existed before Jesus Christ—that love for one's mother is the most holy form of love, and, as with all myths, the discovery that it isn't true, in the experience of a particular person, is shattering. A person is shattered if they discover in themselves not love but hatred towards their own mother—or their own child. They realize that they are fallen, that they are outcasts, they have defied the order of things. You can fight with God or be an atheist, but hate your own mother—that you can't do.

Once, years ago, I attended some do at the theatre and beforehand I went backstage with a lovely group of women—all of them writers or actors or artists or directors, what have you, working in the theatre, and as we were waiting for the show to begin we sat and drank coffee and told each other stories—there was a wonderful atmosphere. And I decided to try out one question on them: did they want to be like their mothers? A howl went up and one and all replied: No! They couldn't imagine anything more dreadful than to turn out like their mothers!

SL   One of the most striking features in this story is the disparity in the mother's behaviour towards her son and her daughter: her adoration and pity for Andrei and her constant fury and despair at Alyona. It's especially striking because of the brutal way Andrei treats Anna, his mother—on the face of it he's the most difficult character to feel sympathy for.

LP   But imagine the life of a young man who's been crippled by prison! Andrei feels destroyed as a person. How can he go on living? And imagine a mother's feelings when the life of her child, this separate life which she can't control, is turned upside-down before her eyes! What suffering, incomparable, Homeric suffering!

I'm sure that you'll come in the end to understand Andrei and pity him. Because his is the story of a person who's heading full tilt towards death. I simply didn't have the strength to see that story to the bitter end—because *she*, Anna, wouldn't have the strength to bear it, not that. There were a lot of things that had to be left out in the end, that were beyond limits.

At the beginning, for instance, I was strongly tempted to develop the daughter's diary, which Anna, the mother, presents to us and comments on so scathingly. But the structure of the novel demanded brevity—and I realized in the end that the diary as it stands was enough.

At first I'd made the diary much more genuinely erotic—but Russian readers aren't used to that sort of thing and I felt sorry for them! So later I made it much more humorous, interrupting the diary with Anna's various interjections. Her comments put paid to any eroticism that remained!

SL   Alyona's assigned a pretty poor role in her mother's account of things, isn't she? All the teenage emotions she expresses in the diary are made a mockery of. We see her as a hopelessly gullible character, like so many of your young heroines—incapable of controlling her own life, constantly getting pregnant by men who don't care for her and depending on her mother to come to her rescue.

But putting together the evidence of Anna's own life we realize that she was just as feckless as her daughter and just as much the object of her own mother's disapproval. Both Anna's children were 'mishaps' too, and she remains just as susceptible to men as Alyona. And in the end we see Alyona after all taking charge of her own life, proving her mother redundant. So between the lines she emerges as a much stronger, more valiant character than her mother gives her credit for.

LP   Anna is the heroine of the novel, it's her story, while her daughter remains in the background, she's seen only through her mother's eyes. But it quite often happens that someone tells us a story about another person, perhaps a rather negative story—and later on we meet this same person and find they're quite different from the way they were described to us, which in turn makes us relate to the original story-teller quite differently. It dawns on us that perhaps the negative character isn't the one we heard the story about, but the story-teller herself. The harshest judges are often those who deserve judgement themselves.

Anna thinks she understands her daughter perfectly—that she knows exactly what motivates her behaviour. But what she knows about her daughter is what she knows about herself. And that's terribly offensive to Alyona, who thinks of herself as being completely different from her mother.

A mother should never be too intimately involved in her daughter's affairs or a father in his son's—it's terribly damaging for an older person to impose his experience on a younger one, to assume that the younger person is as corrupted as himself. A parent has so much more experience than his child, has seen so much more, has so much more reason to fear. He can spoil the innocence of his child by his own imagination.

So in the novel the thread of the daughter's life flows somewhere beneath the text. We can see that her story is terrible in many ways—the story of a person who loves and is constantly rejected, who knew from the beginning that she came second to her adored brother. A child who feels unloved will always have problems and go in perpetual search of love elsewhere. Alyona has been deprived of a father and to all intents and purposes a mother too: hence her desire to compensate by creating her own big family, to develop through them the self-esteem that her mother never allowed her.

And then—so we understand from the little epigraph at the beginning—the mother dies (we never know when or how) and the daughter reads this text, these 'Notes from the Edge of the Table', including her mother's hurtful commentaries on her daughter's diary—and Alyona forgives her mother, forgives her everything.

The fact that she hands over these notes—anonymously, without seeking any reward for herself—testifies to the fact that she has come to think of her mother as a separate person, that she no longer thinks of her through the film of her own egoism—and that she wants to leave a trace of her mother's life on earth. In doing so she proves herself already a different person from the daughter her mother described. She's not only rejected the past—she's become older and wiser than her own mother. She's forgiven her. Neither the grandmother, Anna's mother, nor Anna herself was capable of that! And that's the note of hope that the novel gives—we are allowed to hope that with Alyona's act of forgiveness the vicious circle, that endless circle of revenge and recrimination, will at last be broken.

sl So the novel isn't quite as 'black' as it appears at first?

lp No—one of the purposes of that little explanatory preamble, the epigraph, was to take away some of the shock of the ending, where we see Anna left alone and defeated, forced to realize that nobody needs her—not even her beloved grandson.

I wanted to let the reader know that the story was over now, it was all in the past. I know from readers, even so, how shocking the ending is—people write and tell me that this is the hardest thing they've ever read. I always tell them that they ought to read the novel a second time and they'd find a good deal to laugh at in it—in the diary, and in Andrei's dreadful conversations with his mother, and in Anna's wishful thinking about the awful men she meets. She's always absurd when she imagines herself still a great beauty!

So I hope that the second time round readers will cease to take it on a purely tragic level and see the humour in it.

sl The same applies to a lot of your work, especially the plays—there's so much grotesquerie as well as tragedy in the way your characters behave to one another.

lp I want readers to enjoy themselves. In the end that's why I write, in the hope of readers who can appreciate and smile at a word or a phrase that's just right, at some precise observation, at the way that words can magically transform things. I want readers who won't take everything literally—who are capable, let's say, of looking at a painting of St Sebastian and not just bursting into tears but saying—how beautiful it is!

A work of art should be taken as precisely that, and not as a record of this or that person's suffering.

SL Part of the pleasure in reading your work is in fitting together the jigsaw of different voices and reading between the lines. When can we believe what Anna's telling us? Much of the time she's just unconsciously comical, but she can also be very clear-sighted and witty.

LP Anna's own assessment of herself constantly changes. It's a fantastic thing the way a person's view of himself can change in the space of ten minutes. A person can never get at his own secret—never. He will create himself in a certain image one moment but ten minutes later that image will start to double and triple and eventually disappear altogether—and something quite different will replace it. It's the most mysterious thing, the way a person defines himself—or rather, the way he lacks any firm internal portrait of himself.

But of course I do give some clues to figuring Anna out. I offer a direct key to her suffering in the scene where she goes into the kitchen and sees the young people standing there—sees that 'the light of youth' shines in them—and realizes that there's no place for her there beside them. And she's quite right. That's when she sets off to see her mother, the only person who needs her now, needs her in particular—her intervention, her kindness, her heart.

A child is a creature who immediately arouses other people's protective feelings, whereas who needs the old? Dreadful, smelly, mad, who needs them? Their children are all they have, the only people left to love them. The Lord God brought children into this world armed with beauty and tenderness and light, whereas the old have nothing to offer. God leaves them to the mercy of those around them, those who are capable of stepping onto a higher plane and taking on God's mercy themselves.

SL I imagine that the most difficult thing of all—especially perhaps after living with the novel so long, putting so much into it—was to find the right ending or realize that you *had* an ending.

LP That's always the most difficult thing. I knew that I had to find some resolution—there was so much energy packed into this novel, it was like a tightly coiled spring. And at the same time I wanted to leave the door open, not seal it totally. I had to find that one point—that small detail—that would hold it down and yet leave it ready to spring open every time it was read. Art is the only form of *perpetuum mobile* there is, it has to work afresh every time or it isn't real art. The reader must be jolted every time—jolted I hope, in the end, into tears. Because tears are a release. You have to weep—not so much over the hero or heroine as over life itself, the world.

I searched a long time for that little detail that would leave readers with a sense of relief—with tears. I knew there could be no victory for Anna, for the heroine—she had to be defeated if she was to become a person, *holy*, a true poet. She had to give in, give up the struggle, become human.

SL For the foreign reader one of the most striking features of the life you depict in your work is simply its material poverty. A sociologist could take any number of your plays or stories and say: here's the stark truth about everyday Russian life in the 1970s and 1980s—food shortages, cramped flats, family quarrels.

LP Well, I don't think the essential things I write about—mothers and children, family relationships—differ so much from one country to another, but there's no doubt that conditions here, especially the fact of all the generations being crammed together, can aggravate things. One of Bulgakov's characters [Voland, in *The Master and Margarita*] says something to the effect that the Russians would be a fine people if it weren't for the question of apartments! Everyone living together in one apartment makes life very difficult.

SL We've talked a lot about the problems children have with their mothers—but of course children bring grief as well as joy to their parents. Sometimes it seems from your work that a parent can *never* win—as Anna says, 'Love them and they'll tear you to pieces, don't love them and they'll leave you all the same ...'.

LP Well it's true, you know. There are many paradoxes in life. We want parents to love their children but if a child grows up surrounded by love he may spend the rest of his life searching for it—and who will give him such love again? And he'll go through terrible suffering when his parents die. In a strange way love in childhood can disarm a person.

SL I'm reminded by what you say of a paradox that emerges constantly in your work, which might crudely be summed up by the saying 'You have to be cruel to be kind'. Ordinary human kindness isn't a quality one comes across much in your work, whereas apparently cruel acts are seen sometimes at least to have good effects.

LP You know, even the most selfish and egotistical people can play an important role in life because they awaken our pity. The longer their self-absorption continues, their solitude, the more they look like prisoners of themselves—the more sorry people feel for them.

Egoists in our society play a role similar to that of the caste of beggars in India who don't have the right to work—not just that they can't find work but they don't have the right to lift a finger: all they can do is ask and beg. Their role is precisely to uncover the sources of kindness in other people.

SL One effect of your having waited so long for your work to be published is that your earliest work has been read almost simultaneously with your more recent writing. Looking back on your earliest stories now yourself, do you think you've changed much as a writer?

LP I would like to think that I've maintained the level of those first works—that I haven't fundamentally changed. I don't want to! I think of myself as a documentary writer, collecting documents about people's lives and reworking them, and I hope that I can still 'process' these documents today with as much strength and love as I used to—with as strong a pity.

But I'm afraid I have changed lately—to my great regret. One of my recent stories—'The Way of Eros'*—even has a happy ending, or at least the possibility of a happy ending!

* 'Po doroge boga Erosa', first published in 'V sadakh drugikh vozmozhnostei: rasskazy', in *Novy mir* (1993).

SL The hero and heroine in that story at last find the way to each other's hearts, don't they?—and the dream of a woman 'becoming young again' seems finally to be vindicated.

LP Yes, and that story won the hearts of a lot of people who hated me before and convinced a few others who weren't sure! I've been writing a lot of fairy-tales too, and fairy-tales have to end happily. No doubt in some way I've been influenced by the changes around me—in any case, these things are beyond one's control.

But in essence I don't think I've changed that much, and the right people have always understood me. Horrible people and fools, as I've told you, are never going to like my stories—so luckily the people who surround me have always been clever, nice, generous, shining people!

Like a woman I knew, a children's doctor—she was a simply wonderful person—fantastically good, kind, clever. She devoted her life to looking after children and looked after her husband like a child as well, earned the living for both of them while he pursued his endless studies. She died very young, her youngest daughter was only 19 years old, but the most fantastic thing was the way she died. She was ill for three years, in the most terrible way—she lost her mind, went senile, and no longer recognized anyone. But in those three years she gave her family the chance to love and care for her, to feel that they were good people too—the chance as well to get used to her dying so that when death came they experienced it not as a grief but as a liberation.

They looked after her wonderfully and at the end they could feel they had done their duty—that was also her gift to them. You see how God looks after us! There was such justice in that story. It's sometimes said that people who've led a saintly life die easily, but it's not true. So many fine people have had terrible deaths. Think of all those who died in the camps, in Kolyma. Such things deserve to be studied. In general, you know, this world of ours is such a wise, clever text. It deserves to be read.

◆   ◆   ◆

Six Years Earlier

SL Until recently your plays were known only to a very limited circle, and you are still waiting for your first collection of stories to be published. How do you feel this lack of recognition has affected you as a writer?

LP Up until now my whole existence as a writer has been in question—and even now it's by no means assured. But oddly enough I've always considered that state of affairs to be not just natural but even essential for both my life and my work. You can see plenty of cases where mass publication and acclaim, and all the material benefits and public status they bring, have subtly or not so subtly altered the outlook of a writer.

My family belonged to the Moscow intelligentsia, and like any child who grows up surrounded by books I naturally wanted to write. I studied journalism at the university and later worked as a journalist, and all that time I was writing away,

Interview recorded in May 1987.

trying to imitate my favourite writers: Joyce, Proust, Bunin, Bulgakov, Thomas Mann. But all that early writing—before I found my own voice—was just nonsense, pastiche, parody.

I was terribly conscious of the huge moral demands made on writers in Russia, the passion and modesty required of them. As you know, Russian literature has been a kind of religion in this country—a religion based on the moral position of writers, on their suffering. All our greatest writers have been sufferers and saints: Pushkin, Akhmatova, Tsvetayeva, Bulgakov—all of them. Our literature has been the substance and essence of my whole life, as it has for millions of ordinary people, for whom it has provided the only source of light throughout their long, hard lives. The great classic writers of the nineteenth century and the early part of the twentieth represented the heights for us, the snowy peaks of literature. Alongside them most Soviet writers—those who got printed, that is—looked paltry and insignificant. The memory of those great writers, many of whom never knew peace and respect in their own lives, casts a brilliant light over all of us still today.

SL Do you not see writers today who belong to that great tradition?

LP Of course there are fine writers in each generation. For many years now I've been reading the manuscripts of young authors, all of whom write much better than the people who get printed, but for the most part they're unable to find any outlet for their work. Many of them simply stop writing, or turn to writing children's books or film scripts instead—or leave Russia. Or leave life. To survive these conditions as a writer you have to have—I don't know, something out of the ordinary.

SL You mentioned 'finding your own voice' in your writing. How did that happen for you?

LP I've been writing, as I say, for as long as I can remember, but all of it was worthless until I was overtaken by ordinary life, until I joined the ranks of the millions of ordinary people who know the meaning of loss and suffering. My family were dependent on my being able to work, and if my son fell ill it meant disaster. My first husband was struck down by a terrible illness, he was paralysed for six years before he died and received only a miserly pension. He was a saintly man. From time to time it seems Jesus Christ appears in the world in the guise of ordinary people, and he was one such person. In general I've been very lucky in life: I've known many, many extraordinarily good people.

Five years after my first husband died I married again; we had two more children and now I'm a grandmother. My second husband saved me. Spiritually I was in a terrible state. But those years of struggle and loneliness opened my eyes. I felt the life of ordinary people enter me and demand some outlet. The doors were closed to most ordinary women; I wanted to open them at least a chink, and that's how I started to write properly. About the lives of people I knew; about my friends or just people I'd met in passing.

Many people have told me the stories of their lives—on trains, in queues, in hospitals, at bus stops. People are forever telling each other stories, but not many people set store by them and not many people have tried to write them down. I carry these endless monologues around inside me and I remember them forever. Not a single thing in my stories and plays is invented.

Of course it would be immoral and hurtful simply to serve up straight a single person's life story, and it wouldn't be real art. But all the raw ingredients I use come from real life, and they turn out to be much more powerful than anything you could invent. I believe all the best writers have essentially worked in that way. I used to study them endlessly, all the classics. Except Chekhov. You can't learn from Chekhov. He's so simple, so pure, his genius is invisible. It's a fantastic thing. The same with Pushkin. Who could learn the 'technique' that makes his *Tales of Belkin* so great?

But when I started writing properly I stopped trying to imitate and wrote just as simply as I could, without metaphor or simile, in the voice people use to tell their story to another person on the bus—urgently, hastily, making sure you come to the point before the bus stops and the other person has to get off. And then you know that the story will get passed on, and that's the beginning of folklore—not traditional folklore, with all its embellishments and repetitions, but city folklore, that unrecognized murmur of city people that goes on all the time—the folklore of chance encounter. Such stories have to be told at speed, and the plot is never the point—sometimes they begin at the end, and the story consists just in explaining how that end came about. Sometimes there *can* be no end in the traditional sense. . . .

Of course my circle of readers has been artificially limited by the fact that I've been so little published, and I don't allow my work to be passed around and copied in typescript—people feel free to steal and plagiarize your work if it isn't published.

I feel desperate now to get at least one book out. I wrote a letter to Gorbachev and the message was very simple, it was a cry from the heart: I won't live to see my book published, help me! How long are we going to go on publishing writers only after they're dead? My book of stories has been doing the rounds since the 1970s, and the publishers keep putting it off and putting it off. How long can they go on? I'm still waiting, I'm still standing in that never-ending queue.

Well, I got a letter from one of Gorbachev's secretaries and it looks as if my plea may have worked, but you can never be sure. I went through the same process with *Three Girls in Blue*, appealing to Chernenko to have it staged.

SL But hasn't the climate changed radically since then?

LP Of course things are getting easier now. Mind you, all the same old bureaucrats are still in place and you have to work round them. But you can feel the pressure exerted by decent people now, there's a rising tide. We work like the Mafia—like good mafiosi!—recognizing one another and doing our best to help. Decent people were always there, but the possibilities for helping one another are much greater now.

The press plays an enormous moral and social role these days—my husband is permanently sunk in the newspaper, there's so much interesting stuff to be read, and many writers have turned to writing articles, what we call *publitsistika*. Literature's a strange thing, though. Readers still have a thirst for it, for real books.

SL Do you see youself as a 'women's writer'? Do you think there's such a thing as 'women's literature'?

LP I don't regard myself as a 'women's writer'. I write above all about children, not about women; the land I inhabit is a land of children, not of grown-ups. What happens to the children when people treat each other the way they do? Do we have the right to treat each other like that? Those questions are at the heart of all my stories and plays.

People often accuse me of not having 'positive heroes'. But my positive hero is the reader or the spectator. When people sit together in the theatre watching a play and all of them weep or laugh or clap simultaneously it's a fantastic thing—it means that the same thoughts and emotions have entered all their hearts at once.

SL How do you explain the fact that it's been somewhat easier to get your plays published or performed than it has been to publish your stories?

LP I think my plays will always be more successful and popular than my stories because, for a start, the humour in them is more obvious. You have to give the audience a chance to relax and laugh; Shakespeare knew all about that with his Falstaff. It's such happiness to sit and laugh in a theatre in a human way—not at somebody else but at yourself, at human beings.

Mark Zakharov, the director of *Three Girls in Blue*, said that at first the actors kept asking 'Why is it all so black?' They treated the characters as people apart from themselves at first. Then they began to pity them, and finally they understood that the play was about *us*. And you could feel the way their acting changed as a result.

In the theatre people have the opportunity to be together and create a kind of common humanity in the face of suffering. The catharsis they experience when they laugh and cry together is a great victory over themselves, over everything in them that is evil or absurd. Stories don't give you that possibility. You're alone as a reader, with no support from others, and a person on his own has much less strength. That's why my stories will always be regarded as more 'difficult'.

This year I've had stories accepted by two journals in Russia, *Avrora* and *Neva*, and one journal in Estonia—people who used to have their hands tied are now free to use them. Moscow, my native city, is the most difficult nut to crack though—as always there's a great battle going on for a place in the sun, and I sense there's no place for me here at the moment. Perhaps there never will be.

SL Is it possible to pin-point the things that have made you an 'outsider'?

LP I'm an outsider partly because I'm out of step with my own generation. Chronologically I'm a member of the Thaw generation of writers that came of age in the 1960s—the so-called *shestidesyatniki*—though I'm a bit younger than the best-known names: Yevtushenko, Voznesensky, Akhmadulina, Aksyonov. But I was never part of that set anyway because I began writing properly quite late, when I was nearly 30 years old. Those writers were already famous when I was just starting.

Before the Revolution many wealthy people were ashamed of their wealth and did their best to help poor people as much as possible, but it isn't like that today. Soviet people who've done well—including writers—are mostly quite stingy about giving help to others, they're too interested in buying a new car or whatever. They have a bad influence on young people, who've become very demanding. I see the difference even in my own children. My oldest son had quite a deprived childhood and he still refuses to dress well, almost as a matter of principle. My younger son expects much more materially.

In general, though, I don't think people change that much from generation to generation. That's why literature will always be needed. People will go on seeking the truth about themselves. You can't change human beings: Jesus Christ first undertook to do that 2,000 years ago, and look where we are today! But you can help them just a little to understand who they are, and what their lives are all about.

3
Vladimir Makanin
(b. 1937)

Vladimir Makanin is a professional outsider: someone who, like many of his heroes, has always lived on borderlines and resisted belonging. A Muscovite with strong roots in the Urals, an intellectual with a pronounced practical bent, Makanin has retained, in his writing, something of the austerity and rigour of his first profession, mathematics. Neither 'official' nor 'dissident', at odds with both his own generation of 1960s liberals—*shestidesyatniki*—and with the younger 'School of Moscow prose'* to which critics, at one time, sought to assimilate him, Makanin was to write for almost two decades before finding a secure place in the literary mainstream.

To the combination of opposites which Makanin embodies, it is perhaps worth adding that, physically, he is a strong, vigorous-looking man who resembles, with his big frame and slightly Asiatic features, the Cossack grandfather whom he describes in the interview that follows. But he also walks with a pronounced limp, the result of a serious car accident in his early thirties which left him confined to bed for two years. The shock of this accident reverberates through Makanin's writing, informing recurrent images of abandonment and helplessness. Yet many of his 'weakest' characters—the sick or simple-minded—prove to have a hidden strength, while, conversely, the physically strong may turn out to be impotent and doomed. Tatyana Tolstaya,† speaking of Makanin's objectivity and 'coolness', has stressed the 'masculinity' of his work, a quality underscored by abundant imagery of hard, physical labour: digging, hacking, tunnelling. But a feminine principle is equally at work, finding in weakness a gift and a dignity.

Makanin's peculiar status in life—as both member of and outsider in so many camps—may have contributed to the preoccupation, in his writing, with estrangement, loss, and the nature of belonging. But it has also afforded him a kind of

---

* See Introduction, p. xxi.

† Tatyana Tolstaya discusses Makanin's work with Karen Stepanyan in *Voprosy literatury*, 2 (1988).

Olympian vantage point, allowing him to survey, with easy authority, multiple dimensions of human life.

Born in the town of Orsk in the Urals, Vladimir Makanin grew up in a mining settlement on the border of Europe and Asia. Images of life there in the hungry, post-war years, as well as from the myths and legends of the region, would later shape much of his work. In 1954 he moved to Moscow to study mathematics at Moscow University and, after graduating, worked for a time at an institute specializing in weapons research, later publishing a monograph on the military application of linear programming. In 1965, following the successful publication of his first novel, *A Straight Line*, Makanin abandoned his first career, and after a brief excursion into cinema (he studied screen writing at VGIK, the All-Union Institute of Cinematography, from 1965 to 1967) he turned full time to writing and settled permanently in Moscow.

Based on his experience at the military research institute, *A Straight Line* had been relatively conventional both in its implicit attitude towards issues of the day—the threat of nuclear war, the problem of cynicism and complacency in the workplace—and its narrative technique: the novel privileges the ethical standpoint of its first-person narrator, the moral innocent Volodya Belov, over the attitudes of the collective he confronts, and adheres to strict chronology in its presentation of events. It was published, to modest acclaim, in the journal *Moskva*; Makanin later reworked it as a screenplay for a film released by the Gorky studios in 1969.

But the works that followed were less easily assimilated to the conventional aesthetics and didactic traditions of Soviet literature, and in the 1970s Makanin found himself shunned by the editors of the prestigious Moscow monthlies. His stories and novels appeared in book form only (a marginal form of publication in the Soviet Union at the time) and throughout the 1970s received little critical attention.

Like *A Straight Line*, early works such as *Orphanhood* (1971) contrasted the anachronistic idealism of the hero with the growing materialism and self-serving ambition of post-war Soviet society. But Makanin's distanced, ironic treatment of his 'superfluous' heroes suggested an interest in their social dislocation more sceptical and far-reaching than that sanctioned by liberal social criticism. What makes some individuals adapt and thrive, while others falter, resist, and get left behind? Or by what process does a 'normal' person, apparently well attuned to life, lose his bearings and find himself cast out? Already in these early works, such questions pointed to a pessimism about the tractability of human problems that was at odds with both official and liberal ideology at the time.

By the late 1970s, works such as the novella *A Portrait and its Surroundings**[*] (1978), and the stories 'Citizen in Flight'[†] and 'Klyucharyov and Alimushkin'[‡] (1979) had begun to extract these questions from their specific social milieu. To be sure, the familiar settings are still there: the settlement in the Urals, the Moscow apartment. But the form of these stories makes clear that we are in the realm, not of social history, but of existential puzzle or parable.

---

[*] *Portret i vokrug* (1978).
[†] 'Grazhdanin ubegayushchy' (dated 1978, published 1979).
[‡] 'Klyucharyov i Alimushkin' (dated 1977, published 1979).

Indeed, the term 'stories' is a misnomer to the extent that it evokes expectations of chronological order, tension, and resolution. 'Klyucharyov and Alimushkin' thwarts such expectations at the outset by presenting its entire 'story', or premiss, in the opening lines, with the bare precision of a mathematical formula or a scientific hypothesis: 'A man suddenly noticed that the more good luck he had in life, the more misfortune befell another man.' What follows is an investigation of this hypothesis—or, to use a musical analogy, the elaboration, in a series of variations, of a simple initial theme. The number of such variations is theoretically infinite, and each, inviting us to review the theme in different moods, gives satisfaction precisely in its changed reference to developments already known. In *A Portrait and its Surroundings* the first-person narrator—one of Makanin's several *alter egos*, the writer Igor Petrovich—invites us to examine, from contrasting points of view, the ambiguous personality of his powerful acquaintance Starokhatov. But in the course of this examination the writer himself becomes an object of scrutiny, part and parcel of an experiment whose conclusions are necessarily provisional.

Makanin's search for forms adequate to his principled scepticism led to the incorporation of openly self-reflective, authorial passages in *Voices* (dated 1977, published 1982), his most ambitious work yet. Incorporating, in chronological disorder, several disparate historical periods, from the legendary past of the Urals to the post-war period and the present day, *Voices* signalled Makanin's urge to pursue his investigation of archetypal human patterns down the vertical axis of history and myth, in a text as fragmentary and outwardly chaotic as the evidence by which the archaeologist reconstructs the past and makes audible its voices. Later, Makanin would use the same montage technique in *Loss* (1987) and *Our Way is Long* (1993).

Voices marked a critical breakthrough for Makanin, attracting the admiration of younger critics with its innovative form and free narrative technique. But it was the publication of *The Precursor* (1982) that brought him to the notice of a broader public, exciting widespread interest by its presentation of a visionary healer, Yakushkin, as its central character: at the time, such healers were the talk of Moscow. Is Yakushkin merely a quack—as his patent recipe of herbs and toothpaste suggests—or is he possessed of genuine spiritual powers? Presenting his hero in shifting guises, Makanin typically leaves his reader to decide.

Suddenly in the limelight after long years in obscurity, Makanin sparked further controversy, in 1987, with the publication of his novel *One and One*. The novel (whose Russian title, *Odin i odna*, plays untranslatably with the distinction of gender in Russian), tells of a 'man of the sixties', Gennady Pavlovich, and his female counterpart, Ninel Nikolayevna, both of whom suffer from a debilitating nostalgia for the past: he for the brief, glorious period in his youth when he was an outspoken hero of the post-Stalin Thaw, thronged by admirers, a member of his age; she, as hopelessly, for the moral and cultural values embodied in nineteenth-century Russian literature. Both, now in middle age, find themselves estranged from the times, lonely, cut off, their will to live depleted. Many readers, as Makanin relates here, were shocked that he should thus 'defame' his own idealistic generation, whose later capitulation to the dreary ethos of Brezhnev's Russia had already come under fierce scrutiny in the new 'thaw' of the *glasnost* era.

Both novels in that sense could be read as social commentary on fashionable issues of the day. Yet both, at a deeper level, represented a further development of Makanin's meditation on the theme of estrangement and loss—Yakushkin's eventual loss of his healing gift in *The Precursor*, and the sense of irreversible exclusion experienced by both protagonists in *One and One*, to the point where each has lost the ability to connect or love. The titles of the two novellas published concurrently with *One and One*—*Loss* and *The One Left Behind*—might just as aptly have been given to these two works.

The term *otstavshy*, 'the one left behind', mirrors the word *ubegayushchy*—'fleeing', or 'escaping'—used in the title of Makanin's earlier story 'Citizen in Flight'. Together the two words signal Makanin's awareness of a profound ambivalence in the individual's relationship to the collective, the 'crowd': both a dread of exclusion and a longing to escape. Only in Makanin's first novel, *A Straight Line*, is this relationship conventionally construed, with the hero's distinction from the common herd presented in morally heroic terms. Subsequent works make plain that Makanin's concern is not to judge the guilt or innocence of either party, but to explore the dynamics of the relationship itself.

In 1991 Makanin published *The Manhole*, an apocalyptic story in which Klyucharyov, hero of several previous works, is found struggling for survival in a city divided between an underground realm of safety and plenty and an overground wilderness in which human society has virtually ceased to function: the lights have gone out, stray, frightened figures scamper between dark buildings, rape and robbery take place unremarked, and the dead are left unburied. From time to time the eerie silence is broken by the baying of a huge, rampaging mob, out of control, purposeless, and lethal. In the midst of this Klyucharyov struggles to dig a cave to shelter his family—his wife and their overgrown, retarded son—and to find a way to bury his dead friend, crushed to death in one of the stampedes. He is the only figure in the story who has access, through a hidden manhole, to the underground world. There, civilized men and women sit round, converse, and drink, discussing the philosophical issues that have troubled Russians for centuries. They attend to Klyucharyov's cuts and bruises—descent through the manhole is painful and difficult—offer him spiritual and alcoholic refreshment, and enquire solicitously about the situation 'overground'. Klyucharyov returns to the overground armed with the things he needs: a pickaxe, a crowbar, a shovel, some candles. But the manhole is narrowing; soon, he fears, he may be cut off altogether. Nor is the underground realm quite as safe as it appears at first. There is plenty of light down there—in contrast to the world above, fixed in a state of permanent twilight—but oxygen is in short supply. From time to time people die discreetly and are carted away.

The Manhole contained clear allusions to the chaotic and threatening state of affairs in Russia at the time, but it also presented, in transparently bifurcated form, the two faces of 'the collective', whose properties Makanin was to make explicit in 'The Theme of Levelling', a series of four connected stories-cum-essays, published the following year. Framed as a meditation begun in a queue for food, 'Levelling' almost physically enacts its subject: squeezed and jostled by the queue, the writer simultaneously watches a huge crowd swarming into the metro and experiences a vertiginous desire to flow down with it into this 'underground pharynx'. Orwell, writes Makanin, saw how people could be cowed by terror, but he did not anticipate that they would in due course come instinctively to 'level themselves', to cover their tracks, to seek invisibility in the crowd. The impulse is suicidal, self-castrating; at the end of 'Levelling', Makanin tells the story of a retarded boy, sunk in his idiot's bliss as a prostitute from the queue, giving him his heart's desire, meanwhile robs him of his purchases—his 'selfhood'. Escape, however, entails its own terrors. 'Levelling' also records the fear of an orphaned boy, fleeing across a river to escape the Red Army; years later, his fear would resurface in the nightmares of his young son. The boy was Makanin's father, and all Makanin's works can be seen, in some way, to stalk the nightmare he inherited.

In a novella published in 1993—which won the Booker Prize for the best Russian novel that year—Makanin appears finally to have tracked down his prey. In this moment of confrontation with the theme that haunts him, history and landscape are dispensed with: the scene is reduced to a bare room with the minimum of props. The title of the work is just *A Baize-Covered Table with a Decanter in the Middle*. Not a very suggestive title to a Western reader; but to most Russians, above a certain age at least, its meaning is painfully obvious: we are back in the interrogation room. Not necessarily in prison; perhaps just seeing the boss, or some authority; applying for something, asking permission. The point is that you are on one side of the table, 'they' are on the other; they are the ones who ask the questions, you are the one who has to explain himself. In a way Makanin had employed an interrogator's tactics with his title, extracting from his readers an admission of complicity. So you recognize the furniture? So you must have been there too.

Table is a profoundly personal work. Makanin, here, is pitiless with his hero: again and again, in memory and anticipation, he drags him back to the 'primal' scene of inquisition—of being laid bare, uncovered, dismantled. Yet his anatomization of the hero's vulnerability and entrapment is, at the same time, highly abstract. Fear on the one hand, authority on the other, are seen as functions not of temperament or experience or even a fixed distribution of power, but of a relationship to the 'table', the symbol of collective authority, in which the people on either side are in principle interchangeable, and all are accomplices in investing 'the table' with power.

Makanin has been thought a 'difficult' writer by many of his critics. There are few sunlit landscapes in his work. Many of his characters seem to exist in the same perpetual twilight that eerily pervades the overground world in *Manhole*; some, like the blind men hired to dig the tunnel in *Loss*, are literally confined to darkness. At the end of *Our Way is Long*—one of whose protagonists finds life so brutal that he voluntarily confines himself to hospital—the whole cast of characters is found crouched by camp fires in the bare, dark expanse of the steppe, warming themselves like their primeval ancestors while they wait in vain for a helicopter to see their flickering lights and rescue them.

Makanin offers no rescue. As Tatyana Tolstaya said of him, 'he's a writer for grown-ups', not a pedagogue or healer. To enter his world is not to go on a tour, with a fixed destination and a guide to point out the sights, but to enter a private laboratory with the words 'Silence, experiment in progress' affixed to the door. Yet we are invited to watch the experiment as it unfolds, and if we pay attention there are clear signs to tell us what is going on. For all the abstract precision of his work, Makanin's subject is after all human beings in their complexity and ambivalence. The world they inhabit is concrete, three-dimensional. In fact, Makanin is deceptively easy on first reading. His style is straightforward and realistic, and although hardly any of his works are based on one simple, linear plot, each incorporates multiple different stories, told with the unhurried ease of the natural raconteur. The openness of his narratives, moreover, gives them an air of spaciousness, of potential infinity: with Makanin, one always feels there is more to be said.

◆   ◆   ◆

sl Tell me about your background. I know you were born in one of the most fateful years of Russian history—1937, the height of the Terror.

vm In a fateful year and a fateful place. I was born in Orsk, a small town on the Ural river. I had to cross the river every day to go to school and, as it happens, the river marks the border between Europe and Asia, though it isn't all that big. So I crossed the border between Europe and Asia every day—that was a symbol of bifurcation that I grew up with.

I felt it very clearly. There we were, right in the middle, between Siberia and the European part of Russia. So whenever you took a train there were two simple choices—either to go to Siberia or to Moscow. A total polarization. Already as a child you understood what was what: that way lay Moscow, that way Siberia—everything was comprehensible straightaway.

sl What sort of town was Orsk?

vm It was just a small place then, though it's grown bigger since. But in fact I grew up not in the town but in a nearby settlement, across the river. It had developed around the factory that my father had built and where he worked as an engineer. We lived close by, about five kilometres away.

sl The settlement is a central image in your work—the location for many of your stories. I suppose you could say that it too is an 'in-between' place, neither town nor country?

vm Yes, it was a very artificial environment that I grew up in, a kind of micro-climate—neither the village with its traditional ways nor a proper city. It was a typical creation of those years, when everything was geared around work, indus-trialization, the big leap forward.*

In the first years after the war, before we got a proper apartment, we lived in barracks. Those were very difficult, hungry years. The system was very harsh; no one living in the settlement was allowed to work anywhere except the factory. But bit by bit vegetable gardens sprang up, pigs were kept, cows—just so that people could feed themselves. So on the one hand there we were, an intelligentsia family, my father a first-class engineer—but at the same time, like everyone else, we kept a cow! There was something unnatural in the whole situation, although

Interview recorded in December 1991.

* A reference to Stalin's drive for the rapid industrialization of the Soviet Union in the late 1920s and the 1930s. This period saw huge numbers of former peasants drafted in from the countryside to work in newly constructed plants and factories, living in overcrowded barracks in settlements such as Makanin describes.

at the time it seemed normal to me because I'd never known anything different. It was only when I went to the country proper that I understood that this was real Russia, old Russia—and I immediately began to see things quite differently.

But the good thing was that it was an eclectic background. I got a proper education and was able to get into Moscow University without any difficulty. So there was sufficient room for intellectual development, but at the same time we were somehow close to the earth. There was one very difficult year after the war when my father decided he'd have to buy a pig to feed us through the next winter—there were four of us in the family then, four sons. So he asked a couple of workers to help him build a pigsty and got a pig; we called him George. That was in 1947. We had a more difficult time during those post-war years than we had during the war itself.

That was the time my younger brother died. My father had been arrested on a trumped-up charge—Stalin had launched a new campaign in the late forties, all sorts of people were being arrested, and my father was one of the victims, accused of 'sabotage'. So for a time we had no father and of course our material situation immediately deteriorated; my mother had to work a double shift as a teacher, and we started going hungry. Anyway, my brother gradually got weaker and weaker and in the end he died of some infection. We were told afterwards that penicillin would have saved him, but there was no penicillin to be had then.

My father was released to come to the funeral. You can see us here [Makanin showed me a photograph], standing round the little open coffin, my father still with his head shaven, just out of prison.

The scene of his release was something out of a movie. He would normally have spent ten years in prison—that was the usual sentence in those days. But it happened that I had an uncle who was a Civil War hero, a partisan, an old, lame man with a wooden leg. He had a pistol at home that he'd been allowed to keep, and he took this pistol and went straight to the procurator and said, 'Release him, otherwise I'll shoot you.' 'How can I?' 'That's your business.' 'I can't, Grigory.' But at the same time the procurator knew he shouldn't argue with my uncle, a hero. 'Go on, release him,' my uncle said. 'He's got children to feed, they need him. I've got nothing to lose,' he said, 'I'm a Civil War hero and they won't touch me, but I'll definitely shoot you if you don't do what I say.'

Well of course the procurator couldn't just acquit my father, that was never done, but he changed the charge against him from sabotage to negligence, and as my father had already served eighteen months by that time, they released him—though for the next five years he was deprived of half his salary as a so-called 'conditional punishment'.

Those were the kind of stories that happened in those days.

SL Your novella *The Blue and the Red*,* where we meet your hero Klyucharyov as a young boy in the 1940s, records the struggle between two grandmothers—the 'blue-blooded' one and the 'red' one, the peasant—to claim the boy's soul and direct his future. Is that an autobiographical story?

VM Loosely speaking, yes. There are two strands, two different Russian traditions running through my family, or through me: the 'gentry' line was my father's, and

---

* *Goluboye i krasnoye* (dated 1981), in *Predtecha: Povesti* (1983).

the 'simple' my mother's. Actually they were a kind of peasant aristocracy, my mother's people: they were Cossacks, which meant that they'd never been serfs and they owned their own land. So everything was fine on her side of the family. Somehow or other the Cossacks have always lived well; they still do. Other people are afraid of them, even the authorities. They're a very stern, tough people. You look at the men and they're great square types, like the samurai—they've been warriors for so many centuries.

My mother's father, my grandfather, fought in two wars—the Japanese war and the First World War—and lived to the age of 99. He first fell ill when he was 97—I took him to the hospital with appendicitis. I remember giving him his bath and being amazed at the size of him. He complained he was falling to pieces, but he was a great hulk of a man with the heart of a youth, so the doctors said, still able to eat a whole bucket of fish for lunch.

On my father's side things weren't of course so good. His father was an officer in the White Army. You can see him here [Makanin showed me a photograph dated January 1917], still wearing the uniform of the Tsar's army. On the other side of the photo there's an inscription: 'God is with us, we will be victorious in Russia.' He was taken captive by the Reds and died in captivity.

My father landed up in a children's colony. He was born in 1911, so he was still just a little boy when the Reds came to Penza. An old woman warned him: run, boy, and he ran, escaping across the river into the country. He was eventually picked up as a homeless waif and taken into one of Makarenko's colonies for homeless children.

You'll find a bit of his biography in 'The Theme of Levelling', in the first story there. He was a very good student, had no trouble at all, but he told me later that he went out of his way not to excel. You see how early that complex begins! It wouldn't have cost him anything to get the best marks, but he tried not to stand out in any way. He was an orphan, alone, deeply marked by everything he'd seen—fire, slaughter. All the same he did well at school and—against his will at first—was sent to a construction institute in Samara and got a good diploma. That was in 1934. He could have gone to Moscow to continue his studies, but instead he went to the Urals and built a factory, and there he met my mother and settled down. That was their wish—to stay in the Urals, out of harm's way. Right from the beginning you see it, this desire not to stand out, to blend in with everybody else. It's something almost biological.

Later on, when I grew up, he couldn't understand my wish to go to Moscow. It was my mother who insisted that I went ahead. My mother was less well educated than my father but she had amazing instinct, intuition—she understood people instantly. She believed in the Revolution, she believed in the Bolsheviks, unlike my father, who was always a sceptic.

SL Did you discuss such things in your family?

VM No, but his attitude was perfectly obvious. 'Who's that Bulganin?'* he'd say, 'He can't even speak Russian properly!' Things like that.

---

* N. A. Bulganin (1899–1975), Chairman of the Council of People's Commissars of the RSFSR (1937–8); Deputy Chairman of the Council of People's Commissars of the USSR (1938–41); later Minister of Defence (1947–9 and 1953–5) and Prime Minister under Khrushchev (1955–7).

SL Some people say there was so much fear around in those days that even within the family people tried to conceal their real feelings.

VM No, it was different in the Urals. Everything was much softer there than in the big cities. And the people were different, they were freer spirits. They'd never known serfdom, which is very important, never in the history of Russia.

 The Urals was a bit like America—the people who went there had either been exiled or were independent people who'd gone east of their own accord. And then the Urals were simply far away—though there was no escaping the KGB even there. People like my father still got arrested for nothing, but his rescue by my uncle was typical of the Urals. You couldn't have imagined that in Moscow.

SL Obviously your work has been nourished by the historic traditions of the Urals, the legends and stories you grew up with, and you return frequently to images from your own childhood there—in *Voices*, in *Loss*, and elsewhere. There's an obviously nostalgic impulse in *Loss*, in the story of the third protagonist who returns to search for his roots in the Urals, and we see something similar in your elegiac novella *Where the Sky Met the Hills**—with the composer Bashilov going back to his native home in the Urals, only to discover that the musical traditions that nurtured his talent have since died out. Is that partly a biographical story? Do you feel a strong nostalgia for your own childhood?

VM Of course I do. The thing is that, despite everything, the hardships and social problems remain somehow external. In childhood you have your own internal world. The world still seems harmonious to you—not necessarily beautiful, but harmonious, whole. As soon as you grow up you lose that sense of harmony—the world turns into ladders and swings and roundabouts. It's only in creating, in working, that you may for a short while get back that feeling of harmony, recover a sense of equilibrium. That's why you do it, that's what the impulse is.

SL You came to Moscow, didn't you, just as the post-Stalin Thaw was getting under way? What was its impact on you?

VM I came to Moscow to study mathematics in 1954—so, yes, just before the real Thaw began with Khrushchev's secret speech. But I can't say that Stalin's death and the revelations that followed had any immediate impact on me. Things didn't seem quite so black and white then as they appeared later on. People didn't immediately link Stalin with the KGB: they thought the KGB were swine, but they didn't see Stalin in the same light—Stalin was Stalin after all. It took people a very long time to figure out what had really happened—a generation had passed before the whole truth started to be revealed.

 As for me, I was a good student, very caught up in mathematics, and I felt somehow removed from politics. Not that we didn't discuss what was happening. Everyone was reading the same things—novels like Dudintsev's[†] *Not by Bread Alone*, which seemed to us quite extraordinary, and all the things that appeared in *Novy mir*. But it didn't go very deep. The point was that all this coincided with our youth, with the sudden expansion of our world in any case, the rush to learn new things. I had lived in the Urals and then come to Moscow, and of course my

---

* *Gde skhodilos' nebo s kholmami* (1984).

† See note on Dudintsev, p. xv.

world changed completely—but I tended to attribute everything to Moscow, not to the times.

We were certainly flooded with new literature in those days. We got to know loads of Western writers whom we would never have been able to read before. I remember reading Hemingway in my third year at university, and Faulkner, and later Sartre and Camus. I grew up very fast: there I was, a boy from the provinces, suddenly reading the French existentialists! It was a time of tempestuous intellectual development, but perhaps I didn't really take stock of it until much later, when I was able to pause.

SL Your first novel was published in 1965, and subsequent works appeared regularly all through the 1970s and 1980s. In that sense you appear to have had a rather successful and straightforward career as a writer. Yet it took fifteen years or more for you to gain proper critical recognition. How do you explain the fact that you remained an outsider for so long?

VM I think the problem for me for a long time—as for certain other writers—was that I never belonged to any clearly defined political camp. In the old days, crudely speaking, there were the socialist realists, who depicted life in this country from their own ideological standpoint, and then there was a group of writers—so-called progressives or liberals—who were ideologically opposed to them and sought to depict the more negative sides of our reality. But both groups were, in a sense, similarly dependent on Soviet reality for their subject-matter, and both groups began to fade away or become less important when that reality disintegrated.

Those who are in the forefront of literature now are precisely those whose work was ignored or criticized before because it represented not just a comment on public affairs but a depiction of the artist's own inner world. It couldn't be easily categorized in political terms. An artist is someone who can't express his thoughts directly—or rather he can, but only 10 per cent of what he means will come out. If his idea can be expressed directly—in an article, say—then there's no need for him to write a whole novel. There are relatively few people for whom art is the only possible means of expression, for whom it is a way of life.

My own career, as you say, has been quite strange. For a start it took a very long time for me to be published in journals. You know there is a tradition here that a writer is either made or unmade by journals. Books here don't play such an important role; in general a writer publishes his work in a journal first, and it comes out in book form only afterwards. Most important, the critics only read the journals, they don't bother with anything else.

This tradition was left over from the nineteenth century when a journal was a kind of vehicle for comment of all kinds—social, philosophical, aesthetic. Pushkin, Dostoyevsky, Nekrasov all ran their own journals. But in the twentieth century this tradition was abused and subverted by Soviet power. The journals were turned into departments, they became a means of selection and control. The point is that it was much easier to control journals than to keep an eye on a whole sea of books. The editors could be carefully appointed and the censors would go through every page, stamping their approval or withholding it as the case may be. The government were able to make what they wanted out of the journals, and literary life was still structured in such a way that they alone had the power to 'make' an author. A 'book author' was the lowest of the low, someone too negligible to have found a proper home for himself in the established literary world.

SL So what happened in your case—did editors just think: Makanin isn't 'one of ours'?

VM It was never straightforward. Even if they published me once, editors would find all sorts of ways of putting me off afterwards—let's wait a year, they'd say, so you'd wait a bit and then try again. You'd go round and have tea with an editor, show him something else, and he'd say that this or that needed to be 'corrected'. They wielded enormous power.

A certain aura grew up around these journals; they gathered writers around them in cliques and to a considerable extent influenced what they wrote. Of course the journals differed from one another—not a great deal, but to some extent. Some concentrated on young writers, some were more liberal or more reactionary. But there wasn't an obvious home for me in any of them.

I started out with the journal *Moskva* when it had a relatively liberal Editor-in-Chief, Popovkin. Later, under Mikhail Alekseyev—a terribly gloomy fellow—it became a bastion of reaction and they wouldn't take me any more. I went through similar difficulties elsewhere.

SL How do you think this lack of recognition affected you as a writer?

VM Badly! And yet there were pluses and minuses. Nobody knew me, but the plus side was that I had, as it were, my own laboratory in which no one interfered. I wasn't well connected, and I wasn't obliged to anyone. And so I was able to grow, think, read. Of course, I felt lonely, and like any other young writer I wanted recognition. But later I understood that this wasn't my fate, my journey. And since I was a mathematician I knew what it was to work alone on a problem and how important in a way this solitude was. Gradually by yourself you build up experience and gather force, independent of the powers that be. I matured as a writer outside the limelight, and when the critics started taking notice of me— with the publication of *Voices*—I was ready for them.

After that the journals started to adopt me too. But the reaction of critics was very mixed. My world, my style, my approach as a writer were unfamiliar to them. Some reacted by just swearing at me. But bad reviews are better than none: they acted as a kind of advertisement for my work—intelligent readers would seek me out, wondering what I'd done to provoke such hostility. So I became quite fashionable all of a sudden, fifteen years or so after I'd started writing.

SL One criticism voiced early on by critics—Natalya Ivanova, for instance—was that you were too 'cold', too 'clinical' in your dissection of human relationships. What do you make of such criticisms?

VM Perhaps they see a certain pessimism in my work. The point is that I've always been concerned with the theme of the individual, with the nature of individuality—and since my own fate marked me out as a 'loner', it pushed me further in that direction. Writing demands honesty, and I couldn't pretend otherwise. But the theme of individuality—of loneliness, if you like—has been very little discussed in our society. Individuality has been deeply suppressed; it really appears only at the moment of death. Only in death can a person finally be liberated from concern about what other people think of him.

So the theme of death as such has attracted me—death as a moment of emancipation. Both in my story 'Anti-leader'* and in *The Precursor* you see typical examples. In *The Precursor* the central character, the healer Yakushkin, doesn't at first recognize what's tugging at him—he thinks that perhaps he's sick or mad, and it's only in prison that he understands that life is over for him. And suddenly at that point he becomes larger than life, bigger than himself.

SL　It seems to me important that by no means all your heroes are exceptional individuals in an obvious sense. Of course, some are marked out by a special destiny or gift—like Yakushkin, the healer, or Pekalov, bent on digging his tunnel under the Ural river in *Loss*. Others are excluded—or exclude themselves—by some special curse, like the hero of 'Anti-leader', who's fatally driven to violence by the sight of another's success. But, for example, Klyucharyov, who recurs in different guises as the hero of several works, bears no obvious stigma—gift or curse—of that kind. In a way he's everyman, or 'keyman', as his name suggests.

VM　You know, in a strange way the assumption of an archetype—an archetypal role—can help the individual in his struggle against the collective. He can't simply depart, separate himself off, or he would be annihilated, he would cease to exist. He can make himself manifest only by using those very values which are contained in the collective itself.

Klyucharyov, as you say, has been the named hero of several stories, most recently *The Manhole*. Now I plan to bring all the Klyucharyov stories together as a single novel, and when they're published together I'll be able to see this hero of mine more clearly. To a certain extent Klyucharyov is undoubtedly me—but there are moments in my work when I speak as 'I', moments when I speak as the writer Igor Petrovich, and there are moments when I take on the guise of Klyucharyov. If you like, there are three different levels of self-distancing in my work.

Klyucharyov, let's say, is a rather typical member of our intelligentsia, with all its pluses and minuses. Of course he is not identical to me, he has certain particularly Soviet features which I might view in a certain way, and he would view differently—perhaps as I saw them once or as my brother sees them or someone else. At any rate he is typical of our time and generation.

When I put him in *The Manhole* I dared to change certain details about him—for example, he has a son instead of a daughter, a handicapped son moreover. It was a rather bold move but I felt it was necessary for the text—and it didn't seem essential to keep the image of him exactly as it had been before. In fact I could have changed the biographical details completely and he'd still be the same Klyucharyov. Biographical realism of the kind you had in the nineteenth-century novel doesn't seem to me important. The important thing is that the hero should develop consistently as an individual of our time.

SL　Did you conceive each story as part of a larger whole—in other words, did you know you would return to Klyucharyov?

---

* 'Antilider', in *Mesto pod solntsem* (1984).

VM No, he appeared of his own accord. My work seems to me like a tree: the different branches grow and grow and by and by there's an apple hanging there at the end of a branch and I pluck it. And for the time being it would seem that's it. But after a while another starts growing—so by all means let it grow! There's no plan to it. And the form of the story, the situations my hero finds himself in, are always quite different. The situation in *The Manhole* is completely different from that in 'Klyucharyov and Alimushkin', for instance; my hero there is being tried out in totally new circumstances.

I'm lucky as a writer in that I never feel a shortage of material; it's just a matter of choosing what I want to write about now.

SL *The Manhole* seems in many ways a departure from your earlier work. It's at once more nakedly symbolic—the world that the hero inhabits is manifestly imaginary—and yet, it seems to me, it relates more obviously than any of your previous work to the experience of what is happening out there, right now, in Moscow.

VM I think that what I write has always been related to the situation 'out there'. Stories such as 'Anti-leader' or *The One Left Behind* were about the reality of our life too. The difference is that that essential reality—the reality that interests me—is much more exposed now, it's come out into the open. Before—under Brezhnev, say—what we had on the surface was a very false reality, one that concerned only journalists and politicians: it was completely uninteresting for a writer to deal with. The real structures, the deeper processes of our lives and our society, were buried underneath. Now of course things are different, everything is much more naked—but it's the surface reality that's changed, not my interests as a writer. I've always been interested in the essential, the archetypal; I've always written to understand my own myths and the micro-elements that make up my consciousness.

The Manhole is built around one of my favourite images—the image of the hour-glass. It came to me as I pictured a man squeezing himself through a very narrow gap, like a grain of sand through the neck of a glass. The image has an obvious historical reference, to the idea of reversal, of things literally being turned upside-down: as they have been lately, and as happened most dramatically in 1917, when the top people went to the bottom, and what came to the top were the most ordinary, coarse elements of society.

SL It's obviously crucial to the story that the world it describes is divided 'vertically', not 'horizontally', into these two realms: like Pekalov in *Loss*, digging his legendary tunnel under the Ural river, Klyucharyov crosses his boundary by literally squeezing himself into the earth.

VM That image isn't artificial or abstract for me. For a start I was born in the Urals where everyone had a passion for digging into the earth, hoping to find gold. This idea of burrowing, getting into the earth, has always been very strong in Russia generally. I don't know if you've noticed, but the Russians have always been very fond of the dug-out—or at least the idea of the dug-out—as a place to live. So the idea of living 'upside-down', under the earth instead of on top of it, has a rather literal meaning for me.

You can even see it in the way we've built our metro here. Down there in the metro everything's beautiful, everything works, whereas on top it's the reverse!

Usually, you know, it's the other way round. If you go to Paris the metro's nothing to speak of, whereas the streets up above are shining and beautiful. But everything's upside-down here.

SL   The underground realm that Klyucharyov enters bears a striking resemblance to the clubbish world of the Moscow literati in 'the good old days'. In fact you could almost swear when he first drops into it that he's landed right in the middle of the cosy basement café in the Moscow Writers' Club! But I take it that the 'underground' here represents the situation of the intelligentsia in Russia generally—both their privileges and their estrangement?

VM   There have been many interpretations of what that world stands for, the crudest one being that the underground represents the West—a place where you can live in comfort and buy everything you want. Some people even said that the manhole itself represented the customs, in the days when the KGB stopped most people from going through, so that you almost had to tear your flesh to get to the West and collect your foreign goods!

I think that what you say is a little closer to the truth. We live in a very bifurcated society, without any middle class to speak of. Soviet society has been split between the working people and the intelligentsia, and the intelligentsia has always occupied a rather special, in some ways cosy and protected place.

SL   Does it still?

VM   The split is certainly still there. You know there's been a long literary tradition of what we call *intelligentnost* in Russia—the idea of a section of society that has an elevated sense of responsibility but very little direct contact with the rest of society. It's only art and literature that can unite these two worlds—and if that contact ceased it would be catastrophic. There must be circulation between them. So the only hope of salvation is through this 'manhole' of culture—however small, however narrow it is.

SL   The underground in this story is clearly the realm of civilization, the spirit, the higher things of life, but at the same time the image of digging or burrowing has a clearly 'regressive' sense in your work. One of the characters in *Loss* longs to dig through cold layers of earth to get back to the 'warmth' of childhood, and in *Manhole* you give clear signals for a Freudian interpretation of Klyucharyov's urge to squeeze into the earth.

VM   Of course there is that as well. On the one hand the hero is trying to dig down into the earth, to get into the woman, to fulfil his masculine principle; but the earth is also the mother—in that sense the 'manhole' is the hole he came out of.

SL   Should we take the devastated landscape of your overground world in *Manhole* as a reflection of your fears for the future, or as a symbolic description of the country's devastation now?

VM   Well, what can one say? In a sense it's both. Of course the country is going through particular suffering at the moment. It's a dramatic moment, one in which the whole of the Russian people is absorbed.

Above all our people have suffered a terrible blow to their vanity. The point isn't just that the whole country's in economic chaos, but that the entire journey towards this moment has proved to be mistaken. Perhaps this is the overwhelming sense you have in *The Manhole*—the idea that people have built and built and thought and thought, and in the end they discover that the whole thing has been done much better elsewhere. Yet they can't run away, because after all what they've built is theirs; it's all they have.

What everyone understands now is that the enterprise was mistaken from the very start, it wasn't just that we took a wrong turning after the Revolution. Everything followed from Lenin. This is a terrible weight to bear on the soul. The nation is in a state of shock. The English ought to be able to understand this, as an imperial nation that lost its empire. It's as if when the empire's there and the nation feels self-confident it's very easy to make decisions, there's plenty of energy for everything—but take it away and the nation doesn't know where to start from again. This search for a starting-point torments us.

For the Germans in that respect it was easier. After Hitler their guilt was obvious—they had destroyed the Jews, and not only the Jews. Whereas the Russians, of course, had destroyed one another, which is a completely different thing. They hadn't said that they were better than everyone else, they had said that socialism was better than everything and everyone else—and that made the process of repentance much more complicated. The Germans were able to say: yes, we were wrong. Whereas the Russians find it harder to repent, because it was above all Russians who died in the camps—and precisely the flower of their nation. It's impossible to explain, and the sense of horror stems precisely from this.

Materially there have been much harder times than this in our history, but details such as what one can get to eat are trivial by comparison with the sense that everything has collapsed, been ruined, and that what has collapsed above all is this [he points to his heart].

sl And the sense that all the earlier hardship and suffering were for nothing?

vm In actual fact they weren't quite all for nothing, but it's too early to say that yet— if you said that now nobody would listen to you. It's a complicated business, but if one were to sum up: Russia as a country based on the peasant commune had never been through the Enlightenment; Russians before the Revolution had never been through the experience of seeing themselves without God. During the last seventy years we were forced to go through this experience in a terrible form. Yet it's been precisely this which has enabled us to begin to see ourselves—ever so slightly—as individuals. Totalitarianism destroyed a great deal, including the traditional commune—but the fact is that otherwise we might to this day have failed to pull ourselves out of that way of life. Now people are returning to the Church, to religion, but already with a different, a Western understanding, not the Medieval understanding we had before.

sl Already with a conscious sense of loss?

vm Yes—and that's very important. Of course the sacrifice has been terrible—and we are going to have to do a lot of searching now. The central question is whether we try to cross out the past seventy years, or in some sense inherit the past and carry on from where we are. Only when we've resolved that in our minds will we be able to start working again. People have got to get over their shock first—the shock of those millions senselessly killed, the flower of the nation hacked down, the churches destroyed, the economy ruined—and so on. But when that shock passes, if the organism survives and its roots are deep, we'll start seeing leaves again. The main thing, in my view, is that the roots themselves shouldn't be dug up. People now are in a state of moral distress, they keep shouting 'Horror! Horror!' and they want to rid themselves of all of it, the whole burden. But the fact is that we have nothing else to inherit. We don't have another life.

sl The generation after yours—not the youngest, perhaps, but those now in their late thirties and forties—seems to have sought a way out in irony and absurdism.

vm Irony—yes, that's true. But irony doesn't allow you to move any further, it isn't enough. First you escape into irony and then you escape from the country altogether, that's how it often ends. People—good, sincere people—say it's impossible to live here, there's no future, and they run away, but that's a great pity for the country.

The idea of socialism wasn't of course a Russian idea—but when an idea is in the air it's impossible that it shouldn't be tried out sometime, somewhere. Someone had to go down that turning first and discover that it was a dead end. It happened to be the Russians who did it. And meanwhile everyone else marched on and we got left behind. That is our tragedy, but we have to come to terms with it.

sl You say that the Soviet experiment destroyed the traditional Russian commune—but in one sense it merely transformed it onto a mass scale. It's a central theme of your work that the collective, at least as an ideal, has continued to exert a very powerful force in this society: even the intelligentsia have continued in some sense to be hypnotized by it.

vm It's true that the idea of the community, the *obshchina*, has always been important for the intelligentsia here, for their self-perception, perhaps because they've never properly belonged, they've always been 'superfluous people'. Part of this feeling may stem from guilt: in Russia for centuries there's been this sense of guilt before the common people. There's a wonderful story by Chekhov, where a servant helps an old professor with some small task—hanging up his coat or something of the sort—and the professor enjoys the fact that he's speaking to the servant in the same kind of language that he once used himself.* Maybe there is an element of nostalgia in this desire to be back in the common herd, because there among the crowd it wasn't so painful—or if it was, it was painful for everybody, whereas now life is painful for you alone. Sometimes one just wants to hide and say what will be, will be, and wherever we go, we'll go altogether, as the people, the *narod*. It's a very characteristic Russian feeling.

The Soviet regime offered the intelligentsia a way into the collective, so long as they were prepared to conform, and in many ways it was very seductive. In my own career as a writer I've seen it very clearly. As a member of the Writers' Union you got all sorts of advantages: they looked after you if you were ill or disabled, as I was after my accident; they might appeal on your behalf to the Moscow City Council to get you an apartment or a kindergarten place for your child; they guaranteed a good rate of pay for your writing, provided writers' retreats and so forth. These trivial details play their role. Now that the Union of Writers has fallen apart everyone suddenly realizes that they used to live rather well, precisely thanks to the Union.

---

* Probably a reference to 'Skuchnaya istoriya' (A Dreary Story), in which a professor enjoys talking to the porter at the university.

But of course the Union of Writers, like any other trade union, had a political edge to it: it guaranteed all these material advantages, but in exchange you had to write as they wanted you to. You were faced with a living organism that followed your movements with great attention and concern, but at the same time it had you under its microscope the whole time; it knew you inside out. Under such circumstances it's an enormous labour to go your own way and remain an individual.

SL In your novel *One and One* you suggest that one reason why the intelligentsia of your generation—'the men of the sixties', *shestidesyatniki*—look back nostalgically to the period of the Thaw is that it provided for them a kind of idyll of togetherness, a renewal of shared ideals.

VM Yes, and they still hold on to that 'togetherness'. It was precisely those people—the liberal *shestidesyatniki* represented in *One and One*—who were very offended with me over that book and the portrait of themselves that they found in it.

SL Even though your portrayal of Gennady Pavlovich and Ninel Nikolayevna, the hero and heroine, seems to me, in the end, a very tender one—isn't it?

VM Well, but you see, those liberal 'men of the sixties' were also what we now call *sovki*, people who, like it or not, were still Soviet types brought up on Soviet myths.

They claimed that they were fed up with socialist realism, but what was socialist realism? The most important thing in it was the idea of the hero. And these people thought of themselves as heroes. So when they saw in Gennady Pavlovich a portrait not of a hero but of someone more like Oblomov,* they were terribly offended. They thought of themselves as warriors, crusaders, ready to go to prison to defend their beliefs. In fact none of them actually went to prison themselves, that was left to a tiny minority of active dissidents, but in their own imaginations they were all sufferers, sufferers on behalf of the people, even though all of them had found some post or other under Brezhnev and lived perfectly well. I had tried in *One and One* to describe the 'stagnation'—the word wasn't even used then—as it really was. And they were all terribly upset with me. How could you do this to our generation, they said, it's not fair!

They wanted to have it both ways: at one and the same time they blamed Soviet society and the era of 'stagnation' for turning us all into such people—and yet they themselves wanted to be depicted as heroes. They wanted there to be something of the Solzhenitsyn romance in Gennady Pavlovich—even if he hadn't been in prison himself, perhaps he could have sent a parcel to someone who was! Although they themselves of course had done nothing of the sort. But no, they said, you're not fair, you should have invented some wicked boss who would have attacked Gennady Pavlovich—and Gennady Pavlovich would have refused to do his bidding. Or you could have kept your Gennady Pavlovich as he is but then shown how he was *forced* to be like that. There needs to be some element of struggle. You see, all of them still have something of the Bolshevik inside, they're just a tiny bit Bolshevik themselves.

---

* The eponymous hero of a novel by Ivan Goncharov, first published in 1859. Oblomov's chief characteristic is his indolence—his inability or unwillingness to use his talents to any effective purpose (he spends a large part of the novel in bed). Hence the term 'oblomovitis' (*oblomovshchina*), first coined by Goncharov himself and subsequently used by numerous critics of Tsarist Russian society, including Lenin.

SL   I must say that when I first read the novel I didn't take it only as a portrait of your generation. Of course, you see Gennady Pavlovich's helplessness and depression. But above all you see the inability of these two solitary characters—Gennady and Ninel—to relate to each other.

VM   Their problem is that they don't recognize one another, even though they're so similar. If you like, that is part of the diagnosis of 'Brezhnev man': they're trapped by their 'Brezhnev' psyche. They've lived intensely solitary, private lives, and naturally what happens with people in their situation is that they become deeply suspicious and afraid of one another. Twenty years on they'll still remember that so-and-so, once upon a time, claimed he was ill just in order to get out of turning up for a demonstration—and they'll condemn him for it, even though they were no different really themselves. That's typical of our generation. And this inability to love, inability to recognize one another—that was a mark of the Brezhnev era in its purest form.

I don't condemn them at all. But they didn't want pity either. A hero doesn't need pity. That's why people were so offended.

It so happened also that several people were convinced that Gennady Pavlovich was a scurrilous portrait of some particular individual—several possibilities were named—because all the details happened to fit. In fact those details had arisen naturally from the image of the person I'd created. But what a swine Makanin is, they said, copying the whole story straight from life! For several days all Moscow was buzzing with gossip, the telephone never stopped ringing, articles appeared—but then it all blew over and other people wrote more intelligent articles saying that wasn't the point.

SL   But it seems to me that the novel could be taken as a comment on a more general human malaise, not necessarily confined to Brezhnev's Russia.

VM   You can think of it, yes, as a story about twentieth-century people in general. A French critic used the term 'anti-love' to describe it. In the classic love story the man and the woman try to find one another, they have to overcome various obstacles to be together, but in the end they're united, even if it's only in the grave. Here the opposite is true—everything is arranged so that Gennady Pavlovich and Ninel should be together, the narrator even forces them into each other's company, but they draw further and further apart—so it's a novel about anti-love, or an anti-novel, if you like.

SL   That idea perhaps has a broader application in your work. Your narratives very often embark from, or present right in the middle, scenes that in the traditional novel would constitute the resolution. In *One and One* we learn in the middle that Gennady Pavlovich dies in a car accident—but that isn't the end of the story, and afterwards we return to incidents preceding his death. Or again in your story 'The Simple Truth'* we arrive early on at the dead end of a romance—but again this isn't the point or conclusion of the work. One effect of this constantly backtracking style of narration, it seems to me, is to give a kind of 'objectivity', an almost three-dimensional reality to the world you present, as if it were available at any point to be picked up again and examined from some new angle. The reader

---

* 'Prostaya istina' (dated 1976), in *Otstavshy: povesti i rasskazy* (1988).

understands straightaway that the traditional ending, happy or unhappy, is not the point here.

VM I think all this may be connected with the fact that at one time, as you know, I studied the cinema, and perhaps as a writer I've spent my whole life trying to escape from and outgrow its influence.

The cinema was my first passion; I grew up under the spell of its aesthetics. That was typical of my generation, at least for those of us who grew up in the Urals and Siberia. Of course we read the classics, Pushkin and Lermontov, but it was the cinema that really caught our imagination.

For a start we could see it for free. In the summer we had an open-air cinema, so we boys used to climb up the surrounding trees and sit there on the branches to watch. Sometimes we'd watch the same film two, three, five times over. You might go home and have a bite to eat and then come back and start watching all over again. So I saw films like *Richard III, Robin Hood,* masses of others, all in the epic style that was the direct twentieth-century successor of the great realist nineteenth-century novels—Balzac, Dostoyevsky, Dickens. Cinema was the all-powerful thing. I was 8 or 9 years old when I saw Shakespeare for the first time; I couldn't have read him then but as a spectator I could understand him. So I'm very grateful for this upbringing—but in the end, in order to develop as a writer, I had to part with it.

I had to concentrate very hard on the nature of words, what words can do. When you've mastered that, writing becomes very rewarding work, very peaceful and calm. You realize that the material you can choose from is endless, unbounded. Usually a writer reaches this point around his fifth book.

My breakthrough came with *Voices.* Suddenly there I felt the possibility of working without all the props of cinema, in a more private way, without the epic story. I felt winged, I was flying.

SL Although it seems to me that there is still a strong cinematic or scenographic element in your work, as if the lighting and staging of each scene were fully imagined.

VM Well, later on it was possible to return to what I'd learned in cinema—for example there's a great deal of visual symbolism in *The Manhole.* But I already feel that I'm using the cinema to serve the word, not vice versa. Cinema can never fully convey the inner workings of someone's mind. The power of cinema is in its brightness, its immediacy—but a writer must tear himself away from all that.

SL The critic Lev Anninsky, among others, has written about your ability to create a very specific atmosphere, a specific climate in each of your works, and I wonder whether your experience of cinema has contributed to that?

VM Atmosphere depends on language. I think Anninsky tends to understand 'atmosphere' in more realistic terms: how truthfully, for example, you've represented the atmosphere of a barracks or a communal kitchen or whatever. But it's less tangible than that for me. I'm interested in finding words that will convey an emotional atmosphere, not just evoke a time and place.

The atmosphere of solitude, for example. For me the fullness of individual life is always connected with a sense of regret that it will end, that it's unrepeatable—it always has a smell of tragedy about it, like looking at a butterfly and knowing that it will only live for two days. On the one hand that gives one a sense of the exceptional, miraculous, one-off nature of life, but also of its finiteness, of mortality in the end. That's perhaps the central thought behind all my work, and the atmosphere I try to convey.

◆   ◆   ◆

Postscript

SL In your new novella—*A Baize-Covered Table with a Decanter in the Middle*—you deal in the most explicit way yet with the motif of confrontation between the individual and the collective. The work has a confessional feel about it. Can you say what prompted you to write it at this point?

VM It's a strange, naked work. The most important thing in the story is the idea of the table itself as a symbol of the scene of interrogation. Of course, I could have written about it in an essay—written a history of interrogation, say. But for me the idea was uninteresting without the phantoms that attend it. They're phantoms that I've lived with since my very childhood. They've changed over time but they've always been present. That's why I chose not to go for an essay but for a story, because it would be impossible to express them otherwise—they're alive, they have lived with me constantly, and I couldn't find any other way of showing why they had lived with me for so long.

The table is what gives these phantoms power. Take it away and they'll be just ordinary people, you or me, completely insignificant. But as soon as a person appears behind that table he turns into a social category, a member of the intelligentsia, a worker or whatever—categories defined by power.

The most important point for me was that these people were exactly the same, no matter what situation I found myself in. They were identical wherever you went. In that sense they are reflections of myself—they *are* myself. Other people will have different judges, they'll fill the places at the table differently. Someone else, for example, would invariably have a 'Party man' sitting there—whereas for me that wasn't an essential category.

Incidentally, in *One and One* there's an episode in which the narrator, Igor Petrovich, comes and sees the heroine of the novel, Ninel, and she describes how she's been summoned to see her boss at work, how they want to get rid of her. And the narrator goes to her place of work and sees the table that awaits her. But for him this scene, this table, is alien. He can't even come into contact with it—because these are not his people, they're not the ones he has to deal with. So the sight of it doesn't affect him. That's why he can do nothing to save her—he has to say, it doesn't work, Ninel, even though he tries to intervene on her behalf.

So this theme crops up everywhere in my work; it's just that here it's been given a kind of special treatment. I found I could breathe more easily once I'd written this thing. While I was writing it I sometimes wondered whether I should publish it at all. I thought perhaps I should just take one of these phantoms and write a different story about my relationship with him. But then I decided why not, after all.

Interview recorded in June 1993.

sl It seems to me an almost painfully personal work, like the revelation of a personal nightmare.

vm Well, you know, I tried in a certain way not to be myself in this work. In real life I'm a tougher person than my hero in this story, quite capable of not giving in, not turning up. On the one hand I've been a member of the intelligentsia all these years, but on the other I'm still a boy from the Urals who's always game for a fight. Whereas my hero can't fight. So he represents only part of me.

sl I was reminded, reading this story, of the hero's father in *The One Left Behind* and how he too seeks to get rid of the phantoms that haunt him—by expressing them, by telling his son about them.

vm I hadn't thought of that—but yes, one way and another these thoughts have been there in my work all along. Another scene you may remember: there's a small episode in *Voices* where a bird has all its feathers torn off, one by one. That's like a miniature version of the trial scene, where the people you love—and who love you—slowly tear the feathers off you till you're completely naked.

sl Do you think that's a specifically Soviet nighmare?

vm I think it's Russian rather than Soviet. These phantoms existed before the Revolution. You can see them in Dostoyevsky's *Devils*, for example. I think this essential scene—of powerlessness before an inquisitor—has a long history in Russia.

sl You talked before about the atmosphere of solitude in your work, and that's something one feels intensely here.

vm Face to face with the table a man is necessarily solitary, he's absolutely conscious of his solitude. I had thought of having a twist in the story, where the man would have a daughter, or someone else who was vulnerable—but that would have changed the psychological atmosphere completely. I also imagined that the hero might see himself there, his double, behind the table—but the whole thing would have become too literary then, turned into a literary game.

sl You talk of yourself as someone who is always ready for a fight—but so often your heroes are people who have lost their strength, they're incapacitated, they can't resist or don't even want to resist.

vm That's true—even in a case like the protagonist in 'Anti-leader' who's incapable of solving his problem in any way other than violently. Sooner or later he always realizes that it's pointless, but then the need to fight rises up in him again—and he sees that there's no way out, he's powerless to prevent it.

I've often had moments myself when I've understood that I won't get anywhere with fighting. It may help you for a day to feel like a living person. But by tomorrow that's already gone—and again you're alone and again they are many. *Table* could have been called 'The Field after the Battle'. You've already fought and fought and it's no use at all. It doesn't make it any easier to know that you've beaten somebody up. Nothing changes as a result of that.

If these people on the other side of the table had been conventional villains it would have been a completely different matter. But here you feel there's a secret, a mystery. How is it possible, you ask yourself, that this person is sitting there and saying these things when only two hours ago he was cleaning his teeth like a normal person? What happened to him between 9 o'clock and 11 o'clock in the morning?

I'm reminded of our dog. He used to be very docile, rather a coward. But once he noticed that a small child was afraid of him, and that suddenly awoke the dog in him: he now expects people to be afraid of him and he's ready to take you on! People can change in the same way. Not that they become dogs, of course not, but in exactly the same way they start to persecute you, anticipating your reaction.

In Soviet times someone who steered away from the collective was considered somehow improper, it just wasn't done. Pasternak suffered not so much from the fact that the secret police were after him as from the fact that out on the streets ordinary people started to react against him, reproaching him for sending his stuff to the West and so on. You've betrayed us! they'd say. And they really thought he had betrayed them. And the worst thing was that he came to believe it too. Pasternak himself was convinced that he'd taken a desperate step. He really did think that he was a bit of a traitor—which is why he was afraid when he sat down at that table. He wanted to hear a kind word from them—he felt that he was still with them in a way.

SL Have you had any direct experience of such persecution yourself?

VM No, there's been no such event in my life, nothing that changed my fate. At the moment I'm working on a small essay called 'The Beautiful Biography'. In a way it can be a kind of luck for a writer to be persecuted just a little—to have been punished, for example, for taking part in *Metropol'*.* It gives you a *beautiful biography*. A writer may be ruined by such things, but sometimes he can be helped, as Brodsky perhaps was helped by being exiled.

Of course it's a difficult, sometimes a fatal experience to be put in prison or expelled from your native country. I haven't had any experience of that kind, and thank God for that. But sometimes the 'table' in a person's life consists not of one grand judgement but of a thousand little incidents. That's how it's been for me.

SL Some readers might be puzzled by the fact that you have chosen this moment to publish a work that, for all its general human reverberations, seems nevertheless to relate to an experience specific to the Soviet era. Is the explanation partly that you felt unable to write such a direct and devastating analysis earlier, knowing it couldn't be published, or does it represent a way of parting with the past?

VM I could have written it earlier, whether or not it could have been published. But maybe you're right that this is my way of putting an end to that era, those phantoms; maybe it was their last chance!

SL So the situation you described there no longer exists?

VM No, of course it does! It's one thing to say that I feel a certain freedom in having exorcized myself of these images, quite another to say that the phenomenon itself has disappeared. The form may have changed, the ideals of the collective may have changed, but the collective itself is still there, still keeping an eye on you, still ready to pounce on you or blame you or denounce you for doing something wrong.

Just recently, for example, there was a false rumour that I was going to publish something in the reactionary newspaper *Den'*. Straight away the telephones

---

* The almanac edited by Vasily Aksyonov *et al.* and published without permission of the censors in 1979. See Introduction, p. xxiii.

started ringing—how could you do this, it's a fascist newspaper! And though in fact I'd given nothing to *Den'*, I felt I was right back there at the table being judged. The norm has shifted, but still if you depart from it just slightly, or fail to pin your colours clearly to the mast, the judges are ready and waiting to pounce.

I was fascinated by their reaction: how everything came to life, flared up, got moving straightaway. It's still the same mentality; it's very easy to destroy some-one's reputation—and that's what people here still love to do, especially young people. They regard themselves as so bold. They sit in judgement over Pasternak for appearing at the First Congress of Soviet Writers—all of them are so much bolder than Pasternak, of course.

I'm not saying that nothing has changed at all—that would be absurd. But something of the same sensation remains, even if there's no real fear involved any more. 'We're so proud of you, how could you let us down'—that sort of mentality remains even among our so-called democrats, though they hate me, of course, for saying so. It will take a long time for these people to become individuals. For the moment they're still a herd with the manners of the herd.

4

Andrei Bitov

(b. 1937)

Andrei Bitov was born in Leningrad in 1937 and, except for a brief period during the war, spent his childhood and formative years in that beautiful, haunted, never-quite-Russian city. Several generations of Bitovs had lived there before him, and the survivors in his day—grandmother, parents, aunts, uncles, and grandchildren—all lived together in one big apartment. Members of the old St Petersburg intelligentsia, their tastes and values harked back to pre-revolutionary times and formed a partial bulwark against the contemporary Soviet world outside. Bitov later wrote of his home that it formed 'a whole world and comprised my whole life, and it strengthened a certain isolationism in me . . . providing an abundance of the best, the finest, people, painlessly dividing my life into two indisputable, a priori categories, my own personal world and the external one'.

Leningrad forms the backdrop to Bitov's early stories and is a central feature of his best-known novel, *Pushkin House* (1978). But from childhood Bitov had also loved to travel; his mother, he wrote, 'infected [him] with space', travelling with him around the Soviet Union and inculcating in him a permanent 'love for displacement'. This passion for travel influenced Bitov's first choice of profession: after graduating from high school, he entered the geological research department of the Leningrad Mining Institute, earning the chance to go on research expeditions with his fellow students to Central Asia. This experience provided the raw material for early works such as 'One Country' and *Such a Long Childhood*;* and travel writings in the broadest sense—stories and essays prompted by journeys to Uzbekistan, Armenia, and Georgia—have remained a central part of Bitov's *œuvre*.

The Mining Institute served a further purpose in Bitov's literary career, for its students ran a literary society that was attended by some of the city's most promising young writers. Bitov went to their meetings and was encouraged to try his own

---

* 'Odna strana' (dated 1960), in *Bol'shoi shar* (1963), and *Takoye dolgoye detstvo* (1965). Both have recently been reprinted in *Zapiski novichka* (Notes of a Novice), 1997.

hand at writing. This was in 1956; the Thaw was just getting under way; young people suddenly had access to contemporary literature, film, and music from the West. Fellini's *La Strada* (1954) made a huge impression on Bitov; for the first time, he wrote afterwards, he realized that art could relate to contemporary experience—and that his own feelings and impressions were fit material to start on. In his enthusiasm to try his talent—initially in writing verse—Bitov neglected his studies and was temporarily expelled from the Institute. Later he was reinstated, graduating eventually in 1962, but by that time it was clear that his real profession lay elsewhere. In 1958 he had published his first short story—a comic sketch called 'People who Shave on Saturday'—in an *émigré* almanac,* and in 1963 his first collection of stories, *The Big Balloon*, was published in the Soviet Union. From then on Bitov abandoned geology and turned full-time to writing.

The 1960s saw the publication of three further books: the novella *Such a Long Childhood* (1965) and two further collections: *Dacha District* (1967) and *Apothecary Island* (1968), each containing a selection of earlier work alongside new stories. This became the pattern of Bitov's later publications, each new volume reflecting his changing perception of the overall shape of his work. Thus *Lessons of Armenia* (dated 1967–9), first published separately in *Druzhba narodov* (1969), later appeared in a disparate collection entitled *Way of Life* (1972), but was subsequently republished in two collections (*Seven Journeys* (1976) and *The Book of Journeys* (1986)) that established the 'journey' as a constant theme of his work. *Days of Man* (1976) similarly drew together several stories concerning a single hero, Aleksei Monakhov, in a 'proto-novel' (variously titled *The Role, The Lover*, and *Vanishing Monakhov*) to which Bitov continued to add new chapters.

This rolling style of publication, resulting in a 'new' book every three or four years, disguised the fact that a major part of Bitov's work had been suppressed. From 1964 until 1971 Bitov had been working on the novel *Pushkin House*, whose penetrating study of the impact of Stalinism made it unpublishable in the Soviet Union at the time. At first Bitov compromised by publishing selected chapters from the novel (under the title 'The Young Odoyevtsev, Hero of a Novel') in *Days of Man*, but two years later, in 1978, he sent the novel abroad to be published in its entirety by Ardis.

Bitov's fate in this respect was similar to Fazil Iskander's, who had also been driven to publish his *magnum opus* abroad. Like Iskander, Bitov compounded his sins by participating, a year later, in the publication of the uncensored almanac *Metropol'*, to which he contributed three stories; and like Iskander he became, for the next few years, *persona non grata* on the 'official' literary scene. The three collections of his work which appeared in the early 1980s consisted almost entirely of rearrangements of earlier material. By 1986 the climate had softened, and under the title *Articles from a Novel* Bitov was able to publish, alongside other articles, the literary essays which had formed the various appendices to *Pushkin House*. But the novel was first published in full in the Soviet Union only in 1987, coming out in book form two years later.

---

* 'Lyudi, pobrivshiyesya v subbotu', dated 1958, first published in *Chast' rechi, Al'manakh literatury i iskusstva*, 2–3 (1981–2); repr. in *Teatral'naya zhizn'*, 16 (1987).

The year 1987 also saw the publication of three new stories, including a science-fiction sequel to *Pushkin House*, 'The Photograph of Pushkin'. But the heady political climate of the late 1980s, culminating in the *putsch* of 1991 and the breakup of the Soviet empire, proved—on Bitov's own admission—a distraction from his literary work. Able for the first time to travel abroad, he participated in numerous conferences and seminars in the West; at home he busied himself with journalism and interviews. Not until 1993 did he succeed in completing *The Monkey Link*,* a three-part novel whose philosophical outline he had plotted almost twenty years before.

Most of Bitov's early stories are intricate psychological studies in the everyday behaviour, thoughts, and emotions of a character who, under various guises, is clearly the author's contemporary and in some sense himself. A few stories—'The Big Balloon', 'Grandmother's Cup', 'A Trifle', 'Apothecary Island'†—go back to childhood, drawing on Bitov's early experience of war and evacuation to explore a child's sensibility and perception of the world. But in most we encounter the hero already grown, at first on the brink of adulthood—struggling to achieve both a sense of separateness and a proper connection with those around him; later adjusting to new roles as husband, father, adult son, and professional writer. In the cycle of 'Monakhov' stories, Bitov documents the waxing and waning of the hero's first love, from adolescent self-deception, through detachment, to a pained sense of loss in adulthood.

From the outset, what interests Bitov is not so much the events of his hero's life as the state of his consciousness. Many of the stories in fact focus on non-events: in 'The Door',‡ an adolescent with a crush on an older woman spends an entire night waiting for his beloved outside an apartment door; in 'A Trifle' a young boy spends an afternoon doing everything but his homework. Indeed, the hero is frequently found in a state of truancy, caught at the junction between thought and action, both elated and discomfited by a sense of dissociation from the mainstream of life. The hero of 'The Sun'§ spends his day observing the play of sunlight on his room and the busy street outside, instead of attending to his own list of 'things to do', while the 'Idler',¶ in the story of that name, skives off work and drifts in fantasy, apparently incapable of concentrating on the tasks before him. 'I am ashamed and depressed that I am not like everyone else,' the hero confesses. 'Something in me is arranged wrongly. I have no right to walk among people and pretend I am like them.'

Recording in slow motion the passage of his hero's thoughts, Bitov locates the source of this shame above all in the failure to confront and recognize himself. The condition of his re-engagement in the world is not the reflex resumption of everyday business, but a proper awareness of the very things that have distracted him. Resolution, at the end of 'The Idler', comes as a result of an inner 'skirmish': a final decision to turn away from 'everything in the office' and train his vision elsewhere.

---

* The part of the novel entitled 'Ozhidaniye obez'yan' (Waiting for the Monkeys) was published in *Novy mir* in 1993. The entire novel, published in English as *The Monkey Link*, came out in Russian as *Oglashennyye: Roman-stranstviye* (The Possessed: A Travel Novel) (1995).

† 'Bol'shoi shar' (dated 1961); 'Babushkina piala' (dated 1958); 'Fig' (dated 1959), all in *Bol'shoi shar* (1963); 'Aptekarsky ostrov' (dated 1962), in *Aptekarsky ostrov* (1968).

‡ 'Dver'' (dated 1960), in *Bol'shoi shar* (1963).   § 'Solntse', ibid.

¶ 'Bezdel'nik' (dated 1961–2), in *Aptekarsky ostrov* (1968).

The words of his boss dissolve as the hero focuses, now fully alert, on a vision of sky, snow, and street, caught in a bubble on the window-pane.

'The Idler' is thus one record of the hero's birth as an artist, one whose vocation is to seize these very 'moments of reality' and find a language adequate to describe them. But such moments are by definition elusive and transient. The nature of this cognitive grace, and the struggle to achieve it, remain a constant theme of Bitov's work. In 'Life in Windy Weather',* written a year after 'The Idler', we see the hero, Aleksei, reach a sudden epiphany on a walk with his infant son; pointing out the sights of the village—stream, tree, boy, house, goat—he discovers 'a kind of genius in this nominative simplicity of things and words, and felt as if he were on some higher threshold beyond which everything truly begins'. But this epiphany is reached only after a series of inner battles. En route, Bitov records with punishing exactness the hero's strategies of evasion, his inability to settle down, the quarrels he provokes to ease his own tension.

'Life in Windy Weather' shows the hero, almost uniquely, finding eventual peace of mind within the setting of his own home: here, a momentary estrangement from the world—and a consequent rediscovery of meaning—is borrowed from the fresh vision of his own son. Bitov's *Journeys*, by contrast, record the search for necessary distance through literal departure. *Lessons of Armenia* (1967–9) and 'Choice of Location'† (1970–3) are essays prompted by Bitov's travels, on various assignments, to Armenia and Georgia, and their motive is transparently a form of escape: from self, from Russia, from a singular identity, and from those things which—as he later wrote ruefully—distinguish life proper from first thrilled acquaintanceship: 'the ordinariness, the workload, the disillusionment'. Turning himself voluntarily 'captive' of the Caucasus, the author discovers what it is to be a stranger: neutered, silenced, a temporary idiot, ignorant of local language and history, he's at once enchanted and unnerved by his encounter with cultures more ancient and 'authentic' than his own. The 'lessons' of Armenia are thus lessons in humility; one mark of a civilization, Bitov concludes, is the ability to respect what you don't understand.

Yet the author's position as a stranger is also equivocal. For Armenia and Georgia are not truly 'abroad': they are part of the empire, an extension of home. The author's footsteps there are dogged by his Russian literary forebears—Pushkin, Lermontov, Tolstoy; and in his search for a fresh location, a setting for his own soul, he repeatedly blocks his own view. Thus the lessons he draws are in part lessons in the limitations of self, and his reflections on the culture of Armenia and Georgia turn inevitably to reflections on his own identity as a Russian, a member of the Soviet empire, a writer who is himself 'co-authored by time and environment'.

The nature of that time and environment is explored at its fullest in Bitov's great novel *Pushkin House*, which he was working on concurrently with the *Journeys*. Here, for the first time, the inner world of the author/hero is explicitly related to the experience of his generation. The struggle for connection, for meaning, for a sense of membership in the world, explored elsewhere in psychological or existential terms, acquires here a historical dimension. Borrowing from Lermontov, Bitov

---

* 'Zhizn' v vetrenuyu pogodu' (dated 1963–4), in *Dachnaya mestnost'* (1967).

† 'Vybor natury', in *Sem' puteshestvii* (1976).

ironically titles the second part of his novel 'A Hero of Our Time', and suggests that he, like Lermontov,* has set out to explore the 'vices' of his era.

The hero of *Pushkin House* is Lyova Odoyevtsev, a young scholar attached to the literary institute in Leningrad from which the novel draws its name. Whereas Bitov had chosen, for his earlier hero Monakhov, a name ('the monk') which emphasized his solitary path in life, Odoyevtsev's name suggests his rootedness in aristocratic and literary St Petersburg. His father and grandfather are (or have been) scholars as well, and, in a city steeped in literary tradition, Lyova works as a curator of culture. In the central event of the novel, however, he fails to fulfil his role: appointed to guard the institute's museum over the 7 November holiday (the holiday marking the anniversary of the Revolution) Lyova gets drunk and wrecks the exhibits, fighting a ludicrous duel with his enemy Mitishatev and ending up dead (or possibly just dead drunk) on the museum floor.

This is the position we find him in on page 1, and in a sense the entire novel can be read as a whodunnit or, in Russian terms, a 'Who is to blame?' Written in circular form to arrive at its opening, it traces the numerous vicious circles in which the hero is entrapped, through his attachment to the agents of destruction in his life (alcohol, Mitishatev, the woman who scorns him) and an inability to connect with the forces for good.

Bitov had written of his earlier, 'proto-novel' (*Vanishing Monakhov*) that it was 'in part about a person's failure to evaluate the present, tied as it is to an undigested past'. In *Pushkin House* the sources of that failure are made clear. Though never mentioned by name, the figure of Stalin looms over the entire novel, his influence manifest in each severed connection and individual betrayal. Lyova's father, it emerges, has built his scholarly reputation in the Stalin era on the repudiation of the work of his own father, Modest Platonovich. When Modest Platonovich, by now a broken man, is unexpectedly 'resurrected', after years in Stalin's camps, Lyova discovers the betrayal and in turn rejects his father.

Orphaned psychologically within his family, Lyova suffers a parallel sense of cultural disinheritance. Revolution and terror have shattered the nation's vital links with its past; a guardian of pre-revolutionary culture, Lyova can no longer claim a straightforward place in its tradition. In an essay that forms one of the appendices to the novel, Lyova compares the work of three poets, Pushkin, Lermontov,* and Tyutchev, and betrays his own ambivalence towards a literature that both engulfs and excludes him. In Lermontov's 'adolescent' protests, he recognizes his own resentment at having arrived 'too late' on the literary scene. Conniving with the 'devil', Mitishatev, in desecrating Pushkin House, he mimics the secret hostility to Pushkin which he identifies as the central motive of Tyutchev's work.

The novel itself in turn enacts the ambivalence of its hero. In its multiple allusions to the classics of Russian literature—Dostoyevsky's *Devils*, Pushkin's *Bronze Horseman*, Turgenev's *Fathers and Sons*—Bitov pays homage to 'the house that Pushkin built', but he also comments ironically on the current tenant of that house, the

---

* Mikhail Lermontov (1814–41), poet and prose writer, best known for his psychological novel *A Hero of our Time* (1840), set in the Caucasus.

† Fyodor Tyutchev (1803–73), lyrical and romantic poet and contemporary of Aleksandr Pushkin (1799–1837).

contemporary Russian *intelligent*. Lyova inhabits a world of literary images—his very city appears written in ink—but the images are by now distorted, the quotations garbled, and Lyova himself a pale copy of Pushkin's or Lermontov's romantic heroes. His duel with Mitishatev, fought with the museum's antique pistols, belongs more to farce than tragedy. At the end of the novel the author himself steps in to help clear up the wreckage he has caused, and resurrects Lyova to continue his scholarly work. But this act of contrition leaves Lyova—unlike his author—still trapped in the museum.

How, Bitov asks in *Pushkin House*, can we rescue literature from the 'dead house' of the past, and life itself from literature? The answer is partly suggested in a manuscript—another of the novel's 'appendices'–which the hero entrusts to the author at the end of the novel. In it, Modest Platonovich, the hero's grandfather, describes his own act of self-liberation in refusing to lie to the authorities before his arrest. Had he not told the truth, he concludes, he might not have been able to 'look up at the sky and know that he was free'. His words can be read as a description of Bitov's own act in writing. In its irreverence, its truthfulness, its disregard for conventional genre, *Pushkin House*—like all Bitov's work—presents a demonstrative act of freedom.

If the novel, in that sense, concerns the author's salvation rather than his hero's, it nevertheless conveys an uneasiness about the manipulative power of words and ideas. Both in *Lessons of Armenia* and in *Pushkin House* Bitov draws implicit parallels between Peter the Great and Stalin, identifying the mark of dictatorship in their realization of a pure abstraction—a perfect city, a total ideology. Both are seen to interfere with some natural, God-given ecology of things. But if Stalinism (or Leninism) is the logical outcome of man's urge to redesign the world, is there not a potential for destruction in the very act of creativity? Even to describe the world, Bitov suggests, is in some sense to destroy it. 'Reality does not survive being described,' he wrote later. 'Either it perishes or it gains full independence.'

Such thoughts form the philosophical underpinning to Bitov's latest work, *The Monkey Link* (*Oglashennyye*). In three interlinked 'tales', written at separate times between 1971 and 1991, Bitov sets out, as translator Susan Brownsberger puts it, to pose the questions: 'What is man's role in relation to other biological species? To God? To humankind? . . . [and] to himself?'

The first tale, originally published in 1976 as 'Birds: New Information about Man',* finds the author/hero back at the place where he had retreated to work on *Pushkin House*: an ornothological research station on the Kurish Spit, at the westernmost border of the former Soviet empire. From the first page, Bitov introduces the idea of 'the border', both spatial and temporal, as man's uncomfortable habitat: wedged between sea and sky, neither fish nor fowl, man originated 'exactly where any other species dies out. No warm fur, no terrible teeth, no lupine morals. Trousers, the bullet, religion . . .'.

Bitov's interlocutor in 'Birds' is the ornothologist Doctor D., a man committed to the specialist's singular description of the world around him. Ever the uncommitted outsider, Bitov's role is to disrupt the scientist's patient, 'sluggish' thinking with questions from outside the boundaries of science: What 'sets the limit on

---

* 'Ptitsy, ili novyye svedeniya o cheloveke', first published in *Dni cheloveka* (1976).

enjoyment if there are no obstacles in its path?' What is the nature of paradise? Which laws, in general, 'does science pluck out for study'? Strolling along a shore where sea, earth, and sky seem to meet at their most elemental, eliciting from his friend information about the life of birds, the author reflects on the nature of human aggression and civilization, and on our attempts to name and explain the world from our own precarious niche in the natural order.

He finds a willing partner in these meditations in the interlocutor of his second tale, 'Man in a Landscape'.* Pavel Petrovich, a landscape painter, is similarly impressed by the contingent 'narrowness' of both our physical life and our capacity to understand it: 'What we live in,' he declares, 'what we see, perceive and comprehend, what we call reality, is also a range, beyond whose bounds we perish in the same way that we freeze to death or suffocate [without air or water].'

Amply fuelled by drink, the author and his new companion discourse on the nature of man's creativity in relation to God's, on the artist's difficulty in removing himself from the landscape he paints, on his search to overcome his own solitude. But in the course of this marathon dialogue, staged at a restored historic site somewhere outside Moscow, the author is also taken on a hallucinatory tour of Russia's past, entering—through Pavel Petrovich's own apparently timeless biography—an unending series of banishments, seizures, resettlements, imprisonments, humiliations, and betrayals. Having passed, in this sense, through several 'layers of reality', the author/hero then awakes, in the present, to a heightened sense of the world around him and a corresponding loss of self—'As whom have we awakened? Who awoke?'

This awakening takes place at sunset and, as the final part of the trilogy makes clear, the hero's confusion—both his hope and foreboding—relate to the sense that his country, too, is beginning to unravel around him. 'Waiting for the Monkeys' tracks the author on a last twilight tour of the empire, shifting both in time, between the invasion of Afghanistan and the *putsch* of 1991, and geographically, between Moscow, Azerbaijan, Georgia, and Abkhazia, where—in a motley company that includes his two former interlocutors—Bitov has gone to investigate, for satirical purposes, a colony of 'free' monkeys on the Black Sea coast. History overtakes intention, however; the author never quite reaches the colony, and in the mean time his manuscript is burned to a cinder in a conflagration that seems, for a moment, to signal the end not only to the empire and history but to himself as an author.

Bitov's restless companion on this journey is by now just his *alter ego*, an unidentified 'he'. Ellen Chances, in her study of Bitov's work, has pointed out that the single pronoun 'he' is not only used, in *Pushkin House*, to refer covertly to Stalin, but resembles, in Russian script, part of the chemical formula for alcohol—OH. The 'he' of 'Waiting for the Monkeys' is likewise a traitor, an enemy of literature, agitating, often successfully, to douse the author and his work in drink. But at the same time he stands, unabashedly, for life, and in a final reckoning with this *alter ego* Bitov shows that 'he', too, has reason to feel betrayed by the author's detached, fastidious, literary persona.

Though the end of 'Waiting for the Monkeys' suggests a provisional reconciliation with self and Russia, it is nevertheless the most self-punishing of Bitov's

---

* 'Chelovek v peizazhe', first published in *Novy mir* (1987), subsequently in *Chelovek v peizazhe: povesti i rasskazy* (1988).

works—satirical of his earlier escapes and epiphanies, distrustful of the very enterprise of literature. As a whole, indeed, *The Monkey Link* shows Bitov at his most difficult and 'subjective', its seemingly chaotic structure held together by obscure references—to literature, to history, to Bitov's own biography, even to the animals of the Chinese zodiac—that will be lost on the uninitiated.

Such charges have been made, by his detractors, about Bitov's work in general. At times a tease, a provocateur, a self-confessed show-off, capable of crudity as well as brilliance ('shit and roses', as he puts it in *The Monkey Link*), Bitov has been unashamedly concerned, throughout, with the workings of his own heart and mind. More than with most writers, to read Bitov is to encounter him personally, and temperament may account for whether one is infuriated or inspired, impatient or charmed.

To me he is the most companionable of writers, and that despite—or because of—the sense of solitariness he conveys. 'The heart is incarcerated in us as in a prison,' says Pavel Petrovich at the end of *The Monkey Link*. 'That's why we all have the same thoughts, and yet our hearts are lonely.' In Bitov's unfettered musings on himself and his art, there is an invitation to investigate our own bafflement, our need at times to throw off the guises of maturity—profession, family status, worldly experience—and to ask the childish and unaskable questions.

◆　◆　◆

SL You've written that the writer is in principle 'homeless', and certainly the search for some kind of spiritual home—or the exploration of what it is to be homeless—seems to me to motivate much of your work. Do you see yourself as someone whom history or circumstance has made particularly 'homeless', or just as someone who has recognized this as the condition of human beings—'the son of man has nowhere to lay his head'?

AB As it happens I was talking about this just recently. You know, all my life I've thought of myself as a person who was made for just one home and one love, and everything that actually happened to me in my life seemed to me conditional, accidental, not characteristic of me at all. But I'm nearly 60 years old now and I finally have to recognize that my 'homelessness' isn't a matter of chance.

I think I grew up with an idea of 'home' that was already impossible to imagine in the Soviet system. Our family kept a kind of insurance by living all together—several different families, brothers and sisters, all lived together in one big apartment, and because of that we were able to keep a certain way of life as it used to be, before Soviet times. For the rest of my life it gave me a feeling of what 'home' was, the feeling of a place to return to.

As a young man, as you know, I was trained as a geologist and it was part of my professional life to travel all over the place. But I was constantly returning to the place of my birth, to my mother's home, and I went on doing so right up until 1980 when the apartment was finally sold and my mother moved.

Meanwhile I went through all sorts of marriages and divorces and was

Interviews recorded in June 1993 and May 1994.

constantly leaving home. So my life has been chopped into little bits, and looking back now I can see that the different parts have more or less coincided with different phases in our history. Stalin's period, Khrushchev's, Brezhnev's, Gorbachev's—they all meant different lives, different homes, different children, as if one's intentions in life were somehow governed by these things. Certainly, my childhood and youth were Stalin's time, my first love came just before his death, my first marriage coincided with the Thaw, then came the 'stagnation', and I escaped to Moscow and remarried, and finally the Gorbachev era brought a further change, like life after death—I married once more and had one more child.

So—I don't see myself as a 'victim', but I do think I've reflected my time. I always used to think of myself as an independent person, but I see now that it isn't true. Recently I was invited to talk at an exhibition in Vienna on the theme of Stalin's architecture, and I had to say that I counted as an exhibit myself, I was one of Stalin's skyscrapers. And as I was talking I remembered Nabokov, and the house of his childhood which we know from *Speak, Memory*. His family was one of the six richest families in St Petersburg, and his father—a great Anglophile—ordered all his purchases from abroad, mostly from England; he owned one of the first automobiles in Russia. Which explains why Nabokov never experienced any culture shock when he found himself in Europe. But the point is that he never, after leaving Russia, had any home of his own; he always lived provisionally in rented rooms and hotels, very expensive hotels when he became rich, but hotels nevertheless.

SL   Because nothing would ever compare with his home in Russia?

AB   No, just because he *had* a home already. And there was something of that in my case. I didn't come from a particularly rich or fashionable family, but it had its traditions. And it made it very difficult for me to start again. I know I can't go back, the roots are dead, they died after the Revolution, but—new people will have to start again. That's my feeling. And maybe subconsciously it's like that: I'm building homes that aren't suitable for me—they are for the next generation.

SL   I'm reminded of Brodsky's essay 'In a Room and a Half ',* about the death of his parents, the disappearance with them of his first home—which was of course a very modest one—and the sense that nothing that he creates, no home of his, can ever have for him the same sense of necessity and inevitability as the things that he was born with—just because he created them himself, he knows their origins.

AB   I know this even from my daughter, who was born in our family home. She was just 5 years old when we moved, but she still lives there in that lost house.

SL   So perhaps—as you imply in a very early story, 'One Country'—there's no contradiction in believing in 'one home, one country, one love' and being constitutionally restless. One can see in your work that both things are true of you: you're both the poet of a particular place and time—the Leningrad you grew up in—and a 'writer-in-travel', always on the move.

AB   I have two definitions, yes, I'm a Petersburg writer and—not so much a writer-in-travel as a writer of the empire, an empire which is now lost.

---

* Joseph Brodsky, *Less than One: Selected Essays* (New York: Farrar, Straus & Giroux, 1986).

One of the most complimentary reviews I've had referred to me as the poet not just of Petersburg but of one particular place, Apothecary Island, the name of one of my first stories. This feeling of the island is very important to me—a British person can understand that. Because, you see, the whole country—Russia—is lost in history and in time, its tragedy is the tragedy of space, enormous undeveloped space. It's natural in such a vast space to move like a nomad, without developing any kind of civilization. But within this huge space St Petersburg itself represented a kind of island; it was the product of Peter the Great's 'island' thinking—this idea of building a window to Europe. And within this island I've had my own island, a particular space that I've cultivated.

Petersburg is a very strange place. It was a planned system, in the same way that socialism was a planned system, organized and built from the mind, but at least it was built from images of Europe, and European architects were involved in the building of the city. Later on life took its own direction and the place became part of a tyranny, of totalitarianism. But it's both the most awful city and the nicest city—Europe combined with this imperial thing. Very strange. But what we received, what helped us—as Brodsky has often emphasized—is that we shared the same physical space as its past inhabitants; Soviet power had not destroyed that space, so that although we led a 'socialist life' in socialist times, and we were cut off from our own culture, we had no way of reading even our own literature, still we lived in the same space as our cultural ancestors, in the very same buildings.

SL But you weren't absolutely cut off from the culture of the past, were you?

AB Not, of course, from nineteenth-century literature. But what was written during the Soviet period, especially the literature of the twenties and the early thirties— none of that was known when I was growing up. My family were not 'Soviet', they weren't communists, they were intelligentsia of the old regime. But the point was that this literature—the literature of their time—simply wasn't published, there was no knowing it unless you had personal connections. So for us, of a younger generation, there was no Mandelshtam, no Platonov, no Nabokov ...*

Now I have to come to terms with what has happened in my life; I have no other, I have no other history. In a way this *tabula rasa* that I was presented with was a sort of privilege. As a young man I knew I was craving for something, I wanted something, I spent a lot of my energy body-building, trying to prepare myself—I didn't know for what, that was just something I invented for myself. And then accidentally I found this group of people, young people, maybe just a bit older than I was, people who were attempting to write contemporary literature. And that astonished me. Because for me literature wasn't contemporary at all. It was something in the past, like God was in the past, like life was in the past.

And then there had been this kind of awakening—it was probably the most important period of my life, though I can't remember it at all. In my last year in school I invented all sorts of excuses not to turn up, I simply walked about in my city, learned my city by heart. I can't imagine what I was doing—it was a kind of meditation.

* Osip Mandelshtam (1891–1938); Andrei Platonov (1899–1951); Vladimir Nabokov (1899–1977), writers whose works were fully published in Russia only after *glasnost* (in the case of the *émigré* Nabokov, none of his works was published in Russia until 1986).

SL Were you already writing at the time?

AB No, not at all. But afterwards, after I left school, I met these people, these writers—in 1956, just at the time of Khrushchev's report on Stalin, the beginning of the Thaw. I was looking for friendship, I suppose, for some kind of connection with people. And I discovered these people were poets and decided they were 'my' people.

SL Did they include any names that subsequently became well known?

AB Yes, there was Gleb Gorbovsky* and Aleksandr Kushner,† the most outstanding poets of that generation—of those still living in Leningrad. Brodsky came a bit later and belonged to another group, Akhmatova's circle. Later on, several other groups emerged; I could draw a whole cultural map of that generation in Leningrad, but at the time this was the only circle, and I was invited to join them as a poet. I have to confess—I've confessed already—that I started out with a piece of plagiarism. They told me: you're a nice guy, but you do have to write something if you want to join us. Well, my brother had written some very bad poems in the style of Severyanin,‡ and I knew them by heart because I'd watched him composing them (we shared a room), so I went ahead and recited these poems. In other words I started my career quite professionally, just stealing someone else's verses. But after that I was trapped; I really did have to write something, and I started writing a long, long poem, a bit in the style of Mayakovsky. When I read it to them they all congratulated me, and then they admitted that the stuff I'd read the first time round was awful ...

The truth was that my own poem was awful too. It was on the theme of art belonging to the people, it described all these visitors to the Hermitage who had no connection with the art world. But I can analyse it now and see that in some way I was already writing about Pushkin House.

SL *Pushkin House* is both a homage to Russian literature, to the house that Pushkin built, and an act of vandalism on it: it registers horror at what happens when culture is desecrated, but also a profound unease about the way that literature has been rendered in some way untouchable, out of bounds, something that belongs, as you say, to the past. Do you see that uneasiness as something uniquely Russian, a result of the peculiar relationship between Russian literature and history?

AB We're very proud of our literature. But one can't help reflecting on the enormous gap between our culture—which is built first and foremost on literature—and our actual standard of life. We're not yet civilized. Our history has consisted of a series of tragic changes; we've constantly shot off in different directions, always on the brink of civilization but never quite reaching it. And it occurred to me that maybe there's been some kind of spiritual mistake. Our literature has been the result of this mistake. It's sacrilege to say so—but maybe our literature has been *too good*. If our culture had developed more slowly ...

---

* Gleb Gorbovsky (b. 1931), Leningrad poet whose first collections, *Poiski tepla* (In search of Warmth) and *Spasibo, zemlya* (Thank you, Earth) were published in the early 1960s.

† Aleksandr Kushner (b. 1936), one of Russia's finest poets this century, whose first collection, *Pervoye vpechatleniye* (First Impression) appeared in 1962.

‡ Igor Severyanin (1887–1942), poet and founder in 1911 of a movement dubbed 'Egofuturism', combining symbolist elements with the new technological vocabulary of the age.

SL There might have been room for something else?

AB Yes, yes ... and yet one can't say it would have been better if the literature had never existed. In this novel I was thinking above all of Pushkin. And how could one say it would have been better if there'd been no Pushkin—it's unthinkable, of course.

SL And yet the ambivalence is there, isn't it, in the hero of *Pushkin House*. Lyova Odoyevtsev allows the vandalism to be perpetrated, he allows the museum to be destroyed before putting it together again.

AB You know, that whole story originated in an anecdote I heard—I was told that something like that had really happened when the guard on duty at Pushkin House got drunk. I was completely hypnotized by this story; I wanted to analyse how a guardian of culture could destroy culture—and then restore it out of a certain kind of fear. That was the start of the whole novel for me. I tried to analyse his reasons, and the whole novel—which started out as a short story—was built on that.

SL In the novel we see Lyova Odoyevtsev sharing many of the difficulties of your earlier hero, Aleksei Monakhov—in telling the truth, in understanding himself, in relating to those close to him. Elsewhere in your work—in 'Birds', in 'Man in a Landscape'—we see these difficulties treated at a more existential level, as part of a general problem of cognition about oneself and the world. But in *Pushkin House* the hero's experience is related much more explicitly to the historical experience of his generation, your generation, the generation that came of age in the fifties and sixties. Do you see yourself—as critics have tended to see you—as a writer of your particular epoch, a *shestidesyatnik*, a 'man of the sixties'?

AB I'm not very keen on this labelling of people in terms of epochs. These sorts of classifications tend simply to spoil relations between people. But of course I belong to my time: just as a cucumber consists of 90 per cent water, so I can't do anything about 90 per cent of myself. I was born in a certain year, in a certain country, and went through such and such experiences, and there's nothing I can do to change that. And yet I do have a soul of some kind and certain things that concern me, and it seems to me that I went along this path in a fairly solitary way, as one has to.

Kurt Vonnegut, in a passage I like, asks what 'community' means and says that it refers simply to the community of people who have met each other on life's path. I like that, it's very simple and free. He distinguishes between a community of that kind and the fake community of the political party, or the generation, or the high school year or the football team. Obviously in Russia we're not alone in labelling people by these 'fake' communities, but perhaps we've relied on them more markedly because our society wasn't allowed to develop naturally; many of the older ties and distinctions—of family, of class—were distorted or abolished.

As far as *Pushkin House* goes—I was of course much younger when I finished it. And now I think that I was simply governed by certain intuitions. In a way the energy that went into that novel was very primitive. We lived then—or at least I lived—with the idea that life was wonderful before 1917. Maybe it was, maybe it wasn't, but in my consciousness at that time there was just hatred towards a system which had ruined my culture, ruined my past, ruined my tradition, ruined my perspective, made it impossible to prolong that former life. Those were the impulses and energy at the time I wrote *Pushkin House.*

Now I'm no longer so sure. Since the fall of Soviet power and the Soviet regime it's been possible to see continuities, to see the aspects of 'old Russia' that continued under the regime, and which paradoxically may be lost now. Not that I have any nostalgia, not that I think those were good times. I'm happy about the changes. But, for instance, the empire we had—the empire we've lost—wasn't only a negative phenomenon. Certainly there was a lot of fakery about it—we hated all those fake words, 'Friendship of the Peoples', 'Internationalism', and so on. But still there was the sense that this was a domestic space, that we were a family of sorts ...

SL   You referred earlier to your being 'a writer of the empire' as well as of St Petersburg. What did you mean by that—apart from the fact that your travels to Armenia, Georgia, and elsewhere have obviously been an inspiration for your writing?

AB   I always thought that I would write about the empire, our Soviet empire. This notion occurred to me long ago: in some way I foresaw that the empire would disappear, that I would be its last scribe. I had this—not exactly romantic desire, but the desire of an old-fashioned naturalist, someone like Linneaus, to gather up and describe all this knowledge, as if I was constructing a building under the title of 'The Empire'. Immediately after *Pushkin House,* my novel about St Petersburg, I thought of writing a novel called 'Moscow'—and then there'd be a novel on the provinces, and to this I'd add my travels round the empire—so the whole thing would be a harmonious construction, a nice fat tome.

It hasn't turned out quite like that, but I think you can still see traces of that idea, although it's hard for me to say; I don't like rereading what I've written. In any case, it's too late now—the empire has gone for good, the job no longer needs to be done.*

SL   In your travel-writings about Armenia and Georgia you're clearly haunted by the writers who've been there before you—Tolstoy, Pushkin, Lermontov: you quote from them, you make clear that your quest is in some way to rediscover their enchantment. But your 'use' of your experience is of course very different from theirs. Did you set out consciously to 'invent' a new genre with these writings—part travel memoir, part philosophical essay?

AB   Certainly there's been no established genre of this sort in our literature. In general Russian literature—for all its greatness—has been rather slow to develop distinct genres. I imagine that in future—as the country becomes more civilized—we'll see the development of literary forms that up till now have been left rather uncultivated here: documentary, travel-writing, biography, essays, even the well-plotted novel. None of these has been developed as great art in Russia, in the way they have in the West.

In my case, my 'travel-writings' only mimic the documentary principle, and there's a paradox involved: when I write about 'reality' I very often end up writing fiction. That is, the reality which I don't invent has to be written about so that it looks invented, and vice versa—things that I've invented must look as if they were

---

* Since this interview was recorded, Bitov has in fact published a selection of his works under the title *Imperiya v chetyryokh izmereniyakh* (An Empire in Four Dimensions) (1996).

drawn straight from reality. People tend to believe the fiction and not to believe the truth, and that's what I like to play on—that gives me my opportunity.

I like the form of the 'travel book' because it's naturally spacious, relaxed, diffuse. You can speak of whatever you like and your thoughts gradually move along with the journey itself. The welding of a novel is completely different; the stress involved is much higher. It's as if in one case—with the travels—there's the creation of an image, in the other—the creation of an artefact.

SL You imply that the development of genre is a matter of 'civilization', of greater sophistication. But in the West—if one can talk in such broad terms—what we've seen, if anything, is the development of mixed genres that collapse or question the barrier between 'truth' and 'fiction'.

AB Maybe I've formulated it too systematically, and of course it's true as before that the most interesting and genuine literature will remain that which invents genre. But at the same time there are defined stages. In European literature the formula of the novel was developed very clearly in the nineteenth century; an author might be expected to produce twenty or thirty novels within the genre, and even today an author in the West works professionally, earning his living by regularly producing new books. He has to count on the public in a way that the Russian writer never has. Maybe the charm of Russian literature lies in its amateurishness.

Perhaps I'm afraid of our losing that here—of our losing the sense of literature as a form of protest.

SL What do you mean by protest?

AB There are forms of protest that aren't just social or political. Every artist makes a form of protest just by reflecting on the situation of the individual in the world. In the end that's what all literature is about, no matter what the subject, the material—and that's the reason we read it, to recognize at a certain existential level our own situation in the situation of the hero. If it's written in the right way we can identify with the hero no matter what colour or sex he is or what particular circumstances he finds himself in.

Books aren't written about the things that are used to explain them afterwards. They're written about the situation 'me and them', 'me and the world'—that's the secret form of literature, and that's what we recognize. For me literature is simply a form of cognition, a method for the writer to understand more about life and his situation than he did before he wrote.

SL So literature in this sense 'protests' not against the world as such but against our established ways of seeing it—the 'protest' lies 'simply' in presenting a new vision, a new truth?

AB This word 'truth' has become a kind of demon for us, because in the old days, in the old regime, it was seen too simplistically: 'truth' was simply the opposite of the official line, it was what lay on the other side of our official life. But what I'm talking of here is a form of artistic daring. Maybe what I mean by 'protest' is simply courage, the courage involved in making up your mind to try to say something that hasn't been said, or to formulate something in a way it's never been formulated before. All this takes courage, takes strength, and it inevitably puts you into a kind of opposition.

SL I see your writing as motivated, certainly, by a search for danger—but the danger consisting not in saying things that aren't allowed but in being thin-skinned, in making yourself naked, exposing the self, exposing the inner processes of thought.

AB But this kind of striptease is very curious, you know—and in fact I should say straight out that it isn't really a striptease. I've said before: the more you make yourself naked, the less other people see. A person who's said a great deal about himself becomes in some way invisible, even more mysterious.

That's why the system of denunciations to the secret police collapsed in Russia—precisely because it became so routine and widespread. There was too much information. No one was able to sort out the truth any more.

SL Perhaps it would be truer to say that you court danger by constantly questioning your own enterprise as a writer—or setting yourself tasks that you yourself define as impossible. On the one hand the world—reality—is tantalizingly *there*, and in moments of grace the hero, or the narrator, is granted the innocence or the inspiration to see it; he suddenly finds that words indeed match the things they describe. And yet the writer is seen by definition to be seeking something beyond the describable—trying, as your character Pavel Petrovich puts it, to get to the other side of this thin 'layer of reality' that we inhabit. What stops us from seeing the truth, you seem to be saying, isn't just ideology or circumstance or our own limitations—timidity, self-deception—but the limitations inherent in human vision and language.

AB Yes, I'm sure now that we're not working with words at all. Certainly our use of spoken or written language can be better or worse, more or less correct or sophisticated, but at the same time we're actually using another language that has no words. What I'm interested in are the things that are certainly present in our lives but which our everyday language—the language of information—doesn't deal with at all. I'm interested in ... this emptiness, these gaps, this air between words, this silence. The reason you write is to use a lot of words in order to explain one non-existing word.

SL It's a form of translation?

AB Maybe. And this is a terrible effort; that's what takes courage. To go beyond the language of information, of the mass media. Because you know that when you use language cheaply there is always some kind of lie. One is told that the world is such-and-such, that this is what the world is like—but it isn't true. Art must be a true description, as true as possible, and that takes tremendous effort. Of course, the image will never be the same as life. But at least if it is beautiful and harmonious then it won't be destructive of life. It can't be used to destroy, to do harm.

Perhaps this idea of literature as a form of *aggression* is peculiarly Russian, perhaps we are peculiar in having used it for such aggressive purposes. But the point is that if a writer can be used in that way it's because he's already aggressive *within* his own art; he is using literature as a form of hypnosis, of slavery. Even great writers—Dostoyevsky, for instance—can be guilty of that. Pushkin, though, never was.

SL In your latest novel, *The Monkey Link*, you suggest that the reason why those in power are nervous of writers is precisely that they create their own form of dictatorship, their own dominion, in which they dispose of their characters. In the last part of the novel the narrator's *alter ego* rises up in protest at what's been done to him in the novel. In *Pushkin House* you reveal a similar squeamishness about the author's power. The author not only revives the hero he'd left dead at the beginning—as if guilty at having killed him off—but he enters the novel himself to help clear up all the wreckage he's caused.

AB But this dictatorship takes place inside your own world—it doesn't affect reality. It's true that I'm afraid of killing my characters, even though I'm dealing in ink, not blood. But what I'm talking of here are more subtle forms of manipulation—subtle ways of upsetting the balance *out there*. There is an ecology of ideas as well as of water and air, there's a stratum where ideas are spread, and this is where the writer can do damage, entering people's consciousness, building the wrong systems, in the end changing history.

Our world consists of a lot of descriptions that don't belong to the real world. Science, money, love, literature—they're all forms of description. Recently on a train I met a man who was a specialist in explosions, and I realized that with the help of his theories you could describe the whole world too—how the universe was created, how life is prolonged, how the heart works. I interrogated my fellow passenger for several hours, exploiting his knowledge—I even invited him to become a character in my book, but at that point he got frightened. But I decided to add 'explosives expert' to the list of Pavel Petrovich's professions in 'Man in a Landscape'. He has a lot of professions already, as you know.

SL In a preface to the English translation of your stories you wrote: 'the past is utterly defenceless against our attempts to reorganize it. I think that for aesthetic reasons it's better not to disturb it.' But the fact that much of your work has been published only long after it was written has given you more than the usual opportunity to 'tinker'. And in fact you've 'reorganized' your own work a good deal, changing names and titles, sometimes even the personal pronouns involved, and placing separate stories in new constellations to suggest new readings. Are you glad to have had that opportunity in the end?

AB All my life I've cursed our system for the fact that I couldn't finish things on time and immediately see them published—but in a certain sense this either made me the writer I am, or at least underlined the character I had anyway. The fact that I was non-engaged, an outsider, always allowed me to throw things aside without finishing them and then return to them later, and in the process they all started overlapping and became intertwined.

Now I can see that I've been writing several books simultaneously over a very long period. There were the various 'travels', which were put together over twenty years, and *Pushkin House*, with all its system of commentaries and so forth, which has gone on for two decades too, and *Vanishing Monakhov*—which went on for thirty years ... and so on. This corpus of work has gradually formed a kind of home for me, or at least the outline of a home. It's still unfinished, it still doesn't have a roof, but the image of the house—the realization that I was building a house—became helpful to me at a certain point; it helped to prevent me from moving out.

In this sense I draw courage from Laurence Sterne, one of my favourite writers, who taught me the virtue of imperfection. The most harmful thing is when everything is clear—then it becomes simply boring. You can only continue by engaging in this endless, restless movement.

sl We talked earlier of your 'homelessness', but it seems to me that in a strange way the epoch up to the mid-1980s, the 'stagnation' era, had a quality of timelessness—of being outside time and history—that made it easier in some sense for a writer, as you describe, to imagine and build his own house. Reality, politics, current events didn't intrude in the way that they must do now. I have the feeling that it's much harder for a writer now to make his own habitable space—too much noise comes in from the outside: history has been cranked into motion and you can hear it permanently grinding away.

ab Those are practically my own thoughts about the situation—of course it's like that. There was a time when I was lazy because it seemed to us that we had an eternity before us. In those days one blamed all sorts of other circumstances for preventing one from writing. But then a new problem arose—one was interrupted by facts, by events, they interrupted the imagination.

I began writing the last part of *The Monkey Link*, 'Waiting for the Monkeys', in the early eighties and it seemed to me that I caught that sound you describe, caught some intimation of it in advance, even while everything was still standing still. But afterwards it became very difficult to retain this sense. In all my time writing prose I've never had such a struggle as I did completing 'Monkeys'. It should have been finished in 1983 or 1984. I already had the basic idea: the idea of the hero setting out to see this monkey colony and never quite getting there, being in a state of constant waiting.

When you set out to do a job like this you have to be properly prepared—you have to concentrate all you have on one point, develop a kind of artificial freedom, arrange your circumstances so that you feel free to concentrate, and so on—and I was all ready and poised to go. But then various events occurred in my personal and family life and I lost the necessary spirit. And two years later history started catching up with the story I'd invented and which should have been told *forwards*, as a kind of prophesy. Everything started to unravel. And then I found myself involved in a new situation—giving interviews, writing journalism, and so on, travelling abroad.

But the main point was that I could no longer use this story as pure imagination. I couldn't any longer write in this secret, elliptical way—this style of the 'stagnation' period—everything was out in the open, my story was coming true.

And then I became a bit desperate because it's a part of my basic metabolism to be writing and it became a problem simply to sit down and write. It wasn't just my problem—other people stopped writing too. But then I was granted the chance to spend some time in Germany, just before the fall of the empire in December 1991. After the *putsch* [the coup in August 1991] and before the fall: because the *putsch* was a false ending which had looked like a full stop, but it wasn't the real end. And I managed to use this two-month period to get moving again. But as I was writing, history kept happening—the whole of Ukraine disappeared. It was very difficult to retain the energy that comes from knowing things *before* they happen, from being contemporary or ahead of your contemporary.

It was hellish work—trying to live simultaneously in today and yesterday. But it's only through this inner struggle that you earn yourself the right to some space of your own and the freedom also to get up and go away and misbehave again ...

Anyway the result is a very strange combination. The last part of *The Monkey Link* involves three different time periods one inside the other, like *matryoshki* dolls.

SL Both 'Birds' and 'Man in a Landscape'—the other parts of *The Monkey Link*—were first published separately as independent pieces. Did the idea of the whole novel emerge only later, or did you conceive of these three pieces going together from the start?

AB Right from the start I saw these three works as having the same form, consisting of a dialogue between the hero and an interlocutor. There was the ecologist Doctor D. in the case of 'Birds' and the artist Pavel Petrovich in 'Man in a Landscape', and the only difficulty was to decide who my next interlocutor should be.

In the end I decided on this kind of *alter ego*, this unidentified 'he'. When I republished 'Birds' as part of the novel, the main thing I added, right at the beginning, was the phrase 'He said or I thought', and in the first version of 'Monkeys', right at the end, there was a mirror phrase: 'He thought or I said', though that was later deleted. Anyway, the result is a kind of detective story about this 'he' ...

SL Aren't both Doctor D. and Pavel Petrovich also *alter egos*, other versions of yourself?

AB Doctor D. was partly based on a friend of mine, and as for Pavel Petrovich—well he just appeared; I wrote about this landscape and I found him there, painting the landscape, and he was a great gift to me; I think he's a great Russian character. Certainly he's me in some form—but I'm a combination of several people, I don't believe in such a thing as a strict personality. Pavel Petrovich is also a kind of composite. But I knew very well he was my *alter ego* in some way—and then, when I was trying to think who this third interlocutor should be, I thought—why not just make him my *alter ego tout court*, just 'he'.

The whole story is about loneliness, the loneliness of the author. I'm a twin—a Gemini—in the zodiac, and people who've lived with me know that I really am a double, they've suffered from my character. All my life I've been exploring these different people within myself. So in this book I divided myself very easily into two—into this more brutal 'he' and this more moral 'I', who was somehow less alive than 'him'. It's not a harmonious combination and I never knew what direction their conversation would take them in.

What I invented with Pavel Petrovich also was a way of expressing certain ideas and thoughts that gave me pleasure but weren't 'important'. He's a sort of intellectual primitive, he's not really educated and he's drunk most of the time. He may say things that have been said seven thousand years ago but it doesn't matter that his ideas aren't original, *he*'s an original. It's a way of discussing ideas without underlining them.

SL The book tilts towards comedy every time your characters start drinking—indeed there's almost an element of farce to *The Monkey Link*, especially to the last part, 'Waiting for the Monkeys', with so much drink swilling around and so many characters confusingly assembled. It seems to me in some ways a very self-mocking book.

AB   Well I just like to have this possibility of not being serious about serious things. The sorts of things Pavel Petrovich discusses are in fact very serious for me. For instance when he says in his boastful way that among all his other professions he's a specialist in watches, and this leads on to a whole discussion of time, the idea that there is no movement in time itself, that time is a kind of dead body from which life emerges, a kind of chrysalis—and that we are in that sense living inside death, living in darkness, and reflecting light from the outside ... all these ideas I take seriously. But if I talk about them with a serious face and voice I'll destroy them.

A critic in Germany who disliked the whole book asked me whether I didn't feel that people reading it wouldn't trust the ideas in it because the characters expressing them were drunk. I tried to tell her that that was the whole idea.

SL   In *Pushkin House* you say that the hardest things to describe are 'the world of the child, the world of the drunk, and the world of the false or talentless man', but in many of your works—including *Pushkin House*—you give a virtuoso performance in the genre of drunkenness. Drunkenness seems to convey a heightened version of the 'unreal' or ungraspable world in which many of your characters live all the time. But it also seems to me to mimic the condition of the writer himself— always steering a perilous course between brilliance and banality—between truisms and moments of truth.

AB   Drunkenness is certainly a metaphor, or not even that—it's a method, a device. But what I can say is that—well, I have plenty of personal knowledge of drunkenness, most Russians have, but for various reasons it hasn't been described much in Russian literature, though it brought us Venedikt Yerofeyev's brilliant work *Moscow-Petushki**. So—I wouldn't pretend to be a pioneer, but I set about my investigations independently.

But now that theme is exhausted and I've stopped drinking with my heroes. In order to write I have to be completely sober.

SL   Pavel Petrovich talks of *kaif*, the Russian—or Asian—version of getting high. Is this kind of *kaif* necessarily different from the 'moments of truth' that your characters—or you yourself—occasionally reach, when the world seems suddenly to fall into place, as on the road from Tiflis to Kutais which you describe in *The Monkey Link*: 'When you no longer ask yourself the question, What is it? You simply inhale and don't exhale ... Look, a cliff! Look, a stream! Look, the sky! ...'

AB   I would call such moments 'moments of reality', and the whole question is about how you reach such moments. The theory of drugs, of 'highs', is like the theory of explosions, it's about everything. Everything depends on the way you get your high, on the kind of drugs you use. If you need artificial ones you're lost; somehow you have to reach this 'high' yourself. That's the great principle of all our activity and all our dreams about the future and happiness and so on. That's the basis for all our ... not our morality, I hate that word, but our moral life, our *nravstvennost*, meaning the system whereby if you do things the wrong way you're punished and if you do them the right way you're rewarded, you get the result you're after. And the first 'honorarium', the first reward, is a sense of your

---

* See Introduction, p. xxii.

own identity. You have to work for it, work to get this 'drug', to get to a state when you can smile and see the world and achieve a normal distance from other people. But if you get more than you're *paying* for—paying for in your own work—the situation immediately changes.

But as a writer you can treat drunkenness as a kind of sociological phenomenon—as I did in *Pushkin House*—or you can use it as a way to compromise the seriousness of your characters' talk, to give yourself a kind of freedom.

SL You seem to me to be deeply equivocal about the kind of freedom you're after. On the one hand there's the sophisticated, sceptical, games-playing Bitov, who enjoys the freedom even to compromise his own seriousness and take to pieces every false 'truth'—and on the other there's the 'simple', puritan Bitov, who knows there's something called truth that's worth working for and that 'freedom' comes from committing himself to it. Or are they one and the same—the 'sophisticate' is the would-be simpleton at his most self-critical and severe?

AB Well, that's why I need doubles—this 'he' and this 'me'. It really is something like that ... there's a kind of primitive puritanism in me. But I've found another term for it, for this kind of writing: cynical romanticism. The empire, the idea of the empire, that was my romanticism ... but it's cynical because of my experience, because of my knowledge of myself.

SL I think of it as scepticism rather than cynicism—this permanent, punishing investigation of your own thoughts.

AB Well, maybe scepticism. Maybe we use the word 'cynic' wrongly in Russia, but I've always used it and heard it used about people I liked, nice people, lost romantics. Uncle Dickens in *Pushkin House* was someone of that kind.

SL Cynicism perhaps has a special meaning in a context—the Soviet context— where the whole realm of ethics has been 'occupied' by the state. The temptation is to become shy—as you are—of using the words 'moral' or 'morality' at all. But in fact you on the contrary have developed your own counter-ethics—a kind of ecological-conservatism that combines a defence of individual freedom with a respect for the 'given', a horror of interference in natural and cultural ecologies. Or perhaps that's being too complicated, and one should just say that you invoke God in your work—God and the devil. Are you a believer? Or is God shorthand for a more private idea of the good?

AB I can't say I'm religious in the sense of belonging to one particular faith. I know that I belong in some sense to the Orthodox tradition, but that's more a question of ethnic background and attitude: I like my churches, I like icons, I like their atmosphere, but I'm not educated, I've got no real knowledge of the Orthodox Church. In so far as I'm a believer—I think I am a believer—my approach is ecumenical. That's what I've built for myself, but I can't explain anything about God. Life makes no sense to me. And the idea of God is developing all the time. But real belief isn't a question of your particular church, of belonging to one or other branch of culture—it's like being inspired. And therefore you can't be a believer all the time. Faith means not hesitating in the presence of God. You can't be in that state permanently. But occasionally you are enlightened and find yourself there—and in a way the purpose of writing is to reach that point. The discussion of faith and religion runs in parallel to the process of writing.

sᴌ *The Monkey Link* ends on an extraordinary, ecstatic note, reminiscent of the end of Blok's *The Twelve*, with a vision of heavenly forces—the legendary angels who'd helped Prince Nevsky in a battle six hundred years ago—coming to the aid of the homely, implausible-looking defenders of democracy in 1991. Artistically it's a triumphant moment, but it also reads like a moment of grateful release for the writer—a sort of yielding up of the self, an acceptance of history taking over. It's the more striking because the book as a whole strikes me as pessimistic— more pessimistic than your earlier work—about the process of writing itself, about the possibility of achieving this sense of rightness, of the heart being 'eased', in your words.

ᴀʙ I hesitated a great deal before using this historic material, but in the end I decided I must. I don't know about the book being pessimistic. But I've said already, I do have this awful thought: maybe there's some kind of strange guilt that hangs over our great Russian literature, a guilt about the gap between our culture and our development in other ways.

sᴌ At the end of *The Monkey Link* it's as if the angels relieve you of that guilt—'it was they . . . who had the heavenly trash of Russian villages stuck to their wings, log cabins, fences, carts, tracks, wells, the ruins of churches and tractors . . .'.

ᴀʙ Russian literature has somehow grown independently from its own soil. Maybe I'm just talking about my own situation, but at the beginning I was sure literature was the only way to be socially free—not because it earned me much money, but because it brought me independence from the state. I could sit and write, even if I had no hope of publishing my work. Now, in the new era, there are a lot of possible occupations, but in the old days the choices were very limited—sportsman, criminal, Party worker ... for anyone who had some energy and some feeling of individuality there weren't many options. I felt lucky as a writer to keep this lacuna, this niche.

That was how it started. But now I sometimes have this desperate feeling. Not because literature has lost its status in society, not because there are fewer readers than there used to be—these are natural developments. But—literature obliges you to stay aloof from life. You know that in order to concentrate, you have to avoid certain human obligations. That's how families get destroyed— you're not properly living with your own people, you're always busy with something other than your own life—and that's very irritating, for your wife, for your children, even your friends. You can give them everything you have—but it's as if you've become a bit colder. In order to write you have to keep escaping, and if that gets repeated throughout your life, you see that—it's not normal, it's not normal.

sᴌ That's a human reason for being pessimistic about the 'salvation' of a writer. But isn't there, as I've suggested, a deeper mistrust of the whole business of putting life into literature—the mistrust one feels right at the beginning of *The Monkey Link*, in the opening of 'Birds'—where you say 'I wouldn't want to find that this had style'?

ᴀʙ 'Birds' is the 'Paradise' of this book and so the hesitation was very slight there. I had just finished *Pushkin House* when I wrote it and I felt myself so young, so mighty, so powerful, so there came this moment of hesitation, of desire for escape—escape from style. I felt that beauty shouldn't come before knowledge, before science. Now I think that beauty is the only goal ...

sl So you disown that first doubt?

ab Yes, yes ... I was young, I felt it was too easy, I had got this feeling of power, a very harmonious state in one way but from my own point of view it felt too easy. And still the pleasure of writing overtook me, I was caught in this *kaif*, this stylistic high. But later on I saw that the pleasure of art is that it does no harm. It brings something to the world but it doesn't steal. Maybe in one's private life as a writer one doesn't feel that. But at least the result doesn't spoil things in the world. It does no harm.

sl When you look at your earliest work now, do you recognize yourself?

ab There was a short period at the beginning when I wasn't really conscious of what I was doing, but starting from stories like 'Penelope', 'The Idler', and 'Infantev'* I see myself as essentially the same writer. The earlier things were more derivative, more pupil-like ... but some people like them, they're very fresh. Thirty-five years have passed since then, and several generations of readers. I know that I have lost some of my readers on the way, but I've also picked up new ones among the youngest generation.

As you get older, though, and especially if there's been a gap—five or six years in which you didn't write—it becomes harder to make the next step. It takes more courage. You know that you have the means to do things at the same level, but will you be able to move on? You have to try, even if it's a failure, but you know that there are limits, it isn't endless. There's the feeling that you can't deal with what's contemporary, that the contemporary belongs already to another generation.

And then this sense of 'homelessness' which we talked about has acquired a very objective meaning now. I'm not a refugee, of course, I'm not an exile, but I spend a lot of time in the West now, just earning money to keep myself and my family, and I don't feel sufficiently at home either here† or 'back home', in a certain sense my country has disappeared.

I've had strange dreams since I came here. I dreamed for example that I'd already turned 60 and various Russian newspapers published their congratulations, and one of them—*Moscow News* it was, I remember—had a very funny heading 'Our Beloved *Izgoi*'. You know *izgoi* is the old Russian word for an outcast, someone who's lost his social position and his means of existence, someone who's fallen out of the social system. And the following night I dreamed that I was buried. I was very angry. I was already lying in my coffin, but then I got out of it because nobody was coming to the funeral. I was expecting my family at least to turn up, my children. There were a couple of other coffins nearby and the people in them were certainly dead. It sounds like a nightmare but I wasn't frightened, I was fighting and furious, I had the energy of anger ...

sl In your next dream you may find yourself in Paradise.

ab Strangely enough I'm trying to investigate the idea of Paradise now, for another book. I'm trying to understand the images I have of it.

---

* 'Penelopa' (dated 1962); 'Bezdel'nik' (dated 1961–2); 'Infant'ev' (dated 1961–5), all in *Aptekarsky ostrov* (1968).

† This part of the interview was recorded in Berlin, where Bitov was staying for a few months in 1994.

SL In 'Man in a Landscape' you said that our idea of heaven is much less developed than our idea of hell—basically because hell was familiarity writ large.

AB You know, I think that the idea of happiness we had in Soviet times was a slave's concept of happiness. The story of Plato's Cave was the very point of Soviet life. And maybe we had a slave's concept of freedom too. Pushkin talked about 'secret freedom', and we always understood this to mean 'secret' because of censorship—and this 'secret' freedom was the artist's goal ... but maybe there is another kind of freedom also. We can't speak about life after death, we have no experience of it. But I'm trying to explore in myself the images I have of it, for this new book, a book about my father in Paradise.

SL Your father—or a father—has been quite a constant figure in your writing, hasn't he?

AB I've thought about my father a lot, especially since his death—he died in 1977. Certainly I liked him, but now I can see that for this or that reason—I don't like Freudian explanations, but for a variety of reasons—there was a kind of struggle and misunderstanding between us, nothing tragic, but something sad enough. I see now that there's no real language for the love between a father and his son. Mothers have this language, but fathers are out of it—biologically. After I lost my father I dreamed a lot about him, and that was the start of this work. I'm really returning my father's love to him after his death. It's like an old wine that gets better with age, to put it poetically.

With my mother it was different. We spent a good part of our lives together, living together, a grown-up son and an old mother. I suffered a great deal when I lost her—but afterwards it seemed to me that the story was finished, it was a closed story: I still love her, but there's been no development. Whereas my father and I missed each other in life. In the story I'm writing the father departs very early—making the son's journey to his father even longer. I want it to be a nice story, very lovable. I hope it will be a bright book.

As for Paradise—I've been working with pictures, looking at the images in old paintings and comparing them with my own. Heaven is always described as if it were a sort of good camp, a *gulag* for clean and brain-washed people. And I dislike that idea. We've had that sort of paradise already, and it's a kind of torture. So my thought was that perhaps Paradise was true freedom, freedom really attained. And I wonder what the atmosphere of that freedom would be, the landscape of Paradise. Perhaps you get invited into this Paradise straightaway, but your self refuses it. You choose instead to go to hell. And that will be your personal decision.

5

Tatyana Tolstaya

(b. 1951)

Tatyana Tolstaya was born in Leningrad into one of the city's most distinguished literary families. She is the great-grandniece of Lev Tolstoy and the granddaughter of the writer, dramatist, and poet Aleksei Nikolayevich Tolstoy (1883–1945), best known for his trilogy about the Revolution, *Road to Calvary*,* begun while he was temporarily an *émigré* in Berlin. Though he had initially been an outspoken opponent of Bolshevism, Aleksei Tolstoy returned to the Soviet Union in 1923 and became one of the very few Russians to maintain a nobleman's life-style while successfully demonstrating his 'loyalty' to the new state: so successfully, indeed, that he was appointed Chairman of the USSR Writers' Union after Gorky's death and won several Stalin Prizes for his work. Aleksei's wife was the poet Natalya Krandiyevskaya, herself from a literary family, while Tolstaya's maternal grandfather, as she relates in the interview that follows, was the distinguished translator Mikhail Lozinsky, whose friends included the poets Anna Akhmatova and Nikolai Gumilyov.

These literary antecedents seem worth mentioning not just for curiosity's sake, but because they perhaps help to explain the sense Tolstaya's work exudes of connection with the past and of aristocratic disdain for (or plain indifference to) the claims of the Soviet state. Tolstaya was born into a family of seven children—itself an anachronism in the hungry post-war years—and grew up in Leningrad, entering Leningrad State University in 1968 to read, unfashionably, Latin and Greek. After graduating in 1974, she married a fellow linguist (they went on to have two sons) and moved with her husband to Moscow, taking a job in the Oriental literature department of Nauka publishing house.

Tolstaya began writing only in January 1983, following an eye operation which meant that she was temporarily forbidden to read. In any case, she was bored with the literature she found in the current journals and felt that she could write

* *Khozhdeniye po mukam*, 1920–41.

something more interesting herself. Eight months later, her first story appeared in the journal *Avrora*. Several more followed, in *Avrora*, *Neva*, and *Oktyabr'*, and by 1986, when four of her stories were published in *Novy mir*, critics were hailing Tolstaya as one of the most original new talents on the literary scene. When her first collection of stories, *On the Golden Porch*, appeared the following year, the entire edition was sold out within an hour. (A new edition of the collected stories, published under the title *Love Me, Love Me Not*, has recently been published in Moscow.)*

One reason for Tolstaya's extraordinary success, paradoxically, may have been that her work was so out of step with the times—so evidently removed from the political and social concerns that dominated the journals and the literary press in the first years of *glasnost*. Her prose was sparkling, her humour sophisticated, her culture evident on every page; and there was a freedom from earnestness that came as a relief after the sombre offerings of political writers such as Anatoly Rybakov or Mikhail Shatrov. While conservatives within the literary establishment regarded Tolstaya with deep suspicion, at first refusing her admission to the Union of Writers, her air of freedom and insouciance quickly endeared her to a Western audience (*On the Golden Porch* was published in English in 1989, to be followed three years later by a further collection, *Sleepwalker in a Fog*). The work fulfilled the promise of the name: these were not stories to be read dutifully, for insight into the sorry lot of Soviet citizens, but for pleasure, for literary delight—in the way that Russian literature used to be read.

Tolstaya, fluent in English, soon found herself invited to lecture at American universities, and since 1988 she has held a series of posts in the United States, most recently as a lecturer at Skidmore College in upstate New York, where we met for this interview in 1993. Since moving part-time to America (she still spends some months each year in Russia), Tolstaya has become known not only as a writer of fiction but as a witty critic and acerbic commentator on Russian and American life, contributing regular essays to—among others—*The New York Review of Books*.

With only some twenty stories published, most no more than a dozen pages in length, Tolstaya's output has been relatively small. Yet the richness of her prose and the compass of her narratives leave one with an impression of greater volume. She is not a miniaturist. Many of her stories are, in effect, condensed portraits of whole lives, some of them spanning the best part of a century. The voices of multiple characters echo through each text, vying with the narrator's voice in snatches of conversation and reminiscence. And although the lives Tolstaya evokes are often apparently obscure and insignificant, the themes she deals in are not. Catholic allusions to literature, myth, and fairy-tale lend these stories of failed love, dashed hope, and domestic *angst* a deeper, sadder, more sinister sonority. The immediate context may be a dusky room, some faded photos, a ticking clock, but the overall backdrop is grander—not so much history or politics (assumed but barely mentioned in her work) as the changing seasons, the stars, the strange mechanics of time. Time—and death—are regular characters in Tolstaya's stories; sometimes, indeed, the only effective agents in them.

But Tolstaya's stories are anything but solemn. Indeed, the immediate

---

* *Lyubish'—ne lyubish'* (OLMA Press, 1997).

impression they give is one of almost irrepressible gaiety. Her narratives move swiftly and capriciously between the lofty and the humdrum, the rhapsodic and the grotesque, from the slow, devoted re-creation of a single moment to the ruthless brevity of a paragraph that captures and dismisses an entire life. In 'Dear Shura' we find Ivan Nikolayevich, the heroine's abandoned beloved, permanently embalmed in summer sunshine on the railway platform where, sixty years earlier, she might have gone to meet him; but as we return, again and again, to this scene, the rest of 'Dear Shura's' life skims by in fast forward: 'After the war she came back—with her third husband—back here, to these little rooms. The third husband moaned on and on ... the corridor was too long. The light was dim. The windows looked out on the yard. Everything was over.'

Tolstaya's lack of sentimentality has led more than one critic to charge her with 'cruelty' to her characters. The very ebullience of her writing seems to chime with the voices of the young and the blithe in her stories, mocking her heroes' and heroines' despair with their laughter and indifference. But the pathos of her stories resides precisely in these juxtapositions of tone. Against the melancholy undertow of her characters' lives, the beauty and richness of Tolstaya's language assert the principle of life. Read in a different light, they offer not a taunt but a solace.

Perhaps the most striking feature of Tolstaya's prose is its extraordinary sensual precision. She writes at times with a Chekhovian economy of effect (here's a city in autumn: 'evening, wet asphalt, the red neon lights in the puddles beneath your heels'), at times with a lush, painterly intimacy that recalls Nabokov: 'Natasha went out on the June porch. An early sun—timid, cold, pure—trembled on high, entangled in the pines ... The earth was black, firm, the grass wet, thick, and under every bush lay a hard block of lilac shade ... Beneath one's feet was a green, prickly country, dove-gray blueberry undergrowth, the green-pea shapes of unripened wild strawberries, whitish pink fields of cockles, and beyond the bright forest—the smooth quiet of a lake burning under the sun.'* Nor is such attention lavished only on the evidently 'poetic'. Tolstaya's landscape is recognizably that of Soviet Russia, but transfigured and redeemed, rescued from politics and history and restored to the senses. 'A long communal corridor ran through Natasha's dwelling; overhead in the half-dark swam wash basin tambourines, dusty Aeolian bicycle harps, and over the exit, rising like a plague cemetery up in arms, the black skulls of electric meters huddled together ...'

The vision Tolstaya imparts is not so much estranged as epistemologically innocent, as if culled from an infant's-eye view of the phenomenal world in which the five senses are still conjoined (the Moonlight Sonata can still smell of lilac), emotion is inseparable from sensation and objects and people alike enjoy animate status. Cheeses snooze on window-sills, gardens wave handkerchiefs, the sun pierces the tree-tops with rainbow knitting-needles, love can be stifled by the action of a tea-cosy, and that Russian sickness of the soul, *toska*, takes you by the hand and stands guard by your bedside.

At first sight this domestic, anthropomorphic imagery appears to make the world a cosier, more populated place. But all too often in Tolstaya's stories inanimate

---

* 'Vyshel mesyats iz tumana' (The Moon Came Out). Translations here and elsewhere in this chapter by Jamey Gambrell (*Sleepwalker in a Fog*, 1992).

things take the place of people as companions and interlocutors. In 'Dear Shura' the only thing heard chattering in the communal kitchen is an abandoned pot of cabbage soup, while in 'Most Beloved' the voice of the elderly Zhenechka is left unheeded in the abandoned receiver of a telephone: it 'lies cosily on the tablecloth, unhurriedly telling the telephone book, ashtray and apple core about its joys and worries'. The gay, laughter-filled voices that echo through these stories belong for the most part to the vanished, dead, or otherwise unreachable.

For many of Tolstaya's heroes and heroines live in a state of irreducible solitude: they are, in the words of one story, 'unfit, unnecessary people'. Some, like the mute boy in 'Most Beloved' or Aleksei Petrovich, the retarded hero of 'Night', are literally 'unfit' to negotiate the world alone: Aleksei's one excursion beyond the safe harbour provided by gigantic, all-powerful *mama* takes him into a realm of terrifying, black, incomprehensible chaos, while the speech of the boy in 'Most Beloved', coaxed into tentative being by the loving attentions of his governess, is crushed the moment she departs by the 'great, rumbling world outside'.

Others among Tolstaya's heroes, while going through the outward motions of life, remain imprisoned by fear, fantasy, or an insuperable Oblomovian lethargy— trapped by dreams of some past or unattainable idyll, or too timorous and squeamish to engage with life. The plain, dumpy Natasha in 'The Moon Came Out' proves unable to make the transition from uncomplicated childhood—where life was just a fresh, unanalysed 'collection of gifts'—to an adulthood to which she herself must bring meaning and purpose. The eponymous hero of 'Peters', similarly ill-favoured, grows out of infancy only at the end of his life. The heroines of 'Dear Shura' and 'Love me, Love me not' are lonely old ladies whose lives still turn on the romances or missed opportunities of more than half a century earlier, while many of Tolstaya's characters, unable or refusing to find consolation in real-life relationships, remain stranded in imaginary love-affairs. Kind-hearted, gullible Sonya, in the story of that name, devotes her heart to a fictional beloved whose lofty correspondence is cooked up, for their own amusement, by teasing friends; the hero of 'Okkerville River' is enamoured of a singer known to him only through her cracked voice on ancient records; while in 'Circle' a married man goes in search of true love by dialling, in a kind of *perpetuum mobile*, the numbers stamped on the laundered sheets of his successive mistresses. In 'Sleepwalker in a Fog'—a title that could aptly be given to several of the stories—the hero, Denisov, after a series of ill-fated attempts to find real purpose in life, fetches up literally trapped behind the locked doors of the 'Fairy-tale' café.

For some, the pain of living requires more radical and fantastic solution. The hero of 'A Clean Page' opts for amputation of the soul, while the squeamish hero of 'Serafim' forswears—with grotesque results—his own human body. Marriage, at best the unsatisfactory backdrop to these characters' lives, offers no solution, in Tolstaya's stories, to the conundrum of living happily with both body and soul. Indeed, in 'Hunting the Mammoth' and 'Poet and Muse' the marriage plans of the female protagonists are seen as a form of spiritual, if not literal, murder. The poet in the latter story chooses immortality as a skeleton in the friendly surroundings of a university lab, rather than a prolongation of existence in the sterile room where his wife has imprisoned him.

A central tension in Tolstaya's stories lies in her ambivalent juxtaposition of 'interior' and 'exterior' worlds. In many of the stories, the interior—the hero's room, the dacha, the communal apartment—is the central location, the apparent focus of light, life, the soul. Outside is blackness, night, rain, the 'great rumbling world', the 'din of passing life'. Inside is warmth and safety, cakes and caramels and tea, photos and mementos, *mama, babushka,* a memory of childhood. Even the neglected abodes of old bachelors, with their ashtrays and old socks and processed cheese, offer the comfort of privacy and familiarity. In 'Heavenly Flame' a family dacha stands as a beacon and symbol of life amid the dark forest into which the ailing hero—a patient at a neighbouring sanatorium—is doomed to vanish each evening, his small pocket flashlight wavering among 'the startled, white treetrunks' as his hosts, with relief, wave him off like departing death.

But domesticity, as we discover, can also be a form of live burial. Shutting out the noise, darkness, weather of the world outside, Tolstaya's heroes seek to protect themselves from mortality—from time, in effect. But by sealing their windows they also seal their fates. Life, shut out, goes on relentlessly outside. The rain, as a reminder, drums on the window-panes.

Abundant seasonal imagery—wind, snow, sunshine, rampant growth, and pungent decay—vie in Tolstaya's prose with her images of domesticity. In childhood, in youth, the seasons are experienced in the pleasant imperfect tense of cyclical recurrence—winter is reliably loaded away in cartfuls, summer beckons and waves as always. But as the adult clock starts ticking, they acquire—for watchful or dispirited souls—an inevitably sinister meaning. The 'four seasons' hat that 'Dear Shura' wears, once an innocent piece of coquetry, rides round on her balding head like an emblem of mortality.

Time past acquires, in some of these stories, an almost physical dimension. The lost or dead wander unreachably 'on the other side of years'. Those in the present are left racking their dreams and memories to find them—but 'all the doors are locked, time had opened and slammed shut'. Curiously, the things that remain to represent those gone are the smallest, most perishable things—fine porcelain, a linen tablecloth—things that miraculously filtered down through the years while 'time's meat-grinder destroyed all the big objects—cabinets, pianos, people'.

The cataclysms of twentieth-century Russia scarcely get a mention in Tolstaya's work. Yet it is impossible to ignore the fact that the doors, in Russia, were slammed loudest of all, not by the action of years in themselves, but by the Revolution and all that followed. Tolstaya's work, for all its surface gaiety, is haunted by a sense of what her century has irretrievably lost or destroyed. Both in her work and in her words here, she shows an unmistakable allegiance to traditions transcending the narrow boundaries of the Soviet state—and to the act of memory itself. Her own past, and that of her family, were the starting-point for our conversation.

SL You grew up in a literary family and in St Petersburg, a city full of literary associations. What have those associations meant to you?

Interview recorded in May 1993.

TT The city I was born in was Leningrad which has now, strangely enough, changed its name back to St Petersburg. I have a very ambiguous feeling about that. On the one hand it was sickening when you realized the name Leningrad was actually connected to Lenin, and as soon as you thought of that you wanted to change it. But the truth was that we didn't think of Lenin when we said it—it sounded like a natural word: Leningrad, Leningrad. And now as a protest I can't call my birthplace St Petersburg. How can this ugly thing be called by that name? Look what they've done to it! Somewhere in its core, in the invisible Platonic world, it *is* St Petersburg, of course. But just look at it, look at the people in it, the people who live in those palaces now!

Bunin* wrote about the peasant soldiers who broke into the locked-up, abandoned dachas of the rich during the Civil War—they'd go in to see what they could find, and then shit in a Chinese vase or something beautiful like that and leave some illiterate, abusive message. That was their idea of desecrating culture. There was such a gulf separating the poor from the rich in pre-revolutionary Russia, and their hatred of the upper classes was so vivid, that they associated culture with oppression and wealth.

It's very easy to kill the rich, of course—Bang! and they don't exist. But to kill culture takes time. And they are still killing it. And fantastically enough it's not yet dead—it's as strong as the weeds that grow out of the asphalt. Culture's a very powerful thing, it wants to live. So it's still there, in that dead city with all its ghosts around. It was dead when I lived there too; to live there was like living somewhere haunted. But now it's even more dead—even more pitiful.

SL Were you very conscious of those 'ghosts' when you grew up?

TT Yes, yes, I was—first of all because of my family, which fortunately wasn't destroyed, though we came very close to it. My very existence is a matter of chance. Well, everyone's is, of course. But there was a strange story behind my birth—mine and my brothers' and sisters'. My father met my mother in 1934, when they were just 18 and 19 years old, studying at the university. My father liked my mother—she was so beautiful—and he wondered how to approach her. They were just good friends. Then came the murder of Kirov in 1934†—and the whole of the Russian nobility, what remained of it, was supposedly implicated in the plot to kill him, so hundreds of them were packed off into exile and later to the camps. Many of those families, cultured people, still live in Siberia today.

Anyway my mother's parents were all set to leave Leningrad along with my mother. My mother's father was a very distinguished translator, Mikhail Lozinsky; he was trained as a lawyer but—typically for pre-revolutionary times—he

* Ivan Bunin (1870–1953), writer and poet, winner of the Nobel Prize in 1933. Bunin, best known as a master of the elegiac short story, emigrated to France in 1920 and lived there for the remainder of his life. His work, unpublished in Russia since the Revolution, began to resurface after 1956.

† Sergei Kirov (1886–1934), head of the Communist Party organization in Leningrad from 1926 to 1934 and member of the Politburo from 1930, was assassinated in December 1934, evidently with Stalin's blessing (a popular figure in the Party, Kirov was seen as Stalin's chief rival). The start of the Great Terror, which reached its height with the purges of top Party members and the show trials of the late 1930s, and involved the arrests of thousands of innocent people, can be dated from this murder, for Stalin used the assassination as his excuse to unleash a wave of terror on all those supposedly implicated in the murder plot.

also spoke six languages, including Persian, and translated Dante and Shakespeare into Russian. And my grandmother, too, my mother's mother, was an educated woman, a museum curator, full of humanitarian ideals and culture. So they were destined for exile like everyone else. But then my father stepped in: at the age of 18 he decided he would marry my mother to prevent her from being exiled with her family. My grandparents agreed to the marriage just in order that their daughter could stay in Leningrad and continue her studies. So it was a fictitious marriage, but slowly and inevitably it turned into a real one, which resulted in seven children, including me.

And in fact my mother's parents weren't exiled in the end, because at this point my paternal grandfather, the writer Aleksei Tolstoy, stepped in as well and asked Gorky* to come to their aid. Gorky still had some influence at the time, and he managed to help them.

All my family were in some way connected with literature, but they belonged, so to speak, to different schools of culture, they had different views of what literature was. For example, my grandfather, Aleksei Tolstoy, and especially his wife, my grandmother, were artists; they had an artistic attitude to culture, a belief that poetry and literature generally were the highest things—while politics, okay, politics was just something you had to put up with. Whereas their respective mothers were involved in what I'd call 'social' writing—concerned with the rights of women, peasants, children, human rights.

SL So your family embodied two central strands in Russian literature?

TT Well yes, and it was no accident that those who belonged to the 'social' strand in my family were bad writers, while those whose orientation was artistic were good—because that's inevitable, there's nothing you can do about it! It's just that politics kills art—it killed it even in Gogol and Lev Tolstoy.

Anyway, the point is that my family was strongly anchored in Russian culture and literature of all kinds. Whether literature is in the genes or is just passed along down the line I don't know, but I certainly got a lot of it, along with the usual human tragedies which accompany war and loss of relatives and everything else—it all accumulated and was passed on to me.

SL In your story 'Sleepwalker in a Fog' Denisov is haunted by the shades of three victims of the Leningrad Siege†—they appear in a dream, demanding that he give them the bread he's bought, and later he's wracked by guilt at his failure to hand over the bread straightaway and by frustration at his inability to get back to these hungry people. And of course the story 'Sonya' ends with the Siege as well—with Sonya saving the life of the woman, Ada, who's been posing for all these years as

---

* Maksim Gorky (1868–1936), the first Chairman of the Union of Writers of the USSR, whose novel *Mother* (1906) became the model for the method of socialist realism, was—in political terms—the leading writer of the 1930s. Despite his periodic departures from the Soviet Union, and his attempts to protect his fellow writers from repression, Gorky retained his 'heroic' status as the prototype of the good Soviet writer. Numerous streets, institutions, even an entire city (his birthplace, Nizhny Novgorod) were named after him following his death.

† Leningrad was blockaded by German forces from August 1941 to January 1944. Cut off from overland communication with the rest of the country, with the only supply line across 30 miles of Lake Ladoga, thousands of the population starved or froze to death. During the first winter of 1941 alone, the death toll reached 53,000.

her fictional correspondent Nikolai. So Ada gets saved and Sonya perishes, along with all the letters she wrote.

The Siege in fact is about the only historical event that comes directly into your work. Did you grow up haunted by its ghosts? What happened to your own family?

TT Well, they all survived. Aleksei Tolstoy was living in Moscow at the time, with a new wife, but his first wife—my father's mother—was still in Leningrad, and so were my mother's parents. They were all saved because of a little wonder that happened to each of them. You can't help thinking about it. My grandmother on my father's side was saved by an acquaintance of hers who just happened, completely by chance, to turn up in the nick of time with a can of juice, just when my grandmother was about to die of starvation. That's the episode that turns up in 'Sonya', though of course with a different meaning, a totally different context. But I couldn't let it go, I had to use it somehow.

As for my mother's parents, they left Leningrad, I think it was in December 1941, when everyone was already weakened by hunger. They were given a place on a little plane that was due to leave from an airstrip on the outskirts of Leningrad. It was snowing heavily and they were old and weak with hunger, so the only things they took with them were some heavy overcoats and two suitcases with the drafts of my grandfather's translation of Dante's *Divine Comedy*. My grandfather was translating the Paradise section at the time, so he loaded himself up with Paradise.

Anyway, there they were, walking along through the snowy fields; it was pitch dark because no lights were allowed, and after a while they realized they were completely lost; they simply couldn't find the plane anywhere—and they decided to die right there and then. So they sat down on Paradise and started waiting for death. And then all of a sudden this figure appeared from out of nowhere and saw this snow-covered obstacle—my grandparents—sitting in the darkness, and he looked at them and recognized them. He turned out to be a young man who'd studied with my father and once dropped in on their house. 'What are you doing here?' he asked, 'Let me help you to the plane.' So that's how they were saved. They went to Yelabuga, the place where Tsvetayeva* hanged herself, and that's where my parents landed up living through the war. In fact they even had their second baby there. Everyone thought they were crazy.

SL So life turned up instead of death.

TT That's right. I grew up on all these stories. My whole family were in love with anecdotes, all kinds of anecdotes. Everyone in my family, as far as I can gather, had a rather pleasant character; they liked to make fun of themselves—unlike the branch of the Tolstoys who belonged to Lev Tolstoy's family; they were deadly serious and still are, especially when it comes to anything connected with Tolstoy's life and his teachings. Whereas there are no sacred cows in our family.

---

* The poet Marina Tsvetayeva (1892–1941), who returned to the USSR in 1939, having emigrated to Western Europe in 1922. Following the outbreak of war, Tsvetayeva was evacuated to safety in Yelabuga in Tatarstan but was unable to publish her work and received no support from the Writers' Union. Her husband had been executed, her daughter arrested and sent to the camps. In despair at her situation, Tsvetayeva committed suicide.

Another nice thing about my family is that they aren't envious; they've never envied other people their success—it just isn't in their genes. I really believe these things are partly cultural and partly genetic. If you like what others do so much, how can you envy them and compete with them? That's always been the attitude in my family. Art is the only thing where there is no competition at all. The point is to love and to create art, not to ask for someone else's love or the love of everyone around—which is something you can't control anyway. So what's the point of envying and competing?

SL Creating art is just pleasure?

TT Yes, pleasure, joy—and hard labour.

SL But did you grow up with any sense of pressure to live up to the literary traditions of your family?

TT No, there was no pressure at all—the only pressure was to enjoy more, to open yourself more, to read more, and to study. My father, for example, wanted me to speak three foreign languages; he himself started studying languages only when he was 18, to be worthy of my mother who spoke three languages perfectly. I'm afraid I only learned to speak two, English and French, and my French is pretty rusty now.

SL In the circumstances of Russia at the time you were growing up, with all the weight of what was happening and what had happened around you, wasn't it a kind of labour in itself to retain this sense of lightness, of pleasure? History has given ample cause for a kind of 'tragism' in Russian literature—a predisposition to view life tragically. How do you keep that sense at bay?

TT Well, you know—from everything I can gather about my grandparents and from what I see of my father particularly, what he passed on to me—there's an ability in our family to handle the blacker side of things and even laugh, while at the same time keeping a sense of the tragic. The dark side of the world is always there, but you look at it not through dark glasses but through one dark glass and one rainbow one.

SL Bifocally...

TT Yes—and at the same time you have a certain source of energy. All of us are energetic—and it allows you somehow to live with both sides of life. Because there are a lot of sad currents underneath, in the character of my relatives—in me. Those currents are always there, but somehow they're in a certain harmony with the energy that allows you to accept the best side of the world. Perhaps the main thing is that all of us have a sense of humour and an ability to laugh at ourselves. The tragic romantic poet with long hair and so on is such an absurd figure; no one can afford to be like that.

SL Maybe when I was talking about keeping tragedy at bay I was really talking about keeping the Soviet Union at bay. It sounds as if your family thoroughly insulated itself from Sovietness.

TT Yes it did, in many ways. The thing is that Sovietness was so foolish that it became comic—so that's the way we treated it. But of course the foolishness wasn't uniquely Soviet, though the Soviets added their own special twists to it. It was a classic Russian foolishness. When you read nineteenth-century Russian literature, there it is. The difference between the nineteenth and the twentieth century is that the nineteenth had some extra layer to it—a thin, creamy layer of culture—whereas Soviet culture didn't have this extra dimension: you had to grow it from within.

SL Though nineteenth-century Russian literature—I suppose I'm thinking of Gogol in particular—is full of the fear of a descent into ludicrousness, into scandal and shame—fear that this veneer of culture is rather thin and can be cracked very easily.

TT Yes, but there were features then of society that have since been lost. Because if you don't use an organ it just atrophies. There was a sense of honour in the nineteenth century—especially among the upper classes—and there was this genuine religious fear.

But I was also thinking about Gogol. And it's true that all of us could instantly recognize and laugh at Khlestakov—the hero of Gogol's *Inspector General*—because we all knew our ability to become Khlestakovs ourselves. He's a creation of genius because he shows how Russian society works—and Russian society still works that way. He's so unscrupulous when he tells his lies that he forgets even to get two and two to make four. And nobody cares, because he's so full of himself that everyone feels there must be something in what he says. And we've gone on behaving exactly the same way.

SL Of course there's terrific artistry too in Khlestakov's lies.

TT Yes, and in order to be artistic you have to be an actor inside. And we all have this ability.

My grandfather, Aleksei Tolstoy, wanted to be an actor and he was a kind of Khlestakov throughout his life. He entertained and fooled many people around him, and I'm sure he still continues fooling people from the grave. He pretended to be a lot of things he wasn't—for example, throughout his life he pretended to be a social drunkard. Every evening he invited guests and there were huge dinners with lots of drinking and he pretended that he drank—and then every morning he got up, made lots of coffee and worked until noon, revised what he'd written until 3 o'clock and then embarked on that dinner again. And my father says that actually he just didn't drink, he didn't drink at all. But it was done in such a way that everyone was sure he was a real drunkard. The fact was that he could be very cheerful just from drinking tea, but he needed great control to be able to carry off that act. And I know that's possible because I have this ability myself. I know how it works.

SL Was it always your ambition to become a writer? You started writing relatively late, didn't you?

TT Very late, I would say. I was 32. But I'd never dreamt of being anything or anyone at all; I'm completely without ambitions. Maybe that's a strange sort of superiority complex, but I just don't have ambitions. What's important to me is my own pleasure—inside—and I can get this pleasure from just looking at people and seeing who they are and then making up little stories in my own head and telling them to others—laughing about life as it is.

SL What were you doing before you started writing?

TT Well, I got married and had children and I worked for a while in publishing, and before that I went to university and studied Classics. But I'm no good at studying,

I'm incapable of doing it regularly—I can't see the point. Or rather, I of course see the point in scholarship or science, but for myself I can't get interested enough to remember the whole lot by heart and sift through all those books with fine print and footnotes. I just can't. I read books. I'm a professional reader. I love reading books and imagining these worlds. So when I started writing I used that ability to imagine and verbalize and put things together—but again only because it's a pleasure.

SL   Did you start writing because you thought: I can create the sort of things I like to read?

TT   Yes. That's exactly right. At a certain point—I started writing in 1983, early that January—I just took a piece of paper and wrote my first story. There was nothing good in the journals at the time—and you can forget about books, the only decent books (I mean even Russian books) came from abroad, the ones published by Ardis in the United States, and one or two other publishers. They were smuggled into Russia by people who worked abroad. There was nothing else to speak of. Occasionally something good was published in the journals. But I was disappointed at the beginning of the 1980s because nothing new and interesting and fresh was coming out. And at the same time we had the feeling that something was coming to an end—though we *never* expected the total collapse of everything; that was unthinkable when Gorbachev came to power. We thought the system was so much stronger than it was.

Later I decided to put the stories I'd written together in a book. I knew it would be difficult—editors could hold on to a manuscript for fifteen years before publishing it—but someone advised me that the best thing to do was to put myself forward as a 'young writer'; you had to attend a special seminar and then get yourself recommended to a publisher. So I was all set to go, but it turned out not to be so easy; you had to get a recommendation even to attend the seminar in the first place, preferably from the Komsomol, the Young Communist League, and I'd long since ceased to be even a theoretical member of the Komsomol—membership ended at 28. So I found out the person in charge at the Union of Writers and simply went to see him; I opened the door to his office and went in. He was just sitting there like a huge bag of sand, pretending that he was doing something on a piece of paper. I introduced myself and said I wanted to be a member of that seminar. And he was just dumbfounded, because no one entered his office just like that. And he said: why? Well, I said, first of all I just want to, and second of all— suddenly I realized that today was my birthday, so second of all, I said, today's my birthday and I'd like a present. And he started explaining that he couldn't do it just like that, it was a long procedure and so forth—he just wanted to get rid of me.

I'd never dealt much with bureaucrats before, but later I realized they all have the same technique: they try to get rid of you simply at first, and then they start to push you. But if they suddenly realize you don't feel afraid—and I didn't feel afraid because I had no reason to fear—they just give up, they collapse immediately as if they were empty inside. And that's what happened. He asked me what my name was again. And when I told him he suddenly said: Oh! are you related to Dmitry Tolstoy? Yes, I said, he's my uncle. Oh! Why didn't you tell me straightaway—of course I know him well, oh yes, we played chess together in the Writers'

Union—oh sure, of course, and he gave me this paper and I went to this seminar and I got a recommendation and I was published. By *Moldaya gvardiya*—Young Guard publishers. And that was that.

SL Although by that time several of your stories had been published, hadn't they, in journals? Had you had problems in getting them published there as well?

TT Of course, but there again there were things that helped—again by chance. I guess I was lucky in many ways. For example, *Avrora*, where I first got published, was a small Leningrad magazine and, as it turned out, there was a woman working there in the prose section whose mother was my first English teacher. So of course she was kind and attentive to me—and she had to struggle for my stories because they had an editor there, I think he was the deputy chief, who hated everyone and everything around; he was a KGB type who'd just been planted on the editorial board. At one point he actually called the printers to stop the publication of an issue because of one of my stories—I think it was 'Okkerville River'—though there was no real reason, it was just his job to make difficulties. But in the end just the odd sentence was censored. There was nothing political in what I'd written, of course, but there were things you weren't supposed to write about—like people drinking, for instance. Your hero isn't supposed to drink in case others get seduced into drinking too! As if they don't drink anyway from the moment they're born!

SL But when the book came out in 1987 it caused a sensation. First of all it was sold out straightaway...

TT Yes, I couldn't buy copies of it myself...

SL And then there was a great furore over it, I remember. Some critics reproached you with being too 'cruel', others with being too stylistically extravagant, others with painting too dispiriting a picture of Soviet folk. Then there was a great to-do about whether you should be admitted to the Union of Writers afterwards, with all the conservatives up in arms about it. No one seemed to know what to make of you. Even the critic who introduces your work in the afterword to that first volume of stories chided you for being 'overly beautiful' in places, and I remember a comic passage where he felt bound officially to excuse the fact that one of your characters, the heroine of 'Dear Shura', isn't exactly the embodiment of the righteous revolutionary past—though she's a dear old lady all the same! It's funny to read these things now, and quite hard to recreate the atmosphere in which they were written.

One critic—L. Bakhnov, in *Znamya*, about a year after the book came out—remarked that perhaps readers would have taken you in their stride a bit more if they'd been more familiar with Nabokov or Pilnyak or Zamyatin,* who got 'unbanned' after you appeared. I felt there was some truth in that. People tended to treat you as a completely *sui generis* writer, because no one at the time was writing anything at all similar.

---

* Boris Pilnyak (1894–1937), author of *The Naked Year* (*Goly god*, 1922) and Yevgeny Zamyatin (1884–1937), author of the dystopian novel *We* (*My*, 1920), both noted for their innovative, experimental prose styles. Pilnyak was arrested and shot in 1937. Zamyatin succeeded in emigrating in 1931, but died of a heart attack in Paris six years later. After the 1930s, Pilnyak's work was not published in Russia until 1976; Zamyatin's not until 1988. See also note on Vladimir Nabokov, p. 81.

TT I was surprised myself at their reaction. I realized that these were not the sort of stories you found in magazines at the time; they didn't deal in a conventional way with Soviet life or Soviet problems. But still that wasn't sufficient reason to create such a scandal.

But I found the whole thing very entertaining—I love scandals, they're a vital part of life. What interests me are people's behaviour and inner motives, and here was a fascinating experiment—it was like chucking an old shoe into the river and suddenly it explodes, turns into a bomb. And suddenly there was a whole bunch of fish and crabs I'd never seen before, never even suspected were there. So I enjoyed myself. The wave I created was very high, but it was absolutely harmless. Of course there were people, the conservatives in the Writers' Union for instance, who meant to do me a lot of harm. But I turned out to be completely immune to that kind of harm. I was made of teflon as far as they were concerned, because I have a different idea of life and different expectations. And I knew I wasn't in any serious danger anyway—this wasn't 'dissident' literature and there was no question of imprisonment.

SL And anyway we're already talking here about the period of *glasnost*.

TT Yes, and I think the point was that *glasnost* had created certain literary expectations and I just happened to satisfy those expectations. If the book had come out any earlier it probably wouldn't have provoked such interest; likewise—though for different reasons—if I'd left it any later. I was lucky in my timing.

SL But at the beginning of *glasnost* all the excitement was about things that were politically daring, like Anatoly Rybakov's *Children of the Arbat*,* or Mikhail Shatrov's[†] plays, for example.

TT Very bad stuff! I think the point was precisely that I turned my back on all that, that I was somehow independent of it. I think it somehow surprised and intrigued people that I dared to ignore their scale of values and went against the grain. Essentially I think Rybakov's novels are just as bad artistically as the novels of any of the conservative Soviet writers, even if you could more or less agree with his liberal sentiments. All these writers, liberal and conservative, were writing in the same spectrum, even if politically they were at opposite ends of it. It was the same with Solzhenitsyn; I'm not talking about the *Gulag Archipelago*, of course, that's a great historical work, but about the novels—which are essentially Soviet in style even if they're anti-Soviet in content.

The reason it was difficult to harm me is that as a writer I just wasn't interested in politics; I wasn't interested in having any sort of social influence, because things are somehow transparent for me. I seem to be able to walk straight through what other people regard as walls. No one can create an obstacle for me. The only obstacles are my own dumbness, silliness, lack of memory, inability to do something on a piece of paper. Loss of creativity is an obstacle—all the rest is nothing.

---

* Anatoly Rybakov (b. 1911) began his literary career in 1948 and was regularly published during the following decades, but came to prominence in 1987 with the publication of *Children of the Arbat* (*Deti Arbata*), his novel about the fate of the Moscow intelligentsia during the 1930s.

† Mikhail Shatrov (b. 1932), playwright, best known for political plays such as *Onward, Onward, Onward* (*Vperyod, Vperyod, Vperyod*): dramatic studies of Lenin and the events of his life which became milestones under *glasnost* in exploring the nature of Bolshevism.

I'm not a very ambitious person, not very curious. Lack of curiosity is a Russian vice—Pushkin said it of us: we're lazy and uncurious. I always wanted to travel, of course, and it was frustrating in the old days when you couldn't do that, couldn't go to countries you'd dreamed about. But I didn't *die* for lack of that freedom; basically I was quite content with my own company, and all I've ever actually needed was a cigarette and a cup of coffee—plus other people who share my values, and like talking not about how great they are but how amazing life is. On the whole you don't find such people among writers. Writers just concentrate on themselves. I like critics and philologists, especially people who know the literature of the nineteenth century and can dig up treasures that I'm unaware of—diaries and memoirs and letters and things. That's what I love!

SL If there's a moral imperative in your writing, it seems to me to lie in your emphasis on memory—the importance of remembering as a moral value in itself. The forgetful and careless in your work are haunted by the forgotten; the dead demand remembrance. 'Sonya' begins with the simple words 'A person lived—and isn't there now' (*Zhil chelovek—i net yego*). Much of your work seems to begin from this simple—or simply-put—mystery. What happens to all those vanished lives? I sense in your writing the consciousness of what it is to be a member of your generation, the last to have any intimate personal association with those who lived in pre-revolutionary Russia. Do you think of yourself as a keeper of memories?

TT I haven't been particularly. Every time someone dies, of course, a whole world dies with them. But when I was young I was such a fool, I paid no attention to all these old people—old ladies, mostly—I just laughed at them and didn't take them seriously.

SL Like the young people in 'Most Beloved', who laugh at their plain, dull, devoted governess Zhenechka, the person who rules their summers in childhood and lovingly tends their dacha garden and gives them countless presents—they don't recognize her love, they leave her out of account, until it's too late and she's gone, and the dacha gets uninhabitable and the garden overgrown ...

TT That's how it was. And now there's virtually no one left. When you're 15, 16, 17 life goes so fast, you're so impatient to become an adult—an adult but not old. The old don't count. And suddenly they all start to die. There are lots of people I remember now, whose stories I know, and of course I can't help thinking about them. I'd like to write all their stories. But you can't endlessly repeat the same plot. They're the best thing in the world, old ladies, I love them, and of course they all have different pasts and stories, but I can't harp endlessly on about them—from a literary point of view it would be repetitive.

SL Many of your stories—'Love me, Love me not', 'Most Beloved'—are written from the vantage point of childhood or youth—careless, hilarious, unsentimental. That's what makes them so touching, but also so 'cruel'.

TT I couldn't have written them from any other vantage point. That's the whole story: the values and tragedies of the old don't affect the young, the young are still morons in that regard. Of course even when you're young you have little pangs of remorse, now and then, but there's a drive that pushes you forward constantly—to live, to love—and that's how it has to be! Think what a sanctimonious bore you'd be otherwise. Always worrying about the old—impossible! There *are* these saints, of course, but everyone tries to avoid them—it's no fun being made to feel in the wrong all the time. As for writing from the point of view of the old—'Look how interesting I am, no one appreciates me, everyone offends me!' No, it just wouldn't do.

SL Many of your 'heroes' and 'heroines' are failures and misfits, unable to emerge from their shells—from their private obsessions, their fantasies, their childhood. Their lives are 'small' and utterly obscure, and that's led some critics to type them as versions of the *malenky chelovek*, the 'little person', in a time-honoured tradition of Russian literature. Do you see yourself in any sense as writing in that tradition?

TT No—not at all. Of course we were all brought up on that tradition in school—the 'little person' was the hero of all our literature classes. Before the Revolution, according to those classes, good literature was literature that championed the 'little person'; supposedly that was what Pushkin was doing with his Yevgeny in *The Bronze Horseman* or Gogol with Akaky Akakiyevich in 'The Overcoat'. But of course good writing doesn't depend on whether you write about princes and princesses or about 'little people'. And whether a character is capable of feeling insulted and humiliated doesn't depend on that either—you can feel humiliated not because you're Akaky Akakiyevich but because you're only a count instead of a real prince. Humiliation is in the mind. There's a wonderful story by Chekhov where someone's sitting in the bath house, washing himself, and he looks at the naked people round him and can't make out who's important and who isn't, who's a general and who's a clerk, and he feels very confused and disturbed.

For me all people were born naked and will die naked, and that's the only thing that actually matters. All the rest is a matter of clothes, clothes, clothes.

SL It seems to me a psychological, not a social, complex that makes so many of your characters outsiders to life—but a psychological complex that's nevertheless very Russian. All your stories play in some way on the contrast between energy and entropy—in Zamyatin's terms—or *eros* and *thanatos* in Freud's; you repeatedly see your characters struggling to act, to love, to grow up, to become part of life, but tugged backwards by a hibernating desire for enclosure, safety, stasis, oblivion. You see that these things spell death, yet you're made to experience the profound attraction they exert—the idyll of infancy may be a trap, death in disguise, but you feel all its charm: warmth, cosiness, *mama*, the safe, interior world of food and tablecloths and tea-cosies—in contrast to the terrifying, indifferent world outside. Denisov lands up under a table in the 'Fairy-Tale' café, and you see that he's trapped—but fairy-tales aren't just traps, they're enchantment, freedom: freedom from the categories of adult logic, adult realism.

This ambivalence about life, about action, about taking responsibility for yourself and going out into the world, does seem to me especially Russian. Oblomov, after all—who's surely the ancestor of many of your heroes—is a uniquely Russian character; you can't imagine him appearing in any other culture.

TT I think that ambivalence is universal. But maybe it appears in Russia more strikingly because Russia is a mixture of East and West, it's on the frontier of both, it's an in-between culture and it has always found it difficult to get its balance. There's a constant feeling of disturbance when you live there, as if you're always in danger of losing shape or form—partly just because the country is so huge, its traditional forms and shapes keep vanishing, getting lost in amorphousness.

When the culture is somehow unsteady, and all the patterns of cultural behaviour are constantly questioned, then perhaps you can afford and allow yourself to be a child all your life—which you couldn't do in a more rigid culture, one that had firmer rules about how to behave, one where you had to hide your identity.

sl That seems paradoxical in so far as Russia had always been so illiberal—politically at least. But perhaps the helplessness that goes with that illiberalism—the inadmissibility or pointlessness of any attempt to change the main circumstances of your life—has conferred its own peculiar kind of freedom, the freedom to regard yourself as innocent—infantilized, perhaps, but innocent.

America in that sense is a convenient opposite. It's ideologically committed to the idea that you can get out and change your life—and that you ought to.

tt Well yes, and you can—but a Russian would say, what's the point? Coming from a Russian background you see that the American idea of success as freedom is just—just designs on the clouds. It's wonderful to own your own house and get your child into college. But you can't seriously believe that this American dream is the goal in life. Fine, a house and a college place—but what comes next? Earning more money? That's the goal of many Americans. But what are the points along that route? Where do you stop? It's like some strange, nightmarish activity—rushing to fill a life that keeps leaking from every hole. Why is that better than those Russians sitting doing nothing? Maybe it's a philosophical question—but what's the point of life?

sl You speak about 'those Russians' as if they were a breed apart. Do you see yourself as in some way different from them? You mentioned before how 'energetic' your family was—not a characteristic common to your heroes!

tt I'm both energetic and lazy at the same time; my energy is spent in my laziness—that is, I'm energetic in some vital sense, but I'm lazy in a practical sense, not getting round to doing things—and other Russians are just worse than I am in that way! But I understand them.

Foreigners who visited us from time to time back in the 1970s—before we could travel at all—were sometimes very bemused by the way we lived—'mild' Russian dissidents who didn't do anything politically but just despised everything around. It was a well-known phenomenon: they liked to invite foreigners to their homes and show them their horrible communal apartments and say: look at these walls, the wallpaper is coming down, and all because of those bloody communists! And the foreigners were completely bewildered: why don't you just go out and buy some new wallpaper, they'd wonder, buy some glue and stick it up—surely the communists don't stop you doing that? People didn't sweep their floors because the regime was all wrong! Of course there's something funny about that. And I'm not just talking about sophisticated Russian dissidents in Moscow and Leningrad who'd make a point of not sweeping the floor. Everyone contributed to it.

There was a film recently—a sort of new-wave Russian film—about an old man living in a Russian hut; he comes back after the war and the hut is half-ruined, and then forty years pass and nothing changes; at the end of the film the hut is still in ruins. So this film was presented abroad and after the presentation people started politely asking questions like: why didn't he repair the roof? Because every time the hero goes into the hut something falls on his head or the rain pours in, but he never picks up a hammer and nail and attempts to repair it. And the director didn't know how to explain. She said it was all due to his distress over the war. But for forty years? people asked. He couldn't get it together for forty years? The film was a work of genius but she couldn't explain it at all, it made no rational sense.

And in fact there was no reason for his complete helplessness, because we aren't rational—Russians aren't rational creatures. I think it goes as far back as the split between the two Churches—the Catholic and the Orthodox. The Catholic—and Western—dogma is that the truth can be searched for—you can look for the truth both through the Church and its writings and through science and logic. So the teachings of Aristotle were somehow incorporated and universities sprang up and one result is that people's roofs stay up in the West and you have proper plumbing. Whereas the Greek Church consigned all that kind of thinking to the devil. God can't be understood, caught, perceived—it's impossible—and logic is just a challenge to God. That kind of thinking permeates everything in Russia. To be rational is to be dangerous and foreign.

SL So being helpless and doing nothing isn't just a failure or a refusal to 'grow up' and face the 'real world'—it's a philosophical outlook?

TT Yes—or it's both. Russians aren't nearly so afraid of the child within them as Americans are. Americans deny their own child-likeness. Though their popular culture in fact is very infantile—all these TV chat shows and so on, they're sometimes unbelievably primitive. They've applied the democratic principle to every aspect of life here [in America], but it can't be applied to everything. Just as there are some molecular structures that are complex and others that are primitive, so it is with things in society—and in order to get culture you have to have a complex structure. If you try to make everything equal, on the same level, you'll reduce everything to hydrogen, the simplest molecular structure on earth. America is reducing culture to hydrogen. It's like being worried that a virus and a human being aren't equal, and arguing that if a virus can't love or vote or write poetry then a human being should be ashamed of these abilities too and try to get rid of them.

SL I have to ask the obvious question—why have you chosen to live in America?

TT Yes, I ask myself! I didn't choose. These things happen gradually. You're offered one nice position and then another, and the years accumulate. And meanwhile I realize that it would be even more difficult now in Russia for anyone in our family to get a job—and I have to think about our children's future, they're grown up now and they will need to work. As for me, I know there's less and less interest in literature in Russia these days. And you can't suddenly change your life in your forties and take up baking pies for a living. And then I'm just afraid of the level of crime there. If you've spent any time in the West criminals assume you're rich even if you're not; you're an obvious target.

SL All your stories to date have been located in Russia; it's difficult to imagine their being located anywhere else. Has moving to America made it more difficult for you to write?

TT Not as such. What's in the mind can be carried away, and can even grow and flourish *in absentia*. Living here doesn't affect my writing in the way that events in Russia do. What's happening in my immediate surroundings, what I see outside my window, doesn't influence what's happening on the piece of paper—or more often these days the computer—in front of me. What I want to write now belongs absolutely in the mental realm in the sense that it's about the past—it relates to the end of last century and the years before the Revolution—to my great-grandmother's life. I have some of her papers—though many were lost and she burned her letters. Burned her letters! Imagine it. I would have loved to read them.

Sometimes I get quite lost and imagine that when I step outside the door I'll find myself in Moscow. The number of miles between me and Moscow is immaterial, it makes no difference whether it's thirty or thirty thousand—except in terms of the money you need to cross it! I know lots of other Russians who live in the same sort of mental realm, living in America but not interacting with it very much. But what's happening in Russia right now does affect me, as it seems to have affected lots of writers. The context has collapsed—and you have to wait until another context grows up, like the grass. But I feel that things are settling down now, or something has begun to settle inside me, and that this period of inner silence—lack of words for what I see around me—has enriched me in some ways.

SL We've talked about your 'entropic' and 'child-like' Russians in general, without making a gender distinction that's very clear in your work: it's the men, for the most part, who wander dreamily about or lie pondering on the sofa, while the women are engaged in a constant bustle of activity: hunting for men, laying traps, buying them slippers, and cooking them dinners and coaxing their shirts to come and settle on their shelves. Far from being helpmeets and muses or the prey of men themselves, they seem taken from the gallery of men's horror fantasies about women—greedy, domineering, petty-minded killjoys, determined to enslave their men in domesticity or keep them in a state of permanent helplessness. Even if your stories can be said, as one Western critic put it, to subvert conventions about gender relationships and women's roles, they hardly do so from a feminist perspective. Do you see yourself as pointing, albeit in comic and grotesque form, to something essential in the relationship between men and women—at least in Russia?

TT I don't think these relationships are uniquely Russian, but in Russia they're more obvious. Women are much more practical and earthy than men. Men on the other hand are very social animals, that's their very meaning—their spiritual health depends on their position in society, while women's doesn't at all. And so when men lose their jobs or feel they're not needed, when no one requires them to do anything or to be creative or whatever, they're completely lost, they lose some essential light in themselves, they don't know what to do, they start drinking or behaving rather vaguely and distractedly, or they simply go out of their minds. While women aren't like that, they can exist without any of that—and they do, they do, that's why they can actually create society. Society is created not because someone conceives the idea but because there are lots of practical jobs to be done—children are born and people have to be housed and fed and have various things, and that's how society starts growing. But men—men are more spiritual beings, they think in more abstract, less concrete terms, that's their way of creating.

So the sorts of controversies about the family that are going on right now in the West, especially in America, are a very sad thing. Men are so weak. Why deprive them of the only things they're able to do? It's very easy to destroy a man as a man—as that very special thing—whereas it's very difficult to destroy a woman, women are indestructible. They're like weeds, they'll survive anywhere, in any society. Put a woman on a desert island and she'll get on with it and do something. Robinson Crusoe should really have been a woman. Really.

As for satire—of course I satirize everything, including myself; it's a way of putting things so that they're not too straightforward and boring and so that you don't sound like a schoolteacher. I try to avoid this schoolteacherism as much as possible. But I do try to show the essential things in both men and women. I think I'm even-handed—neither feminist nor masculinist. Both men and women could be equally offended by what I write about them.

SL Is it meaningful to talk about 'women's literature' in Russia?

TT At some times it's pointless, at other times it makes perfect sense. It depends on the cultural context. In the sixties, seventies, and eighties, the period between the Thaw and *glasnost*, I think there was no difference between men's and women's literature. There was good and bad. When I look back I think that, with all its flaws, and despite all the censorship, it was a very healthy period compared with what's happening now. Because, for all their faults, the cultural élite then, unlike today, genuinely assumed that there was good art and bad art, and that a writer was just a vehicle through which certain messages were conveyed from the place where art is conceived. Whether that vehicle was a man or a woman made no difference—it was just that everyone who contributed to great art was good. But in periods when art is regarded as a secondary device for bringing about social change—as happened at the end of the nineteenth century, with the Populist movement and so on—then of course the cause of women was taken up as well, and you could speak appropriately of a women's literature. But in terms of art you could just take all this literature and throw it away.

The same thing may happen now, if people are crazy enough to listen to fashionable theories—especially American feminist theory; everyone talks about it here and it's started affecting Russians too. Only people with very strong wills can stand up to these stupid ideas. I remember two or three years ago being invited to a conference in New York, something about women in literature. Four women from Russia were invited, and the organizers started telling us how we'd been oppressed, and were still oppressed, and they wanted to hear all about it and how it had affected us. When we denied that we'd been oppressed they started shouting at us and assuring us that we had been, it was just that we didn't realize it. They knew nothing about Russian cultural life, but they wanted us to confess. Yet there I was, one of the few writers at the time who had a wide readership and could sell her books. And next to me was the critic Natalya Ivanova—and just try and oppress her! She'd bite your leg off. For twenty years she'd been one of Russia's top literary critics, in a perfect position to oppress whomever she chose. So I started shouting back, I just screamed that no one had ever oppressed us in

Russia the way we were being oppressed now—being forced to own up to things that had never happened.

SL You mentioned just now the literature of the period between the Thaw and *glasnost*. It seems to me that this is a period that's in danger of being forgotten or ignored. I asked some young critics recently to name their 'top ten' Russian writers from the twentieth century and not one of them mentioned any writer from this period. The literary world in Russia seems to me even more fiercely split by generation than elsewhere.

TT What you're seeing now is just another wave of nihilism. If you look at it that way it helps you to calm down. I've been very irritated by the way some young writers and critics have been trying to rubbish their predecessors, but I try to look at it all *sub specie aeternitatis*. I'm just glad not to have been part of all these fashions and to have rejected them at the time, though no one would listen to me before.

When *glasnost* happened everyone kept waiting for a new writer to emerge in response to what was happening. But I said at the time that it was pointless to expect any such thing: writers emerge not because they are allowed to but in spite of everything, no matter what the obstacles. The obstacles may even in some cases prove to be a help. Homer was blind and Dante was expelled from his home town, and that didn't stop them creating. There's no point in blaming circumstances. You may be distracted by them—sometimes very distracted—but that's all there is to it. There have been great discussions about whether being arrested and sent to the camps was a help or a hindrance to writers, but—short of your being killed or physically destroyed—everything depends on whether they are good writers to start with. Shalamov's* stories were written to prove that there is no positive experience in being sent to the camps—but of course the irony was that he created a great work in the process.

Then after *glasnost* they started all these new styles. Aha, they said, there's no tradition of eroticism in Russian literature, let's create one! But all the results were in very poor taste. They'd failed to understand that Russian literature is in fact very erotic, and just because it is so burdened with eroticism it doesn't talk about plain sex, because it wants to preserve that inner tension and inner feeling. But open a page from any Russian classic and you'll find sex in some sublimated form. All this clinically described sex and intimate physiological detail is just uninteresting. We're all adults. No one can shock me enough that I like it—I'm not an old Victorian lady. Where is the art in it? So these writers—Viktor Yerofeyev, Vladimir Sorokin, Valeriya Narbikova—are actually involved in self-destruction. But this will pass too, it's already coming to an end. All this bold and obscene stuff had none of the tension that creates real art—so now everyone is just tired of it.

SL Don't you think this wave of 'eroticism' is partly a reaction, not just to the primness and euphemistic language of Soviet society—a society that in fact hid numerous real obscenities in its history—but to the traditional Russian elevation of the writer as a moral and spiritual leader? As if these writers wanted to make it quite clear that they had no desire to play this role?

---

* Varlam Shalamov (1907–81), writer, best known for his *Kolyma Tales*, based on his experience of over twenty years in Stalin's camps (*Kolymskiye rasskazy*, first published in 1966 in the New York-based *émigré* journal *Novy zhurnal*). None of these stories was published in Russia until 1988.

TT I think it's an adolescent reaction. And it comes from not reading enough.

A writer plays with words and meanings; the activity of writing as such is purely spiritual. These writers are trying to pull it down from its pedestal. So they stuff their texts with all kinds of bodily functions—but they score an own goal, because it just doesn't work. It's fine to write whatever you wish, but you have to understand that writing's a difficult job, you have to find the right words to get the proper result. If the reader is simply repelled then it hasn't worked.

It's very difficult to write about sex. When human beings are involved in it themselves they don't find it repulsive, but when they read about it they do. We're just constructed that way. For example, it's nice to eat—to use the closest metaphor. But it would be unpleasant and not the least interesting to be able to feel inside someone else's mouth and know the way they chew. Our own physiological functions are okay, other people's are not—unless it's someone very close to us: our babies, for example, can shit all they want and that's fine. Love, warmth, acceptance, the expansion of your own self to include the objects you love does allow us to accept these things with others. And a work of literature can involve me in all these things too, if it's done very well and in some very strange way manages to create something like that atmosphere of love and warmth. But Viktor Yerofeyev, for example, can't do that. And if someone just makes your life miserable you don't want to read them.

SL But how do you yourself feel about the fact that the role of literature in Russia has clearly undergone a change in the last few years—that it *has* been taken off its pedestal?

TT Well, on the whole it's a good thing—but it's sad if literature has fallen from its place for writers themselves. For the rest of the country, fine, because they should get off their backsides and do something else besides reading and chatting on and on about literature. But what can writers replace literature with? Well, money—but money has nothing to do with literature. Pushkin said: 'ne prodayotsya vdokhnoveniye, no mozhno rukopis' prodat'': 'you cannot sell the inspiration, but you can sell the manuscript'. So that's the truth. What is amazing about Pushkin is that he manages to say in a short aphorism the obvious truth—but if it weren't for him no one else would have said it, especially in Russia. He had more common sense than anyone else.

SL I wouldn't use the word erotic to describe your prose, but it's certainly sensual—both in the sense that it's linguistically very rich, so there's an almost gastronomic pleasure in reading it, and in the immediacy with which it conveys the phenomenal world, the experience of touch, sight, sound. And taste. It's not accidental that you mentioned food as the closest metaphor for sex. Food is all over the place in your stories; it's part of that great undertow of comfort and warmth that seduces men into helplessness and indolence, just like the pies that Agafya makes in *Oblomov*, working on the pastry with her big doughy arms—with Oblomov lying on the sofa and watching her.

TT Or what about Gogol—the food in his story 'Old-World Landowners'! Marvellous! Of course there's a great tradition in Russian literature of writing about food. I love it.

SL Many critics have commented on the contrast between the incredible lushness of your prose, the density of its imagery, and the poverty of your characters' lives—Fazil Iskander remarked that the language in some way compensated for the lives. To me it acts as a kind of teasing, provocative counterpoint to them.

Your very first story, '"On the Golden Porch"', starts with an epigraph—a children's counting rhyme—which contains a riddle that seems to me to run through all your work. 'Tsar, tsarevich, king, prince, shoemaker, tailor—who are you?' The riddle is addressed here to Uncle Pasha, the hero of the story: from the child's-eye-view at the outset of the story he's certainly a tsar; the room he rules over is an Aladdin's cave, a realm of magic, crammed with fascinating things. But at the end of the story it becomes just a room full of worthless bric-à-brac. The children are grown up and they've no time now for Uncle Pasha's pathetic baubles. He's no longer a tsar, just a poor old man. But whose vision is 'truer'—the child's or the disillusioned adult's? It seems to me that your language, in a sense, 'argues the case' for the child's-eye view. It shows the world to be full of magic.

TT Whether you see your world as rich or impoverished depends on you.

In Chekhov's story 'Dushechka' (The Darling) we see the heroine going through different husbands and adapting to each and finally being left alone and looking through the window. She sees a bottle standing on the window-sill and a muzhik [Russian peasant] going by somewhere in his cart. And she doesn't know what to think. What do the bottle and the muzhik mean? Not for a thousand roubles could she tell us, Chekhov says. He's a genius. He understands that her soul is an empty vessel which has to be filled with some meaning, and in her case meaning is given by men, who create their own universes.

But all of us have to try to fill this vessel of our souls. I am the same. I don't know what to think about any element of the world unless I fill it with some cosmos of my own, which in my case is constructed with words. I'm trying to elaborate this cosmos, and the richer and more lush my language, the more features of this world appear. Otherwise I feel both empty and yet burdened with unpronounced meanings—and I don't know what to do with them. I think that everyone who is involved in some creative activity feels the same. With literature at least all the words already exist, you just have to combine them. But music, for instance, doesn't exist in the world at all—musicians had just to guess that something like that would be possible. Even the instruments had to be invented first. It's amazing.

In a way in literature you have to construct your instruments too—instruments made out of words that will allow your ideas or images or emotions to flow from you to the reader—though they may affect the reader quite differently from the way they affect you.

SL I'm reminded by your reference to Chekhov's story of the contrasting endings to two of your stories. In 'The Moon Came Out' we see the heroine, Natasha, standing at the window, and 'nothing, nothing could be heard but the din of passing life'. Whereas at the very end of his story, after a series of trials and defeats, the old Peters stands at his window and at last, for the first time, opens it to the world outside and smiles at life—'indifferent, ungrateful, deceiving, mocking, senseless, alien—wonderful, wonderful, wonderful'.

Those were the last words in your first collection of stories and it was impossible not to read them as a kind of manifesto—or a revelation of a very simple truth that had been dogging us through all the other stories.

TT That sentence didn't appear until the very end of the story, and then it just came as a necessity. But many people didn't see the point of it, they didn't see that it was necessary. Some even thought I'd written it to please the censorship! So there'd be something cheerful, after all! 'Life has got better, life has got jollier', just like Stalin said. That's how distorted people's minds are; they're so used to thinking in political terms in Russia. But politics has nothing to do with it—I can transcend politics more easily than anything.

There is no life unless you create it. There is no such Peters, nothing described in these pages exists. But if the story's written wonderfully then life itself becomes wonderful. Everything depends on how you describe things. You can feel the emptiness and meaninglessness of everything—and then all of a sudden life, on the contrary, becomes full of meaning. There's both a poison and a cure in all our herbs. It just depends on what you choose to extract from them.

6
Yevgeny Popov
(b. 1946)

Yevgeny Popov, best known as a short-story writer and master of parody, was born in 1946 in the Siberian town of Krasnoyarsk, immortalized in his work as 'the town of K. on the banks of the river E.'. In the 1960s he studied geology in Moscow, and in 1968, having unsuccessfully applied to the Gorky Institute of Literature and the Institute of Cinematography, he returned to Siberia to work as a geologist. In 1975, he abandoned this first career, moved back to Moscow for good, and thenceforth devoted himself to literature, earning his living with a series of hack jobs.

From the early 1960s Popov had been writing, occasionally publishing his stories in local newspapers and journals. But his real début came in 1976, when *Novy mir* published two of his stories ('I Await a Love that's True' and 'The Drummer and his Drummer-Wife'), with a foreword by the writer Vasily Shukshin. These stories won him immediate popularity and admission, as a promising new name, to the Union of Writers.

His status as an 'official writer' was to be short-lived, however. In 1979 he was one of two young writers (the other being Viktor Yerofeyev) to contribute to the unofficial almanac *Metropol'*, an act which promptly earned him expulsion from the Union and exile to Moscow's literary underground. In 1981 a collection of his stories, *Merry-Making in Old Russia* (*Veseliye Rusi*) was published by Ardis in the United States. But it was not until 1989 that Popov began once more to be published in Russia.

By that time he had accumulated some 200 stories, selections of which were published in *I Await a Love that's True* (1989) and *Aeroplane to Cologne* (1991), and two longer works, *The Soul of a Patriot* (dated 1982, published 1990) and *The Splendour of Life* (dated 1985, published 1990). The publication of this large 'backlog', together with a steady flow of new writing, has made Popov one of the most visible and popular writers of the 1990s. Subsequent works, such as *The 'Beryozka' Restaurant* (1991) and *On the Eve of On the Eve* (1993), show his imagination energetically at work on the absurdities and incongruities of life in more recent times, and he vigorously denies that the fall of the old regime has left him short of a theme. Yet, along with Venedikt Yerofeyev, Popov is surely one of the great poets—and clowns—of the vanished empire in its declining years.

Many of Popov's stories are set in Siberia; not, however, in the romantic wilds but in the streets and apartments of his native city, or a literary version thereof. 'The town of K.', *circa* the late 1960s and 1970s, operates as a central 'chronotope' for Popov in much the same way that 'Mukhus' and 'Chegem' do for Iskander. The same names, the same streets recur in different stories, giving the reader, as with Iskander, a sense of recognized reality.

But the difference in mood and landscape could not be greater. The town of K., far from being exotic, is ordinariness itself, a remote, provincial, quintessentially Soviet place of anonymous apartment blocks, where citizens quarrel, watch TV, grumble about the rubbish disposal system, engage in petty theft, blame one another, and drink. Against this backdrop the search for fulfilment goes on: people 'feel in need of happiness, and go to the cinema, and again feel in need of happiness ...'. Love, in these stories, is elusive or non-existent, the relations between the sexes fraught, suspicious, and brutal.

Many of Popov's stories, in this sense, recall Petrushevskaya's in their bleak comedy. Here, however, we see the male side of the story: where men, in Petrushevskaya's tales, are routinely missing, assumed drunk or otherwise departed, here we gain insight—often through a first-person narrator—into their thoughts, meanderings, and drunken conversations. Not that the overall picture is objectively very different. In 'Beyond Culture'[*] we find the hero desperately trying to claw his way out of a hangover, and the debris of two days' partying, by writing 'verse'. His wife, returning from a visit to her mother, curses him for his drink and his drivel, cleans up the kitchen, makes him some soup, and threatens to leave him for good. 'Sure, go to hell,' the wretched husband replies. In a typical Popovian coda, the narrator takes his part. Why couldn't the wife love her husband? he asks in sorrowful wonderment. Tall, curly-haired, a blue-eyed boy—was he any worse than the next man?

For all their immersion in humdrum, everyday reality, however, many of Popov's stories have about them a whiff of the mystic, hallucinatory, and supernatural. To be sure, the virtual omnipresence of alcohol may partially account for such phenomena as the appearance of an extraterrestial at the trolleybus stop, or the way God's eye, abroad in the street, winks and gloats at passing girls. Most of Popov's narrators are inherently unreliable—anecdotalists, purveyors of tall stories at second and third hand, or moist-eyed sentimentalists whose exclamations and admonitions do little to illuminate 'the truth'. Some of the stories, in their rhythmic, repetitive structure or blatant illustration of a moral ('Caution is the Highest Form of Wisdom'[†] is the motto of one) demand indeed to be read as fairy-tales.

But what Popov conveys, through his constant juxtaposition of the banal and the bizarre, his heightening of incident to render it grotesque, is the sense that reality itself is somehow unstable, unconvincing. When the hero of 'Dear Little World'[‡] is struck on the head by a wafer of falling plaster, we register an unwarranted alarm, as

---

[*] 'Vne kul'tury', in *Samolyot na Kyol'n* (1991).
[†] 'Vysshaya mudrost'', ibid.   [‡] 'Slaven'ky mirok', ibid.

at some laden and sinister portent. The narrator's mutterings, at the end of 'Two Dried Fingers out of Five',* that something in the story is 'not quite right', confirms an intimation of some other, inaccessible dimension to life, some missing clue to the meaning of things.

Such intimations may be, at root, no more than an expression of desire, a reaching-out of the soul for something beyond the TV set and the shambles at work. Many of Popov's stories turn on a moment of epiphany, a glimpse of loftiness inspired by some minor change in fortune. For some, the acquisition of a new apartment becomes the symbol of ascent to higher realms. In 'Dear Little World', the hero gazes out from his new fifth-floor apartment and seems, for an instant, to grasp the essence of things: as the tiny figures down below labour to shift his furniture, he sees a lifetime construed in a series of key verbs: 'To drag. To stand. To work. To sing. To dance. To drink. To fall'. In a gesture of liberation, the hero flings his hat out of the window—alas, hurling it into a neighbouring apartment and thereby provoking an unseemly row (the narrator warns from the start that his story will prove 'embarrassing'). Likewise, the view from a magnificent new tower block in 'The Green Massif'† inspires grand reflections on the beauty of Siberia—until, that is, the central character falls from his thirteenth-floor window (or, just possibly, is pushed out by his wife) after eating a surfeit of buttered pancakes. Other stories record a similarly violent descent from grace. In 'The Electric Accordion'‡ the hero, entranced by the beauty of this new-fangled instrument, heard by chance on the way home from work, is unable on returning home to reconcile himself to the ordinariness of life, and picks a furious quarrel with his wife.

These tales of frustrated escape and fleeting euphoria thus serve, in the end, only to reinforce the sense of entrapment in Popov's world. *La dolce vita*, if it exists at all, must necessarily be somewhere else—perhaps in the far-off West, where only the elect few are destined to go. In 'Aeroplane to Cologne',§ a foreign bigwig, Mandeville Makhur, is due to stop off at the town of K. on his way abroad, and a magnificent ceremony is planned at the airport to honour his arrival. Typically, however, the plan misfires. With excruciating clarity, we see Makhur lean back in the sky and shake his head contemptuously at the recollection—those comic Russians, their barbaric food—while, back in K., the locals go into the usual spasm of mutual recrimination. Similar humiliations are visited on a local sculptor from K., the narrator's friend Kishtakhanov, when a group of Western tourists, on arrival in the town, are invited to view his new sculpture 'symbolically representing the heroic past and happy present of the mighty Siberian River E.'. Alas, the attention of all concerned is diverted from this work of art when the tourists (one wearing a T-shirt declaring 'I am sexy') start offering chewing-gum to the local children, brought out in force to sing 'Bandera Rossa'.¶ Even the story 'Drawn to Native Villages'‖—where a local drunkard, Sheponin, succeeds against all odds in swapping his apartment in

---

* 'Dva sushonyye pal'tsa iz pyati byvshikh', in *Veseliye Rusi* (1981).

† 'Zelyony massif', in *Veseliye Rusi* (1981).

‡ Elektronny bayan', in *Zhdu lyubvi neverolomnoy: rasskazy* (1989).

§ 'Samolyot na Kyol'n', in *Samolyot na Kyol'n* (1991).

¶ 'Glaz bozhy (God's Eye)', ibid. (1991).

‖ 'Vlecheniye k rodnym derev'yam', ibid.

K. for an abode in Paris—ends in mortification for the narrator and his friends, left behind in K. and forced to accommodate, as their new neighbour, a disreputable Frenchman whose dog fouls their stairs.

These stories, for all their comedy, are studies in embarrassment and wounded dignity. How do you carry on in the knowledge that the world you have been fated to live in is somehow second-best, a world of kitsch and sham? How, in particular, does the artist function, where the local models of man-made beauty are at best a heroic sculpture in dubious taste, at worst a rubbish dump and a row of tower blocks, where everyday language is riddled with an alien jargon, and where the very notions of loftiness and beauty have been usurped?

The difficulty is summed up in Popov's story 'The Only Instrument',* where a young man laments to friends at a party that he possesses not a single thought of his own about eternity or love, that all his attempts at poetry are a grimace, an affectation, and that, for all his musical talent, the accordion is the only instrument he has been able to master. Can one play a Bach fugue on an accordion, he asks? Perhaps the only consolation is that no other fool would dream of attempting anything so ludicrous?

Playing the clown, the story suggests, may be the best option under the circumstances; and in the story the young man reaps his clown's reward—he makes a beautiful girl at the party laugh. Popov, in a sense, reaps his reward as well. All his stories can be read as exercises in clowning—in making comedy out of discomfiture. Some, like 'Deficit'† (the scenario for a tragic ballet on the theme of shortages in the record industry) are pieces of outright grotesquerie. In others, the very notion of telling a story is mocked: the narrator goes off at a tangent, decides he should be talking of something quite different, or simply gives up and loses his nerve half-way. In 'The White Steamer'‡ the narrator pauses mid-stream in his tale to consult the opinion of his friend, the writer Fetisov. 'Is it meant to be a satire?' Fetisov asks of his story; and as the two sit gazing meditatively at a white steamer passing on the River E., he suggests a quite different, more tragic plot, in which the hero ends by hanging himself. With this option still dangling in the air, the two authors characteristically abandon the reader and go off alone to drown their sorrows in drink.

Like a clown's make-up, a pair of outsize inverted commas surround all these tales, screening the author's private thoughts as he assumes, with virtuoso mimicry, the voices of the sanctimonious official, the Major in the Armed Forces of the Fatherland, the indignant man-in-the-street, the scowling drunk, and the despairing poet. And yet it would be wrong, as Popov suggests in the interview that follows, to use the term 'irony' of his work. Popov does not look on his characters *de haut en bas*; in a sense, he is there in the story too, drinking alongside them. Their voices *are* his 'only instruments', and the effect of using them undeniably comic. Still, as the young man in the story said of his Soviet accordion, it may be 'shrill, wheezing, hysterical. But it does have soul . . .'. A will to live, a striving for dignity, propels Popov's characters even as they reach for the bottle or hit out at their wives.

Popov's depiction of the Soviet soul, in all its odd tenderness, was unwelcome to literary officialdom in Brezhnev's Russia, and by the end of the 1970s Popov had

---

* 'Yedinstvenny instrument', ibid.   † 'Defitsit', ibid.   ‡ 'Bely teplokhod', ibid.

added to his clown's repertoire the role of outcast poet, struggling against the odds to maintain his productivity and self-esteem. In 1982, bored with writing short stories ('I knew I could easily write another 200 in the same vein', he said in an interview in 1988), he embarked on a longer work, *The Soul of a Patriot, or Various Epistles to Ferfichkin*. The 'author' of these epistles is none other than the writer 'Yevgeny Anatoliyevich' himself, whose many friends and acquaintances include his 'brother in literature Ye.' and 'the philosopher K.' (easily identifiable as the real-life Viktor Yerofeyev and Vladimir Kormer), as well as the fully-named poet Dmitry Aleksandrovich Prigov.

The 'epistles', whose mythical addressee remains obscure, take the form of a diary, beginning with great ambition as the record of the author's reflections on Russia, its past, its landscape (the opening missives are penned on a long train journey), and the fate of the author's own relatives, including his Uncle Kolya, whose chief claim to fame was the bringing of a recipe for Russian 'home-baked milk' to one of the greatest restaurants in Vienna. Roughly a third of the way into the work, however, 'life intervenes' to cut short these rambling reminiscences. For on 10 November 1982, the day when the author was setting forth his recollections of his Granny Marisha, a momentous event occurred: Leonid Brezhnev finally upped and died. From this point onwards the author devotes himself to an account of this historic moment, as witnessed principally by himself and the poet Prigov, whose tour of Moscow-in-mourning, with frequent stops for discussion and liquid refreshment, is recorded (and graphically mapped out) in minute detail.

Typically, however, what should have been the crowning scene—the pompous funeral itself—is all but passed over, the author confining himself to recording, on the eve of New Year 1983, the few cryptic jottings he had made while watching the event on TV six weeks before. Far more space is devoted to the author's more immediate concerns: excited speculations about the future, biographical digressions, meditations on the eternal meaning of New Year and spring, and above all the desire to turn over a new leaf, write more, and fulfil his literary plan (the work is riddled with calculations concerning pages per day and roubles per page)—a desire constantly frustrated by the intervention of life at a more mundane level, as when the lavatory breaks down on 29 December, and the author is obliged to break off his work to fix it.

Like all Popov's work, *Soul of a Patriot* is, in this sense, profoundly self-mocking, its historical truthfulness residing precisely in the author's failure to carry through his heroic intent. History on the grand scale cannot be written from obscurity; an author of the underground, himself unpublished, is in no position to confer immortality on others. Yet history consists in the trials and ceremonies of the obscure as well—consists even in their survival. The author's homage to his friends and family, to their obscure lives and times, has about it an unmistakable air of celebration—of triumph against the odds.

To the extent that it was prompted by a vision of change, the celebration in *Soul of a Patriot* was slightly premature. After Brezhnev's death the real-life Popov continued to labour in obscurity, and among his labours, as he describes in the interview, was a detailed reading of the Soviet press, from 1960—the year that he had begun self-consciously to write—to 1985. *The Splendour of Life* (1990) was the fruit of those researches. Subtitled 'Chapters from a "Romance with a Newspaper" which will never be begun or ended', the book consists of twenty-five chapters (one for each of the years in question), each containing a selection of headlines, snippets of news, slogans, speeches, public pronouncements, and suchlike from the relevant year, together with two fictional texts—one written concurrently with the newspaper extracts, and one, so to speak, retrospectively. The book could thus be seen as the literary equivalent of a 'docudrama', juxtaposing fictional scenes with documentary newsreel, and recording the development of the artist against the background of his times.

But whereas newsreel excerpts in film serve classically to anchor a fiction in some 'objective' reality, Popov's bizarre extracts read like fiction themselves. To be sure, they lend a certain 'authenticity' to the fictional texts; in presenting them, Popov reveals one of his richest sources of anecdotal and linguistic material. But he also, conversely, highlights the aesthetic properties of the 'official' texts themselves; in this context, they turn into museum pieces, grotesque literary curiosities. Deprived of ideological power and purpose, they become, in other words, part of the manifold 'splendour of life'.

If this 'romance' (or 'novel'—*roman* in Russian may mean either) remains in principle unfinished, it is mainly—as Popov suggests here—because life itself remains inexhaustibly rich and curious, regardless of the political forms under which it is enacted. But subsequent works may lead us to construe his subtitle in other ways. Works such as *On the Eve of On the Eve* (1993) reveal Popov's continuing preoccupation with the peculiar personalities of the bygone era, here depicted struggling to adapt to the realities of the new. They also, of course, testify to the persistence of social patterns and forms of language, not to mention physical settings, beyond the immediate remedy of politicians. Soviet Russia has not disappeared overnight, and continues in its death throes to exert a fascination.

But at a distance, now, from the Brezhnev era, and the odd claustrophobic world of the underground he once inhabited, Popov himself can be seen as a writer of older and wider allegiances: a satirist who owes his extravagance and seriousness, his clowning and his melancholy, as much to Swift and Petronius as to Gogol, Zoshchenko, and the Russian absurdists of the 1920s* to whom he pays tribute in the interview that follows.

◆   ◆   ◆

---

* The 'absurdists' included Aleksandr Vvedensky (1904–41), Daniil Kharms (1905–42), and Nikolai Zabolotsky (1903–58), together known as the 'Oberiuty' after the acronym of the writers' association which they founded in Leningrad in the late 1920s (the satirically named 'Obedineniye realnogo iskusstva', or 'The Association of Real Art'). All three were arrested under Stalin and their names obliterated from Russian literature until their rehabilitation in 1956 (posthumous in the case of Kharms, who died in prison, and Vvedensky, who was executed). Mikhail Zoshchenko (1895–1958) was a writer of humorous short stories who achieved immense popularity in the 1920s, before he too came under attack for his satirical representation of everyday Soviet life. In 1946, together with the poet Anna Akhmatova, Zoshchenko was singled out for attack by Stalin's cultural watchdog Andrei Zhdanov, and his work was vilified and for the most part banned until his rehabilitation in 1956.

SL   Russians seem particularly fond of talking in terms of generations—the 'men of the sixties', the 'forty-year-olds'. It's often said of your generation that you were the ones who suffered most from the period of 'stagnation' under Brezhnev. How would you describe your generation's experience?

YP   I won't give you a writer's answer: 'we are the generation that was forgotten.' My generation is the first post-war generation—the generation of those who in many cases were conceived during the war. I can't say that we had a worse time than anyone else. The so-called 'stagnation' was just a part of the whole seventy-year period of totalitarianism. It was a terrible time, or rather, not so much terrible as hateful, disgusting. But there have been much worse times—the 1930s, the war, in fact virtually every period beginning with 1917 was a terrible time.

Our generation suffered only in the sense that we were held back. We didn't enjoy the immediate success of the 'sixties' writers—people like Vasily Aksyonov, Bella Akhmadulina, Yevgeny Yevtushenko. But in the end—I can say this now—perhaps God knew what He was up to. Because the fact that our generation was immediately confronted with a kind of concrete wall meant that we were forced to go in another direction, we were forced to think a bit more, to read a bit more, resist a bit, get a bit more angry. So that our generation never identified with Soviet power, absolutely never. Well, maybe at the age of 12 or 13—but that was it. Whereas that generation, the 'sixties', *had* identified with it, they'd gone through the romance of joining the Young Communist League and hearing all these myths and stories about good communists. They'd been seduced by this subtle lie. People agreed that the times were bad, but they felt it was because the ideals of communism had been distorted.

We never felt that. Our only hope was that we might get away with it just a bit, cheat the system a bit, maybe publish a few things. That was our rather minimal ambition.

SL   What kept you going as a writer during the Brezhnev period? How did you keep your life afloat?

YP   In a practical sense I sustained life with all sorts of jobs. All the way through, and even now, I've never lived from my literary earnings. In the 1970s I published perhaps one short story a year, so that wasn't enough to live on.

I worked in masses of different places, but the main job I had was working for the Artists' Union Fund—it was idiotic work, but it had the advantage that I had to travel a lot; about once a month I'd be sent to some provincial town to formulate some agreement and sign a contract, and on the way I met all sorts of people and got into all sorts of conversations. Then in 1978 I was accepted into the Union of Writers, but I was expelled almost immediately, so there was no real chance for me to become a professional writer.

Luckily I was able to keep my job with the Fund, even though the KGB went to see them and said it would be a good idea if they got rid of me. But they said that they had no grudges against me—we don't know anything about his being a writer, they said. As far as we're concerned he fulfils the plan. They weren't bad people.

Interview recorded in December 1991.

It's nice to have a lot of money but it's not so bad to have a little, and that's what the Fund gave me for doing virtually nothing. And then I had some 'black' work translating from the languages of the different nations of the USSR—I did it from a crib, a literal translation that had to be turned into something more literary. There was an official translator who sympathized with me and passed on some of his work to me, and it would be published under a pseudonym. I must have translated about ten books during that period and they brought in quite good money. The books were absolute rubbish—average, grey prose. But I always take a responsible attitude towards any kind of literary work, and I'd try to make out of this average stuff something that was just a little better. In its own way it was a kind of literary game.

So none of this was unbearable, unbearable isn't the word ... but it was simply melancholy, very melancholy, watching what was happening around us, communism and more communism, and wondering when on earth it would end. In fact mostly it seemed it would never come to an end.

SL And that time wasn't passing at all?

YP Not shifting an inch! We felt that for evermore and eternity there'd be a portrait of Brezhnev hanging there on the wall and someone singing some communist rubbish on the radio. So however much we laughed at Gorbachev, we should all remember very clearly that he played an absolutely enormous role—who he *is* is another question, but what he *did* was very important. Because it could have worked out very differently. Many people say now: well, if there hadn't been Gorbachev another one would have turned up. And that's obviously true, but it might have happened five years later, or more, and even five years is a very long time and many chances could have been missed.

Meanwhile literary life in those years—the life of the literary underground, that is—was quite tumultuous. Official literature during those years was in a state of total marasmus, total decay, supercretinism ... but underground life was extremely interesting. There were writers around like Dmitry Prigov, Timur Kibirov, Venedikt Yerofeyev, Viktor Yerofeyev*—a whole lot of names you could mention.

Venedikt Yerofeyev was already a 'classic' of the underground. Viktor would make speeches and write about everything under the sun and read his stories. And there were loads of other people, especially wonderful poets—Sergei Gandlevsky, Lev Rubinshtein, Olga Sedakova, and in Leningrad Viktor Krivulin, Yelena Shvarts, the prose writer Mikhail Berg†—these were all people who were formed as writers during those years, people of my age, who started writing in the late sixties, early seventies, though their 'dawn' came later—in the early 1980s.

SL How did you get to know one another's work, if it wasn't published?

---

* Dmitry Prigov (b. 1940) and Timur Kibirov (b. 1955), poets of the Moscow 'underground' in the 1970s who gained wider recognition only after they began to be officially published in the late 1980s. For information on Venedikt Yerofeyev, Viktor Yerofeyev, see Introduction, pp. xxii, xxiii.

† All the writers mentioned here were born in the decade after the war and were members of the 'underground' avant-garde whose work remained largely unpublished in Russia until *glasnost*, although it began to attract the notice of critics from the early 1980s. For a perceptive study of their work, see Mikhail Aizenberg, 'Nekotoryye drugiye', in *Teatr*, 4 (1991).

YP It was like an underground network—like some new literary underground party. I might never have met a particular writer, and he might never have been published officially, but I knew that in Leningrad, for example, there existed this poet Viktor Krivulin, because someone or other had shown me his poems, or perhaps he'd already been published in the West. And then when we did meet we wouldn't be strangers to one another—he would know my work too.

I made friends with Lyudmila Petrushevskaya in the early seventies too, when I was still living in Siberia. She was living in Moscow and she read my stories in the editorial offices of the journal *Novy mir*. They were lying around in some cupboard there, and she read them and wrote me a letter, and a lively correspondence ensued, although at the time we never met one another.

SL What made you finally move from Siberia?

YP Well I'd been studying here in Moscow in the 1960s, and I went back to Siberia only because my mother was ill and alone, and I had to be with her. I finally moved here after she died, in late 1975; I swapped apartments and got a quarter of a barracks here, and I was very pleased with that and am still very pleased. I was young, I had friends, and here in Moscow I could immediately get hold of books that it was difficult to find anywhere in Siberia, so life started moving along. Three years later I got involved in *Metropol'*—so I arrived on the scene when everything was getting going.

SL When you met together as underground writers in those days did you feel any sort of danger?

YP Not really, because there was nothing in us that the KGB could destroy. I've always said that Brezhnev didn't prevent me writing, and Gorbachev didn't help either. Nobody could 'help' in that sense. The conditions for getting printed were another matter, that was pretty much unthinkable at the time. But there were always these little circles in Moscow where lovers of literature—not necessarily even writers—could gather. For example, there was the salon of the physicist Sasha Krylomazov—he had a unique collection of literary tapes, because once a week or once a fortnight some writer or other—[Vasily] Aksyonov, for example, or some lesser-known writer—would come and read his work at his salon, and there would be an audience of twelve or fifteen and a discussion would follow, and Krylomazov recorded the whole thing. This went on regularly for years. Of course there was a certain danger, the police arrived once and took down all the information from people's documents—someone had reported that there were these gatherings going on. But there were no very serious consequences.

Then there was a doctor who also had his 'salon', where people associated with the 'sots-art'* movement gathered—Dmitry Prigov, Lev Rubinshtein. Once I remember he put on a wonderful happening, a great spectacle, a celebration for

---

* The term 'sots-art', which combines implicit references to both 'pop art' and 'socialist realism' (often abbreviated in Russian to 'sots-realizm'), was coined by its practitioners in the late 1960s to denote forms of art or literature which played on the established values, images, and narratives of socialist realism, and the sacred rituals of Soviet society, estranging and, in Vyacheslav Kuritsyn's words, 'profaning' them by placing them in an alien, ironic context (see Kuritsyn, 'Postmodernizm: novaya pervobytnaya kul'tura', in *Novy mir*, 2, 1992). The Russian version of 'conceptualism', to which Vladimir Sorokin refers on p. 149, and of which the poets Dmitry Prigov and Lev Rubinshtein, mentioned here, are among the leading practitioners and exponents, is a part of this movement.

all the underground Moscow literati in honour of the fact that Prigov had written 7,000 verses. So he staged a sort of parody of an official celebration, with a proper programme—a pompous ceremony at the beginning, some amateur theatricals, and a concert, and finally a buffet and dancing. I made a ridiculous speech, Prigov read his poems, then there were congratulations from grateful workers and pupils and artists, and we baked an enormous cake with the figure 7,000 emblazoned on it—I remember 15 kilos of flour went into it. Prigov was wearing a kind of military cap, and there was the poet [Lev] Rubinshtein, and both of them in their glasses were leading the dances; it was absurd—a wonderful event.

sl You didn't have a folk ensemble to play?

yp Of course we should have done—but the apartment was rather too small for that, unfortunately! Anyway, there were these sorts of gatherings, in Moscow, and we were all very busy.

Leningrad meanwhile was in a rather special position. In 1981 a writers' club had been set up—'Club 81', it was called—and given semi-official premises for its meetings. All of this was done under the eyes of the KGB, of course; they simply decided that it would be better to gather these writers all in one place than have them scattered everywhere in little apartments. Leningrad had traditionally been a more policed city than Moscow, right from the time of [Iosif] Brodsky's arrest [in 1964], but in this instance it turned out to be freer. So we writers from Moscow would go up there to Leningrad and read in the Club—Victor Yerofeyev, Dmitry Prigov, Vladimir Sorokin too. The Leningrad people got scolded by the KGB— we've given you your own place, they said, and it's bad enough having you lot as it is, but why drag in all these swine from Moscow?

But the Club reduced the pressure a bit because before that there'd been a lot of incidents with the police. For example the episode when Viktor Krivulin* had his manuscripts snatched from him on a train when he was travelling to Moscow—at one of the stations the KGB simply threw him off the train and took all his manuscripts away.

sl Is it strange for you to think of these events now?

yp You know, it's still too close for me to detach myself from it all. Maybe in five or six years I'll be able to think of all this as a curiosity, a trifle—but now it's still too vivid.

sl But not in the sense that you think it could happen again?

yp *That* can't return. Maybe there'll be some other variant—some kind of nationalist, military dictatorship. But restore that ideology, in all its force—that's impossible. The ideology has collapsed as an aim. It exists only in fragments, sparking up now and then when old men and women, hard-line communists, meet up and shout their slogans—but as an all-embracing ideology it doesn't exist any more.

---

* From the 1960s onwards Viktor Krivulin (b. 1944) was one of the key figures in the Leningrad literary underground. In 1975, following the failure of his initiative to publish an anthology of 'unofficial' Leningrad poetry through official channels, he helped to set up the samizdat publication *37* and in 1980 organized a 'Free Cultural Workshop' as a meeting-ground for the city's young poets. These activities inevitably attracted the attention of the KGB, who in 1980 searched his apartment and confiscated his typewriter and manuscripts. The incident which Popov refers to, however, probably occurred later.

Because its representatives, those same KGB people and old communists, are themselves turning into capitalists—so they have a vested interest in not going back either. Once upon a time, let's say, you were the head of some small department in a District Committee of the Party, with fifty bosses over your head, terrified that someone would report you for some misdemeanour, so that although you might fancy the Western way of life you'd keep your mouth shut for fear of losing your position. Now you're your own boss, you've made off with the Party cash and can travel abroad and spend lots of money, even buy yourself a house in the West. So why hanker for the old days? It doesn't make sense.

So no, I don't think it could return although, touch wood! I don't even like to speak of it. At any rate I don't have any nostalgia at all for that era. It was a hateful time. I like to be able to read Krivulin in the newspapers or hear that he's gone on a trip abroad. That's much better than hearing him read his poetry in some tiny kitchen and feeling sorry for him and for all of us.

SL You said that, at the outset, you did have some 'minimal ambition' to play the game and get published. But right from the beginning your stories dealt with 'difficult' subjects—drunkenness, brutality, corruption, official incompetence, not to mention ordinary human despair. The picture of Soviet life they present is comic, painful, humiliating. And none of your narrators can be relied on to offer sensible judgements or solutions. In fact they're at their most suspect when their pronouncements are most unimpeachably 'Soviet'. In the context of the 1970s it was perhaps surprising that *any* of these stories got published—your 'minimal' ambition sounds quite ambitious.

YP Well, for the most part I wasn't published, and that didn't surprise me at all. Although it's a bit more complicated than that. I tried to play by the rules of the game. I wrote what I wanted and sent my stuff to publishers and journals, like any other writer. And in that way I developed a kind of name for myself, people knew there was this writer who lived in Krasnoyarsk.

My situation was much the same as, say, Petrushevskaya's. Both of us got only a few things published at the time, but we were more widely known—at least to editors!—than that would suggest. It was different with someone like Venedikt Yerofeyev, because he never had any truck with official publications at all, he immediately cut himself off from everything.

At the beginning, in the late sixties, I got a few stories published in Moscow under the rubric 'humour'. Journals would take out the tragic side of what I wrote and print the story—roughly a couple of stories a year.

SL What sorts of things would the censors cut out?

YP Well, it was all right to have a bit of drunkenness, a bit of good fun, but death for instance shouldn't be mentioned—that was too much. One editor even suggested a good solution—I could keep the stories just as they were, but transfer all the action to America!

SL I can't imagine *any* of your characters being mistaken for an American!

YP No, I'm afraid not. But then in 1976 I had a lucky break when Shukshin* wrote the foreword to those two stories in *Novy mir*. That was my real beginning, both

---

* The writer, actor, and film director Vasily Shukshin (1929–74): see Introduction, p. xxi.

in the sense that it brought me recognition and because for the first time hardly anything got cut out of those stories at all; they appeared as I'd written them. Shukshin was extremely popular at the time and his endorsement ensured their respectability—he said my stories were 'necessary', which isn't the word I'd use, but it was the sort of thing you had to say at the time. And it was as a result of this publication that I was accepted into the Union of Writers, which I really hadn't expected at all. But these stories and the ones in *Druzhba narodov* the following year were really my only 'big' publications before I got chucked out of the Union and banned in 1979.

SL Did you feel on balance that it was worth accepting the cuts made to your earlier stories for the sake of getting published in some form?

YP It was better than nothing. And I don't condemn the people who tried to make my stories presentable—on the contrary I'm grateful to them, because they did what they could. And after all I was free not to give them the stories in the first place.

SL Shukshin's name is associated with the 'village prose' movement of the 1960s, which lamented the destruction of rural life and traditions in Russia, contrasting the wisdom of simple peasants with the shallowness of urban folk. You decidedly don't belong with the earnest moralists in that movement. But do you feel some affinity with Shukshin—his humour, his liking for 'simpletons', his knowledge of brutal everyday life in the backwoods? A character like your Grandad Pronya, who comes to town and hears a radio for the first time in your story 'The Benefits and Dangers of the Radio',* seems to me straight out of Shukshin.

YP You know, sometimes stereotypes get in the way of reality. For example, Shukshin—who was a great friend of mine—couldn't stand Aksyonov. Outwardly they were completely different people—Shukshin, the village prose writer and Aksyonov, the super-sophisticate and Westernizer. But in fact there were many points of connection between them. For instance the hero of Aksyonov's story 'Half-Way to the Moon' is a real Shukshin character, a simpleton, a *chudak* from exactly the sort of social milieu Shukshin was interested in.

It's very difficult for a writer to judge himself, especially if he lives the sort of dog's life we've had here, where in order to survive a writer absolutely had to belong to one group or another. Shukshin was regarded as belonging to the village prose movement, but if you actually analyse his work you see that his later stories, especially, are much more complicated, they showed the influence of Bulgakov and Gogol. The language he uses in his late work is completely different from that of the conservative village prose writers. Shukshin understood about irrationality and illogicality, 'madness'.

So Shukshin is certainly one of my mentors, my 'masters'—but so was Aksyonov, even though theoretically they belonged to two completely different poles.

SL Perhaps one of the points you have in common with both is a very acute sense of 'Soviet language'. Shukshin remarked on the precision of your dialogues, but one of the most striking features of your work generally is your ability to shift key

---

* 'Pol'za i vred radio', in *Samolyot na Kyol'n* (1991).

linguistically—from officialese to vulgarity to loftiness to whatever. That makes it very hard to pin you down as an author. Are all these forms of 'Soviet language' yours, or are you using them all ironically?

YP   It's impossible to escape that language. Look outside, look at the air out there. Of course one could put on an oxygen mask. But most of us are obliged to go out on the street and breathe the air we're given. It's the same thing with language.

I wouldn't say I used that language ironically. I don't like the word irony. On the one hand the term itself is compromised in the Soviet context. And then it implies some kind of estrangement, as if here I am, sitting in my tower, while everyone else is walking around below, and I'm looking at them through a telescope and laughing at them. But I live here, you see, so I can't do that.

I'd rather use the term that Likhachov* uses to refer to a whole strand in Russian culture—he refers to a 'culture of laughter' which encompasses grotesquerie, and absurdity, and even tenderness, if you like.

SL   The source of laughter in your stories is very often your narrative posture. Sometimes your tone is deliberately 'inappropriate', morally obtuse; your narrator expresses views that are the radical opposite—one may fairly guess—of the writer Yevgeny Popov. Sometimes you adopt the guise of the writer 'Fetisov'—a conduit for bad verse and unlikely plots. But sometimes your narrator bears a suspicious resemblance to Yevgeny Popov himself—and sometimes he even bears his name. How do all these narrators relate to one another?

YP   At the beginning I went along a traditional path, inventing this character Fetisov, who appears in many of my stories, rather like Zoshchenko, who invented Mr Bluebelly, or Pushkin, after all, who invented Belkin as the author of his tales.† But more recently I decided to give myself a more complicated task—to invent a character, but present him as if he were me.

A narrator is always an invention in some sense. The everyday person who stands in queues and the person who appears on paper are always different people. They exist in different spheres of life, they can't relate to one another. I've always been suspicious of people who regard themselves as 'bearers of truth', or, to quote [Aleksandr] Galich, 'I'm wary of people who know who to live.' It seems to me that life consists of various uncertainties, and it's only God that can have the whole picture. No matter how great a man is, he can't see it, because any fact can be interpreted in a lot of different ways.

SL   Another way of saying that is that everyone speaks a certain truth—as the narrator says in the story 'Two Dried Fingers out of Five': 'Everyone is always right.'

YP   Everyone is right in his way. Look for instance at those dreary, grey houses out there. On the one hand what you see is a terrible, nightmarish, totalitarian

---

* Dmitry Likhachov, b. 1906, member of the Russian (formerly USSR) Academy of Sciences, author of numerous works on the culture and literature of Russia from the 10th to the 17th cents., including *Laughter in Ancient Russia* (*Smekh v drevnei Rusi*), co-authored with A. M. Panchenko and N. V. Ponyrko (Leningrad: Nauka, 1984).

† The satirist Mikhail Zoshchenko invented a comic character called Mr Bluebelly (Gospodin Sinebryukhov) as the fictional narrator of his *Rasskazy Nazara Il'icha, Gospodina Sinebryukhova* (1922). The latter's chief characteristic is an inability to adapt to post-revolutionary life, even as he mouths the new slogans of the age. Similarly, Pushkin invented Ivan Petrovich Belkin as the supposed author of his *Tales of Belkin* (*Povesti pokoinogo Ivana Petrovicha Belkina*, 1831).

landscape. But then when you remember what people's homes were like before these blocks were built—how people lived in communal apartments and bashed each other over the head with various kitchen implements—these houses begin to look very fine. Both views are true.

The point is that a character can express any view he wants. A character has no obligations, he's not bound, he has no responsibilities. So by inventing an 'I', I get rid of some of my responsibilities as a person in real life, jostling in the queue. In real life, speaking as myself, with my real name, I've got to watch my words. Whereas my character is more free, he's not in the real world. It's a form of sublimation.

SL In your novel *The Soul of a Patriot* the narrator shares your name, Yevgeny Anatoliyevich—and he also shares your time, your historical experience.

The novel's devoted to one very particular moment in history—the death of Brezhnev—but at the same time it carries a sense of all the weight of Russian history behind that moment: a sense of its cycles and repetitions. What did you set out to do with that novel? What was your aim at the start?

YP You know, when I began this book I thought it might turn into a novel of a thousand pages. It begins with this scrupulous account of the narrator's family, his ancestors. But then life intervenes, and it gets concentrated on the present moment.

It's a new kind of novel, a novel of the end of the twentieth century, when everything has fallen apart, language itself has fallen apart, and truth as well. So instead of writing those thousand pages, and explaining in detail who all these characters were—I realized it was perfectly understandable who they were in any case, their particular identity was not important, and I ended up, in the final toast in the novel, simply by listing them all, listing this whole crowd of people who've lived or are living, establishing a historical link between them simply through the device of this list.

SL Was the novel written concurrently with the events it describes—in other words, did life intervene for you as an author as well?

YP Yes, some of it was written absolutely directly at that moment, the moment of Brezhnev's death. Later I rewrote it, but some of it is to a certain extent automatic writing.

Very often it happens with me that I start with just a phrase of some kind, perhaps some witty remark that I've picked up on the street, and I start writing a story without knowing how it's going to end. Sometimes I have a plot, a kind of anecdotal scheme, but 90 per cent of the time I don't. I start writing one thing and something completely different emerges. And that's what happened with this novel too.

So the first third of the book is an attempt, if you like, at a vertically constructed history, a re-creation of things that have been flung into the past. But at a certain moment this stops, the history stops and we start moving on a completely different, horizontal plane—like in a Salvador Dali picture, where you move surreally from one dimension to another. So whereas hundreds of years pass at the beginning of the novel, in the next part we're dealing practically with just one day, or even a few hours.

SL Did you see the novel as a kind of parody of the classic autobiography—Tolstoy's *Childhood, Boyhood, Youth*, Herzen's memoirs, Paustovsky's? The narrator seems to start off with an ambition for that kind of amplitude and detail—but then gets defeated not just by the intervention of history but by a sense, perhaps, of his own impoverishment, the inadequacy of his language ...

YP The writer can't really invent anything new—there's a given set of plots in life, and the main ones are childhood and maturity. That's why every writer writes about practically one and the same thing—because these things are the essence of literature. But the means of fulfilling that essence are in each case completely different.

As far as language goes, of course, in a sense my narrator is working with a language that's impoverished, grotesque even. The characters in the novel are 'poor' people, if you like. And yet the novel is also an attempt to understand why these people haven't become finally, absolutely poor—crudely speaking, why they haven't finally turned into wild beasts who wander round with clubs and torches, but are nevertheless trying on their own level to hold their own on this slippery slope that leads to the abyss. I'm not ironic about them—about us. Even the title is not intended to be ironic.

SL I take the title to be descriptive: here is an analysis of the soul of a man who for good or ill is deeply bound up with his country, its history, its future.

YP Well, it is that, but at the same time the title belongs of course to the culture of laughter in the sense that we know how the word 'patriot' has been used; we can't avoid its official connotations. But I genuinely like the word 'patriot', as I like the word 'comrade', and it isn't my fault that the Bolsheviks compromised these words and turned them into their own icons.

SL The novel ends with a toast, a homage to all the people whom it has immortalized. In a way the end comes back to the beginning, by giving all these individuals their place in history, memorializing them as characters in a potential epic, even if the epic hasn't actually been written. Do you see it as an optimistic ending?

YP You know, the very last thing that the novel ends with is a question mark—it ends with the words 'Shall we drink?' There, again, I would say that there isn't so much irony as a sense of the imperfection of the world ...

SL And a sense that celebration of any kind must be provisional?

YP Yes—and yet there *is* a celebration, it's New Year, there are pies being baked in the oven, and just for a moment you can forget about all that ugliness and poverty out there. And at the same time something really has happened—Brezhnev has died—and so the future is in doubt, it's not clear what will happen next.

Now we can see that the death of Brezhnev really was a significant moment—because it was the beginning of the end of communism for us. The *putsch* this year [August 1991] was the real end, the real finale. Now, as I say, the word communism in Russia will never have any real meaning again, it will be looked upon as something exotic and strange, much as it is in the West. But the death of Brezhnev was the beginning of the end—not just to oppression, but to that evil atmosphere, to an atmosphere steeped in something fatal to human beings.

SL It also marked the return of 'time'—of history.

YP That's absolutely true, yes, and one had a quite graphic sense of it. The preceding period—before Brezhnev—had clearly been one of great events—don't accuse me of cynicism, but even the Terror and the War were great, cataclysmic events, you could never say that nothing happened during Stalin's time.

Whereas in Brezhnev's time there was none of that, it was as if the country had been drugged, it found itself in this state of oblivion, almost bliss—Brezhnev wandered around, listlessly making pronouncements from time to time, while drunken Russians wandered from shop to shop listlessly cursing Brezhnev. The whole country was drugged ...

SL I see the inconsequentiality of many of your stories—the way they drift off at a tangent or come undone as the narrator decides to go off and have a drink—as a reflection not just of that feeling of timelessness, of not going anywhere, but of the difficulty of being a writer under such circumstances: of constructing a story at a time of non-stories. That seems to me partly what *The Soul of a Patriot* is about. In your account of your wanderings round Moscow with Prigov you parody the pose of the self-important writer, pronouncing judgement and recording history for posterity, but you also mock yourselves ...

YP There are, of course, these elements of parody—you see these two comrades sitting there self-importantly in a bar, naming each other as bards and kings. There are direct hints that they compare themselves to Herzen and Ogaryov, swearing to each other not to let history go unrecorded*—indeed there are references there to James Joyce writing his *Ulysses*, not to mention Dante and the *Divine Comedy*.

But I would say there are elements not just of parody but of playing the fool in the ancient Russian sense—making oneself out to be self-important when one knows one isn't important at all.

SL And thereby mocking other people's sense of self-importance?

YP Yes, and I'm afraid plenty of my literary colleagues do have that sense. They're very pleased with themselves, they discuss important things like the meaning of life and happiness and are ever so proud of themselves, proud of the smart clothes they wear and the fancy suitcases they carry around.

SL Like the writer in your story 'Realism' who comes to Siberia from Moscow and boasts about his beautiful jacket ...

YP That's right. I remember once going to visit a friend who studied at the Literary Institute.† I couldn't get into the hostel where he lived because there was this porter there who kept a very strict eye on everything and wouldn't let people in. In the end I summoned the Komsomol Organizer,‡ and the guy came out drunk and informed me that my friend had been put in a drying-out clinic and was being treated for alcoholism. 'But what's this all about?' I asked this Komsomol guy. 'Why can't I get into this hostel in the normal way just to visit a friend?' And this

* Aleksandr Herzen (1812–70), writer and radical political thinker, describes in his memoirs how he and his friend Nikolai Ogaryov (1813–77) swore a solemn oath on the Sparrow Hills above Moscow not to forget the example of the Decembrists, the group of liberal aristocrats who plotted to overthrow the autocracy in December 1825. Similarly, in *Soul of a Patriot*, the narrator and his friend the poet Dmitry Prigov swear on a bench by the Bolshoi Theatre not to forget the momentous events surrounding Brezhnev's death.

† The Gorky Literary Institute. See note on p. 2.

‡ A member of the Young Communist League (Komsomol) was routinely appointed in such hostels to maintain 'discipline' among the student residents.

fellow, completely sozzled, replied: 'What are you talking about, we have to be guarded here! After all we are future writers—we're going to form the opinions of the nation!' This drunken idiot was planning to form the outlook of the entire nation ...

I think this notion that writers have to be great prophets has destroyed more than one good writer. Rasputin,* for example—the fact that for years he was told from dawn to dusk, Valentin, you're a genius. His every word was hung on by choirs of millions—and that has an irreversible effect on a writer. On the one hand these inflated authorities were created, absolute soap bubbles, official writers—but this deformed the whole structure of literature and affected good writers too. A writer should occupy a more modest place in society. But in those days it was always a case of being judge or prosecutor or counsel for the defence, or a priest, or a political scientist, whatever. As a result writers accumulated such a bunch of obligations that there was no room left in their brains for literature as such.

sl I'm reminded by what you say of the marvellous conversation you have about the meaning of life with the philosopher in your story 'Billy Bones'.†

yp Well, actually I should tell you that one of the protagonists in that story was based on a real person, the late Vladimir Kormer,‡ who really was a wonderful philosopher and writer. He wrote a marvellous article called 'The Double Consciousness of the Intelligentsia and Pseudo-culture'. He was a great friend of mine and a very intelligent fellow, but it was only after he died that I realized how intelligent he was—because usually when the two of us got together it was when we'd drunk a good deal, and I'm sure a lot of our conversations were pure nonsense. In fact usually they were about very mundane details like where you could get more vodka ... so anyway in that story, in 'Billy Bones', I turn him into the Philosopher K. and demand that he give an analysis of the current situation, and he answers me as he would have done in real life, and it creates a comic impression because he says quite trivial things, parodying these people who with serious faces pronounce complete banalities about the current economic crisis, for example.

sl Your writing is full of 'in' jokes and references that could only have been understood by a small circle of people. It's as if, at the time, you'd entirely given up on the idea of having a wider audience—as if you were writing from a hermetically sealed world.

yp In *The Soul of a Patriot* there's even a direct passage about that, a reference to the fact that all of us (though I loathe saying 'us' and 'we') have disappeared a long, long way from the world. It's true, we were sealed off, and the literature of the time reflects this, it's turned in on itself.

Now there's a quite different situation and it's not clear what will happen. [Dmitry] Prigov, for example, is extremely popular, though it's not clear how seriously he's taken. I consider him a great lyric poet, whereas many of his imitators—who come nowhere near his level—have seen him only as a parodist.

---

* Valentin Rasputin (b. 1937), writer. See Introduction, pp. xxi, xxvi.

† 'Billi Bons: peizazh i zhanr', in the anthology *Vest'* (1989).

‡ Vladimir Kormer (1939–87), writer and philosopher who worked as an editor on the journal *Voprosy filosofii* (Questions of Philosophy).

SL In *The Splendour of Life* it seems to me that you carry on—in a sense lay bare—this analysis of your own estrangement as a writer by juxtaposing your own stories with an official discourse that existed in parallel. On the one hand we see your development as a writer, and on the other hand the development of this official discourse whose content changes but whose essence and form don't fundamentally change at all. What changes is your attitude towards this discourse.

YP You know, it was quite strange how that book came about. When I was excluded from the Union of Writers I still had my ticket to the writers' library, so although I was no longer 'official' I went there virtually every day and read twenty-five years' worth of Soviet newspapers. There was this old lady there, a librarian, who was very fond of me. Sometimes I caught her glance, and I saw how she felt such pity for me. I even felt that I was somehow in the way, that I was somehow transferring my misfortune to her—for what normal person would sit reading twenty-five years' worth of Soviet newspapers? I'm afraid it must have made a very sad impression on her ...

But I found it extremely interesting, and I made an extremely important discovery for myself. I discovered that it wasn't true that the Soviet press shied away from talking about certain things. On the contrary, it reflected on every aspect of life. *How* it did so is quite another question. Everything was there—philosophy, rock music, the Beatles, sex—but discussed in a language that made it completely unrecognizable, so that you got a completely distorted picture of the world.

You know there are these halls of laughter with distorting mirrors where everyone appears to be either immensely tall or immensely fat. That's what the Soviet press was like.

I remember for example the story of the Beatles. The first version was that once again the West had thought up one of its routine forms of poison—the Beatles were translated as the 'beetles', and in Russian a beetle is a very bad person, very sly. Next what they wrote was that the Beatles were wonderful working-class lads from Liverpool, and then later on we heard that these good working-class guys from the slums had been destroyed by bourgeois capitalist interests, and we were told all about their depravity, their trials, and so on. Still later they more or less got absorbed into communist mythology; they became harmless 'classics'.

There were a lot of other themes that were treated in this way. And what interested me most was the effect of language, the way that no matter what they wrote about became repulsive in the process; it created this sort of monstrous atmosphere. So what I wanted to do was to show the life of the country through the eyes of the government, through the newspapers ... and in the stories, counterposed with this version, the life of the country from the point of view of one of its inhabitants.

One of the things that the government periodically waged war on, over the years, was vodka. Every time there was this noisy campaign, dozens of speeches, although always from a slightly different angle. One time they said that you shouldn't drink vodka but it was okay to drink dry wine, and then beer turned out to be the best thing, and then it turned out you weren't supposed to drink anything at all ... and on and on it went.

And the citizens would listen to all this, look at it, and spit on it, and carry on doing exactly what they wanted.

Or there'd be campaigns about building more houses for people, and more houses really did get built, more towns. But then everything got stolen that possibly could get stolen. If there were bricks lying around they were absolutely bound to disappear because it was considered they didn't belong to anyone. People would be told, you have to work hard, and they'd say, yes, of course, they'd have to work hard and then they'd go and do absolutely nothing. So there was this complete rejection of official speech in ordinary people's consciousness: you're in power, they'd think, you get on with building communism, and meanwhile if you don't mind we'll just get on with living, because you give us absolutely nothing, nothing.

But on the other hand—and that's there in my stories too—you couldn't help but be affected, and especially in the sphere of language. Everyone's language, mine too, became sullied by Soviet jargon. So a kind of schizophrenia developed: there was this mimicry of the official language, the language of communist ideals, and at the same time there was this utter nihilism, this spitting on everything—let the whole country go to hell—this urge for destruction in the clearest form.

There was this slogan, 'the People and the Party are united', and in one sense it was laughably untrue, but in another sense, objectively, it *was* true—because the People and the Party destroyed the country together. It wasn't that there were the honest masses on the one hand and this wicked party on the other. In the end the masses turned out to be dishonest as well.

SL One of the things that always struck me about the Soviet press was its obsession with order, decency, *prilichnost*. I loved those articles about morality and etiquette; they breathed such a fear of the abyss all around, the horror of *skandal*, the need to keep up appearances.

YP That was very understandable psychologically, because no matter how they twisted their pronouncements and sayings, in the depths of their souls these people understood that they really were criminals and scoundrels—and they slept very uneasily. So your perception is quite accurate. The person at the top of the pile knows very well that he is a thief, and he understands that ultimately there's a higher judge than him, and he is genuinely afraid that one day this higher judge will say, Fedya, you're a thief, and will punish him very severely for it. So people at all levels of Soviet society were really afraid that they'd be chucked into the abyss, and that concerned even—or above all—the strongest people, the biggest bosses. Because on the one hand they would declaim about communist justice and so on, and on the other hand they were the biggest thieves in the country. The idle worker who stole a bit of iron piping was completely innocent compared with Brezhnev who'd appropriated twenty cars and God knows how many villas and so forth for himself.

SL The impression is of hearing a waltz with the volume turned up to drown out the noise of desperate swearing down below. Yesterday I saw this play, *Evening in a Madhouse*, based on the work of the *Oberiuty*—Kharms and Vvedensky, the 1920s absurdists.* And that was just how it ended—with wild swearing on the one hand, and this peaceful music going on at the same time. I was reminded of your

* See note on p. 123.

grotesque scenario for a ballet, 'Deficit'. Do you see yourself as writing in the tradition of those early Russian absurdists?

YP I've certainly thought a lot about the *Oberiuty*; in fact I was thinking about them recently, about the fact that they were the genuine 'socialist realists'. Because through this eschatological sense, this split consciousness, this awareness of the grotesque and absurd they depicted our life as it really was. Whereas the people who were officially called socialist realists were extreme formalists and modernists. They invented an entirely new kind of novel—one in which families discussed from dawn to dusk the need to build new houses, and how you needed to build them from left to right, not from right to left, and in these discussions there'd always be the statutory 'pessimist' and the statutory 'progressive', and so on and so forth. And in fact all this was a kind of élite writing, written on the basis of some obscure aesthetic formula, incomprehensible to most people, whereas strangely enough it was these aesthetes, the *oberiuty*, who captured the real spirit and consciousness of the masses, who strangely enough dealt in a form of naturalism ... swearing and music, just as you say.

SL You said just now that the phrase 'the People and the Party are united' had a genuine meaning—they were united in guilt. In several of your stories the opposite view is taken—or at least, all the characters are determined that they at least are innocent. In 'Aeroplane to Cologne' an official fails to turn up to an important ceremony, and everyone denies it was their fault—the buck gets passed and passed, till eventually it's the secretary Glafira who gets the blame, or rather, the influence of Western bourgeois propaganda on her sexual behaviour. Or in 'The Cold'* it's the freezing weather that's assumed to be responsible for the fact that all the characters drink themselves senseless. 'Because of circumstances that were nobody's fault' is a recurring phrase in *The Soul of a Patriot*—indeed you use it in your autobiographical foreword to *The Splendour of Life*. I assume it's one of those phrases that means the opposite of what it says?

YP If the circumstances are nobody's fault, if they depend on nobody in particular, then of course they depend on everybody together. It's impossible to blame any one person. Who's responsible for the fact that a huge harvest rots away? You could blame the Minister of Agriculture. But he'll say that it wasn't his Ministry's fault, it was the Ministry of Transport that was responsible. And the Minister of Transport will say it wasn't his fault either, there just weren't the necessary vehicles for transporting the harvest. And so the blame extends and extends and gradually evaporates. In the end all you can say is that it's everybody's fault. There's a Russian saying: fear is worse than robbery. We won't get anywhere until everyone starts admitting their share in the guilt, even if they were only passive participants in the whole crime, even if they only participated by being afraid.

Everyone, including writers, is so busy blaming one another now. You were a Communist, they say. Yes, but I wasn't active. But didn't you go to meetings? Yes, I did. Didn't you vote? Yes, I did. But still you didn't take part? Of course it sounds like nonsense. But on the other hand the ex-Communist is right too, in his way, for, yes, he took part in all these meetings, but then he'd go home and listen to the

---

* 'Kholod', in *Samolyot na Kyol'n* (1991).

Voice of America, and he knew that everything he'd discussed at these Party meetings was nonsense.

SL In the old days there was a tendency in the 'underground' to praise everything that couldn't be published and damn everything that could. How do these two 'strands' of Russian literature look today, now that everything can be published?

YP The split no longer exists, and Russian literature has become unified in several senses: we've seen not only the publication of 'underground' works but the 'return' of literature from earlier generations, including the works of *émigré* writers. Not to mention the return of Western classics of the twentieth century, including maybe the most important publication of the *perestroika* period—the publication of Joyce's *Ulysses*. From a literary point of view that was much more important than the publication of political writers like Orwell.

The literature of the underground has now acquired its full legitimacy, as well as that part of officially published literature that was worthy of the name. When people say that all this official literature was rubbish it's obviously not true. There were people to whom God gave this gift and who for this reason or that were able to get published. For example, I very much admire Yury Trifonov, or to my mind the best poet of the sixties generation, Bella Akhmadulina, who lived freely and was able to publish what she wanted and write what she wanted. Although by the end of the 'stagnation' period she had in effect become part of the underground—some of her best work couldn't be published here.

But things have taken their normal course now and for that I'm really glad. Now in a single newspaper you can find a piece by Pyotr Vail, who lives in New York, and a piece by Volodya Potapov who lives in Saratov—and this has ceased to seem exotic.

Mind you, all of this is very recent. It was only a couple of years ago, at the end of 1988 or 1989, that I myself was allowed for the first time to appear on television, together with a critic who's now the editor of the magazine *Stolitsa*. We had to go to a rehearsal for the programme and we gathered that there was going to be some slight reference to the *Metropol'* affair, but it was hinted that we shouldn't mention [Vasily] Aksyonov by name. Without consulting one another we said that we didn't want to say anything at the rehearsal, because we wanted the actual programme to be fresh and lively. So when it came to the live programme, mention was made of *Metropol'* and this critic started talking about Vasily Pavlovich Aksyonov, and a bit later I started saying 'As Vasily Pavlovich Aksyonov once said . . .', and altogether we mentioned his name about five times. So when the programme was over we asked, well, was that all right? And they replied rather wanly that yes, it was okay. But then the next morning somebody rang me, the executive producer, and said with great warmth, 'Yes, everything really *was* okay.'

SL You mean they'd checked in the mean time and got the programme officially endorsed?

YP I think it was more that there was still this self-censorship at the time. Because nothing had been said officially—everything depended at that point on the individual. Now of course Aksyonov is a member of the editorial board of the journal *Yunost'* and the main literary weekly, *Literaturnaya gazeta*, so the whole thing sounds like a funny story. But I simply want to illustrate how that 'exotic' element has gone. Aksyonov is published here and lives his pleasant life in Washington—and that's fine, no problem, there's nothing exotic about it any more. So that's been a real achievement for good literature.

As for the minuses, they arise simply from the nature of writers. The point is that there were just as many scribblers, just as many graphomaniacs in the underground as there were in the Union of Writers. It's as if all of us have been deprived of our rights now. The official writers have been deprived of their material privileges, their status—and the unofficial writers have been deprived of their own peculiar privileges too. They can no longer wear their halo as Dostoyevsky's injured and insulted. And yet many of them are sincerely aggrieved and consider that life has once again been unjust—because there's freedom all around and they're still not published. But the reason is very different now—for the most part it's just because they're no good, not interesting.

Other writers of the former underground simply want to reverse the situation—'Those guys have had their turn in power,' they say, 'and now we want ours.' There's been a terrible struggle for power in the old Union of Writers. But these people fail to understand that the kind of status writers had in the old days has gone for good—and there are no more material privileges to be dispensed these days.

In the old days it was written in honest Russian that the writer—an official writer, a member of the Union—was the helper of the Party, the Party's right-hand man. So it was absolutely fair in my view that the Party should have paid its best helpers—the really orthodox writers—the best money. And it was natural that they wanted to be rid of the dissidents or the anti-Soviets; everything was quite straightforward and logical.

Now there is no Party and there are no helpers, so everyone's on his own now; there are no bosses and everyone just has to get on with the job by himself. That's my understanding of the situation. But it seems to have created a problem for many of the former underground writers. They want their turn in power now too—maybe Uncle Freud should take a look at that.

So what troubles me now is that many people are spending more time quarrelling than writing. Literary material occupies perhaps one-tenth of *Literaturnaya gazeta* at the moment. The rest is just polemics—about whether so and so was a Communist or not. If earlier they were all striving to kiss the Party's arse, now they're competing to show who hated the Communists most. Maybe I'm being a bit malicious—but that's what's happening.

No doubt it's a temporary phenomenon. I see a pattern in our history—the Russian always has to go to a certain limit in his life, that's how it seems to me—and we've come to this limit in literature and now it will all go along on a different basis. Not that writers will make millions or have millions of readers, but 100,000 isn't such a bad number of readers, or come to that 10,000. There's a lot of discussion at the moment about the fact that the circulation of journals has gone down, but if you look at the figures they're just closer now to what they were at the end of the 1970s—it was just a passing aspect of *perestroika* that you could get circulations of one and a half million. Now, with the freeing of prices, books are going to cost more, but the fees for writers should be higher as well, and who's to say it's not fair that the richest writers won't necessarily be fancy intellectuals but the writers of soap operas? The others will have to put up with a modest way of life like everyone else, and they'll have to work hard.

SL So talk of the 'death of literature' here is premature?

YP The Russians have always had two favourite occupations—reading and drinking vodka, and I don't think there's any danger they're going to give up either. There simply won't be these grossly inflated print-runs any more, nor will there be the set-up whereby a writer is provided for by the Party, so long as he behaves loyally, no matter what the quality of his writing. I hope that gradually everyone will come to realize that it's better this way, even if you remain a bit obscure and not very rich and not very influential. At least dissident writers won't have to work as stokers, as they did in the past. The model of the writer-intellectual will be much closer to that in the West, or for that matter in nineteenth-century Russia.

Writers in the last century worked very hard and didn't consider that they were superior to everyone else. So writers today, too, will have to remember that they can do other things besides sit at their desk—they can teach or work on magazines or in television or radio. If a writer really wants to write he'll find ways of earning a living. It's possible also to imagine that in the future there will be a system of grants or subsidies, as in the West. The journal *Solo*, which I'm one of the editors of, has more or less been taken over by a business, as an act of cultural philanthropy—it doesn't bring the business any profit, although it doesn't actually make a loss. This kind of thing will grow gradually. Bad writers will get by writing horror stories and pornography, and good writers will have to make do with glory instead.

That's what I think about the practical future of literature. As far as its content goes—well, the theme of the individual versus the totalitarian government is over now, although people will still reflect on it. Our generation has enough nightmare recollections to last a lifetime. But gradually this theme will wear out, it will become a historical theme—like the colonial wars and the stories of grandfathers in India in your literature. People will become more philosophical about these things, more existential. And perhaps they'll find it's time just to write a simple love story about how a young man came along and fell in love with a girl, and the parents were against it ...

Postscript

SL When we last met you foresaw that the grand political themes of the Soviet era would eventually 'wear out'—and writers might even find themselves writing 'simple love stories' again. Now you yourself have written a novel with a title and plot inspired by one of Turgenev's novels, *On the Eve*. But *On the Eve of On the Eve* isn't exactly a simple love story, is it? It reads more like a comic 'spoof' of Turgenev's romantic novel.

Interview recorded in June 1993.

YP *On the Eve of On the Eve* is part of a triptych. The first part was *The 'Beryozka' Restaurant: Poems and Stories about Communists*, published in *Znamya* in 1991. That was really just a bunch of stories about ordinary life under communism, joined together in a mad *poema*, a poem in prose. *On the Eve of On the Eve* is the second part, and as you say it's based chapter-for-chapter on the scheme of the Turgenev novel; you can recognize the same characters under different names, but the action is all transferred to our times, to the post-*perestroika* period—though some of it looks back to around 1985, and some forward to the end of the century.

Turgenev set his novel in a dacha near Moscow, whereas mine takes place near Munich and all the characters are *émigrés*. One of them, Vladimir Lukich, is rather like Lenin, one of them resembles Gorbachev, one of them's convinced that he's the heir to the Russian throne—and then these three drunkards from Moscow turn up, Dmitry Prigov, Viktor Yerofeyev, Yevgeny Popov. And of course there's the dissident Ipsanakharov who is—as it were—the hero Insarov from Turgenev's novel. He lives in exile in Germany and dreams of freedom, just as Insarov dreamed of freedom for Bulgaria, and there's a love story in my novel too, so you have the whole Turgenev plot. But as far as I was concerned this wasn't meant to be a parody, and it's not 'postmodernism'—if anything it's a parody on postmodernism.

There are plenty of 'spoofs', if you like, but there's a serious side to the novel too, if you look closely. It's meant to be about our times. It's about a world that suits grown-ups well enough—but nobody thinks about the children. Of course, that's been said by Dostoyevsky. But nobody believes it ...

SL I'm reminded of the last line in your story 'A Nice Blockhead'—'Let's at last quit playing the fool. Let's finally be like children!' One never quite trusts that these things aren't said tongue in cheek. It seems to me that you haven't quit playing the fool and the 'Moscow drunkard' yet. The predominant tone of the novel, at any rate, is comic ...

YP Well, if you recall, the lines just before those you cited were about laughter: 'Let's at last stop being melancholy and have a good laugh—openly, cheerfully, happily, lightly ...'

Readers seem to have found this novel funny. It's a bit like *Alice in Wonderland*, a sort of allegory. People talk and drink and talk a bit more, everyone talks about freedom, but nobody does anything—which is just how it is in Turgenev, by the way.

SL Part of the comic effect comes from your mixing the nineteenth century language of Turgenev with contemporary jargon—your characters speak in a mixture of both.

YP There's a funny story about that ... the editor at the publishing house Tekst, who undertook to publish *On the Eve of On the Eve* as a book, told me he'd just like to draw my attention to a few places where my style was rather awkward. He pointed them out and I laughed—they were all Turgenevian constructions, gallicisms of the kind Turgenev used, because his writing was just very slightly un-Russian, very slightly displaced. It's going to be very complicated to translate.

SL In the Turgenev novel Insarov, the revolutionary hero, dies in Venice before reaching his homeland—and we never learn whether his wife, the heroine, really succeeds in transporting his body back to Bulgaria. In your version the hero is struggling to get back to Russia via Finland, but as he approaches Russia he keeps diminishing in size, becomes tinier and tinier—and he's microscopic by the time he manages to get his visa back into Russia. Was his literal diminution symbolic— suggestive of the way that Russians feel themselves 'diminished' outside their own homeland?

YP I don't know—I always write without reflecting, and then think about what I've written afterwards. It's up to the critics to sort out the symbolism. In Turgenev's version Insarov gets ill and starts fading away, but it occurred to me that it wasn't a literal illness—it was just that the fellow started getting smaller.

Anyway, in my version the hero's saved at the crucial moment by a drunken Finn, who manages to sort out his visa problems. That was a portrait of my Finnish translator, a great drunk and a very good friend.

The third book in the triptych is going to be set, strangely enough, at the time of the Soviet–Finnish war, though with hints at the contemporary scene as well. I've been doing research on it in the War Museum, and it's extremely interesting.

SL I can't immediately see what will hold these three works together.

YP No, it's a very complex construction—at the beginning I wanted to write a single novel, but as if written by three different writers. Now I don't know, I think it may be too artificial to join them together, I may keep them as three separate books.

SL All your earlier writing, it seems to me, was deeply informed by the mood of the 'stagnation'—both your melancholy and your clowning were a reflection of that mood. One can't help asking: have you found yourself unsettled, as a writer, by the disappearance of the old life—however glad you may be of it as a person?

YP I don't have any nostalgia for the old days, neither as a writer, nor as a person. I think we still haven't realized fully how that whole period affected us as writers—how much energy was wasted having to think about people who had nothing to do with us, having to hide out and protect ourselves.

It's strange now hearing all these conversations where people say: you've nothing left to write about any more. As if life had disappeared! Or death or love or illness or eternity. Prince Hamlet didn't live under the Bolsheviks—but I suppose he had his problems too.

7

Vladimir Sorokin

(b. 1955)

Vladimir Sorokin is one of the most gifted, and certainly the most notorious, among the group of younger writers who surfaced from the 'underground' in the late 1980s. Their hallmark was a general iconoclasm: the rejection of realism in all its variants; frequent reference to sex, bodily functions, and other taboo subjects; an emphasis on style and linguistic game-playing as opposed to ethical content, and an avowedly detached, ironic stance towards political and social questions.

Sorokin was educated as a mechanical engineer and graphic artist, and until recently has relied on his skills as a book designer to earn his living. He lives with his wife, a piano teacher, and their twin daughters in a tower-block apartment in one of the amorphous modern suburbs of Moscow. In the 1970s and 1980s such apartments were the incongruous meeting-places of a group of writers and artists who dubbed themselves 'conceptualists' and who included, among others, the poet Lev Rubinshtein and the poet and artist Dmitry Prigov. It was among them that Sorokin first made his name, initially as an artist, in the late 1970s.

Like many terms borrowed from the West, 'conceptualism' acquired its own meaning in the Soviet context. As in America, it represented a response to an all-pervasive mass culture. In the Soviet case, however, this culture originated not in commerce but in ideology, deeply permeating the language as well as the visual landscape. The Russian conceptualists took as their premiss that this culture was inescapable: the writer or artist had no language of his own, but must operate within the prevailing system of 'signs'. At the same time, his attitude to these 'signs' was remote and estranged. In the context of his work, the language and symbols of Soviet culture became aesthetic objects, deprived of their original meaning. At an extreme, words ceased to function as such, but were transformed into elements of meaningless sound or arbitrary components of graphic design. In several of Sorokin's works, as in Prigov's, 'literature' disintegrates into typography, a mere pattern of printed signs on paper.

These days such experiments might seem, at least to the Western reader, a bit puerile and dated. But in the Soviet context they were fuelled by more than a fashionable speculation about the possibility of meaning in general. For all his claims to detachment, Sorokin's work, in particular, can be read as a passionate response to a society that lived on hypocrisy and sham, combining grandiose pretensions to moral righteousness with an almost unparalleled capacity for violence. In such a society, language itself gets abused, becoming an instrument of control and denial instead of a means of communication. Violence is done to meaning as well as to human lives.

Sorokin's work 're-enacts' this violence at several levels. His narratives include graphic descriptions of, among other things, rape, murder, incest, cannibalism, mutilation, sado-masochism, coprophilia, and straightforward defecation. The shock these scenes administer, however, derives above all from an incongruity of language. Sorokin typically embarks on his gruesome tales in styles reminiscent of the 1930s socialist realists, the village prose writers of the 1960s, or even Turgenev and Tolstoy. The language employed, the settings involved, evoke comfortable expectations of moral uplift and meaningful resolution. This cosy manner is maintained even as the narrative abruptly departs into scenes of bewildering violence, raving, and obscenity. The effect, even on those forewarned, is shockingly grotesque.

Almost all Sorokin's short stories turn on this device. 'Start of the Season',* for example, tells of two men, young Sergei and old Kuzma Yegorych, going on a hunting expedition in the heart of the Russian countryside. The forest scene is lyrically evoked, and as the two men walk through the woods they talk of themes dear to the 'village prose' movement—the decline of the village, changes in the countryside and the local wildlife. The first sign that something is amiss occurs when the two men fish a tape-recorder out of a rucksack and laboriously fix it to a tree. Presently the husky voice of the singer Vysotsky is heard. The voice acts as bait for the huntsmen's prey, who turns out to be a human being. The story ends with the two men chuckling comfortably and exchanging rustic pleasantries as they swiftly disembowel the corpse and prepare to cook and eat the dead man's liver.

'Passing Through'† begins with similar decorum in the offices of a district Party Committee, where the assembled company listens respectfully to the views of a visiting official, Georgy Ivanovich, from the regional centre. There is talk of factories and percentages, and Georgy Ivanovich addresses these issues in the tone of mixed gravity and camaraderie approved in numerous novels of socialist realism. After the meeting he drops in on Fomin, the head of the propaganda department, with whom he discusses a planned jubilee album devoted to the fiftieth anniversary of a local factory. A dummy version of the album is presented and admired, but suffers badly when, shortly afterwards, Georgy Ivanovich squats down on the office desk and proceeds at groaning length to relieve himself. This procedure is described in graphic detail. The pale-faced Fomin is left holding the results as Georgy Ivanovich, business-like as ever, departs from the office unperturbed.

---

* 'Otkrytiye sezona', in *Vladimir Sorokin: Sbornik rasskazov* (1992).
† 'Proyezdom', ibid.

This pattern is pursued, with imaginative variation, in numerous other stories. Some, like those outlined above, develop the opening setting in considerable detail, and—like their heroes—maintain an aura of unruffled normality right through, even as the narrative turns to torture, murder, or some exotic variety of sexual interplay. Elsewhere the signs of immanent madness are more blatant and immediate. 'Railway Incident'* and 'Competition'† both unravel into obscene gibberish, while in 'Possibilities'‡ and 'Love'§ the opening decencies are dispensed with after a mere paragraph, the rigmarole of an old man's reminiscences being replaced, in 'Love', by a series of dotted lines which give way to words only when the burbling narrator has worked himself into an orgasmic pitch of recollected violence. The dots make plain that the opening rigmarole is literally meaningless, a ritual collection of words that may be abandoned at any moment or replaced at whim by sounds and signs from some quite other semantic realm.

To read these stories, in short, is to find oneself in a schizophrenic world in which the stock characters of Soviet literature—solid officials, eager young men, wry old codgers who have seen a thing or two—turn out on inspection to be monsters and perverts, and where everyday Soviet language—the language of apparent sense and morality—is seen as no more meaningful than the raving of lunatics. The failure of Sorokin's characters to register any 'appropriate' response to the chaos that befalls them leaves the reader, moroever, with a sense of abandonment—forced, so to speak, to bear the shock of the narrative alone.

Sorokin secures our acquiescence in this exercise above all by his gift of mimicry. Herein lie not only his wit but the nightmarish plausibility of his narratives. Their 'realism' derives not only from their conscientious accumulation of detail but from their precise rendering of an accepted style. Narrative conventions, Sorokin shows, exert a ritualistic power over our will to believe—which is why their dismemberment is experienced, shockingly, as a form of sacrilege.

Sorokin takes this mimicry to extraordinary lengths in his novel *Roman*, written in the late 1980s but first published in 1994. Written in classical, nineteenth-century prose, *Roman* is at first sight the pleasant, meandering tale of its eponymous hero, whose name in Russian also means 'novel' or 'romance'. Set somewhere around the end of the last century, it follows the hero through his sojourn on his uncle's estate, where he paints the rustic scene and partakes in various traditional festivities— Easter, haymaking, hunting, mushroom-gathering, and so forth—while meditating on the nature of the Russian peasant and the gulf that separates him from the nobility. These 'genre' scenes, lovingly depicted, occupy some three hundred pages, in the course of which Roman also discovers true love in the form of one Tatyana, and engages in various heroic exploits, including the symbolic rescue of an icon from a burning hut. Finally, however, Sorokin unleashes his own, long-postponed act of vandalism: the novel ends with a series of staccato sentences, consisting of little more than subject, verb, and object, in which Roman, after hacking all the villagers to death with an axe, then disembowelling and dismembering them, proceeds to desecrate the church with their remains and the products of his own body—and in the final sentence (this one without an object) dies himself. With this unexpectedly

---

* 'Dorozhnoye proisshestviye', ibid.   † 'Sorevnovaniye', ibid.
‡ 'Vozmozhnosti', ibid.   § 'Lyubov'', ibid.

literal solution, Sorokin puts paid to two centuries' worth of Russian meditation on the philosophical puzzle 'Who whom?', stripping away the soothing cadences of literature to reveal an underlying grammar of pure violence.

The Hearts of the Four is elaborated at similar length, but here, by contrast, the violence takes little time to surface. Short-listed (in manuscript) for the first Russian Booker Prize in 1992,* this latest novel is set in Moscow on New Year's Eve 1991, and concerns the exploits of its four heroes, who—despite evident differences of age and character—are united by their pursuit of some mysterious 'goal'. Their quest through Russia at the end of the communist era takes them eventually to the radioactive ruins of the Siberian city Chulym, abandoned in 1964 following an explosion at a nuclear power plant. It is there that the mysterious 'goal' is reached. While conversing in a mixture of sentimental cliché, obscure officialese, and pure gibberish, the four central characters engage in a series of bewildering rituals, alternately pampering and mutilating their own bodies while casually disposing of other   people's. Here, as in many of the short stories, the grotesque effect derives not just from the acts described, but from the singular neutrality of the narrative, its failure to shift key appropriately—as if language itself, like the mutilated bodies described, had lost some vital conduit to the heart.

Whereas The Hearts of the Four begins, like the stories, with a scene of reassuring 'normality'—an encounter between a young boy and an apparently benign old man—The Thirtieth Love of Marina (first published in French translation by Lieu Commun, 1987) reverses Sorokin's traditional device, moving this time from chaos to pseudo-decorum. The heroine, Marina, is a nymphomaniac, lesbian, political dissident, and petty thief, the disturbed product of incest and abuse in childhood, who eventually finds salvation through the discovery of orgasm with a stalwart Party worker (her thirtieth lover)—at which point the previously anarchic narrative settles down into the strict wooden tones of Pravda, and Marina becomes a solid Soviet citizen.

If many of these narratives suggest a masochistic element at the heart of the Russian psyche—or in Sorokin's analysis thereof—A Month in Dachau (1991) confronts this issue directly. Here, as he records in his 'diary', the narrator goes on vacation to a concentration camp, where he offers up his body, and a soul freighted with Russian history, literature, and lament, to torture and eventual union with a twin-headed German female. The tone is mystical and ecstatic, cries of excruciating pain alternating in the narrative with invocations to God. Meanwhile the hero's language is similarly tortured: German words increasingly intervene as Russian grammar disintegrates. Here, as in The Hearts of the Four, the hero's physical destruction is seen as part and parcel of his pursuit for spiritual 'salvation'.

It goes without saying, perhaps, that none of the above works could be published in Russia during Soviet times, though several were published in translation abroad. As late as 1992, indeed, the publishers of his short stories (a collection simply titled Vladimir Sorokin) encountered an unexpected obstacle when the first printers

---

* The Hearts of the Four (Serdtsa chetyryokh) has been published since this interview was recorded in the periodical Konets veka (1994).

engaged refused point blank to handle the work on grounds of its obscenity. Since then, the Moscow publishers Obscuri Viri have brought out two further works, the novel *Roman* and its twin *Norma* (a miscellaneous meditation on the notion of the Russian 'norm', analogous to *Roman*'s study of 'romance'), while *The Thirtieth Love of Marina* was published in 1995 by Elinin (Moscow), and other works have appeared in the periodical *Konets Veka* and (most surprisingly) the conventional newspaper *Segodnya*. A screenplay, *Moskva* (Moscow), is to be filmed by the director Aleksandr Zeldovich, and the Moscow publishers Ad Marginem have meanwhile undertaken to publish Sorokin's *Collected Works*.

Surprisingly, however, Russian publishers have been slow to reissue Sorokin's first novel, *The Queue*, first published in Paris in 1985. By far the least 'offensive' of Sorokin's works—and perhaps the least estimated by the author himself—*The Queue* stands on a par with Venedikt Yerofeyev's *Moscow-Petushki* as a melancholy masterpiece of the Soviet era.

The novel employs none of Sorokin's customary shock tactics, but displays at its subtlest his gift for mimicry. Set in a Moscow suburb around the late 1970s, it consists entirely of the conversations, exclamations, sighs, groans, and other sounds emanating from a gigantic queue. It is summertime, it is hot, and the queue, some 2,000 strong, winds round the block, down a side street, and in and out of the courtyards of houses. Night falls, and the queuers, each memorizing his or her place number, dispose themselves on benches round the square. As they drop off to sleep, the pages grow emptier, the last random sounds giving way to blankness as the queue falls into total oblivion. Then dawn breaks, the queue reassembles, and the words on the page resume.

The object of this monstrous queue (like the 'goal' in *The Hearts of the Four*) is never quite clear. At times it seems to be a Yugoslav coat with a special kind of lining, at others a chest of drawers with fake bronze handles or a pair of designer jeans with orange stitching. Whatever the object, it holds the queuers in thrall. Present discomforts are relieved by the prospect of future bliss, the value of whose attainment—like that of communism or heaven—is only elevated by the length of the wait.

Sorokin serves his queue neat. There are no stage directions, no narrative voice, no formally identified characters. But such is his skill in presenting his voices that we are left in no doubt as to who is speaking at any one time or what is happening around them. And amid the general cacophony we soon identify the hero of the piece, following him as he courts a girl, loses her, goes on a drinking spree, and eventually finds salvation in the arms of a woman. The latter not only rescues him from the queue and the rain, offering him unhoped for joys in kitchen, bed, and bathtub, but proves, by a miracle of coincidence, to be the chief purveyor of the very goods he was queuing for.

The sounds of the pair's blissful coupling are graphically reproduced, with the sighs and cries of one partner appearing at various stages upside-down on the page. The same scrupulous care is given, earlier in the story, to recording the list of names in a roll-call of the queue, the quantities of change handed out at a drinks stall, or the grunts of diners in a handy canteen. Here, as elsewhere in Sorokin's work, the language of judgement and discussion gets disenthroned, accorded no more weight than all the other sounds of human life. In contrast to the purposeful, highly edited narratives of socialist realism, *The Queue* presents a form of hyper-realism, in which disparate phenomena are presented all on a par, each with the same indiscriminate exactness.

The lack of discrimination is only apparent, of course, for *The Queue* is tuned and orchestrated with the utmost care. Like all Sorokin's works, it may be read as a devastating document on a society where the human capacity for judgement and meaning has got lost, abused, fatally unhinged. Here, however, the shock of reality is administered with an unmistakable tenderness. No one reading *The Queue* could fail to register an awed and appalled compassion, or to feel the pathos in these creatures' blind acquiescence and heroic patience.

◆   ◆   ◆

SL You've said of your novel *The Queue* that it 'belongs outside the frontiers of literature'. With no narrator, no formally identified characters, can one even call it a 'novel'?

VS In a purely formal sense, I would say that *The Queue* is a conceptual version of the traditional Russian novel that describes the salvation of the hero—for example, Tolstoy's *Resurrection* or Dostoyevsky's *Crime and Punishment*. But it's written in a somewhat different language and the situation is somewhat different. The action, that is, takes place in a specifically Soviet situation—an enormous queue. But it follows the plan of those earlier novels in that there's a central character who is saved by a woman. The hero lands up with her quite by chance—he meets her outside the door of her apartment when he's taking shelter from a rain-storm. But through her, he escapes from the monstrous situation of the queue and finds all his dreams fulfilled.

SL Though it's his body that gets saved rather than his soul, isn't it?

VS Yes, perhaps—and yet the woman gives something to his soul as well. What I wanted to emphasize was the distinction between the public, social world of the queue and the intimate, private one of the woman's apartment. The hero is saved from that outside world and brought inside by a woman. For me this is very symbolic. This contrast between what goes on in the street and the cosy mini-world of the private apartment reflects our Soviet situation in general. That is, the street is the space occupied by ideology, while there's very little ideology in the apartment. I can't say that there's none at all, because all of us grew up steeped in ideology and some version of *Homo sovieticus* remains inside us whatever our particular beliefs or attitudes to the authorities. So it's only to a certain extent that the private world can be contrasted with the harsh, social world. And it's only in a formal sense that this is a novel of 'salvation', because unlike those serious novels by Tolstoy and Dostoyevsky it offers only an ironic kind of salvation, a pseudo-salvation if you like. Because even when the hero's been granted this wonderful thing—this woman, and the goods he's been dreaming of—he remains somehow pathetic and impoverished. He doesn't fundamentally change.

Interview recorded in May 1987.

In fact I should emphasize that there are two main characters in *The Queue*: the hero, and the queue itself. To a certain extent the queue turns out to be the protagonist, the victor in the situation. That's to say, it crushes the particular individual and all attempts to run away from it turn out to be pitiful. We see Vadim, the hero, escaping from the queue, but he's like a rat that manages to crawl into a hole somewhere and sit out the storm—he doesn't try to do battle with the queue itself.

sl Formally you set yourself a very difficult task—to describe a situation and tell a story without any narrative voice. One effect for the reader is that the queue becomes much more immediate—one becomes a kind of participant oneself.

vs Right from the start I rejected any kind of descriptive language—literary language. Because that would mean looking at the queue from the outside, from the point of view of an observer, and where there's an observer there's also a personality—which means there's also a personal literary language. There would no longer be this sense of the multitude, of a single gigantic organism. That's why I wanted to describe the queue in its own language, or rather, force it to speak up in its own language.

Some years ago I got acquainted with the circle of the Moscow conceptualists,* and I was drawn to the idea of conceptual art. In principle the conceptual artist doesn't have his own language—he uses only the language of others, as Andy Warhol, for example, used the language of cliché, mass language. This idea seemed to me very natural; it had an obvious relevance to our situation here, to our attitude towards the language of our state, its literary language. I feel acutely that I can't be *inside* this language, because to be inside it, to use it as mine, means that I'm *inside* this state—and that's something that I've always feared, I've always felt myself to be out on the edge. What I mean is that, for me, the only kind of freedom there is, is the freedom to choose different languages, make use of them, and remain an outsider in the process.

That's why this conceptualist consciousness is so close to us: the idea of remaining in principle non-partisan, refusing to get aesthetically involved. Ethically we've long ago been caught—because we live here after all, we're part of this huge body, we can't avoid that. But aesthetically we can remain outsiders.

sl The queue can be seen, of course, as the perfect symbol of Soviet life, of a life spent in waiting for some radiant future to come ...

vs That's very true. Recently, going past some shop or other, I saw a large queue out on the street. Everyone in the queue looked absolutely vacant, blank, bored stiff. I went up to one of the people in front and asked 'What's this queue for?' and he just said 'They promised'. They promised! It didn't matter *what* they promised, the important thing was the promise itself.

Soviet man doesn't have a present tense. He either lives on nostalgic ideas about the past—imagining the sweet, friendly life people used to live—or on an ideological notion of the future, a future he's continuously striving towards. For seventy years now people in this country have been living on hope, on constant promises. At the first Congress of the Komsomol Lenin said: 'We old folk won't

* See note on p. 126.

live to see communism, but you young people will live to see it.' And this promise was repeated in quite concrete terms right up to Khrushchev's time; everyone wrote that communism was our aim and that it would be realized in the foreseeable future. Now of course the goal has been infinitely postponed, no one talks in terms of dates any more, but it still exists—the slogan hasn't been wiped away. And this means that our actual, real, present life is devalued—it doesn't really exist. People are continually asked to wait for something, starting from the most mundane, ordinary things—you're promised that if you wait just a bit longer you'll get a new apartment, a pay rise, a place for your child at the nursery—right up to things on the global, mystical level: our descendents, if not we ourselves, will live to see the dawn of communism.

It's a curious fact, but if you look around you'll see that we're living in a realm where the culture of *things* is not respected at all. All the man-made objects that surround us have been extremely badly made, as if they're just temporary, makeshift things. Everything, from ball-point pens to aeroplanes, is inferior to the equivalent things in the West. It's as if the manufacturers have said to themselves: here's an aeroplane that will do for the moment; we'll just fly it around for a while, and then later on we'll make something *really* good. All this creates a kind of mythological consciousness in people. It's as if we don't really live here, or we're just sort of incorporeal beings.

SL At the same time we see in *The Queue* that 'real life' isn't totally postponed—it partly gets incorporated within the queue itself: we see people doing business, forming attachments, discussing life, playing games, as well as eating, drinking, sleeping ...

VS To a certain extent, yes. Standing in a queue isn't just existence, it's a form of life, a whole world which has its own laws and its own rituals. Maybe they're rather impoverished rituals, not very varied, but by now they have a history, an evolved form. The Soviet queue goes right back; it began just after the Revolution. In the old days it was called a 'tail'—the present term, *ochered*, meaning 'turn', came in after the war. During the war there were huge queues for bread and people used to write their numbers in the queue on their hands. Sometimes neighbours would swap with each other: so-and-so would stand for one hour, and someone else for another. In other words they'd take turns—that's how the new word arose.

SL Your queue in the novel goes on for several days. Do such gigantic queues really occur?

VS Well, I did see a queue more or less like the one in the book, it must have been around 1975. They were selling American jeans somewhere near the Moscow *Univermag*, the 'Universal Stores'. I was going home late one night, after the metro had closed down, and I saw all these people sitting on benches near the store. Some of them were sleeping, some were smoking, talking. I went up to them to find out what was going on, and some guy told me that this was a queue for jeans. I remember too how my wife and I, just after we got married, decided to buy a sort of kitchen suite, a hideous thing, and got involved in a quite fantastic queue for it. The queue didn't appear to be moving at all. You had to clock in three times a day—at noon, at 3, and at 6. All our names were written down in a notebook, and they'd call them out one by one. I don't remember what our number was—about 700, I think. It took a whole week for us to buy this absolutely pathetic kitchen suite. So what I described isn't pure myth. Nowadays in fact there are more queues than ever, you can check for yourself just walking along the street. I think it's because people have more money to spend these days.

sL Though it's always seemed to me that money as such is relatively unimportant here—the key point is whether 'they' have decided to hand out the goods, not whether you can afford to buy them. If there's something good on offer you'll borrow the cash if necessary—because the opportunity may not come again.

vs That's true. The key word here is 'giving', not 'selling'. The state is supposed to 'give' you such and such, whether it's an apartment or a pair of jeans. You're put in the position of a perpetual supplicant, a petitioner—they're doing you a favour if they sell you something. A Soviet person experiences a feeling of humiliation just by going into a shop. First of all he has to ask the person behind the counter to pay some attention to him, and then get her to say whether something or other is available, and finally persuade her to sell it to him. This happens everywhere. It's what happens with taxis, for example. You wave your hand to catch a taxi, and the driver—if you're lucky—will stop a bit further up the road. So you run up, breathless, to ask if he'll take you where you want to go—at which point as likely as not he says no and just drives off. So at the most trivial junctures you constantly feel this opposition between the power of the state and the needs of the individual.

sL All the characters in *The Queue* seem to accept this situation as the natural state of affairs. Of course they grumble now and then, but they don't fundamentally question the need for the queue or oppose the authorities in any way.

vs No, because every Soviet person drinks in with his mother's milk a fear of the punitive force of the state, which at any moment may be visited on him personally. So you'll never hear any outright opposition in the queue; at most there'll be a few malicious murmurs. I've often heard people in queues cursing the government, but their complaints are always at a very basic level, about the housing shortage, for instance; they never involve some deeper, argued-out criticism. And these complaints are partly just an extension of the ritual muttering that goes on the whole time in the queue: abuse of the government goes on in parallel with phrases like 'Look, they've pushed in again' or 'We're not moving at all'. But right from the start people understand that there's no alternative. So the only thing to expend your own will and energy on is attempting to understand the mentality of the authorities, understand how best to get round them. It's impossible to escape from this reality altogether. Everyone feels that, and that's why they go on standing in the queue to the bitter end.

But as a phenomenon, as a microstructure, the queue's a very curious thing, and it's curious that it hasn't been researched and analysed at all. You could take a psychoanalytic approach to it and see it as a vehicle for expressing collective ideas, the collective subconscious if you like.

sL One can hardly talk of an 'exchange of ideas' in the queue. In a way, spoken language in the novel is represented as just one variety of human sound, on a par with the grunts we make when sleeping or eating or making love.

vs The queue speaks its own language. There are no attempts to make this language literary. I feel very clearly the difference between literary language and the language of the crowd. This language is absolutely not functional, it's ritualistic by nature. Its purpose is not to exchange information or ideas—it's designed for finding one's place somehow in this gigantic mass of people. The way a person speaks and behaves is very important; it gives him his place and his role in the queue. And then this language acts as a kind of glue which holds people together. Because if you deprived them of their voice, the situation would be unbearable for them, even allowing for the fact that these are Soviet people who have grown up in these monstrous circumstances from childhood, who've seen and perhaps even understood everything there is to see. But the act of speech and conversation is the only kind of freedom granted them—the only thing that depends on them alone. So it seems to me that speech itself is a kind of subconscious attempt to withstand this dreadful situation of the queue.

sl The sounds of the queue are reproduced so scrupulously and indiscriminately, it's as if you've simply hung a microphone round the neck of the central character and transcribed the recording, unedited.

vs There's no editing, in the traditional sense, because there's no writer. But it's important that the microphone is hung not just round the neck of the hero, Vadim, but round the necks of everyone. The queue is not just one recording but an endless collection of recordings, including the recording of silence which we see on the blank pages. They represent the time when the tape is running but there are no sounds to be recorded.

sl Do you think *The Queue* will ever be published in the Soviet Union?

vs I don't know and I don't really care. I printed it here myself—admittedly only in one copy—and it's been printed in Russian in Paris, albeit with some changes to the design which I didn't like—but at any rate my bibliophilic ambitions are satisfied. But for some reason I'm much happier about the fact that it's been translated into other languages; I find it interesting to imagine the Western reader glancing in for a moment at a Soviet queue.

Who knows what will happen with the present government—it's a Pandora's box still waiting to be opened. It's certainly out of the question for the moment that *The Queue* should be published here—let alone any of my other books! *The Queue* is by far the least offensive thing I've written.

sl You're in the curious position of having had quite a number of articles written about you, despite the fact that no one can read your work officially in print.*

vs Yes, there was an article in *Moskovskaya pravda* just recently [20 April 1986] which said that I was a malicious fantasizer. I was very flattered, it sounded beautiful, and it's perfectly true. And I wasn't persecuted as a result, because *perestroika* was already under way. If the article had appeared any earlier I wouldn't have been able to avoid some unpleasantness—it would probably have cost me my job, if not more.

sl What do your colleagues know about you at your work?

---

* Sorokin's work began to be published in Russia five years after this interview was recorded.

vs They don't know that I write. If they did they might relate differently to me. So far the rumours haven't reached them.

sl You must feel you lead rather a schizophrenic existence?

vs Yes, it's a double world, a double life.

sl It's strange sitting in this flat, with its view over the hills, and picturing you as an 'underground' writer.

vs Most of the writers in my circle live more or less like me. On the surface, that's to say, they live a normal, quite bourgeois existence. But when we meet up together it's a different matter. I'm very glad that I had the opportunity to meet these people, the Moscow 'conceptualists'. They're very principled people. Each one of them has opened out his own territory, created something that's aesthetically completely distinct and original. I regard them all as classics.

◆   ◆   ◆

Five Years Later

sl When we last met, five years ago, you said that *The Queue* was by far the 'least offensive' of your books, and you were sceptical that any of your work would be published in Russia. Now your latest novel, *The Hearts of the Four*, has been short-listed for the Russian Booker Prize. It's certainly as shocking as anything you've written—an account of various macabre and barbaric acts performed by a group of people who appear, on the surface, to be quite 'normal', and indeed often speak in rather lofty and spiritual terms. What's the novel about? Is it a reflection on the state of humankind generally, or rather on the state of Russia now?

vs Both, probably. But it certainly arose from our 'local' conditions. What I've always liked in the Russian mentality is this combination of mysticism and anarchy, and to a certain extent that's what the novel's about. It's about the hidden content of this closed world—a world of chaos and aggression, but a world of the sacred also. It seems to me that my heroes have this Russian ability to live several different lives at once. I've thought a lot about this problem—about how people here have learned to exist on several different planes simultaneously. A friend might turn out to be a KGB agent and, vice versa, a bad man may suddenly turn out to be a Buddhist. This is typical of Russian metaphysics. You can share a bed with a person but you will never learn about these other lives of his.

There's a good term, nomadism, for our kind of society. My characters, the people in this novel, are nomads, meaning people with no possessions of their own, no property, no shelter. They're continuously on the move, and this is reflected in their mentality.

sl How are we to decode the mysterious rites they perform? And how are we to judge them, if not morally?

vs Maybe one needs to look at them, not even from the point of view of aesthetics, but from the point of view of energetics, of dynamics. Universal moral criteria can't be applied to these characters because their behaviour is actually incomprehensible. They have no obvious motivation. Maybe there's some kind of magic ritual they're performing, but one can't see what its purpose is. Maybe they're mentally ill, and yet in certain ways they appear to be quite sane. It's incomprehensible what it is that forces them to behave in this way, what it is that's directing them—because the final act doesn't reveal anything, doesn't throw any light on the problem at all. And that was precisely the sensation that I was aiming for in this novel.

sl Can you say that this is a society in which such motivation is lacking in principle?

vs I think that's especially true of our society now, post-totalitarian society, because even the last vestiges of a moral code have been destroyed. So that this period—the period that the novel is set in—is like a landscape after a battle. Many people seem to lack any criteria for evaluating reality at all.

sl Maybe it's just more obvious now. Weren't you dealing with the same moral chaos in your earlier works?

vs Yes, probably. I've always been interested by this 'unfixed' nature of people in our society. I'm attracted by it. I lived for eight months in the West, and there everything is the opposite, people are much more 'fixed', and that annoys me there—the fact that people can't permit themselves even for one minute to lose track of themselves. A Western person can't permit himself a gesture that would destroy his conception of himself. All of which is to say that in the West people lead a singular life, and it's a much more open, less shadowy society than ours.

sl Clearly your characters themselves, as you say, are not guided by any moral criteria, at least in any conventional sense. Yet the book is surely calculated on the knowledge of what those universal criteria are—on the knowledge that, by any 'normal' standards, your characters' behaviour is monstrous, grotesque.

vs Of course I understand that reaction. But I see the novel as an attempt in some way to overcome the human world, or rather as a description of an attempt to overcome its reality, to go beyond human relations, human society ... it shows an attempt to go beyond the limits of the human generally.

It's important to remember that there are different kinds of monstrosity, and there isn't a clear hierarchy among them. Rape and murder and so on are monstrous, but who's to say that they are necessarily worse than the activities of some grey *chinovnik*, some Party hack, who issues various decrees without staining his hands himself? The characters in my novel and their various manipulations are indeed monstrous, of course they are, but this monstrosity defines their unhappiness. In a certain sense they are unfortunates, they are tragic individuals.

An image I had in mind with this novel was the image of a single, gigantic crystal which it's impossible to put a bullet through. But if you search and search there's just one place in the middle of this crystalline network, where, if you probe with a needle, the whole thing will fall apart. In principle my characters are seeking this place, seeking by the method of trial and error, because they have no rules to guide them. That's to say, they're typical Russian people who are seeking an answer to the meaning of existence, searching for it in the most tortured, passionate way—searching for this one spot which will make the whole structure come apart.

I should add that I didn't make up anything in this novel. All these horrific manipulations and rituals are completely typical of Soviet man. For seventy years people here have been living according to a new kind of moral code in which killing and torturing and humiliating people is quite okay provided it's in the service of a higher aim. So the behaviour I describe here is completely natural—these characters could quite easily have existed. The monstrosity isn't something I've given birth to myself.

sl   In that sense *The Hearts of the Four* could be seen—like all your work—as a challenge to a particularly vicious kind of hypocrisy, an attempt to lay bare the grotesque underside of a supposedly decent, orderly society.

But it demands to be read on a more metaphysical level as well. The 'crystal' that your characters are probing seems to me to be not just a social structure but an existential one. To 'go beyond the limits of human life', as I see it, means among other things to go beyond the limits of the human body, the condition of the flesh. The human body is seen in your work at its most debased and debasing, a grotesque, comic, torturing prison from which the soul necessarily seeks escape. Is that how you see it yourself? Do you have any respect for the body as such?

vs   Life—including our bodily life—in general seems to me a heavy thing. That's to say—I understand that life's a kind of camp. And of course there are different types of camps with different 'regimes', as they say here—some more severe than others. In the West the regime may be marginally more civilized than it is here. But in principle the world's a camp, and we've received a certain sentence to live in it. Why, what for, is not a question that's generally asked, it's considered inappropriate. All you can do is sit out your sentence honourably ...

sl   What does honourably mean in this context?

vs   Simply that you can't run away. For a start, that would be, so to speak, ungentlemanly. Second, one doesn't know what the consequences might be. Maybe one would have to sit it out a second time. So I try to sit it out honourably; which means also trying to remain a person, not sinking to the level of swine.

But at the same time I don't respect this camp, which consists not just of this country and the relations among people here, but of the body itself, the body which subjects us to so much dependence and torment. So in that sense, no, I don't respect the body. And you are right that this novel—and my other work—is in some way a debate about this problem, the problem of the flesh, of bodiliness.

sl   You speak of your characters as being 'unfortunates', and in some way it seems to me that a compassion for your characters—no matter how monstrous their behaviour—is smuggled into all your work.

vs   I always relate well to my heroes! I don't respect the body but I don't despise human beings. I understand man's weakness and his lack of freedom. Of course the characters in *The Hearts of the Four* perform horrible things, but for me nevertheless they are innocent. They are innocent in their desire to seek an exit from the situation. Almost all my novels can be seen as descriptions of a search for an exit; they are all in some way about the salvation of their heroes.

sl   I'd be interested to know how you relate to Freud. There's such rich material for Freudian interpretation in your work—it's almost as if you're goading us to analyse it in Freudian terms.

vs   I don't regard Freud's work as science, because in principle there can't be a single, scientific description of psychic phenomena. I think Freud's ideas—and Jung's—have to be regarded as metaphors, not as science, and I use these metaphors with pleasure when they seem to me relevant. I think, for example, that it's interesting to interpret history with the help of these metaphors. The Second World War could be seen, for instance, not just as a social phenomenon but as the collision between two collective unconsciousnesses, the Russian and the German, the collision between two collective bodies, or two different psychotypes. For example, you could define the Russian type as genital-masochistic, and the German as anal-sadistic ...

SL　That was obviously the starting-point for *A Month in Dachau* ...

VS　Yes, and it was interesting that that work seemed to touch a chord in Germany. I've been quite surprised in general by how well they understand my work there, and maybe it's because our mentalities are somehow parallel, quite close to one another in certain ways.

Incidentally, there was a curious story associated with the publication of *A Month in Dachau*—you know that it was published—in Russian—by a friend of mine in Germany, the painter Igor Zakharov-Ross. He used to live in Petersburg; I met him back in the seventies when he belonged to the circle associated with the artist Igor Ryukhin. The KGB in Leningrad at that time were terrible, Ryukhin was constantly persecuted, and eventually the KGB set fire to his studio and he died from inhaling smoke. Igor Zakharov-Ross emigrated after that, but last winter, fifteen years on, he was due to have his first exhibition here, in the Tretyakov Gallery. So over in Germany he packed up this huge container with just about all his best work, including around six hundred copies of this book, *A Month in Dachau*, which he'd designed and printed himself. So when this container crossed the border into Russia, around Smolensk, the driver stopped to have a sleep, he got out of his truck, and when he woke up he found that the whole container was engulfed in flames. The only thing the driver was able to grab was his jacket. Everything else was burnt to a cinder. No one knows the cause. It was as if Igor lived under the sign of fire. So nearly all of these books were burnt ...

SL　Unlike any of your other works, *A Month in Dachau* is written in the first person—as if the writing of it was a kind of masochistic act in itself. To what extent do you see your work as an exploration of your own personal psyche?

VS　I've actually written an article on this theme, or rather a kind of memoir about my own early childhood traumas. I'm convinced that virtually all great writers have been traumatized in some way—either by some serious illness or by the early loss of people who were close to them, or in other ways by the conditions they lived in. And I'm sure most writers make use of these early traumas in some way in their work.

In my own case, for example, I remember going through various early erotic experiences, having various fantasies while I was still at kindergarten and being unable to sleep there when I was supposed to. And there was a particularly severe nurse there, a sort of old maid type, who caught me playing with myself and threatened to fetch the scissors and cut off my penis. It was after that that I started stammering badly.

So that was one trauma I remember, and any sort of trauma separates a person from the rest of the world. I have the feeling that in general I dropped out of the world, so to speak, very early on. I had the feeling that I was divided off from the rest of the world by a sort of glass wall—and that sensation formed very early and hasn't changed at all since my childhood. I remember for instance when we were putting our coats on at the end of the day, waiting for our mothers to collect us from kindergarten, I would look at the other children, watch them joking and fooling around, and I felt estranged from them even then.

So I think literature is a way of overcoming this sense of the abyss between one-self and the rest of the world. In general I consider that any creative work—however 'realistic' it is, however apparently impersonal—in some way bears the stamp of the author's childhood. Think, for example, of Dostoyevsky and his hatred of his father, which is evident in some way in all his novels. It seems to me that any really healthy person—mentally healthy—won't feel the need to write. Real literature—creative literature, I mean—has a kind of necessary, forced char-acter; that's to say, it's an attempt to compensate for something that's been lack-ing in the author's life, a way of overcoming some trauma, and at the same time perhaps a form of defence.

sᴌ The 'simple' reader might say: that's fine, write away if it helps, but why inflict all these traumas on other people? To which one might reply that what you reveal in your work is not just the traces of your own 'pathology' as an individual but a reflection of a more general, national trauma. This is a nation that's had to repress a whole series of terrible memories, that's tried to stuff them away beneath a façade of order and decency and euphemistic double-speak, and which has lived as a result with a constant sense of unease and shame and immanent horror. Your work could certainly be read as a kind of amplified record of that experience.

vs I'm not against that interpretation, although it's difficult for me to judge. But I suspect that if that weren't the case, my work wouldn't have aroused such inter-est. I've been very surprised by the interest people have shown; it was quite unex-pected for me, but it may be that I've acted as a kind of vessel or medium, so to speak, for the internal movements of this collective body. By itself the collective body can't speak—it can just give out certain impulses which a writer may more or less unconsciously express, and which his own experience may in some way have reflected or been part of. That's how I explain the interest in my work, because if it were just the record of my personal feelings it wouldn't be of any interest to anyone.

sᴌ One of the most striking things about your work is that you obviously know the language of this 'collective body' inside out. That's what lends an eerie realism, a kind of spurious normality, even to your most violently surreal works.

vs I seem to have some mechanism in me which enables me to identify with 'the masses', to know almost in advance how people are going to think or act. Some-times for instance I can very easily imagine, say when a bunch of people are swearing at each other in the shops, just what words they're going to use next. But I suspect that all of us have this 'mass' language inside us—you only have to turn the right tap on and it will start pouring out.

sᴌ You talked of life being essentially a 'camp' which you have to sit out—a pretty pessimistic view, to say the least! Are those who find satisfaction and happiness in life, or who imagine that they are doing something worth while—are they simply deluded, in your opinion? Are you an out-and-out cynic in that sense?

vs I certainly don't reject the term 'cynical'—I relate quite positively to it. But of course everyone is different, everyone has their own psychosomatic nature. There were people, for instance, who got so used to life in Stalin's camps that they simply didn't want to leave. For them, life in the camps was real life—they were completely unprepared for life outside, they felt that there was nothing to look forward to out here.

sl You've said that you don't despise human beings as such, you feel compassion for them in their efforts to find an 'exit', yet I sense in you a scorn for people's efforts to improve life, to make the world a better place to live in.

vs I feel scorn for attempts to find palliatives. If you wander round any city in the West, look into the shop windows, you begin to get the feeling that death simply isn't reckoned with over there, there *is* no death. Man is born just to consume, to enjoy, to get pleasure—and he's a slave to this consumption. So, after a long stay in the West, that begins to annoy me.

As far as I'm concerned the West and Russia are just two forms of cancer ward. In the Western ward it's as if there's no fear, you're well provided for, you don't feel too bad. Whereas over here the ward is dirty, the beds are rusty, there are no medicines, everything hurts, and there's a gloomy, unshaven doctor walking around and telling you straight out: 'The prognosis is bad.' But at the end of the day I'm not sure which ward is better.

sl I think any cancer patient could tell you which ward he'd prefer to be in!

vs We're all 'cancer patients' in the sense that we're all doomed to die. And I'm saying that I'm not sure it's better to be in a place where death isn't reckoned with at all ...

sl But to reckon with death doesn't necessarily mean to give in to it. If one believes there's something valuable in life, the effort to fight death—if only just to postpone it—isn't pointless.

vs Everyone is free to choose. But as far as I'm concerned these superior medicines and so forth aren't radical enough. Recently, on the other hand, I heard that the Japanese were working on the development of artificial wings ... Now, there's a different matter! That's something that could really give us hope.

sl You've said before that the reaction of your readers doesn't really interest you. Yet it seems to me that all your work is in some sense *about* the relationship between author and reader. I mean that your shock effects are calculated on the breaking of a certain unwritten contract between the two: by constantly violating the reader's expectations, you expose both the nature of those expectations and the way in which the author can manipulate them. In that sense your work could be read as an 'exposé' of literature itself, the mechanisms by which it operates and exerts its power.

vs I understand what you mean—but that's not exactly right. At least, I've never got any sort of pleasure out of shocking my readers. I don't enjoy giving public readings, for instance. And every time a book of mine appears I experience a sense of deep shame. I've never had any feeling of triumph or exultation over my publications. Right from the start, I don't calculate on my reader at all, I count on myself.

I get colossal pleasure out of what I do, but for me the reaction of the reader is entirely mysterious.

SL But you surely know what effect your work will produce?

VS No, because people are quite different. There are, of course, people who are shocked or disgusted by what I write, and then there are others who are prepared for this sort of literature, and their opinion interests me because they're professionals, they're rather clever people, though there aren't very many of them; it's a very small circle that understands what I'm trying to do.

But basically what concerns me is the manuscript itself. When it becomes a finished book, an industrial product, bought by a reader, then it becomes part of a completely different process, one that's absolutely closed and mysterious to me.

SL But what your readers are buying is not just an industrial object, a bunch of pages bound together by glue. They are buying the book as a work of literature, a creative work that expresses a certain view of the world. It's surely disingenuous to say there's no continuity between the reader's and the writer's understanding of what a book is: both understand it as a form of expression or communication, which as such is bound in some way to intersect with its readers' lives or thoughts on life.

VS I don't know why people buy my books! But at a certain level all they're buying *is* a bunch of paper covered in printing signs. And it's important to recognize that, because that's after all what distinguishes literature from life. The people in books aren't real, the things they do aren't real, they have to be judged by different standards.

I always distinguish between ethics and aesthetics. Aesthetics is the realm in which everything is permitted, if only because in life itself far from everything is permitted. What I permit in literature I would never permit in life, but for me there's no contradiction there, whatever the reader may feel. There's no problem for me about morality in literature, because morality ends outside the limits of our body, it ends so to speak where our hand ends. There another space begins. Literature itself is inanimate. It's just paper. It can't do anything to you.

Even my little daughters manage to make this distinction. They understand that they have to separate me as a person from what I write, and that writing is essentially just a private occupation involving paper and ink.

Of course I understand that my readers, especially here in Russia, may have a different idea of what literature is. The relationship to literature has been very complicated here. For example, one printing house refused to print my book of stories. The printers, not the publishers, rejected it! The book was completely ready, all they had to do was print it, but they refused—these workers who are incapable of speaking without swearing in the foulest language. Swearing is the most powerful glue that holds these people together; it's the language of their collective ethics. But as soon as these printers saw these 'bad' words in the context of Russian literature, they were terribly shocked.

Most literary critics here can't stand my work either; they consider it sick; they assume my aim is simply to shock. They can't tolerate simple writing, writing that doesn't respect the great myth of Russian literature. I understand their reaction and I'm not offended by it, but I have to repeat, that's not the level I work on, I get no pleasure out of shocking people.

SL What the critics are referring to—what I'm referring to when I speak of your 'shock-effects'—is of course the device which you established in your very first stories, and which is used in some way in nearly all your works: the device of embarking on some apparently harmless, anodyne story, painting a series of genre scenes in the manner, say, of socialist realism or village prose or classic nineteenth-century realism—and then, at a certain point, allowing the 'plot' to disintegrate into a kind of moral and semantic chaos, so that the characters are found performing a series of barbaric rites even as the same bland narrative burbles on.

In each case the conventional opening could be regarded as a virtuoso exercise in parody, whose ironic intent is punishingly revealed in the outcome of the story. But one senses that this is much more than a literary game for you. For one thing, your 'openings' are so prolonged. It's as if you revel in impersonating the chosen style as completely and convincingly as possible—in the case of *Roman*, you go on for over three hundred pages before the 'attack' is launched. And of course the longer the punishment's delayed, the worse it is—or rather, the anticipation becomes part of the punishment.

VS One critic said that I was actually a genuine socialist realist. He was referring to the same thing, the fact that I set out my stories with such patience. Any normal person, he said, would have started joking long before, making clear that the whole thing was a spoof.

I don't see myself as writing parodies, and certainly what I write isn't just a literary game for me. Many people have related my work to the work of the absurdists, the so-called *Oberiuty*, but in fact I'm a romantic; I'm genuinely concerned with the idea of salvation, as the nineteenth-century writers were, and I see myself much more as the heir to that tradition, the tradition of Tolstoy. If you read Tolstoy, you see there's such convinced madness in him.

But I don't really know why I do what I do. I just do it because it gives me pleasure to be a different person for a certain time. It probably springs from a deep hatred towards myself and a desire to get out of myself even for a moment, to lose myself, to exist for a while in a different guise, with a different mentality. For instance, I've written a cycle called 'Normal Letters', a dozen letters written as it were by mentally sick people, and I got colossal pleasure out of doing that. But there's no element of parody in it at all.

SL Does the language create the person?

VS Yes, undoubtedly, yes. It's by his language that you judge a person. There's no mysticism to that at all.

SL You've said elsewhere that critics have failed to appreciate that socialist realism was, in its own way, a genuine literary movement with its own aesthetic rules and its own masterpieces. For all you've subverted the style in your work—exposed its pretensions and hypocrisies—you've in one sense stuck faithfully to its aesthetic rules. I think it was Aleksandr Genis who said of *The Hearts of the Four* that it was the last great socialist realist industrial novel.

VS I wouldn't say that I was exactly working with socialist realism in that novel— *The Thirtieth Love of Marina* was really the last novel where I dealt with socialist realism as such.

sʟ But what one might call 'Soviet' language and aesthetics clearly remain ...

ᴠs Yes, Soviet language—and it's true of course that socialist realism is a very significant ingredient in that; it's a powerful tradition that has influenced ordinary speech. It's enough to hear the speeches of deputies in parliament today to hear the same inflections that you find in those 1930s novels.

I do think that we haven't yet had time to appreciate the art that came out of that movement. Not enough time has passed, it's still too close. But there were works of genius there—especially in the cinema. In the case of the literature of the thirties it wasn't so much that there were individually great artists, but what's wonderful is the fact that they developed a certain canonical language. Within the genre they wrote identically well, if you can say that!

But in the cinema especially there were real works of genius, like *Volga, Volga** or *Party Card*† or *Happy Fellows*‡ or *Kuban Cossacks*.§ What I love about these films is just their wonderful quality, their professionalism. They really understood cinematography, those directors. Compared to them Tarkovsky¶ is just a child.

sʟ When we first met, in 1987, you said that your writing belonged outside the frontiers of literature. Has literature widened its boundaries since then?

ᴠs Probably it has, but in principle I still have an extra-literary relation to literature. When critics say 'this isn't literature' I'm inclined to agree with them. Unlike real writers I can't be recognized by my style because I have no style of my own. I think if you read, say, *The Queue* and *Marina* together you wouldn't be able to recognize that they were written by the same person. I can only be recognized by my devices.

sʟ Do those devices still work?

ᴠs No, I can't use the same devices any more, and since *The Hearts of the Four* I've deliberately taken a pause in my writing. I was very tired after that novel and I understood afterwards that it represented the last stage of a certain experiment. Crudely speaking, I had exhausted a mine.

sʟ So what happens next?

ᴠs I can't say. I only have a general premonition, but I want to play the game by different rules now. I want to get rid of the harsh modernistic devices I've used up till now. It's telling that at the moment I love reading very un-ironic things. Perhaps irony has started to irritate me.

sʟ Is that connected with the fact that there is no longer such obvious reason for remaining detached from the life of the country itself?

ᴠs Well, that may be one reason. But I think that irony has simply ceased to work here, as it ceased to work a long time ago in the West. In the West it's obvious that irony's simply boring.

---

* *Volga-Volga*, dir. Grigory Aleksandrov (1934).
† *Partiiny bilet*, dir. Ivan Pyrev (1936).
‡ *Vesyolyye rebyata*, dir. Grigory Aleksandrov (1934).
§ *Kubanskiye kazaki*, dir. Ivan Pyrev (1950).
¶ Andrei Tarkovsky (1932–86), internationally acclaimed film director. His films include *Andrei Rublyov* (1971) and *The Mirror* (*Zerkalo*, 1975), poetic works notable for their strong 'spiritual' content and sophisticated approach to narrative.

sʟ Many people speak now about 'the death of literature' as such in Russia.

ᴠs I think they're referring to the end of the myth of the writer. Soviet power succeeded in preserving the myth that grew up around nineteenth-century literature—the Communists made use of it and inflated it even further, turning literature into a government department. A writer became a kind of government worker. Novels, works of pure fantasy, were read and discussed very seriously. Soviet power was the last preserver of this tradition, but now it's exploded and gone for good.

sʟ You've spoken of your liking for a kind of irrationality in Russian life, the combination of anarchy and mysticism. Are you afraid that this element may disappear in Russia as it becomes inevitably more 'Westernized'?

ᴠs I think there'll be plenty to last my life-time! Any change will be very slow; the nation can't simply be reborn, it's impossible. And then there's the question of physical space as well, the fact that physical space here is so . . . unformed. That has its effect as well. And that will never change.

8
Zufar Gareyev
(b. 1955)

Zufar Gareyev was brought up in an orphanage in Bashkiriya (now Bashkortostan), a republic in the Urals that is part of the Russian Federation. Subsequently he served in the army and worked as an unskilled labourer in a variety of jobs. In his late twenties he moved to Moscow, where he continued to earn his living as a porter, loader, and odd-jobs man while getting acquainted with the literary 'underground' and with established writers such as Andrei Bitov and Bulat Okudzhava. Eventually he enrolled at the Moscow Literary Institute, from which he graduated in 1990. Married with three children, he now supplements his income with regular free-lance journalism.

Gareyev started writing young, but his attempts to publish his work remained unsuccessful until the late 1980s, when a few sketches appeared in newspapers such as *Komsomol'skaya pravda*. By that time his manuscripts had already 'circulated widely in narrow circles', and critics alert to new trends began to mention Gareyev as one of the most interesting writers of 'alternative' prose. His real breakthrough, however, came in 1989 with the publication in *Novy mir* of his story, 'When Other Birds Cry', followed by 'Holidays' in 1990. Subsequently his stories and novellas have appeared to critical acclaim in a number of journals, including *Volga, Kontinent, Solo*, and *Znamya*, and his work has twice been nominated for the Russian Booker Prize. A collection of his novellas, *Multiproza*, was published in Moscow in 1992.

Gareyev's prose follows two quite distinct trends. Works such as *Multiproza* (1991), *Stereoscopic Slavs* (1991), and 'Second-Hand Autumn' (1994), together with his (mostly unpublished) one-act plays, belong to what Gareyev himself calls 'game prose': stylistically ebullient, burlesque works that mix the real and fantastic, the lofty and grotesque to present a comic-horrific portrait of Russian life. Such works can be seen as an offshoot of a Gogolian tradition which extends through the absurdists of the 1920s to writers of the 'underground' such as Yevgeny Popov. Several of Gareyev's works, however, are written in a more straightforwardly realistic style and reveal a quite different authorial persona: serious, lyrical, at times even sentimental. In practice, as he suggests here, Gareyev seems to use the different styles as mutual antidotes, alternating between them according to mood.

Multiproza might be translated as 'comic strip' or 'animated prose', and consists, as its title suggests, of quick-shifting scenes in which a great array of characters—a bunch of drifters in Krasnoyarsk, a savage herd of old ladies in Moscow, neighbours of all sorts in tower-block apartments—undergo a series of knockabout adventures, literally losing their heads, gobbling up each other's minds, disposing of each other down rubbish chutes or, in the case of the old ladies, giving birth to identical replicas of themselves, complete with compulsory string shopping-bags. The language in which they converse is rich in oaths, and violent death occurs cheerfully on almost every page.

The prospect of extinction gives rise *en route* to moments of grandiloquent reflection, as when a certain Gnusavy, good-for-nothing in life, goes out in spectacular flames of glory. But for most of the old grannies, at least, the passage to eternity is unceremonious. One sees her entire life 'flash before her' as she dies, but the vision consists entirely of stampeding queues. Another (crushed to death by shopping-bags on a tram) starts her voyage to paradise by trying busily to arrange her own funeral and to retrieve, for sustenance in the afterlife, the freshly bought chicken she has just been forced to abandon. Life is seen as a fraught scramble for advantage, and heaven as unlikely to provide any let-up.

Here, as elsewhere in his 'game prose', Gareyev deals manifestly in types, or stereotypes, rather than in character. The various players may be introduced *en masse* ('a bunch of bearded, balding intellectuals') or, Soviet-style, by their professional or generic titles—'Saleswoman Valentina', 'Old Man Mosin'. But there is no pretence of getting into their minds. Or rather, when their minds are revealed—splattered across the page or snatched and installed inside somebody else's head—their contents mirror precisely the world outside: queues, quarrels, shopping lists, revenge. Individual 'personalities' are swapped, stolen, or discarded, and in a final apotheosis an entire heap of grey, worn-out bodies and brains is seen to decompose into a single featureless mass.

If this vision of life is redeemed at all, it is not so much by the characters' own lapses, now and then, into bathos or enthusiasm, as by the stylish gaiety of the narrative itself. Gareyev's own viewpoint is Olympian: he presents each sequence as part of a swiftly choreographed whole, in which disparate and apparently meaningless events are seen to occur synchronically and to acquire, together, a macabre energy.

This emphasis on synchronicity is evident in an earlier novella, *Park*, in which a similar array of low-life and 'respectable' characters converge, within the space of twenty-four hours, in a provincial city park in summertime. Here, Gareyev plays overtly with the conventions of story-telling itself, drawing comic contrast between his characters' subjective sense of purpose and their 'objective' function in the narrative. We are privileged to a panoramic view in which the various dramatis personae—the emblematic Young Man, the Cleaning Lady, the Comrade who ideally represents the inhabitants of all those five-storey boxes in the town of T.—become unwitting performers in a highly synchronized literary dance.

In *Stereoscopic Slavs*, the idea of multiple coinciding events, or of a single moment seen from different perspectives, is taken one step further. Here, the 'grand perspective' is that of the cosmos itself, and the various parallel scenes are set in motion by a wild magnetic storm that rocks the entire earth. The storm, which flings buildings apart and sends girls in panic running through the city, affords the characters momentary, hallucinatory glimpses of their own condition: thus the sleepy Mikhailov, emerging from the city's ruins into a 'vacuous pink evening', watches his own family pass by in a terrible, ghostly procession and is momentarily pierced by 'the cold of mystery'. 'It seemed as if they were gnawing something as they walked, their jaws working rapidly. Their eye-sockets, veiled with a pink membrane, blind, were fixed upon the back of each other's heads.' But for the most part the various characters remain transfixed in habitual action: leafing through official documents, conducting a slow-motion fight in the courtyard, quarrelling hoarsely in high-flown gibberish, and falling into such deep and befuddling sleep that entire seasons pass them by, or appear, on the contrary, to have occurred simultaneously.

Here and in other works Gareyev offers an estranged vision of his own local species—Soviet and post-Soviet citizens in the late twentieth century—by casting them, not only in unfamiliar dimensions of time and space, but in unexpected literary language. In *Stereoscopic Slavs*, the scene of a fight between a driver and a security guard is described in richly poetic terms, while in 'Second-Hand Autumn' (1994) military officers converse with ineffable sweetness in language blended from the rituals of eighteenth-century courtship and Soviet bureaucratese. While an elderly colonel sits knitting contentedly on a swing, the sunlight flashing on his needles, the cream of the Soviet army is seen sighing and prancing about the arbours and columns of an autumnal garden, and a young Lieutenant, exhausted by love, is transformed into an exquisite statue, astonishing an erstwhile comrade 'with the classical fragility of its arms, and especially the filigree of the fingers forming cupped hands full of diamante sparkle'.

'Second-Hand Autumn' (which was incidentally translated in a Gay issue of the magazine *Index on Censorship*) reads on the surface as a piece of satirical camp—quite extraordinary in a context where any mention of homosexuality was until recently taboo, and the army itself considered sacrosanct. Yet for all its comedy there is a charming innocence about the story, an unsatirical tenderness, as if this fantasy of graceful men, tuned to love one another rather than fight, offered some genuine alternative to the savage, squabbling society that Gareyev depicts elsewhere.

In an interview in *Literaturnaya gazeta* (15 December 1993), Gareyev says that he has always been interested in unconventional relationships, and several of his 'serious' stories deal precisely with this theme. 'Holidays', one of his best and simplest stories, subtly analyses the feelings of an adolescent boy with a crush on a male friend. Unable to express his feelings, the boy spends a dismal evening trailing, with another school-mate, after the friend and his sweetheart. 'When Other Birds Cry' describes a young girl who returns to the village where she grew up and was ostracized as a teenager. Estranged from her parents, she seeks refuge in an old bath house with a boy she remembers from childhood, himself an outcast in the village.

Both these stories are anchored in realistic settings and are rich in unusual, well-imagined detail. The prelude to 'Holidays' is a quarrel in the boy's family, centring on the problem of his deaf old grandfather and the valuable living space the latter occupies in the family apartment. In 'When Other Birds Cry' the tension between the girl and her parents is exacerbated by the presence in the village of a television crew who have arrived on the scene to make a carefully staged pro-gramme about village life, doubling the father's anxiety that his daughter will create some embarrassing disturbance. In both stories, the stifling atmosphere of home is contrasted with the yearnings provoked by the long, empty summer days which are a recurring lyrical theme in Gareyev's work.

'Fever' (1993) is set in summertime in the southern resort of Pitsunda, where a Moscow journalist, Krasheninnikov, is sent on an assignment. Feeling alienated from his wife, who is also spending her summer at the resort, he is drawn to the figure of a barefoot, half-wit girl first glimpsed at the railway station in the company of a young boy, possibly her brother. Curious and disturbed, Krasheninnikov later follows them through the city park to the shelter they have made for themselves outside the town. In the course of his wandering he catches a chill, and in the ensuing fever reviews the central relationships in his life, revisiting—in dream or hallucination—his dead friend Andrei and his unhappy, childless wife. As if removed to another dimension of time and space, his wife ceases to be the difficult companion of his everyday existence and becomes, in his fever, an archetypal vision, 'the small, gentle woman who had been coming towards him throughout her life'. Similarly, the banal, dusty, provincial city park is transformed into a virtual Garden of Eden, a paradise at once regained and known to be lost.

In 'Fever' the parallel presence of this other dimension is signalled not only by the strange girl, who seems to exist outside the boundaries of ordinary life, but by the appearance of an 'ancient, grey bird' that is a recurring symbol in Gareyev's stories. It appears, for example, in *Stereoscopic Slavs*, in 'Second-Hand Autumn', and in *The Allergy of Aleksandr Petrovich*, a semi-fantastic novella in which the hero, an anonymous office worker, is crushed in the opening page by a mysterious force ('a multi-armed, bronze-faced God') and gradually thereafter retreats from the city and from life itself, failing to comprehend the rules by which ordinary people sustain their existence. His sole companions are a stray dog and a little runaway girl; when they disappear, Aleksandr Petrovich gives up entirely, and his obscure demise—signalled by the recovery of his childhood name and his mother's voice—is seen precisely as a return to some other (and better) dimension.

The appearance of identical motifs—the grey bird, ancient trees, seasonal cycles—suggests a fundamental link between Gareyev's apparently disparate works. Works such as *Multiproza* provide a comic, grotesquely stylized vision of the society in which the individuals of his 'serious' stories live, but it is recognizably the same society: one in which human values—love, tenderness, beauty—have got lost in the routine battle for existence. In the midst of chaos, Gareyev suggests, we can either laugh, or drink ourselves to sleep, or struggle to remember that we belong to a bigger, grander universe governed by laws other than our need simply to get by, crush our neighbour, and jump on the crowded tram to work.

◆   ◆   ◆

sl Tell me about your upbringing. I know you come from Bashkiria, but I must admit I had to look up Bashkiria [Bashkortostan] in the atlas, and even then it was hard to find.

zg To be honest I'm rather vague about where it is myself. Basically if you travel due east from Europe to Asia you'll come across this small republic of Bashkiria, somewhere in the southern Urals, south of Perm. And there the writer Gareyev was born. For seven years I lived there in a little village with my grandmother. And then I was put in a children's home in Duvai, also in Bashkiria.

sl Who were your parents?

zg I don't really know. I vaguely remember my mother, but I don't remember my father at all. I stayed in the children's home until I was 17, by which time I'd finished school, and then I left for Ufa, the capital of Bashkiria. I worked at an oil refinery there, and afterwards I served in the army for a couple of years—in the southern Urals, around Perm—which I survived. And then I set off to Siberia, to Krasnoyarsk Territory, near where Yevgeny Popov lived in his famous town of K. on the River E., though I had no idea of that at the time. I lived in the less famous town of Lesosibirsk, and worked there for four years, in the timber industry. It was a very big place for timber.

sl What did you imagine yourself doing, in the future, at that stage of your life?

zg I always wanted to be the person I've turned out to be. That is, even in the children's home I wrote a great deal, mainly poetry. I probably started to write when I was about 14. And I carried on when I was in the army. I used to hide my exercise books in my boots. In one I'd have poetry, in another stories, in a third a big novel I was writing, something *à la* Tolstoy which I later burned; it was awful.

sl Where did you acquire such ambition? Were you a great reader?

zg I was the best-read boy in my class. I was also the smallest and skinniest; the other children looked like giants beside me. But I was definitely the best read. And maybe that counted for more there than it might have done in other circumstances. I was just cleverer than the other kids—cleverer and nicer! Where I got it from I don't know. Anyway, I always had this ambition to write. And you have to fulfil your dreams.

sl What are your memories of the children's home? Was it a terrible place?

zg I don't know. I was an orphan, and it's a difficult fate to be an orphan. But I can't say the children's home was either particularly terrible or particularly jolly. Or it was both. I remember when I was in seventh or eighth grade—around the age of 14, 15—I was very good at physics and mathematics, and once I was sent off to take part in the regional Physics Olympics. And I remember coming back at around nine in the evening to the children's home, and my supper had been left out for me. So I sat alone in the big dining-room and ate this supper, which consisted of a plate of very stiff porridge, so stiff you could have turned the plate upside-down and it wouldn't have fallen out, and a glass of milk and two pieces of bread. But I thought it was very nice. I felt very contented. And I fell in love for the first time in the children's home. I had a lot of romantic feelings. There were the fields flowering all around in spring, in June, and a lot of sunshine, and friends, and my first taste of getting drunk—all those things.

Interview recorded in December 1993.

sl So you didn't have the feeling of being an outsider, cut off from ordinary life?

zg No, I never had that feeling. Sometimes the other boys would say: 'Let's go and beat up the homies'—the kids that lived at home. And we'd start a fight. But it would be twenty against twenty, so you didn't feel lonely.

There was no real feeling of envy, I can say that. But on the whole I don't like to dwell on all this. All my life the one thing I've dreaded is having people feel sorry for me for being an orphan. I've never been able to accept that. Perhaps when I was younger, when I first came to Moscow in my mid-twenties, I played on the experience a bit. I wrote a story about the children's home, and I knew I could have made a whole career out of it, become the sort of Komsomol writer that says how awful it was not to have a mother—pity me! pity me! But I dread all that, I hate it, though objectively it's true that my life has been difficult—earning my living in Siberia and so on.

sl What brought you to Moscow?

zg I had the vague feeling that I needed to go to Moscow, and my best friend, who was also writing, was already here. I'd been living in Siberia hauling timber—you can't imagine, dragging these logs and loading them up for transport, day in day out. That's how I got my muscles. But I was also reading a great deal. I was this sort of weird fool living in a small town in the middle of nowhere and subscribing to all the big literary journals—*Novy mir, Yunost', Oktyabr'*, you name it. And I was also writing a lot—I don't even remember what, novellas, plays—and sending all this stuff to Moscow. Where none of it was published.

sl I imagine your work-mates must have thought you rather odd.

zg Yes. Although they didn't know that much about me. We worked together in the day and then I'd go back home to my rented apartment, and they'd go back to their homes, and there wasn't much contact between us, though I think they regarded me as a pleasant sort of fellow.

sl So what happened when you came to Moscow? Did you already have any contact with literary people there?

zg Well, my first contact was the friend I mentioned, who'd settled in Moscow, got a job as a porter, and was writing poetry. I stayed with him for two whole years. My wages in Siberia had been very good, relative to Moscow, so I had enough money to live for those two years without working. So he and I sat about and chatted a great deal, and went out and met people, and drank a good deal, and I felt very happy with my room in the centre of town. This was in the early eighties. Then the money ran out. And I started working on a building site in Moscow and wrote and went to publishing houses, but with no success.

And then after a while, in 1983, this friend and I decided to go and see the poet Bulat Okudzhava. It so happened that Okudzhava lived in a block very near where we were staying. It was a Writers' Union building, a nice brick-built apartment block with everything you needed—lifts that worked, a proper entrance hall. Whereas we lived in a two-storey building infested with rats where nothing worked at all. But anyway, we went to visit Okudzhava—my friend took along his poetry, I took along my prose, and Okudzhava took an interest in my writing and sent it to the journal *Druzhba narodov*, where, as usual, they turned it down. This was still the period of stagnation, remember.

But then Okudzhava said to me, Zufar, do you think you're the only person who writes like this? And he gave me the phone number of Yevgeny Popov, who read my work and said all sorts of nice things about it, and began showing it around the place. So that's how he and I got to know one another.

sl And before that you'd not read any of these 'alternative' writers?

zg No, because none of that stuff was published at the time, you needed to know people personally. I'd immersed myself in the classics—I adored Tolstoy, I must have read *Anna Karenina* ten times over, and I knew my Shakespeare and Thomas Mann and so on, and now and then you'd catch a glimpse of something else: a fragment of Joyce's *Portrait of the Artist* in the *Foreign Literature* magazine. But in those days we still didn't have Kafka, we still didn't have *Ulysses*, let alone any contemporary avant-garde stuff. But when I met Popov he told me: this is it, here we are, the Russian avant-garde. 'Super-realism', he called it. And he told us there were two decent people around, among the older generation that had established a name—Okudzhava and Andrei Bitov. So we went to see Bitov too. I remember the first time we visited him—we found him sitting at his desk, deep in piles of stuff, manuscripts, bottles, God knows what, and he read my prose and liked it. We even got quite friendly; that's to say I started going to visit him and we'd always find a lot to talk about.

Bitov took an interest in the new generation, his successors—people like me and Valeriya Narbikova,* for example. It wasn't that he singled me out particularly, but he took the trouble to keep mentioning my name among the handful he found interesting, and that helped me a good deal. We've remained friends, he understands me, though I can't say my writing is especially close to his heart.

sl Is his close to yours?

zg Well, in those days, against the background of all those official writers, that grey army of Proskurins and Markovs† and so on, he really stood out—even compared with someone like Yury Trifonov,‡ he was different, a completely free spirit.

When you read Bitov you suddenly had the feeling that there was another world out there—you got a whiff of Europe, of civilization. That's what I always associate with Bitov. He's a genuine European writer. And you felt his freedom straightaway. He could do what he wanted. It's associative writing, he never bothers with plots, but the writing flows along; let's say an apple appears in it and you eat it and enjoy it—that's Bitov.

And I've always enjoyed talking to him. We've had wonderful conversations. But the main thing is that he's someone who understands young people; he's always taken an interest, which is a rare thing.

sl So when did you finally manage to get into print?

zg I had a journalist friend, Yura Sorokin, who was a rising star on the newspaper *Komsomol'skaya pravda*, and he said to me: write us a sketch about bread. At the time I had various odd jobs as a loader and janitor and garbage man, and I went and wrote this sketch about my life and about bread, and they did publish it in

---

* Valeriya Narbikova (b. 1958): avant-garde writer who began publishing in Russia in 1988.

† Reference to Pyotr Proskurin (b. 1928) and Georgy Markov (b. 1911), conservative writers and functionaries of the Union of Writers.

‡ The writer Yury Trifonov (1925–81): see Introduction, p. xxi.

Komosmol'skaya pravda. I'd been trying at that stage to enrol at the Literary Institute in Moscow, and they'd slaughtered my prose; they said it was all wrong, but
then I showed them this piece in *Komsomol'skaya pravda* and they accepted me.

So that was my first publication, and then there were two or three other pieces
in other newspapers. But my stories were rejected everywhere.

sl Did your studies in the Institute help?

zg My studies? I don't know. I went there with the idea that you have to get a piece
of paper somewhere; without paper you're a nobody, and if you're a writer you
should graduate from the Literary Institute. I knew perfectly well that it wouldn't
help me in the sense of helping my creative work, that's to say it wouldn't make
me a writer. And I didn't actually spend much time there, I found the whole thing
boring—all this raving nonsense about Marxism-Leninism. I was there off and on
for six years, graduating in 1990. By that time we'd been through *perestroika* and
glasnost and I'd often thought of chucking the whole thing in, but I decided I
might as well get my diploma. And perhaps it helped me to get officially accepted.
While I was there I published my first story in *Novy mir.*

sl Despite your 'piece of paper' you've continued to earn your living doing manual
work, keeping your job as a janitor. Have you never wanted to switch lanes and
get professional work as an editor, say, or teacher?

zg God forbid! I like my work. I take it seriously. I like being active, shovelling snow
and dirt. I'd do it anyway even if I wasn't paid for it. I feel a physical need to get
outside and use my muscles and use up some energy. It's only then that I feel at
peace with myself, able to reflect a bit. I couldn't bear sitting indoors all day.

But of course the problem nowadays is to earn enough money to live; in a practical sense life is harder than it used to be. So I take what I can get. Recently I've
earned some extra by distributing a publication called *Yeshcho*, a sort of porno-
graphic thing, I'll show you. It's quite funny.

sl You don't object to its contents?

zg Why should I? It's harmless stuff, and maybe it fulfils a need.

sl Your life has certainly given you access to a kind of demi-monde that many of
your readers won't know about—the world of cleaners and porters and builders
and drifters. You've made rich use of such 'types' in your work; you know their
language inside-out. Is that one reason why you've decided to steer clear of
'cushier', professional jobs—to keep contact with this other world?

zg I think the point is more that I'm someone who makes contact quite easily with
all sorts of people; it doesn't matter to me what position they occupy in life or
what strange orientations they may have. I'm quite good at finding the right language to talk to different people and in that sense, yes, I have a rather varied circle
of acquaintances. That's always how it's been with me. And maybe I can draw on
that to convey certain types of language, certain styles of behaviour.

But there's no cunning behind all this, behind my rather marginal kind of life.
To a certain extent the life I lead—and other writers of my generation lead—
hasn't been our conscious choice, it's just been our fate. We don't have the sort of
celebrity that older writers have. In the old days writers like Andrei Bitov were surrounded by foreigners on the one hand and KGB men on the other—the more foreigners, the more KGB men, and vice versa—and then of course the whole of the

Moscow intelligentsia got interested and concerned and tried to help out. But there weren't enough of these people, these foreign specialists and KGB men, to dance attendance on the likes of us; we never had that sort of celebrity, and times have changed anyway—no one can play the role of 'dissident' any more. So we've carried on in our obscurity, doing our jobs as janitors and cleaners, and because that's the life we lead, that's what we write about.

sl You sound almost bitter about it.

zg No, I'm not bitter! That's just the way it is. Maybe those who enjoyed a certain kind of prestige in the old days—on either side of the fence, official or 'underground'—might feel they'd lost something, but that was never my case. I see the present situation as quite normal—no one's going to take special care of us, why should they, so we must just get on with our lives like everyone else, earn our living, and write as best we can and hope to publish our work not in millions of copies but in a decent ten thousand or so.

sl Perhaps 'bitter' is the wrong word. But in your work it seems to me you play ironically on the contrast between life 'above stairs' and below, between the janitor's-eye view and the view of those with, let's say, greater cultural pretensions.

zg It's not so much that I look ironically on all this; the irony is inherent. It's true that I've always wanted to juxtapose, or rather show the irreconcilability between a sort of academic culture in our society and the idiotic absurdity of our actual life. But the point is always to try to bring this life I describe *into* our culture, to see it as part of our culture. That's what I'm trying to do.

sl Of course there's a long tradition in Russian literature of the 'little' man, the humble anonymous man-in-the-street whose obscure, hard fate stirs our conscience and evokes our pity. Your view of the 'little man' is anything but sentimental; sometimes it's even malicious. But do you see yourself in any sense as writing in that mediating tradition, describing the underside of life to a reader who may be ignorant of or indifferent to it?

zg Well, I'm not sure who my reader is, exactly. If anything, I imagine him or her as someone like me, someone who occupies a rather uncertain position in life, who has no vested interests, who's interested in everything and nothing.

As far as traditions go, I've spent my whole life reading the classics, reading them and fighting them off, and no doubt that leaves its mark. Certainly I can't get rid of Gogol, he was the greatest. But the tradition of the 'little man'—I don't see myself there. Objectively my characters—in *Multiproza*, say—may be very unimportant, but that's not how they see themselves. Someone like my cleaning lady at the Kremlin, Klyashchuk, who regards herself as a Minister and writes all these resolutions—'this I'll grant, but that I won't grant'—she's immensely powerful even though she's a nobody. So the idea of the 'little man' is given a sort of absurd twist.

sl Do you see yourself as poking fun at such people—looking at them from a superior position?

zg Not from a superior position, but as an outsider, certainly. The writer is necessarily an outsider, an individualist; he resists being part of the crowd. Indeed anyone who's remotely intelligent and thoughtful is going to feel some contradiction between himself and the world around him, to feel himself displaced, irrelevant, an anachronism.

SL A 'superfluous man', to use another classic stereotype?

ZG Yes, maybe—these types are eternal, though they manifest themselves in different ways. The point is that in real life I'm a nice, ordinary guy who goes round helping old ladies with their shopping bags, but as soon as I take up the pen I find myself cocking a snook at the standard view of these old folk. Of course they're pitiful in a way, our whole life here is pitiful, pathetic, but I don't feel it helps just to go on repeating that, and from a literary point of view it would simply be boring, passé. I'm not interested in simply describing our rotten, ridiculous life. I want to bring a certain kind of gaiety and speed and energy to the thing, not to weep and wail but to give it a certain lightness. And also to show what's true, that many of these people—these old dears and cripples fighting for their kilo of bread—have a fierce kind of energy themselves, they're full of malice and cunning and aggression. They resist our pity; it would be out of place. So I want somehow to capture this energy I observe all around me, the energy of survival, even under the most painful circumstances.

SL I see this kind of hectic energy particularly in *Multiproza*, with its slapstick treatment of life and death.

ZG Yes, it's supposed to be like an animated film, a cartoon. I wanted it to be fun to read. I like cartoons: the dynamics are very fast, the scenes are very short, and they have an easy-going approach to reality. The laws of nature are constantly broken, people undergo numerous deaths and resurrections, because in animation everything is possible; it's like the fable, the fairy-tale. People can eat one another up and tear each other's heads off and get inside one another and carry on gaily.

I wouldn't say it was a new form—there's a bit of Zoshchenko in there, of Gogol—but at any rate I like its lightness. The idea was to speak about this sad, impoverished life of ours in the light way of a child's film, not to speak about it straight but to give that sense of sadness obliquely, more playfully.

SL You say you're not interested in just describing life as it is here, but obviously this Russian reality—the life outside your window here—is your essential source. I couldn't imagine you writing in America or Germany.

ZG Of course this reality is essential to me, I live in it, I'd be nowhere without it. It's like Tatyana Tolstaya says—she can't make do without this Russian absurdity, this strange full-blooded life of ours. If Russia were finished, all of us would be too. But the question is how to describe it, what key to use. Straightforward realism won't do, but it takes a long time to find the right key.

SL Can one speak of a common 'key' that your generation has found—something distinct from that of older writers—or is the 'key' a purely individual thing?

ZG I don't know. When I was younger, ten years ago, I tried to think in those terms, in terms of the style of a particular generation, and it seemed easy then, but if someone asked me to write an article about it now I couldn't do it. I'm rather fed up by now with all these terms—'alternative prose', 'the third wave', 'postmodernism' and so forth; I can't make sense of them any more—I'd rather we just said that such-and-such a work was good and such-and-such was bad, and left out the fancy terms.

Maybe you could say that people like me and Vladimir Sorokin and Valeriya

Narbikova are aesthetes to a greater extent than slightly older writers like Yevgeny Popov. Their generation was orientated by the fact that they were going to be rejected by officialdom, and they attempted to wipe officialdom out of the picture by irony, tried to remove it. I think our generation has been less conditioned by this, or our response to it has been much more oblique, on the level of pure aesthetics rather than ideology. Sorokin, for example, attacks socialist realism by revealing its absurdity aesthetically, from within.

In general I would say that our generation is more playful. Literature for us has been more of a game. The job of rejecting the old has already been done for us; we don't have to fight that fight any more, and in that sense we can afford perhaps to be more individualistic. Certainly we're more playful than the 'sixties' generation. They were much more serious and ideological, more tragic in their attitude to life. Our view of life is maybe less black and white, and that's reflected in our narratives. They're less straightforward, more splintered, they tease the reader more.

But all of this is a generalization, of course.

SL I'm not sure how true it is even in your case. I recognize what you say in novellas like *Multiproza* or *Park*, or in your plays, but some of your stories—'When Other Birds Cry', or 'Fever'—seem to me much more straightforwardly realistic. And there is a strong lyrical element in all your work, it seems to me—a poetic preoccupation with the experience of the natural world, a constant gesturing towards the bigger context.

ZG There are certainly two sides to my work and they reflect a kind of conflict inside me. I feel myself that we may have reached a kind of dead end with our literary games, that the time has come to start saying something serious. We've had our fun, okay, but now it's time to try to say something from the heart, to say what we actually mean. And I think that may prove more difficult for a writer like Sorokin, who has this tremendous facility, but has never written from the heart, as himself. Whereas I've always had this other strand to my work, this more straightforwardly confessional style. Maybe I'll succeed in this direction, at least I would like to believe so. I think that I've kept a sort of naïve principle, something human, and I feel in myself that laughter isn't enough. I know I'm always tossing and turning between tragedy and laughter, and it seems to me that a narrative has to somehow touch both simultaneously. There's a strong sentimental streak in me, I acknowledge it; I know I'm quite capable of laughing ironically one minute and then listening to Alla Pugachova* on the TV and suddenly bursting into tears.

That's why I never belonged properly in what used to be the Moscow underground—people like the poets Dmitry Prigov and Lev Rubinshtein, or Vladimir Sorokin and Igor Yarkevich†—because they could sniff out this sentimentality in my work, a willingness to cry or to grieve. That sort of simplicity is very unpopular among those people I've mentioned; they're even embarrassed about words like love and grief and suffering, these words were excised from their vocabulary long ago. If I appear among them I'm embarrassed to speak about such things, but

---

* Popular Russian singer.
† Igor Yarkevich (b. 1963), avant-garde writer.

when I'm left alone with myself, I understand that I'm stuck with these two or three concepts—the need for happiness, warmth, love.

It's not that I reject what they do, and part of my work belongs with theirs. When I want to have a really good laugh I write a play, when I'm sad I write serious stories—it seems to go in cycles. But I know that I'm not quite acceptable in their circles because I have this other side to me. Maybe I know too much about life; I love life too much for their taste. But I don't belong among the long-faced tragedians either. My writing is too formal for them.

SL You use the term 'confessional' to refer to your more realistic stories. Do you mean that the hero in these stories becomes a vehicle for your own thoughts or experience?

ZG 'Confessional prose' is just one of these terms we've coined. We used to have all these categories—'village prose', 'industrial prose', 'war prose', and so on, and 'confessional prose' was used about people like Trifonov and Makanin to describe what seemed like a new kind of writing, something more personal, stories about individuals, lonely people, people in big cities. Maybe the term 'confessional' is meaningful only in the Soviet context, but for me this kind of writing still has a special sort of charm and tenderness.

The hero in these stories isn't necessarily a reflection of the author, but he must be a thinking person, someone who reflects on himself and his life, an individual and in that sense an outsider.

SL The hero of your novella *The Allergy of Aleksandr Petrovich* is a kind of extreme outsider in the sense that his allergy turns out to be total, an allergy to life itself.

ZG Yes, he's a subtle character, sensitive, complicated, and it's obvious that this idiotic world that he's buried in—this world of jobs and offices and men and women getting up every day and following their routines—he can't fathom out how it works, and it makes him feel physically ill. The world for him consists of allergens, that is of things he rejects—his eyes start to stick together, he feels physically ill. It's another matter that alongside there are things which he loves, for example the dog he gets attached to or the little girl who's also an outsider, who runs away from the holiday camp she's sent to. But they can't rescue each other. The world crushes him, he can't exist in it, and in the end he has to disappear.

SL It appears at the end that he disappears back into his own childhood; he recovers at the moment of death his childhood name and his mother's love—as if the source of his allergic state were a kind of orphanhood, a sense of being nameless.

ZG There are no allergies in childhood! It isn't quite clear what happens at the end, whether he has physically died or not, but there's this beautiful evening sky and the voices of mothers calling their children home and among them the voice of his mother, so his name is mixed with theirs in the sky ... I would like to think that he's died, that he's disappeared from his own suffering body, that he's become this disembodied name flying away up there, where everything's clear and peaceful again ...

But all this was decided, of course, on the level of sensation, of intuition. I'm not quite sure what it means; I'm a bit embarrassed by the pathos of it—though at another level I'm not ashamed of it; I'm glad to have kept these simple feelings.

SL In *Allergy* we see the hero attracted to a little runaway girl, and in 'Fever' the hero is drawn to a half-witted waif he meets in a southern town. Indeed, something similar happens in your early story, 'When Other Birds Cry', where the 'heroine' escapes from her parents' home and spends the night with a down-and-out. What is it that appeals to you in these characters?

zg I think what's most characteristic about 'Fever' is the sensation of summer in the story, a very strong, almost erotic sense of the heat in the little town, the park, the station—and the half-mad girl is in a way the medium through which we experience all this. The girl is intent on getting to know this summer, she loves it so much, loves the trees, loves life flitting by, loves it physically, and that's what's important to me—if there's a beautiful sunset it's never enough for me to say, 'look!', I want to be able to do something with it, to get inside it, to disappear in it. And I think you feel this in her—this almost physiological blending with the air, the heat, with a kind of quintessential summer.

But the story is also about the hero's sense of being somehow rootless and unsettled himself; that's why he's attracted to these wanderers. He wants to escape from this real world into some other realm, and these mysterious waifs—the girl and her brother—seem to beckon from another world, to promise something, to offer a whiff of something different. That's why he follows them, and the whole story develops—he catches a chill and develops a fever, and in his fever he begins to see his own life, and the lives of the people close to him—his friend, his wife—in another dimension.

What interested me, what I was curious to try to describe, was this sense of two parallel dimensions, two parallel times that exist side by side. There is real, ordinary, physical time but there is also, especially in the finale, another, metaphorical time in which real people and places become identified with something ancient and mythological. His wife is no longer the wife he quarrels with in real life but some archetypal woman, the woman he's dreamed of all his life, and the park in this provincial town in summertime becomes a kind of paradise.

sl In this story, and in others, the existence of this parallel dimension seems to be signalled by a mysterious, rather sinister bird that keeps returning and flying silently overhead. Who or what is she?

zg I think you're right that this strange, grey, ancient bird, a bird of prey, is a sort of sign—a mark of this other dimension. It flies and flies, somehow above time, and it no longer has a name because the people who named it have long since died, the language they spoke has been forgotten, the libraries have all burned down. So it's a symbol of—of eternity, I suppose; I've always wanted there to be some breath of eternity in my stories. I don't like the sort of concrete prose that's about the present moment or the last three years, I'm not interested in writing that sort of thing. I'd like to be able to commune with this other dimension myself, so that I could see my tasks in some other context. That's my sense of the world. So it's not surprising that there are these ancient birds flying around or the cosmos yawning overhead, or that Aleksandr Petrovich should disappear among the relics of trees which have been growing there ever since ancient times.

sl In several of your works—notably in *Stereoscopic Slavs*—you suggest the contemporaneity of these different times by eliding the seasons, making them appear to happen simultaneously. One feels not so much eternity here as the collapse of time, its disappearance into a single moment.

ZG The collapse of time and the collapse of subject—that was what I was trying to play with in this story. My idea was to deal simultaneously with several different actions, several different plots, all of them combined at one point, like a *matryoshka* doll that contains several different dolls in one. That's the meaning of stereoscopy. It creates an illusion of solidity from disparate images. I look now at one point, now at another, and when you combine these different angles it's as if it's simultaneously summer and autumn and spring, and yesterday and today.

SL The 'action' in this story takes place in the midst of a wild magnetic storm—the cosmos rages and howls and sweeps at least one character away altogether, buildings collapse, the whole of the earth is illuminated in one great flash. But what creates the peculiar hallucinatory character of the story is that down on earth—on a very recognizably Soviet bit of earth—all the characters appear to be in a kind of trance. In the midst of jotting down some bureacratic resolution, or mumbling some incomprehensible nonsense or having a fight in the courtyard, they keep dozing off. They seem mired in a kind of tragic sleepiness, as in a dream when your limbs get paralysed. Is this—as the title suggests—a peculiar Slavic characteristic?

ZG Of course it is, that's why Slavs are particularly prone to this kind of stereoscopic vision; they love to drink and fall asleep, and sometimes they sleep so long that by the time morning comes it's already winter, and if they drop off again it'll be April in no time; they lose track altogether.

That's why Russian literature is so full of dreams, because of this eternal Slavic sleep. Vera Pavlovna's dream,* the dream of Oblomov ... the heroes of Russian literature are asleep half the time.

SL Tatyana Tolstaya has eloquently evoked this sleepiness as well, and I've noticed with her that it's generally the men in her stories who are prone to doze off and dream. Would you agree that men are the dreamier sex?

ZG Perhaps they are, but it's not just a question of sleepiness. These dreams in Russian literature generally have a great literary burden, an intellectual burden, and if they're given to men it's maybe because men at some level are more complicated than women, they have more of a yearning for—this other thing, more of a yearning to fly off into the cosmos. In ordinary life, in love and so on, a woman is more flexible and intelligent and understands better what's going on, but when it comes to philosophizing—that's more the province of men. But in general I'm not that interested in these gender questions. I think what we're talking of here is a Slav characteristic, a national thing.

SL What other characteristics would you add to your mental 'anatomy' of the Slav?

ZG I don't know. Perhaps the habit of making written declarations. That's something I love about Russians. They're always sitting down to write some pronouncement, to set out a resolution, to grant some great favour or make their protest.

SL Like Gogol's Bobchinsky and Dobchinsky, wanting the rest of the world to know that they exist.

---

* A reference to the heroine of Nikolai Chernyshevsky's revolutionary novel *What is to be Done?* (*Chto delat'?*, 1863). In fact, Vera Pavlovna has four dreams in the novel, the most famous of which is the last, which became prescribed reading for generations of Soviet school children because it presented a vision of the 'radiant' future to come.

zg   Yes, but it's not just wanting people to know you exist—the typical thing is to complain, to declare that things should be done not this way but that way. In one of my plays the heroine spends the whole time making these sorts of declarations. She wants to make clear her view that this or that—the fact that someone went to Moscow and bought a cake and someone got killed in the process—that this is a violation of order, it isn't proper. So I think that's important—this sincere belief of the Russian man in the power of paper and ink.

sl   And a strong sense of what constitutes 'propriety' and 'order'?

zg   Yes, but above all the belief that you can bring order to chaos simply by writing something down. Gogol described this peculiar kind of mentality. It's not exactly that the Russians are passive; on the contrary they can act heroically and actively—but only in extreme situations: a fire, a war, a famine. *In extremis* they're capable of performing wonders, but as soon as the crisis is over, they no longer know what to do, so they fall back into this endless reverie, musing and pondering. But in actual fact they're no good at thinking, the Russians, that's why they tend to collapse into this sort of sleepy passivity.

But the flip side of this is that they can suddenly be awakened to a kind of furious energy over nothing, over something quite idiotic and meaningless. I have this friend who lives in Chelyabinsk, and one day, for no reason at all, someone denounced him as a spy, and this accusation stuck to him so fiercely it was almost impossible to shake it off. Because once someone tells the KGB you're a spy, they'll work on the case for the next twenty years. It would never happen that the KGB looked into a case one day and dropped it the next—sorry, old chum, we made a mistake. No, they'll cling on to it like a dog with a bone, and they won't let go till they've gnawed it to shreds. So that's maybe another Slav characteristic—this eagerness to expend tremendous energy over something completely absurd.

The trouble with Russians is that when the crisis is over, in normal peacetime, they desperately need some rules to exist by, some set of instructions handed down by authority. They can't wait to get to work and start making denunciations and opening files. And once they've got started they'll go on fulfilling instructions and carrying out orders into eternity, into outer space.

Maybe it's a sort of slavery, maybe it's just laziness, but the Russian just doesn't want to think for himself—it's so much easier when someone just says to him: do this. Why are Russians so afraid of thinking? That's the mystery. Maybe one trouble is that we've grown too fond of our own absurdity. To an outsider Russian life might look pretty grim and terrifying but to us it's always been good for a laugh. We've had horror after horror in our history, *putsch* after *putsch*, but when we're not crying we're either drunk or laughing. I drank through the *putsch* of 1991, and now here comes Zhirinovsky* and the whole thing seems a farce. I don't know what's to be done with us before we wake up and say, my God, this is really serious ...

---

* Vladimir Zhirinovsky, leader of the ultra-nationalist—and misleadingly named—Liberal Democratic Party, founded in 1990, which did unexpectedly well in the elections to the State Duma (Parliament) in December 1993. Zhirinovsky had called among other things for the incorporation into the Russian state not only of the former USSR's republics but of Poland.

9

Viktor Pelevin

(b. 1962)

Viktor Pelevin is one of the most popular young writers of the 'post-Soviet' era. His first collection of stories, *The Blue Lantern* (1991), sold 100,000 copies, and in 1993 was awarded the 'small' Russian Booker Prize for the best collection of the early 1990s. His subsequent novels and novellas have been published in the prestigious monthlies *Znamya* and *Novy mir*, and his work has been translated into Japanese and several European languages.

Born and brought up in Moscow, Pelevin was first educated as an engineer and subsequently graduated from the Moscow Literary Institute. He now earns his living free lance, supplementing his literary earnings with journalistic and inter-preting assignments. In this respect, as in others, he is one of a new breed, arriving too late on the scene to partake either of the privileges conferred on official writers under the old regime, or the ironic camaraderie of the erstwhile 'underground'. In his tastes, too, he belongs to a generation that has sought philosophical and cultural alternatives outside the traditional Russian canon—in Chinese philosophy, in Buddhism, in the strange perspectives of computer science, the experience of hallucinogenic drugs, or the 'mystic' or esoteric works of Castaneda, Hesse, and Borges.

These influences are evident from Pelevin's first collection of stories, many of which have a fantastic premiss, taking some ostensibly other world as their setting, or describing the inner lives and adventures of Soviet-style werewolves, talking chickens, or a farmyard barn possessed of soul and feelings. All in some way ques-tion conventional boundaries: the separation of life from death, the animate from the inanimate, the real from the imaginary, the 'I' that perceives from the universe perceived. At their core is a puzzle about the meaning of that 'I' and the extent of its freedom. We are both much less free, Pelevin suggests, than we imagine ourselves to be—and yet less free than we might be, could we but understand ourselves and our situation properly.

What makes these stories distinctive, however—what gives them charm—is their peculiar 'realism'. The riddles of existence are here filtered through the unmistakable experience of everyday Russian life, or, vice versa, we sense that they arise naturally out of that experience. However apparently exotic the setting or the characters, we feel ourselves in familiar territory: for the landscape is that of Soviet Russia, its high-rise blocks, its fume-filled air, neglected playgrounds, and dusty, rutted highways; the characters, whatever guise they assume, speak with the same troubled jocularity or wistful intensity as ordinary Russian citizens. And if they are peculiarly susceptible to physical mutation, to sudden switches of perception or anxieties about the meaning of life, it is in part, surely, because their surroundings impose such melancholy limitations. Their very concreteness invites the question: is this all there is? And if there's such a thing as 'beyond', where is it and how do I get there?

Two of the finest pieces in *The Blue Lantern* implicitly relate the author's metaphysical reflections to the experience of growing up in Russia. In the title story, a group of boys at a summer camp lie awake in their dormitory at night, thrilling and frightening each other with stories of death. They are hypnotized, in particular, by a tale in which the hero comes to realize that everyone around him, though apparently going through the motions of life, is in fact already dead; slowly it dawns on him that he himself can be no exception. The narrator of 'The Blue Lantern' then offers a variant on this theme, bringing the moral closer to home by offering to his friends a story set in their own summer camp, where the children, magically sent to eternal sleep, proceed to live out the rest of their lives in dream. The story concludes with the boy-hero gazing at the mysterious blue lantern outside the window, and failing to notice when he himself has drifted off to sleep.

The notion of growing up as a gradual drift into unconsciousness, or into a state of imprisonment made tolerable only by the dimming of sensation, is spelled out in a beautiful essay included in the collection: 'The Ontology of Childhood'. Here and elsewhere, Pelevin writes with great tenderness about the freedom of childhood, the intensity of its perceptions, and the loss in adulthood not only of those perceptions themselves but of the successive selves that experienced them. That process is universal, and yet there is—so Pelevin's work suggests—something peculiarly dispiriting in the trudging routines of Soviet adulthood. Its attendant disillusionments are the more poignant for the fact that romance, in childhood, was attached so loyally to things that later proved shoddy or make-believe—perhaps even seemed half so at the time. The eager curiosity of boys, their scrupulous attention to the craft of things—particularly to emblems of adventure and glory, like model spaceships and heroic posters—are constantly evoked in Pelevin's stories, as if he still mourned the loss of their appeal, their innocence, and the boyish tribute they once exacted.

This in part is the theme of Pelevin's novel *Omon Ra* (1992) whose eponymous hero dreams, as a boy, of becoming a cosmonaut, to that end undergoes a bizarre training programme, and eventually gets launched on a supposedly 'unmanned' mission to the moon. At its simplest, the novel can be read as a satire on Soviet pretensions to technological splendours way beyond their means: Pelevin's version of the Soviet space programme includes not only standard amputation of the cosmonauts' legs (a tribute to the legless hero of a popular wartime novel), but making do with space-suits padded out with baby's blankets, pedalling a moon-walker adapted from a bicycle, dining on Chinese corned beef in outer space, and accepting one's own death as a routine part of the mission. An unintended survivor of this exercise in Soviet-style sacrifice, the hero emerges alive from his 'moon-walk', only to find himself back in the familiar network of the Moscow under-ground. The stars, it turns out, are as far away as ever.

Woven into this melancholy spoof, however, are the metaphysical riddles that haunt all Pelevin's work. The hero's invented name—which combines the falcon-headed god of the Egyptians with the acronym for a particularly savage detachment of the Soviet police—signals the twinned images of confinement and flight that run throughout the novel. The hero finds himself at various times forced to crawl the length of a corridor in a gas mask, buried underground in the secret headquarters of the cosmonauts' school in Moscow, hunched in a cramped space over his 'moon-walker' and emerging to freedom in an underground tunnel. As messages about our lives, these images require no spelling out. Yet within these dark spaces, Pelevin suggests, our freedom is potentially limitless. The universe is not 'out there' but contained within us. In a sense, cardboard and make-believe *are* all that is required: as a child, the hero achieves perfect flight in the wooden aeroplane of a Moscow playground, while his friend and *alter ego* Mityok, drugged and strapped into a chair for a sinister 'reincarnation check' at the training school, hallucinates himself into half a dozen different epochs and personae before eerily disappearing from life altogether. His fate, we realize, isn't necessarily worse than that of the hero, a dogged survivor in our everyday dimension.

Mityok is one of the several friends-cum-doubles who serve to initiate Pelevin's heroes about the meaning of life. Khan, in the novella *The Yellow Arrow* (1993), plays a similar role as mentor and prompt, jogging the hero into consciousness of his position as a passenger, this time, on a train bound ultimately for a ruined bridge. The train appears to encompass the whole of human life; most of the hero's fellow passengers, long since deaf to the perpetual clicking of the wheels, take their habitat so much for granted that they fail to register it at all. Indeed, it takes some time for the reader to identify the cramped location of the story, such is the lulling, easy movement of the narrative.

Pelevin's gift, here as elsewhere, is to furnish his abstract premiss so naturally that it assumes all the contours of 'normality'. True, life aboard the *Yellow Arrow* bears a particular resemblance to the not-entirely-normal life of the ex-Soviet Union in the 1990s: half the passengers are on the make (or take)—trading in nickel melted down from carriage doors, constructing shady deals around ashtrays and toilet paper, or trying to turn an honest rouble with manufactured kitsch. But as they go about their everyday business—attending the Upper Bunk avant-garde theatre, leafing through Pasternak's *On Early Trains*, or disposing of their dead through the com-partment windows—Pelevin's doomed passengers appear only slightly more absurd than the rest of us, wilfully ignoring the puzzles of our existence just as they wave off the peculiarities of theirs.

Khan's mission is to keep the hero, Andrei, from drifting into the same fatal com-placency as his fellow-travellers. Slowly alerted to the 'messages' that surround him, Andrei eventually succeeds in making his escape—in momentarily stopping the train and walking away from it. As he does so, the train ceases to be a symbol of life in Russia or life as such, and is seen rather as a vehicle for habitual consciousness (or unconsciousness): 'The rumbling of the wheels behind his back gradually faded, and soon he could hear quite clearly sounds he'd never heard before—a dry chirping in the grass, the sighing of the wind and his own quiet steps.'

An awareness of precisely those natural sounds was one starting-point for *The Life of Insects* (1993), written, as Pelevin describes in the interview that follows, after a summer spent in the Crimea. The novel is set in a shabby Crimean resort, with its tawdry 'video bars', its faded posters on abandoned display stands, its landscape of rusting wire fences, tin cans, and weeds and its 'dance-floor filled with writhing, steaming bodies, like a bus at rush hour'. As if to emphasize the death of Soviet ideals, the road from the resort leads past 'a foundation pit with the ruins of an unfinished building . . . [like] a grave for a building that had died'.* The characters who haunt this battered landscape belong, once again, to the rogues' gallery of 1990s Russia: pimps, prostitutes, drug-addicts, racketeers. Their peculiarity, however, lies in the fact that all of them double as insects: one moment functioning capably as post-Soviet humans, the next sporting wings, six legs, and a pair of mandibles.

Pelevin, a specialist in such transformations, engineers these metamorphoses with consummate skill, and presents his strange heroes with an endearing tenderness. The novel consists of several intertwined stories, each of which functions as a separate parable: the tale of the scarab beetles, condemned to push a giant dungball through an obscure 'dung world'; of the moths, forever flying towards the light, and the mosquitoes, who stay alive on blood. Sometimes the characters change species: the prostitute Natasha, who started life as an ant—the offspring of an accordion-playing officer from Magadan—rejects life in her mother's cramped, stuffy burrow and transmutes into a fly. In a more evident progression to higher things, the twin moths Mitya and Dima—purveyors, one assumes, of Pelevin's own Buddhist-inspired philosophy—discover within themselves the principle of light, and turn into fireflies; while Seryozha, who was born to be a cicada, narrowly escapes the drudgery of life as a cockroach, emerging—in an epiphany that recalls the ending of *The Yellow Arrow*—into clear air on 'a windless summer evening, with the purple clouds of sunset gleaming through the trees'. Here again, consolation is offered by the suggestion that, if only we attend hard enough to the inmost working of our beings, an exit into meaning can be found.

If 'reality' is elusive in these tales, it becomes even more so in Pelevin's latest novel, *Chapayev and Emptiness* (*Chapayev i Pustota*, published, after this interview was recorded, in 1996). Somewhat grandiloquently, Pelevin has said of this work that 'it is the first novel in world literature whose action takes place in absolute emptiness'. His description puns on the name of the novel's hero—Pyotr Pustota, or 'Peter Emptiness'—implying that the action takes place entirely inside the hero's head. This, at any rate, is a plausible reading of the novel's fluid narrative, which shuttles the hero to and fro between the dreams of his fellow inmates in a

---

* A reference, perhaps, to Andrei Platonov's great novel *The Foundation Pit* (*Kotlovan*, 1929), which saw with tragic clarity the lethal effects of Stalin's efforts to 'collectivize' the nation.

post-Soviet mental hospital, and his other life as adjutant to the legendary Bolshevik commander Chapayev* in 1919.

As Irina Rodnyanskaya has noted in a perceptive review of the novel,[†] Pelevin here 'corrects' the popular view of Chapayev, transforming him into a Buddhist mystic who acts (like Khan in *The Yellow Arrow*) as a guide to the hero's experience, awakening in him the realization that all reality is a species of dream, or the product—as Rodnyanskaya puts it—of some 'collective visualization'.

The philosophical underpinnings—more apparent here than elsewhere in Pelevin's work—are not particularly original, and may or may not appeal. But what commands our attention—and, in a sense, belies the novel's message—is the very 'reality' of the images Pelevin evokes. If the narrative has the lawless fluidity of dream, so too its scenarios occur with dream-like vividness: convincing, substantial, undeniably *there*. As in all Pelevin's works, the scenes which linger most in the mind are those which, one senses, hold the author's own imagination most in thrall: a drawing-room in 1918, still furnished with an open grand piano; an abandoned country estate, to which the hero is taken to convalesce, or the ceremonial 'office' of a Japanese businessman who, with the florid courtesies of a bygone age, puts the dreaming Pustota through a series of delicate trials, including composing a haiku in the open air at night and tying an imaginary steed to a tree somewhere, one gathers, on the outskirts of modern Moscow.

Pelevin's imagination is labyrinthine, and he has a natural story-teller's gift. One suspects that he grew up telling himself and his friends the kind of strange tales recalled in *The Blue Lantern*; a certain boyishness survives in his humour, his liking for sudden *frissons*, his rather distant view of the adult human emotions that propel most literature (almost all his principal characters, it might be noted, are men or boys), even in his solemnity. But these are tales for grown-ups too—those, at any rate, prepared to countenance Pelevin's disaffection with conventional 'grownupness'. His fantasies are redeemed by a lyrical grace, and have about them the gravity of felt experience.

◆   ◆   ◆

SL Although you began your writing career in the 1980s—already in the era of *glasnost*—you're a 'product' of the Brezhnev era, and many of your stories evoke the dull, melancholy atmosphere of that time. How do you feel it touched you personally?

VP I don't know. I was an ordinary boy, an only child; I grew up in Moscow with my parents; my father was a military officer and my mother an economist. I wouldn't say my writing had any particular connection with my experience as a child. Though I liked riding my bike, and that comes into *Omon Ra*. The hero is riding his bike along the highway, and suddenly he finds himself pressing the pedals of this imaginary moon-walker. That's how I felt. I was always riding and riding to reach fresh air.

Interview recorded in December 1993 and June 1994.

* Vasily Chapayev, killed in action in the Civil War, was immortalized by the Vasilev brothers in their 1934 film *Chapayev*, based on the novel by Dmitry Furmanov (*Chapayev*, 1923).

† '. . . I k nei bezumnaya lyubov'', in *Novy mir*, 9 (1996).

I was touched by this monster of socialism like everyone else. When I was 16 I entered an institute of power engineering—if you went to an institute you could get out of army service, which was like doing two years in gaol, so I went to the institute and I came into contact with the Komsomol [the Young Communist League] there. In those days there were only two roles to choose from—either you joined the Komsomol or you were an Enemy of the People and you got expelled. So everyone joined. Everyone faked it, faked their allegiance, faked what they said. If you asked an improper question that was it, you were out. So I've tasted all that. I got very good marks, at least in the first year. After that I stopped going to lectures and borrowed notes from the girls or just trusted my luck, and I did all right. But you could feel this pressure almost physically.

sl Do you mean you lived in fear of the authorities?

vp No, it was a matter of disgust rather than fear. You felt disgusted with everything. But the difference in those days was that you could put up a kind of barrier to protect yourself. All of us knew that the state was evil. Evil was concentrated on the other side of the barrier. Now evil is diffused everywhere; it's no longer possible to locate the source of it. Or to say who the goodies and the baddies are. So life was simpler in those days. It was simpler partly just because I was younger, but also because—well, for one thing it was easier to be an expert in those days. Standards weren't high. But also because the state participated in every aspect of your life, it controlled what you did, it told you what to do. And that made things easier in some ways. It's hard to be totally responsible for your own life. You feel uneasy looking out of the window if you don't have a regular job and a ready-made programme.

sl So do you feel a certain nostalgia for that time?

vp No. I didn't like living under communism. Of course it's better to live under Adenauer than under Hitler. Maybe there are a few *babushki* around who feel nostalgia for the old days, but it's simply nostalgia for their youth.

sl After you graduated from the technical institute you joined the Literary Institute. Did you gain anything as a writer from your studies there?

vp No. The dream of every student at the Institute was just to make connections. Now I don't need those connections, and it's odd to think back to it. But that was the point. While I was there I started working as a journalist and I set up the 'Myth' publishing house with some friends; we published a few books, including an anthology of contemporary literature, but I packed it in last year.

These days you have to take every chance you can to earn hard currency. So I work for foreign magazines and interpret for foreign correspondents and sometimes do broadcasts on Radio Liberty. And I've translated some occult books into Russian.

sl You're obviously keen on the occult and mysticism.

vp Yes, I read a lot. I'm not a practitioner! A sorcerer tries to influence others. I'm trying to influence myself ...

Anyway the point is that you can't make money as a writer here these days, no matter how famous you are, and even if your books are published in thousands of copies. I sold 100,000 copies of my book of stories, *The Blue Lantern*. If you published that number in the West you'd be regarded as a great success, but there's no money to be had in it here. The only hope is to get your work translated so you earn some hard currency. You don't need that much, although Moscow is very expensive now. People are charging as much for apartments here as they do in Manhattan.

There's a kind of hard currency élite in Russia now, with everyone else just trying to hang on and survive. It's made a big difference to the mood of younger people. Kids now are much more materialistic than they used to be; their only goal is to make money. It was different for us; we grew up in another country. I feel now that I'm slowly emigrating along with all my compatriots, slowly leaving the past behind. We even have a new language, a new slang—people for instance use the word *bucksy* for dollars.

But it's not as if we now live in the West. Everything is much harsher and crueller here. Just to compete in business you have to have criminal connections—the whole society is more criminalized. The point is that this was never a real socialist society, in the way that Sweden, for example, is. There's no culture of kindness in Russia. People here are much crueller than they are, say, in America. America went through this pioneer stuff two centuries ago.

SL Your work appears to have little in common with that of the 'unofficial' writers of a slightly older generation. Did you come into contact with any of the former 'underground'? Did you know their work?

VP No, I've never mixed in any of those literary circles. There was never any question of my joining the 'underground' because it was already *perestroika* by the time I started publishing at the end of the eighties and I never had any problem getting my work into print. But in general I don't have many literary connections. I don't understand these people, or maybe I understand them too well. They're full of intrigues and struggles. Whereas I think literature should be a refuge, a shelter. Maybe it's bad for one's career to look at it that way, but that's how I feel.

I can't say I've read much recent Russian literature. I certainly can't name any particular influences. I liked Bitov's *Pushkin House* when I read it at the time—this romance with nineteenth-century Russian literature that Bitov had—but I doubt whether I'd want to read it now. I like Iskander, his early work that he published in the Soviet era, because it has some real warmth. And of course writers from earlier in the century—Bulgakov, for instance; I was deeply touched by *The Master and Margarita*.

But I'm not interested in most of the younger writers. We share the same world, but we see it differently. I don't like postmodernism; it's like eating the flesh of a dead culture. People like Sorokin I don't care for. Basically he has only one trick—after you've read one story you don't have to read any of the others. It's destructive writing. Somebody had to destroy socialist realism, but now it's dead and you can't keep feeding off it. And in a sense the real socialist realism is more interesting than the parodies of it. It's so weird to read that stuff now.

Who else? I like what I've read of Zufar Gareyev. He's got some peace in him, some calm, and I realize I felt happy reading him. A writer should be a kind of transmitter who connects this time with eternity. That's something Gareyev does.

But I think I've been more influenced by foreign writers. Aldous Huxley, for instance—I like his essays a lot; and Hermann Hesse, *Steppenwolf* especially, and Carlos Castaneda ... and various more obscure people, occult writers.

SL Your writing is certainly more accessible than that of the former 'alternative' or 'underground' writers. You're a natural story-teller, for one thing. Did you set out to write in a more 'popular' vein?

VP No, of course not, but it pleases me that I'm popular and that ordinary people like to read me. You see, it's quite hard to compete with 'the mainstream', with famous names like Vladimir Makanin who get published in the big Moscow journals and receive prizes and all that sort of thing. Not that I see myself as competing, but it's hard to get into *Novy mir* or *Znamya*. So I'm pleased about that, but, you know, it's even harder to compete with the pulp fiction that's printed in hundreds of thousands of copies these days. So I'm even more pleased that I'm able to compete with those trashy writers.

But I don't deal with the reader when I write, I mean while I'm in the process I really don't care whether anyone's going to read me, I block it out, it's a personal thing. In fact I hate absolutely everything about writing except for the few moments when you experience something that's very hard to explain, something that's much better than any drug. I don't think you can get that if you set out to be a best-selling writer and write one book after another, trying to take into account the public's taste.

To me it's quite surprising that they read my books here at all. It's not that I underestimate myself, but it's as if you live in a cave and you have this very peculiar religion which no one in the world shares, and you are the high priest of this religion ...

SL So you write the rules?

VP Well not just that, but you perform the service, you invent the ritual. That's what writing's like. It has nothing to do with what critics write about. Critics have been quite kind to me, but that doesn't alter the fact that most of them are incredibly stupid, mean, venomous.

What I like about writing is that it's private, and you don't need anything to do it. It's not like shooting a film when you need a crew, lights, cameras, loads of money. As soon as you need money and people you're not free, whereas here, in literature, you're absolutely free. You're—not exactly God, but you can create something out of nothing, you can create a whole other reality and transform it into anything you want. There are some rules which govern this world, of course, but if you know them it's really very nice ... It's a kind of trick, I think anyone could do it if they really wanted.

So I like this process of inventing, but I have to admit that I'm not really interested in literature as such. When I read other people's fiction I often can't help thinking 'someone's made this up', and then I start wondering why I should read it. I see the trick, I see how it's done and I can't get absorbed in it. You can't really respect something invented by another human being.

I think in general there's been a trend away from pure fiction; non-fiction is becoming much more popular. What I mostly see in fiction these days is 'irridescent mediocrity', to use Cyril Connolly's beautiful expression. Whereas non-fiction, even if it's not very distinguished, at least contains some information about the world, there's something true behind it. And just the knowledge that it's based on truth transforms every sentence, makes every thought seem more valuable.

So the trick is to make an unreal story real, to make fiction seem like non-fiction, and if I manage to do that one sunny day, I'll be a happy man. Real literature has this quality of being 'true' without really being true. It has to have a certain pressure behind it to achieve that, and it's a miracle when it happens. Everything in life makes sense when you feel the presence of this miracle.

So for me writing is like arbitrarily digging a hole in the ground, not knowing whether I'll find this treasure or not, not knowing whether this miracle will take place or not.

sl Does the 'pressure' you speak of mean telling the truth, in some way, about yourself?

vp Maybe. You know, a writer from Armenia once said to me that there are basically two kinds of writers: those who write about themselves and those who write about other people. I belong to those who write about themselves. I know that I'm using the contents of my own psyche, and that if you do that you have to be honest. That was what was wrong with the entire literature of socialist realism— just that it wasn't honest.

I don't have characters as such in my work. I know that I can write only about different aspects of myself. Every person contains a universe. That's not a metaphor, it really is like that—and at the same time he's contained within this universe too. I'm quite sure I could tell everything about you, just writing about myself, and you could tell everything about me just by looking at some aspect of yourself. What makes people different is the exact point at which they look, and if you are able to shift your gaze it means that you can create other characters and make them real.

But that's not the point for me. There are certain rules to writing, and the main rule is that what you write must be interesting to read.

sl But you've just said that you don't take readers into account when you're writing.

vp Whether your work is interesting or not isn't something that you can arrange. It's just a quality of the writing itself. It does have to do with honesty. If you write honestly, if you write in a way that genuinely interests and corresponds to some part of yourself, it's bound to be interesting to someone else. But making it interesting shouldn't be your objective.

sl You started your career writing short stories and have since turned to novellas or short novels. Do you have a preferred genre? Do you know in advance the scale of a work?

vp A writer has a certain natural distance. I like to write short stories, twenty-five pages, thirty maximum. A novel for me is a kind of necklace which consists of different stories threaded together. I just get bored, you know—I can't imagine how people write novels of 800 pages describing the life of a single person. What interests me in literature is some specific energy, and a single story can contain the same amount as a novel.

sl You've talked about the trick of making non-real things seem real. But you set yourself a particularly hard task in that respect by starting out with manifestly 'unreal' situations—people and things in your stories undergo supernatural transformations or live in worlds seemingly governed by laws different from ours.

VP But the point is, it doesn't matter what subject you take. There is this thing that just makes literature literature and if you can get to it nothing else matters. Your characters can be insects or wolves or whatever. I have this novel about people who turn into insects, and if I described it to you just like that you'd think it a pretty stupid idea—what are these creatures supposed to be? And how did these transformations take place? That's what I'd ask myself. But the point is to write it in such a way that you don't feel the need to ask these questions, you feel the pressure of the story, it touches you somehow.

By the way, I was just thinking about this—it's an interesting question, whether the result of a writer's work is material or not? You see the nice thing about art is that the real product isn't material: what you really produce when you write are feelings, human feelings, the things your readers experience when they read your work.

SL What was the starting-point for *The Life of Insects*?

VP I like insects, and I wrote it because a friend of mine presented me with a small book, a beautiful, glossy book on American insects with very nice illustrations in bright colours. So I read it carefully and I didn't really need any more, because this book, showing you these nice insects and giving you some interesting details about them, served as a kind of notebook for me. So in a sense I felt I didn't have to write the book, or only had to write a small part of it—the basic chapters were already there. Although there were certain things I excluded—for instance a chapter about this plant which eats flies. I thought that might become a bit gloomy and morbid. Anyway I don't know how it all works in a literary sense, maybe it's not that good, but in my world it's still a source of warmth to me; I feel that the novel emanates warmth.

In fact I like it much more than anything else I've written, not because I don't see its shortcomings, but because it's something very personal; it's connected in my mind with the place I describe in the novel and the summer I spent there. It's a place in the Crimea called Karadag, a little village with a sanatorium, next to a volcano. It's near the resort of Koktebel, but much quieter—Koktebel's just a little Moscow, there's no point going there if you want to get away.

I wrote *The Life of Insects* just after I'd spent the summer there, in recollection of the summer, so it has this private association for me—it's like when you catch some fragrance and suddenly remember the situation where you smelled it the last time, and all sorts of things come back to you that you thought you'd forgotten. For me the novel contains a kind of canned summer, like a scent in a bottle.

Maybe this feeling also has to do with what was happening at the time. It was the summer of 1991 that I was there, the summer of the coup, and I wrote the novel the following winter. You see, politics affects you even if you don't want it to. You can be totally withdrawn from politics and social life, but every time they start a coup or bombard the parliament or elect Zhirinovsky,* something

---

* Pelevin is referring here to the coup against Gorbachev in August 1991; the crushing of a revolt by anti-reformist Members of Parliament after Yeltsin's suspension of the Russian Parliament in September 1993, and the unexpectedly large vote for the nationalist Vladimir Zhirinovsky in December 1993 (see also note on p. 177).

changes. You can sit locked in your apartment with the TV switched off, but somehow you still feel it. It's as if the chemical content of the air has changed.

sl All the stories of different insects in the novel—the scarab beetle pushing this huge dungball before him, the ants digging their burrows, the moths always flying towards the light—could be read as different metaphors for our human condition. Are you offering us a choice of metaphors for how to see ourselves? Or is there one which strikes you as more pertinent to our lives than the others?

vp When I write something I know how it should be written but I can't explain it. I think if a writer gave you a choice of metaphors you'd throw up after ten pages, so I hope that isn't what I make you do.

sl But do you think we're more 'beetle-like' or 'ant-like' or 'mosquito-like', or are we all of these things?

vp Oh, that depends ... some people are mosquitoes, some people are ants. In this country we mostly have ants, I think, because the whole society was designed as a giant antheap. In America you have mosquitoes trying to suck blood from each other.

sl There seem to be plenty of those in Russia at the moment ...

vp Exactly, exactly, that's exactly what's taking place. The ants are turning into mosquitoes. In fact you're right, there's probably more blood sucked here than anywhere else.

sl To me the most powerful image in the novel was the image of the beetles, engaged in this endless labour of pushing their dungballs before them and blocking their own view with this accumulation of their selves, their lives.

vp A friend of mine paid me a nice compliment when he said that he'd drunk for three days after reading that piece about the beetles. It's maybe the part of the novel that means the most to me too.

sl It was in this story of the beetles that I especially felt your achievement in making these creatures 'human', touching us with their emotions, and showing the world from their perspective. Suddenly with the beetles we find ourselves in a kind of fog, unable to see beyond this monstrous ball of dung, our view of the world fantastically reduced.

vp You mean that for most people the view is wider?

sl Well, in the novel it seems to me that you play constantly on these changes of perspective—and it's only by contrast with some wider view that you get this terrible sense of reduction in the beetles' case. The focus is constantly changing, so at certain moments we're able to survey the landscape with a human eye, to see the sanatorium, the summer day, the lunch table outside, and the bottle of wine—and at the next we're simply in a fog, we have only the dungball in front of us, or we *are* the dungball.

vp Yes exactly ... but it isn't that the world is suddenly reduced to a dungball, it's more that—you realize that the world, your world, *is* a dung world, and the rest of the world which you're unacquainted with is suddenly left behind. That's what I meant—if I meant anything.

sl The overwhelming feeling in that part of the story is one of loneliness—the loneliness of the young beetle abandoned to his fate, forced to grow up and start pushing his burden alone.

VP I think that loneliness is the natural condition of every human being. There are people who understand that they are lonely, there are people who don't—that's the only difference. I think that I understand that I am lonely. And that I always will be.

SL Much of your work turns on the sorts of shifts in perception we've been talking of—as if different versions of reality could simply be switched on and off, if we could only find the key.

VP The point is not whether they can be switched on and off—the question is who does the switching and what's being switched. In the story of the fireflies the hero—well, let's call him the hero—finds that it's very easy to switch on his own personality, or his absence of personality. These shifts in perception can be achieved in all sorts of ways—with the help of exercises, the sort of exercises that Buddhists practise, or with drugs. But the point is to understand *whose* perception you're shifting ... that's the difficult question.

SL We've been talking of these ideas in the abstract. But what's so striking about your writing is the poetic concreteness you give to these ideas. I was thinking for instance of the scene of the dance floor in *The Life of Insects*—how vividly you convey that sense of summer night in the park, the music, the flickering dancers. It's scenes like this that convince us of the 'reality' of the story, give us the sense of felt experience.

VP Well, I don't know where that comes from. I've never danced in my life. But I admit I like looking at dancing people, especially when the lights get switched on and off. You catch them in glimpses, like a sequence of photographs.

SL In your novella *The Yellow Arrow* the reader is plunged so immediately and naturally into the humdrum life of the train where the story takes place that it takes a while to realize where you are. Your experience as a reader duplicates that of the passengers on the train. At the beginning, in the first few pages, I was mystified. Was this fellow we were reading about living in some kind of dormitory? And where was this café? Were we inside or outside?

VP That was the idea. The reader is meant to understand where the action takes place only when the hero understands it. Because the hero himself also doesn't know at first that he's on this train. He gets up and starts his day and goes to a café and chats and the whole thing could be happening anywhere in this country—a dormitory, wherever. Normal life.

So it wasn't because of my ineptness that you were lost at the beginning. The passengers are lost as well. But I like this feeling that—again, one can suddenly change the whole perspective, make the reader see things differently.

SL Make the reader see that he too is a passenger on a train that's bound for a ruined bridge?

VP It sounds very banal when you say it. The point of the story is that the only ones who go on heading towards this bridge are those who think it's inevitable.

But I'm rather dubious about this story, I don't know if it works.

SL Why?

VP Well, I don't know, I'm dubious about everything I write. But this one—it's too simple, maybe. The metaphor is very simple: life is a train. Life is a journey. When you use a simple metaphor like that you take a very big gamble. If it works then it'll be much stronger for being simple, but if it doesn't it'll just be banal.

SL The reason it works for me is that the metaphor is taken so literally—it's furnished in such witty detail, with a kind of absurd realism. It poses a metaphysical riddle with a wonderfully matter-of-fact air; there's nothing unusual, on the surface, about the passengers' experience.

VP But there isn't anything unusual about it. I think that all human beings have the same kind of experience; the particular details don't matter. What matters is what you do with this experience, how you deal with it, how you understand it. All of us are passengers on this train, but the point—I say it in the story—is to ride on the train without being its passenger. There's nothing much more to be said.

SL It also works because you're a good story-teller. Forget metaphors—as a reader you're engaged, you get absorbed in the story, you want to know how it's going to end.

VP Well that's nice if it's true. Funnily enough there have been a lot of articles about this *Yellow Arrow*, even though it's only sixty or seventy pages long. It seems to have struck people's imaginations. But one critic, in the newspaper *Segodnya* [Today], was rather worried about the ending—he said it only ended like that, with our hero escaping from the train, because I had to end it somehow.

SL The end is puzzling. If the train encompasses the whole of life, what lies outside it? Who are the inhabitants of the city that the hero sees just before he finally jumps off?

VP Well it's another metaphor, I suppose—as if he'd jumped into another metaphor. The ending doesn't mean that the hero departs this life, that he dies or whatever. There's another clue, if you notice, in the story, which suggests that the train isn't so much life itself as a sequence of thoughts, with one thought that calls itself 'I' and which serves as a locomotive for the rest. So it doesn't have anything to do with the so-called real world—everything takes place within, as everything in your world takes place inside you.

SL So the train is a metaphor for a single person's world, or mind?

VP Again when you pronounce it like that it sounds banal. But the thing is, do we have any proof that the world exists? Everything we deal with is perception. It makes no sense to discuss it because it's just a matter of choice, you can choose to act as if something were true or you can choose otherwise ...

SL It seemed to me that the story—like all your work—functions on two levels, both as existential conundrum and as local satire. The train is a very Russian train, or let's say a post-Soviet train: the various social groups—the literary types who discuss postmodernism and quote poetry, and the mafiosi types who are busy trading and doing deals—they're comically recognizable from this society. I even felt that there was something classically Russian in the cosy taken-for-grantedness of the whole situation, the sense that most of these people—apart from the few initiated—show such remarkable lack of curiosity; they accept without question the rather evident restrictions on their lives. But perhaps you'd say that that's true of all of us?

VP Well, of course, societies differ in certain ways, but they have a great many more things in common than we realize—more than the things that differentiate them. I wouldn't say there was anything peculiarly Russian about this train. You can move coaches on it and go 'abroad'.

SL So you wouldn't say there was any element of satire in the story?

VP I didn't plan to write anything satirical. I don't think the story's a satire; it describes what's actually taking place. All the reference to business deals and making business connections and so on—I'm not satirizing these things, I'm relating what I see.

SL At the end of your novel *Omon Ra* the hero—having apparently taken a trip all the way to the moon—finds himself back on the familiar network of the Moscow metro. It's a relief to find him safe and sound, but of course the underground metro is an image of entrapment—we see that the hero hasn't escaped at all, he's back in the dreary familiar world. Is that your own recurring nightmare?

VP I don't have nightmares but I have convoluted dreams. Today I found myself in some sort of Zoroastrian sanctuary in a park in Moscow, and there was no way to get out of this park, nobody knew where the exit was ...

But I don't think this is a personal thing. We're all trapped; the difference again is just that some people understand this and some don't. I've had this feeling ever since I was 14, the feeling that you don't have any real control over your life. You can't change it—you are ruled by outside influences. Of course you can make promises to yourself, promises to change. But it's stupid work, just a way of monitoring what actually takes place outside your control.

Perhaps there is a way out of this trap. I know a lot of people who are interested in Buddhism but I don't think they have the answer. Nor do Christians. To be a Christian is to live according to what Christ said, and in principle it may be a good thing, a very hard thing, but I can't accept its routines—turning up to church every Sunday and so forth. That's not a way out.

But still we have to ponder these things. Everyone has a tuning fork inside himself which he should use. That's what a writer should be doing. The word 'spirituality' has been terribly debased in our society—people, including writers, go on and on about it when all they're really interested in is making money. But still, I don't like fiction that has no spiritual value in it at all. I can't see the point of writing or reading something that has no spiritual meaning.

Omon Ra is about the fate of a man who decided in his soul to go up there, to go to the moon. Then he found out that what he had undergone was not a 'real' journey but—something like a transformation of the soul.

SL It seems to me as you talk about your work that you disown your own wit. *Omon Ra* certainly gives lots of room for 'spiritual' reflection, but it's also, in a melancholy way, very funny—funny about Brezhnev's Russia and all its cardboard and tin-foil emblems.

VP Well yes, the critics wrote that it was a libellous description of Soviet space technology, and of course it's libellous. I never did a moment's real research on it. Too much knowledge is very oppressive when you're writing. The best thing is to know just a little bit, and it wasn't hard to find that much—the odd detail to give the story a sort of 'authenticity'.

I spent my childhood in Brezhnev's Russia, and of course that's partly what the story's about. It has that atmosphere. But what interested me was the ontology of childhood as such. I'm no longer the person I used to be, and some day I'll cease to be the person I am now. But in principle I don't accept the very idea of being grown up. In *The Life of Insects* you see that at the beginning the scarab beetle doesn't have this dungball to push before him. But after a while it begins to form—this individual life, this personality—and in due course it turns out that this is the only thing you're doing, pushing this great ball before you. I wanted to try to capture that process—and recall what it was like before it began.

Igor Pomerantsev was born in Saratov and spent his early childhood in Siberia. When he was 5 his family moved to Chernovtsy in western Ukraine, where he grew up and went to university. After graduating in English, he worked as a teacher and technical translator, moving to Kiev in the early 1970s.

At the time, the Kiev intelligentsia was being decimated by the KGB, and Pomerantsev, though never an open dissident, soon found himself charged with 'spreading anti-Soviet literature'. Had he been Ukrainian he would almost certainly have been imprisoned for this offence; as a Russian, however, he was given the 'option' of exile abroad. In 1978 he left with his wife and infant son for Germany, subsequently moving to Britain, where he worked for several years in the BBC Russian Service. Later he joined Radio Liberty as a producer of cultural programmes, a job that took him first to Munich and then to Prague.

Apart from a handful of poems published in the early 1970s in the Moscow magazine *Smena*, most of Pomerantsev's work in the 1970s and 1980s appeared in *émigré* journals such as *Sintaksis* (Paris), *Vremya i my* (New York and Jerusalem), and *Kovcheg* (Paris). In 1985 a collection of his stories, *Aubades and Serenades* (*Alby i serenady*) was published by Russian Roulette in London. English translations of his poems, essays, and prose have appeared in a number of journals, including *Stand*, the *Edinburgh Review*, the *Times Literary Supplement*, *Index on Censorship*, and the *Fiction Magazine*, and several of his stories have been broadcast on BBC's Radio 3.

In the 1990s, however—after an interval of almost twenty years—Pomerantsev's name has again resurfaced in Russia. Since 1991 his verse and prose have been regularly published in the Moscow magazines *Oktyabr'* and *Znamya*, and since 1993 three collections of his work have appeared in Russia.

Much of Pomerantsev's work is 'autobiographical', in the sense that it draws strongly on scenes and impressions from his own life. But the picture it presents is a complex one: a mosaic rather than a narrative, in which experience is imaginatively refracted through each individual piece, and what counts in each case—what 'strikes home' for the reader—is the evocation of a certain atmosphere, rather than a description of events as such.

Chernovtsy, the town where Pomerantsev grew up, is a key location for his prose: several novellas are devoted to the intense, lyrical, almost tactile recreation of his youth and childhood there; its sounds and colours, smells and accents are echoed in his later travels, and stamp forever the author's—or his hero's—preference for things bright, ebullient, southern, delicious. Elsewhere, however—especially in his poetry and essays—Pomerantsev reveals his cosmopolitan, European self. Communing in imagination with Cavafy and Thomas Mann, with the wine-makers of Ancient Greece and the sons of the British Empire, he shows himself, in the best sense, an opportunist—someone for whom the various accidents of fate, however bitter on the surface, have all offered chances to exercise curiosity and extend imagination.

A novella written in 1975, *Reading Faulkner*, still serves as the best introduction to reading Pomerantsev. In a remarkably compact and daring piece of writing, Pomerantsev marries a critique of *The Sound and the Fury* with a portrait of himself as a young man—or rather as Gena Lyustrin, the main hero of his prose.

Here, in snatches, we first taste Gena's/Pomerantsev's childhood—'grapes, greenery and caraway'—and see it fast-forward, between Julys, to the slap of bicycle tires, first on suburban roads between fields of corn and peas, then on to the cobblestones of Chernovtsy: 'Hunchbacks; madmen; peasants tricked out like painted Easter eggs; Jews—every man a Kafka, every old woman an eternity ...'. We are reminded that this was the town of Paul Celan; see it, Chagall-like, from the air; and rediscover the hero, each time a little older, sampling now the touch of a girl in a doorway, now the poetry of Pasternak, now rain on the roof of a last summer camp. And we discover his parents: in a yellowed cutting of an article written, in 1949, by his journalist father, on 'The Abundant Fruits of the Great Cultural Revolution'; and in a stream-of-consciousness, stream-of-injunctions epistle from his mother that mixes kisses, jam, socks, gossip, and washing instructions with anxious enquiries: 'sonny are you writing the abstract of your thesis remember how much you wanted to write about Faulkner you must do a serious job of it dont skimp it ...'.

The author does not 'skimp it'. He tells us exactly why he admires Faulkner. He loves the way Faulkner works in hints and clues, structuring the first chapter of *The Sound and the Fury* not chronologically 'but, with Benjy's help, associatively', leaving us to draw the conclusions and solve the riddle. He's intrigued by the implications of Benjy's perception: for him 'an event possesses neither logic, nor an end, nor a beginning, but only contours, colours, smell, a degree of pleasure or pain ...'. He meditates on the nature of an author's energy, that elusive quality that shows itself not in plot or theme but dictates the special rhythm of syntax, images, events. Faulkner's energy, he says, 'is revealed through his montage; he marries things that are incompatible ... colliding words, sentences, situations, characters ... Every word is a snowfall in summer.' And the origins of that energy, he believes, lie in Faulkner's attitude to his past, to his own genealogy—'Try finding insignificant parents anywhere in Faulkner'. He praises what he calls Faulkner's 'excess': 'to write with restraint is to play deliberately for a draw . . . Faulkner played to win, for unlimited stakes.'

And so on. It's not hard to discover in these observations a blueprint for Pomerantsev's own writing. All the key features are there: the precise evocation of sensual experience, the belief in the spiritual eloquence of things, the making of atmosphere and meaning through linguistic collision and association; the use—or creation—of roots, of the past; and a sense, too, of the writer as fighter: there is a pugilistic spring to all Pomerantsev's writing, a commitment to a kind of linguistic fitness—the blow must always come from an unexpected angle; the image be taken by stealth and surprise; the reader kept on his toes.

But *Reading Faulkner* is not just a critique or a manifesto; nor is Pomerantsev just imitating Faulkner. The work earns the description 'novella' by its dramatization of a particular encounter. The hero who, upon reading Faulkner, proceeds to 'pour out words, like cherries from a shirt' is still the Russian boy whom this image evokes—the son of his Soviet father as well as his shirt-washing mother, brought up not just on the idylls of summer camps, kisses, and cherries but on the pompous, false pronouncements of the era. At the opening of the story jazz streams from the radiogram, signalling the late 1950s, the Thaw, the opening to foreign things. But nothing quite like Faulkner has come Gena's way before. So this is what literature can do! Not preach, not judge, not explain, but say—see this, feel this, hear this, draw your own conclusions.

More than any of his subsequent works, *Reading Faulkner* is charged with a sense of betrayal: why has all this been kept from me? But characteristic, in this first novella, is the author's determined espousal of the beautiful as the best—the only—defence against ugliness and falsehood. Bitterness, from the start, is absent in Pomerantsev's intonation. Planted in the midst of the author's fizzing prose, the father's grey piece of officialese dies a natural death—it is revealed in all its linguistic helplessness, becomes not so much hateful as pitiful. Why lose one's energy railing against such things, when they speak so dismally for themselves?

In his subsequent writing Pomerantsev would show repeatedly that art must win on its own—superior—terms or not at all: the artist who descends to ideological brawling deserts his own province and risks losing all. 'The optics of accusation, when the accused stands already convicted and condemned, are simply uninteresting,' he rehearses telling a poet friend (*Holiday in the South*, 1990). 'The accuser is always the loser, especially when he's right.'

But to refrain from accusation means to relinquish, too, the role of martyr, prophet, hero. In two plays written after his emigration, Pomerantsev distanced himself from any conventional construal of his own position as exile. *Can You Hear Me?** deals with the relationship between a writer and the KGB, while *Mit Blumen auch Schön* dramatizes the confrontation between two *émigrés* and a foreign student of their culture. In both, however, the heroes and ogres of imagination are missing; what we see, rather, is a kind of wilful non-communion, a dramatic

---

* *Vy menya slyshite?*, published in Russian in *Vremya i my*, 87 (1985), was broadcast on BBC Radio 3 in 1986 in a translation by Frank Williams.

missing of minds. Elsewhere (in *Concise Phrasebook for New Arrivals*),* Pomerant-sev wittily uses the staccato language of the phrasebook—questions, commands, exhortations, complaints—to suggest the hectoring intonation of the *émigré*, deter-mined—and failing—to communicate his message among aliens.

'How *not* to communicate as an *émigré*' might well have been the title of a series of essays and interviews,† published in the late 1980s, in which Pomerantsev took issue with a tradition of criticism that had made the warnings of the wounded the chief province of literature, and imprisonment and torture virtual pre-conditions of Russian authorship. The tone of these essays, however, is never less than genial, aphoristic, charming. Behind them, one senses, is not merely a disagreement with a particular literary tradition, but a temperamental dislike of the miserable—or 'miserablism'—*per se*. 'Why this dismal, rocky shore?' he chides an invisible reader in 'From a Diary'.‡ '[Why] this indifferent carpet of pine-needles? This orphaned sky? Have you really not sensed that a little further on the air is plump and downy, the colouring sweet, the shore unbuttoned?'

From the first, Pomerantsev had chosen for his hero a name redolent of pleasure: in Russian as well as English, 'Gena Lyustrin' carries connotations of genius and glossi-ness, genealogy, lustre, and lute-strings. Gena would later follow the author into emi-gration, doubling for him as husband, father, lover, broadcaster on 'Radio Exile', and expert on wine, in which guise—in *The Hound of the Basques* (1991)§—we eventually leave him wounded, perhaps mortally, by a misfired shot from a terrorist's gun.

But the next time Gena appears after *Reading Faulkner* we are still in Cher-novtsy—and this time the author has let go of Faulkner's hand and is skating freely. In a story dignified by just three asterisks for a title,¶ he delivers himself of a breath-less hymn to love, life, the seasons, and all the champions of his childhood: dogs, athletes, artists, classmates, girls, more girls. Or not just a hymn but a performance, a frenzied dance—the whole story is taut with lust, takes place to invisible applause, as if by sheer ebullience the hero had involved half the town in a musical.

This atmosphere of extravaganza, of carnival, spills into much of Pomerantsev's prose. 'With a Bouquet of Roses'‖ is set in Spain, where 'everyone's invited to the fiesta' and 'the people are twisted from flamenco like polio. . . . They even dance their local Cordovianka at school assembly.' In *Reading Faulkner* we see 'the whole town dancing the tango to Petite Fleur' and in 'A Little about You, Iosip'** the schoolboy hero 'gets everybody hooked on this senseless game which involved leaping out from behind potted palms . . .'. Later, when the genre of the radio play has got entwined with his prose, Pomerantsev sets his *Hound of the Basques* to specified musical accompaniment—Irish romances, Turkish songs, 'The Triumph of Bacchus', Tyrolean yodelling.

---

* *Kratky razgovornik dlya priyezzhikh* (1981).

† See e.g. 'Out of Step' (Interview) in *Index on Censorship* (March 1986); 'Raw Meat: We've Had Enough', in *Index on Censorship* (May 1987), and 'Lost in a Strange City', in the *Times Literary Supplement* (26 June 1987).

‡ 'Iz dnevnika', in *Al'by i Serenady* (1985).

§ The title *Baskskaya sobaka* evokes not only Conan-Doyle's *The Hound of the Baskervilles* but Buñuel's film *Le Chien Andalou*: an alternative translation would thus be *A Basque Dog*.

¶ '***', in *Al'by i serenady* (1985).   ‖ 'S buketom roz', ibid.

** 'Nemnogo o tebe, Iosip', ibid.

Not that the music is always on full blast. The story 'Aubades and Serenades'*— whose cast consists entirely of animals and birds, anxious employees in some doomed, Kafkaesque enterprise—is choreographed to the squeak and rasp of lifts, the banging of office doors, the sinister tinkle of broken glass. And in 'My Mother-land is Solitude',[†] the hush descends completely. Here, the author finds himself in a misty, mountainous, cheese-smelling land where the local language is a multi-nuanced silence, evolved after decades of fearful whispering to supplant the spoken word with delicate gesticulation. Even here there is the sense that the author has got this whole imaginary nation transfixed, shifting them together in ghostly chorus: '. . . theatres were packed to bursting. Tragedies were played out in perfect silence and one could only judge the degree of passion aroused by the dry explosions of applause.'

Where is this eerie place? An otherwise innocent Alpine land transfigured by an exile's hallucinations? Or, on the contrary, a nightmarish evocation of some real place where words are suppressed, poets gagged? Have we inadvertently landed here on some bleak variant of the aforesaid 'rocky shore': 'Slices of blue with wisps of fog. A scaly lake. Stone bell towers'? Or is the oxygen always thin, the sound eclipsed, when the writer—as here—attempts to scale some new peak? For a moment, in this story, we seem to have entered the strange hinterland of the author's own mind, where exile—and its concomitant solitude—is not an acciden-tal circumstance but the poet's natural condition.

But back to Chernovtsy, and all five senses are switched on again. In 'A Little about You, Iosip', a more Jewish-sounding hero has taken Gena's place: to his lot falls the early experience of hospital, but also (in fevered memory) a schoolboy's lust for his first English teacher, and above all the revelation of the cinema—first glimpsed behind rustling foliage on outdoor, summer screens; later experienced, by stealth, indoors—'Latin American films about gloomy, endless stone walls: Czech films from the Barrandov studios, their filtered, hazy landscapes drenched with a cosmic ennui . . .'.

In a subsequent story we find that Iosip has stayed true to this passion, but become more discriminating: in 'Iosip has Made it'[‡] we watch him at work as a film critic, creating his paragraphs between yawns, scratches, and visits to the kitchen, before finally packing up and departing for his next evening's cinematic seance. Like *Reading Faulkner*, this story curls back on itself and its author. We witness Iosip's fastidious craftsmanship, his neat excisions, from the paragraphs he's just written, of excess sentiment, spare verbiage. But we also find, in his critic's com-mendations, the qualities of Pomerantsev's texts. Like the anonymous director whom Iosip praises, Pomerantsev has 'perfect cinematic pitch'; he too knows how to make us hear 'the penetrating whine of a mosquito, rustle of eyelashes, dog's yelp, chain's clank'; knows how to 'shoot weather'; shows an exquisite 'tenderness' in his observations of things.

Both stories, however, involve a second eye, or 'I'. To his heroes Pomerantsev awards, so to speak, the ecstasy of the experience itself. For himself he reserves a

---

* 'Al'by i serenady', ibid.   † ' "Moya rodina—odinochestvo . . ." ', ibid.
‡ 'Iosip dorvalsya', in *Predmety roskoshi* (1995).

cooler, teasing, slightly self-mocking voice—judging, here and there, that an image may not have worked, or implying, in his hero Iosip, a fanaticism he does not quite share. When, later, in *The Hound of the Basques*, he sends Gena off to taste all the wines of Spain, it is he—one feels—who does all the background research for Gena on the history of barrels and corks, stands behind Gena to comment on the paintings of El Greco and Velázquez, and patiently collects up all the beer mats, post-cards, and drawings that serve as absurd illustrations to the text.

It is to Pomerantsev's own voice, necessarily, that his essays belong—spare, elegant disquisitions on quirky subjects that contain just the right mix of information, personal opinion, and imaginative speculation. In 'Danish Babble'* (the title—'Datsky lepet'—puns untranslatably on the Russian for 'baby-talk') Pomerantsev uncovers some of Hans Andersen's more blatantly paedophilic moments, imagines an encounter between the Danish writer and Lewis Carroll, and incidentally expresses his own aversion to Andersen's one 'positive hero', the boy in 'The Emperor's New Clothes'—the sort of boy, he says, who ruins other children's sand-castles and can't see the artistry in the emperor's great pantomime. In 'Colonial Melancholia'† he conjures up the ghost of an English boy who perhaps once lived in the Edwardian house where he now has his apartment in London: did he too, like the author's son, once gaze, perhaps, at a map of the world and take pride in the giant empire he was born into? Pomerantsev then takes us on a journey back to British India, interspersing snapshots of cumbersome journeys and colonial interiors with a history of fans and the importation of ice, before returning to his mental starting-point—his own son's sudden passion for India.

Some of Pomerantsev's essays, like his plays, were written specifically for radio,‡ a medium in which he now has some twenty years' experience, and whose pleasures—deriving from the solitary nature of the broadcaster's craft and the intimacy of his voice—are explored in 'The Age of Radio'.§ Such essays display Pomerantsev's free-ranging curiosity and his enjoyment of serendipity, his craftsman's pleasure in assembling new materials and setting to work on strange facts and new vocabularies. But their atmosphere is also very often personal and domestic. Their starting-point is a map on the kitchen wall, a book taken down from the shelf, a story told by the author's son on returning from school.

The same can be said of Pomerantsev's verse. It is here that we meet the author at his most casual and laconic, undressed, so to speak, in the present tense. The poems are one-off glimpses, thoughts occasioned by a cyclist's kiss, a ladybird on a window, a tell-tale stain, a child in the sand. Wife, son, friends, neighbours enter undisguised, as in a diary; so do a London street, a local pub, moments of pique or sentiment caught off-guard. The verses are written from London, Córdoba, Crete, but their temper is unexotic and everyday. For their true source and location is the author himself. It is his constant presence that makes the new at once familiar and engaging.

---

* 'Datsky lepet', in *Po shkale Boforta* (1997).
† 'Kolonial'naya grust'', ibid.
‡ A selection of these radio pieces can be found in Pomerantsev's most recent book, *News: Stikhi, proza* (1998).
§ 'Vek radio', ibid.

In a beautiful essay on 'Poetry's Housing Stock'* Pomerantsev reviews the different 'lodgings' offered by Russia's poets—the Hall of Laughter that we enter with Khlebnikov, the summer dacha we can borrow from Pasternak—and commends the Petersburg poet Aleksandr Kushner for providing, for the first time in Russian poetry: 'a self-contained, two-room flat of your own . . . with a kettle on the gas and the clatter of the janitor's snow scraper in the yard'. Something of that atmosphere pervades Pomerantsev's verse. To be sure, those particular Russian comforts are gone. But we can be certain, with Pomerantsev, of finding a pleasant berth elsewhere: a bar down a side street of a provincial town, a room with a view of the sea, or just something tasty in the fridge at home. Civilization and its contents. Somewhere distant the wailing, torture, and arguments go on. But this is poetry; we're safe; let's open the bottle and drink.

◆　　◆　　◆

SL As an *émigré* you've had the opportunity to travel widely and exploit that experience in your writing, but Ukraine remains a central source and location in your work—and not so much Kiev but specifically Chernovtsy, the town where you grew up. Your hero—or heroes—appear to be still rooted there. Is that true of you too?

IP No, you know that's a trick of mine, because actually I'm completely rootless. But, as you know, all the great writers—however cosmopolitan they may have been, like Joyce—they all had their small motherland which they exploited and excavated for the whole of their lives. Dublin isn't a great world capital, but Joyce exploited it to the end of his days—precisely because he was so cosmopolitan.

Having no real roots I could have chosen anywhere—Kiev, Baikal. It isn't a question of memory as such but of which memories you choose to recreate, which direction you choose to dig in. Anyway, I chose Chernovtsy as the most charming and intriguing variant of small motherlands. But it's a trick, it's cheating.

SL Of course Chernovtsy isn't just 'anywhere', is it? Even if you use it as a kind of provincial disguise, it has its own distinguished literary history.

IP In my time it was absolutely provincial, godforsaken. There were probably a couple of dozen intelligent people in the entire town. Virtually no one to talk to. But in my writing it's the capital of Atlantis, the capital of a vanished empire, or a kind of mirage situated on the border between two empires, the dead Austro-Hungarian and the Soviet.

In a way, certainly, I was very lucky—firstly because the Austro-Hungarian empire no longer exists, and secondly because in its final period it was culturally so great: some of the most interesting events in the culture of the twentieth century happened there. Later Chernovtsy became part of the Soviet empire, but still in my day it wasn't completely 'sovietized'. I remember once asking my father as a child: Daddy, have you ever been abroad? And he said: Why, we are abroad here! Chernovtsy wasn't the Donbass, it wasn't Sverdlovsk, it was a place where people were arrested for speculating in foreign currency! That was unheard of

Interview recorded in May 1994.

* 'Zhilishchny fond poezii', in *Po shkale Boforta* (1997).

outside Moscow or Odessa. Yet there in the 1960s these great old Jews, geniuses of finance, were sentenced to death for dealing in dollars—as if capitalism had been flourishing on the side all the while, in bribes. And the doors to the outside world were never hermetically sealed, as they were elsewhere. There were always contacts with the outside, with America, with Israel; parcels arrived, people visited, and the Jewish emigration started there in the 1950s, much earlier than elsewhere. The place had only become part of the Soviet Union in the 1930s, and thirty years on you could still get a whiff of its old bourgeois charm—very secret, very decayed, but still as a child you smell these things.

So it's a unique place, and I'm quite proud of myself for having had the cunning, even when I was very young, to choose the right motherland, so that I can pretend for the rest of my days that I come from this mirage, this Atlantis.

SL You can pretend that it chose you rather than the other way around?

IP Well, as a matter of fact, I'm afraid what you say is right, it *did* happen the other way round. Because actually I don't believe in my own intellect or wisdom. I think that Chernovtsy chose me as before it chose the Austrian poet Paul Celan. By the way, when Paul Celan betrayed Chernovtsy and settled in Paris, Chernovtsy didn't forgive him and in the end he committed suicide.

SL What does that example mean to you?

IP I didn't betray Chernovtsy. I still exploit it and still pretend that that is where I come from and that I'm here only temporarily.

SL When did you find out about Celan? He wasn't exactly honoured in the Soviet Union, was he?

IP I must have been about 18 when I discovered him—and then I went on to discover some surviving friends of his, a small, cultivated circle still living in Chernovtsy. Although they were really just in transit at that stage—this was the late 1960s—because shortly afterwards all of them emigrated to Israel.

SL To what extent had Jewish culture survived in the town?

IP There was still a big Jewish population but you should bear in mind that they weren't, say, Hassidic Jews. They were like well-to-do Indian intellectuals, buried away in the provinces, who persist in the illusion that the empire still exists and speak the Queen's English better than most Englishmen—so in the same way these Jews from Chernovtsy kept up Austrian, German-speaking traditions even though the empire had vanished and Atlantis drowned. Right up to the 1930s, all through the period when Chernovtsy belonged to Romania, the language of the *gymnasium* was German. But it was specifically an Austrian tradition—Kafka, say, was cultivated rather than Thomas Mann, and that's not just my hypothesis—Paul Celan's friends said the same thing when I asked this question of them. There was this peculiarly Austrian, individualistic perception of the language and the culture.

As far as Jewishness went, people were of course aware of their Jewishness and kept up certain traditions. One of the most interesting Jewish philosophical seminars—permanent seminars—was held in Chernovtsy. But it wasn't narrowly Judaistic, it drew on a broader culture.

SL Chernovtsy is obviously unique in its particular mix of peoples and cultures, but one can think of parallels—Milosz's Vilnius, for instance.

IP Yes, Milosz is a faker just like me. I remember reading with a certain pride—though I have no right to be proud—how Milosz in his memoirs tries rather humbly to compare Vilnius to Chernovtsy and Trieste: he knew they were the real capitals of Europe! He wanted to be a citizen of Atlantis too.

SL Milosz has an outsider's fascination with Jewishness, whereas you look upon it—don't you?—as a partial insider.

IP Not really. My hero is somehow accepted into the company of Jews, but I never felt completely accepted. They were a kind of élite, that's how I understood Jewishness. We were strangers. My father was Jewish—unlike my mother—but first of all he was a journalist, which meant a Party man, a communist functionary, part of the establishment. Secondly, he came from Odessa—that's where he'd learned Yiddish (which I was very proud of—a foreign language!)—so the Jews from the western Ukraine didn't see him as one of theirs.

Of course when you're a child you don't make all these distinctions, but in retrospect I can see that my friends' parents were probably less open and sincere with me than they were with their own circle.

Later on I realized that my father was a stranger in many ways. He had cut himself off from his own roots in Odessa. Once in London, in the library at the School of Slavonic Studies, I came across a manuscript about the Odessa synagogue in the late nineteenth century, written by a certain Pomerants whose family were closely associated with the synagogue—and I realized these must be my relatives. My father had turned his back on all that. On the other hand he never rejected his own Jewishness, and he certainly experienced anti-Semitism. He had left Siberia for Kiev at the height of Stalin's anti-Jewish campaign, and he wasn't able to get a job on a newspaper there, even though he was an excellent journalist by Soviet standards. Which is how we ended up in Chernovtsy.

SL So you were part Russian, part Jewish, living in Ukraine. How did you relate to the Ukrainians themselves? Did you speak Ukrainian?

IP Yes, I do speak Ukrainian, I was taught it at school. My family never rejected the local culture in the way that many Russians did, particularly the children of Soviet army officers, many of whom simply refused to learn the language and showed what seemed to me an absolutely unmotivated, groundless arrogance towards the whole culture. I learned there what 'imperialism' meant, because they really did behave like imperialists.

I have many, many negative sides but at least I've never been infected by this kind of national or social arrogance; even as a child I couldn't understand it. I think I recognized instinctively that it was destructive—destructive to oneself—and by nature, egotistically, I rejected it; I was simply greedy for everything good and positive. So, for example, I wanted to speak perfect Ukrainian—I remember my tears when I failed to get top marks after learning everything by heart! Later I realized that you can't learn a language mechanically, you have to love it from the inside. Curiously enough I started speaking Ukrainian properly only in emigration, when for the first time I met Ukrainians—the children of *émigrés*—who didn't understand Russian. But I always had—still have—a feeling of intimacy towards that culture.

SL You were born in 1948, just after the war ...

IP 1848 really! I look young for my age.

SL But was there a strong 'post-war' flavour about your childhood? Was it a time of material hardship?

IP No, on the contrary, my childhood was absolutely excessive, baroque, rich, flourishing. Just imagine exchanging Siberia for this land where grapes and apricots grew and people made wine! What luxury! Plus at the simple, political level there was this colossal change—the shift from mass repressions under Stalin, when everybody was afraid of everything because there were no rules of the game, to the epoch I grew up in, the epoch of selective repressions where you knew the rules and could survive perfectly well if you kept to them. Ours was what I've called ironically the 'luxury' generation, in the sense that at least we grew up without fear.

SL Do you know how your parents reacted to the changes at the time?

IP My father hated Stalin—that was absolutely clear. I remember quite clearly seeing my mother crying when the news of Stalin's death was announced on the radio, and my father saying to her: 'What are you doing? What are you crying for? One more despot has died, good riddance!' On the other hand he'd devoted the better part of his life to communist propaganda, so he had to have his arguments and justifications. So Stalin was bad but Lenin and the Revolution were good—he played these intellectual games, like a lot of other people.

And as a child, of course, I had no reason to disbelieve him. What kind of intricate, perverse child suspects his country or his parents of lying to him? I was a normal child, I believed in life, I believed in words, I believed in my parents.

SL So when does suspicion begin?

IP Well first of all I'd received this early vaccination against Stalinism, which stood me in good stead. And then there was my father's permanent, obvious tension about the anti-Semitic atmosphere, which created an inner conflict for him. So, two more or less objective factors. But the third factor is always subjective, it comes from yourself.

For instance, I clearly understood something about the situation of Ukraine, even if I wasn't sure about the whole regime. In my first year at university I remember we had our first lecture on the history of the Communist Party, and the lecturer asked us what language we preferred to be taught in. Well about 85 per cent of the students were Hutsuls, western Ukrainians from the mountains who hardly spoke a word of Russian, and only 15 per cent were Russians or Russianized Ukrainians. But this minority raised such a hue and cry—of course we want Russian! You must teach us in Russian!—that they immediately got their way; the rest of the students just sat there like frightened mice. I saw all this and was terribly shocked—it was all so obvious, and completely repugnant.

So this much at least I understood. Plus by that time I had started writing, and when you start writing with your own hands you begin to understand what others are doing. So when two Moscow writers—Sinyavsky and Daniel—were arrested in 1965 I naturally identified with them, I felt some professional solidarity. And that was also the time that *samizdat* got going and we started reading all those forbidden things. So there were all these factors that created a certain atmosphere and reacted inside me.

sl Did you by that time have a particular intellectual circle where you talked about what you were reading and writing?

ip Yes; you know there were some very nice, fine young people at the university who were mad about literature. Nowadays the fashion might be to listen to rap or techno or whatever, and in the fifties it was jazz that was all the rage, but for us in the sixties it was literature that counted. If I'd been born in another epoch I would probably have been a musician, but literature was the thing we all talked about then. Though at the outset you don't know what you'll choose in the end, and I remember intensive sessions reading philosophy and literary criticism as well.

sl What clues did you use to guide your reading—granted the official curriculum can't have given you much guidance?

ip It gave none at all—except negatively! It was only after emigrating that I realized I was self-taught. I see how my son relies on reading lists and recommendations, how students here trust in their teachers' judgements. Whereas we had to elaborate this intricate system for ourselves.

For instance, you'd get hold of the names of the so-called 'revisionist communists' in Czechoslovakia or Poland, and find the works they'd written before they got arrested. Or you'd gather clues about classical philosophers who were rejected from the official Soviet canon. It was all very complicated, but it gave us good practice, it was a time of intense intellectual research. And we were young, full of hope, we didn't know exactly where fate or life would turn us—so we were greedy for any kind of information, for words, for ideas. I remember cinema played a colossal role. Now and then you'd see some masterpiece of Western cinema. One time it might be Fellini's *Nights of Cabiria* [1956], and you'd live in the atmosphere of that film for six months. Then Bergman's *Wild Strawberries* [1957] would come along, and that gave you air to breathe for another six months, or a kind of air cushion to sit on and carry you through.

I'm not sure we were the poorer for having to discover everything for ourselves instead of having things served to us on a plate. I remember going to an Amnesty International meeting the first year I was in Germany, and I innocently spent the evening discussing Austrian symbolist poetry with one of the organizers, a nice fellow. You know what these Amnesty types are like, you're one yourself. But by the end of the evening I'm afraid he'd decided to leave Amnesty. 'I see now that the situation in the Soviet Union is excellent. If people like you could have grown up there it's not such a tragedy'!

sl So he was a bit disappointed in you?

ip Absolutely. He'd set out to help people who'd been completely degraded, emptied, hollowed out, who'd perhaps make him feel a bit superior—and unfortunately I was naïve and didn't give him the chance.

sl But knowing about Austrian symbolist poetry didn't protect you from being arrested ...

ip No, although if I'd left Chernovtsy for Moscow instead of Kiev I would probably never have emigrated. Moscow was always more liberal and more anonymous— you had to be an outright dissident to attract attention there. Whereas in 1972, when I moved to Kiev, virtually every Ukrainian intellectual, anyone who stopped to think for a moment, was being physically arrested. The KGB was a socialist enterprise, a bureaucracy with a plan to fulfil, figures to notch up, reports to write, and they were beginning to run out of 'dissidents' by the time I appeared. They needed new recruits. In that sense I was dragged into the whole thing. I don't say they had no pretext at all, but more or less any pretext would have done.

These life events are very boring, very banal, but anyway they came for me one day when I was in Odessa—I'd just taken a swim in the Black Sea and was half-naked when two senior officers turned up to arrest me. They could perfectly well have arrested me in Kiev, but for some reason they came to Odessa and spent a week interrogating me there. Perhaps it made a pleasant sort of business trip for them—they could go swimming in the evenings. They were adventurers in a way. But what really gets me is that they paid for all these arrests and investigations out of our own taxes! They arrested us at our own expense!

SL And what did they charge you with?

IP Oh, spreading anti-Soviet literature—Nabokov's *Invitation to a Beheading*, Solzhenitsyn's *Gulag Archipelago*, a collection of articles called *Under the Rubble*. And they were quite right, I can own up now—I did pass those books round to lots and lots of people. And what else—listening to foreign radio stations and having contacts with foreigners. Imagine, in Soviet parlance that one phrase—'having contacts with foreigners'—spoke for itself, it required no further argument!

SL And what about your own writing? Was that 'incriminating' too?

IP They tried to find something in it, and I really sympathized with the poor KGB officer who had to sit down to read all my stuff. I remember him seeing a portrait of Igor Stravinsky on the wall of my flat in Kiev and saying—'Ah! Pasternak!' So the poor man had to wade through all this modernistic, stream of consciousness stuff and try to extract something here and quote something there. And the problem was there was nothing to find. There's no anti-Sovietism in my prose or poetry because I simply ignore it, it's not interesting. I mean it's fine for politics or journalism but for *belles-lettres* it's too superficial a theme, it's not existential, it's simply not interesting.

SL In your play *Can You Hear Me?* we meet a rather sophisticated KGB officer who would surely have understood what your writing was about. He creates a rather witty montage out of the recordings he's made of the writer under his surveillance, a writer whom he clearly appreciates, and who—judging from the views he expresses—is rather like you.

IP But he was from Moscow, he wasn't one of these provincial types. It's clear now that some of the Moscow KGB men really were like the officer in my play: I know of one who's a top intellectual, he can quote Oscar Wilde or James Joyce better than I do, or possibly even better than you do.

SL I'm afraid your play would have disappointed some of our human rights activists.

IP I'm afraid the truth is always unpleasant and disappointing.

SL But when you started to write, did you consciously think of yourself at least as an 'un-Soviet' writer, if not an 'anti-Soviet' one?

IP Literature belongs outside political states and borders. Your family might be Babel and Joyce and it makes no difference that one of them is Russian and the other Irish. It's clear that Pasternak's poetry, say, is closer to Rilke's than to most of Russian poetry, or that Andrei Bely's prose is a kind of Siamese twin of James Joyce's and has nothing to do with Maksim Gorky's. One can distinguish only between their different sensual or intellectual perceptions of the world. But all Europe comes from the same roots. What is the East, what is the West? Byzantium kept more of the traditions of the Roman Empire than Rome itself, which was overtaken by so-called barbarians who later turned out to be not as barbaric as all that.

I was never concerned with this 'Soviet' or 'anti-Soviet' thing. I took it for granted that there were simply people you were fascinated by, kindred spirits, and you were entitled to them and they to you.

sL Still, there seems to me an underlying challenge, almost a provocation, in your first novella-cum-essay *Reading Faulkner*. It's as close to a manifesto as you get: a declaration that *this* is the path you want to follow, not the path prescribed by either 'Soviet' or 'anti-Soviet' literature, and a challenge—let no one dare to take this American away from me!

IP Yes—a manifesto in the sense that behind my words there was, I think, the feeling that my generation had been betrayed—betrayed by our teachers, by the state, actually by our parents. And the only solid ground we had was literature, real literature, art. Books didn't betray us, but people did. That's not an accusation, it's a fact.

sL How betrayed you?

IP They lied to us! And writers didn't lie. I don't want to sound accusatory. It doesn't mean that I criticize my parents or that I'm angry with the state. It's a statement of fact, and that's why my first novella is a manifesto dedicated not to people but to literature—and to Faulkner who was the embodiment of that.

sL Of what? Of truth?

IP Truth? Well, no ... genius. You know how when we're very young we're all maximalists, we ignore mere talents or gifts, we appreciate and recognize only geniuses. So I think that was just a sign of my young maximalism—only the most beautiful would do! You know Dostoyevsky's game: we should be able to love the ugly girls too. I'm afraid I still have trouble with that. Only beauties! Only geniuses! But I'm not quite so maximalist as I used to be.

The point is that beauty's higher than truth, but in the sense that it *includes* it, it includes morality, it includes wisdom and intelligence too. The false or the nasty or the stupid can't be beautiful. I don't mean that great writers can't be stupid or nasty; outside their writing—in interviews, say—many of them sound like idiots, as you may have noticed. Outside their texts they're quite helpless. But if their texts are talented they will be all these things—beautiful and true and wise. There's no competition between these things.

sL Did you believe, when you started writing, that you would be able to publish your work and find an audience in Russia? Or was that one reason why you left— that you saw no future for yourself as a writer there?

IP No, I just ran away in order not to be put in gaol. Plus I was married, my son was 9 months old, and we were living with my parents-in-law in their apartment. I was such a headache and a disappointment to them, constantly at risk of being searched or investigated, and it gave me a bad conscience; I felt I was spoiling their lives. Anyway I had no desire to be a hero, unlike certain dissidents who felt it gave them a certain cachet to be arrested—proof that they were real men. I didn't feel I needed that, so when the KGB advised me to get out I took them at their word.

SL By that time you had had some poems published in the Soviet Union, hadn't you?

IP Yes, a few were published in *Smena*, a Moscow magazine for young people. In terms of quantity it was quite good—the circulation was one million. But the last time I was published was in 1973.

This was the time of deep, deep stagnation, of sclerotic faces, of gerontophilia—as if we were living in an H. G. Wells novel. We'd been flung back in time, we were troglodytes. I knew I had no hope of publishing my work then—but still, it was only the threat of arrest that made me emigrate. It was very bitter, in some ways. Afterwards I sometimes wished they'd forced me to emigrate earlier, when I was younger—it might have been easier to establish myself as a writer here.

SL One doesn't sense that bitterness in your writing. Or at least, you never dwell in your writing on these events—your arrest, exile, and so on—which you referred to just now as boring and banal. It's as if all this, the political situation and its particular impact on you, belongs to some uninteresting outer shell, while the core of life, its curiosities and pleasures, remains completely intact.

IP I think I just have this natural predisposition to take even the most negative, destructive situation and turn it into something creative. Basically I'm such an animal, I have such an instinct for survival. I remember once talking in Kiev to an old Ukrainian poet, a really talented man even though he wrote official stuff about Lenin and so on in parallel—and he looked through my poems and said: 'Why are they so optimistic?' And they *are* optimistic, yes, in the sense that I have this greed for life, this triumphant happiness of pure survival. Maybe it's foolish, but in an existential sense I suppose it is optimistic.

But what a parody of life: here was this officially recognized poet commending my 'optimism'—'We need such poetry', he said—when I was hardly even published, and had no hope of being, however 'optimistic'.

SL Because you ignored the outer realities of your life as somehow irrelevant?

IP Yes, and I think that's the most insulting experience of all—not to be hated, not to be criticized, but just to be ignored. Not included in your landscape or your discussion, simply not to exist in your work at all.

SL Similarly one doesn't feel the 'bitterness' of exile in your work ...

IP Only the sweetness!

SL Perhaps one senses only a slight gnawing guilty conscience in one or two of the poems you wrote immediately after emigration—as if you were annoyed at your conscience for distracting you.

IP I had a bad conscience because I didn't feel any nostalgia.

SL But does exile actually help to tune the memory, to crystallize things, to invest experience with that kind of filmic aura one feels in, say, Nabokov?

IP Looking back in delight—you can't but write sweetly. You can't but do that. Either you love your life, or you don't. I love my life, I love my childhood and youth, and I look back with delight!

Of course exile alters one's relationship to one's subject, but not in the sense you mean. Anyone who emigrates loses something of colloquial language—because colloquial language exists not just in individual dialogues, it belongs to a particular setting where new idioms, new bits of slang are born every day. In emigration that language starts to atrophy. So emigrating made me write in a colder, more literary language—more standard from the grammatical point of view.

If you look at the American tradition—Salinger, Mark Twain, Truman Capote—see how many dialogues they have! Theirs is a truly colloquial tradition, compared to the English, where narrative is still dominant. In that sense you could say that I stopped being an American Russian and turned into an English one.

A second thing that happens in emigration is that you start hearing your own language against the background of other languages—so that you see it as one particular note on a musical scale. And a third point for me was that I discovered here the language of broken Russian—remnants and relics of the language in people who'd emigrated from Central Europe and knew Russian, but interpreted it in their own, let's say Polish, way.

SL Which is the language of your heroine-narrator in *Beloved**—writing to her Russian lover and getting all her stresses wrong.

IP Yes, and all this gave me a colossal new feeling for my own language. In emigration you can hear the whole symphony of different languages and recognize your own note among them—and paradoxically the more distant you are, the more distinctly you hear it.

SL But what of the other emotions that accompany exile? Don't they intrude on your writing at all?

IP The principal emotion you experience in emigration is loneliness. Loneliness makes you angry and anger is a great fuel for writing. But it's like printer's ink—it loses its smell when it dries on the printed page. You won't catch a whiff of the original fuel.

SL What's the anger about?

IP It's a kind of creative anger—it's not against any particular person. It's a fight with the language, but it's like playing chess with yourself—whoever wins, you are the winner.

SL The mention of chess brings me back to Nabokov. Is he one of your heroes? I see a strong kinship in your meticulous language, your focus on the detailed re-creation of sensual experience.

IP Nabokov was a late discovery—I discovered him after I'd written *Reading Faulkner* and other pieces. It was like finding out you have an illegitimate brother: on your twentieth birthday your father takes you aside and says, by the way, you know you've got a brother in Kharkov! I read Nabokov when I'd already become a writer myself—and said to myself: I see, I see, I have a brother in Kharkov!

But we're quite different in the sense that Nabokov always worked with plots,

* 'Vozlyublyonny' [*sic*], in *Al'by i serenady* (1991).

he loved plots. Every piece he wrote was written with a proper beginning, development, and end: you set it on the shelf and it exerts its own separate magnetism; you take it down and you can turn it over in your hand.

I have a different relationship to my own texts. I see them as if from an aeroplane. As a reader you may see only the separate fragments, but for me ... I don't want to sound too grand, but for me it's a whole space that I'm looking at from up here, a whole world that I'm creating, and if I live long enough maybe I'll succeed in finishing it. At least that's my idea, whether I'll succeed or not I don't know. But this is my world that I'm making, it has its characters, some of whom emigrated with me, some of whom got left behind, but in the end it should make something whole, though it won't be a novel in Graham Greene's or indeed Nabokov's sense.

SL Traditionally the novel traces the psychological development of the hero through changing circumstances, and in your work the potential for that is there, even if the 'novel' is a good deal propelled by your own life and in that sense, necessarily, open-ended. But it's as if you disdain to psychologize yourself—you leave that to the reader.

IP One should leave something for the reader to do. If you offer a piece of life, it's up to the reader to deal with it psychologically. It's true that I'm not especially interested in this type of analysis—psychologizing is the prerogative of cleverness, of intelligence, rather than artistic talent, though many people mistake it for literature.

But the point about me is that I'm an impressionist, not a story-teller—and of course I'm absolutely not unique in that. Writers can be divided between those who plot and those who don't. Marcel Proust's great work has a plot only thanks to the fact that he died, physically! My failure to tell 'proper' stories has caused me great trauma now and then—one of my girlfriends left me because she needed stories and I couldn't tell her any; I kept honestly offering her my impressions but—she was quite insatiable.

I'm not saying it's better to write this way or that—there are simply different perceptions of life, people are stimulated and motivated by different visions. For a long time these different ways of writing—Romain Rolland and Marcel Proust—have coexisted happily side by side. It's the same with painting—the Russian realists, say, and the French impressionists. Some paintings demand that you tell the story. But what's the 'story' of *Le Déjeuner sur l'herbe*? It doesn't have one, but that doesn't mean it's not worth looking at.

It's such myopia to start blaming other writers for not choosing one's own path—like throwing stones at one's own greenhouse. When Russian writers—especially abroad—start insulting and dismissing one another, as they're prone to do, they're simply ruining their own house—and the net result is that no one will read them either! Writers above all should know that every word we utter speaks only of ourselves, and that no one, but no one, takes our words just as we intend them.

In this respect I learned a lesson from Nabokov. For years he went unrecognized, and it made him so bitter. If you read his essays on nineteenth-century literature, you see they're marvellous, he writes brilliantly, he has such taste. But as soon as he gets to the twentieth century—Pasternak, Faulkner—he starts hating and condemning, all he can express is his own terrible bitterness.

I've had my moments of bitterness too, but I try to express it a bit more decorously. Like pretending I'm an Austro-Hungarian writer. It's a way of saying: you may not appreciate me, but the Austro-Hungarians certainly do, or at least they would do if they existed.

SL Many writers start out with poetry and then abandon it when they start writing prose, whereas you've carried on with both in parallel. But you've mixed the two genres to the extent that your prose is distinctly 'poetic' and your verse, at least in Russian terms, is quite 'prosaic'. Must there be a clear border between the two? What defines each genre?

IP Writers of both poetry and prose have to define their genres themselves. What I call poetry should be taken by my readers as poetry, and what I call prose should be read and treated as prose. The writer's will and definition must prevail. There is no other way, I'm afraid—it depends on the will and the self-understanding of the writer.

Unlike literary critics, who are paid to worry about these things, readers don't concern themselves with genre—why should they? Their aim is to get a specific pleasure from reading, whether it comes from poetry or prose. The writer's duty is to give them that pleasure, to offer them a good piece of work. After all, when we eat, I don't know, a nice piece of butter, we don't ask ourselves where the cows came from, the Alps or the Carpathians.

If a writer finds a new way of giving enjoyment—a new source of milk—so much the better. What jury or ministry can tell him it's not allowed? We're not children.

SL In your story 'My Motherland is Solitude' the narrator is a traveller who says that he's always been looking for the right place to be, a place where there were 'the ideal proportions of blue, moisture, love, light, wine'. Is travel—the pursuit of this ideal, or simply new pleasures—a necessary accompaniment to your writing?

IP I think my constant travelling is a form of neurosis, actually. Every three months or so I have a need to migrate, leave, travel somewhere. But since I'm a cheater I try to turn this neurosis into something creative and constructive. Plus I think that as a writer I'm a kind of parasite; I'm very superficial. For me 'superficial' is not a negative word. Because I think that appearance, the outside, the external aspect of things is always the most eloquent. To be superficial is to believe in your own eyes. If you want to know what's going on inside, why not start from what's most striking, most evident, most eloquent? So as a parasitic, superficial writer I thank God that the globe is gigantic and that I've exploited just 2 or 3 per cent of it so far. I haven't even exhausted Spain yet.

SL If what you're searching for is blueness and light and wine—forgetting for the minute moisture and love—England was perhaps an odd place for you to settle for so many years.

IP Yes, well, from a sensual point of view—the cup of English tea is not my cup. The liquid theme of my prose is wine, and wine in England exists only symbolically. It's not the kind that gets me excited, or gets into my prose. But a lot of my poetry, you'll notice, is devoted to England—not because it's exotic but because England has simply been part of my life. Especially since my son started going to school there: when a British boy comes home to his family and tells them what's been going on at his school, his parents willy-nilly start living his life too.

But there are many things I love about England. It has its national game, and that's what counts. I've lived in many countries now and it's a terrible thing to say, but many countries have no game at all, no aesthetic touch. France, for example, does have a game—a kind of duel with love; and Holland has this aestheticism of the interior—that's why they don't have curtains; and Russia, as I realize now, at least has this Dostoyevskian hysteria of words, which I've always hated but which I've started to appreciate now, seeing how many people lead completely vitaminless, unaesthetic lives—whereas the Russians at least have a game of sorts, however unappealing.

While Britain, of course, is a permanent theatre. Have you noticed that even when you're robbed in Britain there are certain aesthetic, theatrical rules of behaviour—like the robber apologizing before he robs you? And every word in English means the direct opposite of what it says. English is a form of semiotics that's being invented all the time. So living in England is a very intense linguistic exercise; it requires artistry—you have to keep in good shape or you're outside the game. Speaking is performance, so willy-nilly you become a performer, an artist. That's where the excitement of England comes from.

sL Do you feel that taking part in this sort of 'performance' has changed your own personality?

IP Yes, definitely. When I speak with Russians from the metropolis I feel that I'm less serious than they are. They're interested in the pure truth, whereas I'm afraid England has spoiled me—positively—in that regard. I'm more interested in the conversation itself than in arriving at the truth or building hierarchies of goodness. Thanks perhaps to England I've learned how relative hierarchies are and how illusory 'truth' is. So there are colossal lessons to be learned from England if you're open to them. Whereas the poor Germans—they used to have a wonderful game with soldiers, moving them here, there, and everywhere, but now they've been deprived of their game and they feel bored.

sL I'm afraid anyone reading this would be horrified at your cynicism!

IP Not at all. Cynicism has to do with morals. We're not speaking about morals here but about games, aesthetics.

sL How does it feel after all these years to see your work—some of it written a long time ago—published in Moscow and St Petersburg?

IP If I were younger I would feel so sweet about these publications, and of course they do give me some pleasure now. But I still work in virtual silence. In Russia, at least, there still isn't the kind of literary criticism to deal with work like mine. Writers themselves have to give birth to new forms of criticism—it was Pushkin and Gogol who gave birth to Belinsky, not vice versa, and the great French writers who gave birth to Sainte-Beuve, not the other way round, however arrogantly poor Sainte-Beuve wrote about Flaubert. A new writer offers new possibilities to critics who are open. I read with pleasure a little essay in the magazine *Volga*, written by a young medievalist who'd discovered my work, and I felt that it had been born from my own prose and poetry. But that was an exception. Russian criticism today is so hierarchical, so full of inferiority complexes—that's why Russian critics are so arrogant and closed-minded.

sL You wrote a number of essays in the late 1980s about what you called the 'raw meat' syndrome in the perception of Russian literature, whereby martyrdom and authorship were supposed to go hand in hand. Writers were seen as prophets; the more they'd suffered, the more authority they had, and literary criticism—both in Russia and abroad—ran the risk of becoming less a discussion of art than an account of tortures undergone. Do you think that's less true today? Has Russian literature been to some extent 'normalized' by the demise of the old regime?

IP There are some signs—indirect signs—that Russian letters are in better health these days. You know, literature has its politics and its superpowers—like Tolstoy or Homer, and it has its finance, its fees and royalties; it has its sports—literary prizes and so on—and its current affairs. So when, for instance, I wrote about this pseudo-prophetic motif in Russian poetry, as a social problem of the Russian mentality, that was part of literary current affairs. And unfortunately it's still somewhat current, nearly ten years on. But something has changed. Life has shown writers their place—it's told them: your place is quite modest, quite humble! And writers will have to accept that and stop puffing themselves up like toads.

Perhaps that's been another lesson of England for me, because writers in England do know their place. Of course every writer's an exhibitionist who's eager to attract the attention of the world, if necessary by making grand pronouncements about politics or ecology or whatever. But the wonderful lesson of England is that society has the right not to listen. You can read a writer but you don't have to listen to him pontificating about global problems. So what's good about the English is that they haven't corrupted their writers by taking them too seriously. They've told them: know your place! Go and write a good book! That's much harder than proclaiming your views about the moon or the Soviet regime.

Now writers in Russia are having to learn this too. I met some young poets in St Petersburg recently and they talked exactly like the young Ezra Pound or T. S. Eliot—their only theme was money and banking and publishers' deals. They were a pack of wolves. And I was so glad to see how naturally and immediately they'd reacted to the situation—doubly glad, because meanwhile they're writing very good poetry and prose.

SL You call your polemical essays 'current affairs', but of course they have a strong literary touch as well; they're artistic works. The essay seems to me a genre that suits you: many of your novellas—*Reading Faulkner*, or *The Hound of the Basques*—seem to me as much essay as fiction. But with a few exceptions— Andrei Bitov, for instance—the essay seems an underdeveloped genre in Russian letters. Or am I wrong?

IP No, you're right, in a way this genre has been lost in Russian literature. We've had what we call the *ocherk*, a sketch or feature in a newspaper or journal, which has been a part of 'underground' writing as well as of the official press. But that's different from the essay, which is a genre of the mature personality—and until now there hasn't been a place for mature, independent personalities in Russia. You know, all these millions of personalities got minced up in Russian life: all their energy went on self-defence, on confrontation, on surviving as individuals. That's why there could be no relaxation, no freedom. And a vacancy has consequently been left in the literature.

I think that's one reason why I work so eagerly in this genre—because I feel this

SELECT BIBLIOGRAPHY

Selected Books and Articles on Twentieth-Century Russian Literature

AGEYEV, ALEKSANDR, 'Prevratnosti dialoga', in *Znamya*, 4 (1990).

—— 'Konspekt o krizise', in *Literaturnoye obozreniye*, 3 (1991).

AIZENBERG, MIKHAIL, 'Nekotoryye drugiye . . .' in *Teatr*, 4 (1991).

AKIMOV, V., *Ot Bloka do Solzhenitsyna: sud'by russkoi literatury dvadtsatogo veka (posle 1917 goda): novy konspekt-putevoditel'* (St Petersburg: Sankt-Peterburgskaya gos. akademiya kul'tury, 1994).

AMURSKY, VITALY, *Zapechatlyonnyye golosa: Parizhskiye besedy s russkimi pisatelyami i poetami* (Moscow: MIK, 1998).

ANDREYEV, DANIIL, *et al.* (eds.), *Andergraund = Underground: sbornik molodykh avtorov: poeziya, proza, kritika* (Paris: AMGA, 1990).

ANNINSKY, LEV, *Lokti i kryl'ya: Literatura 80-x: Nadezhdy, real'nost', paradoksy* (Moscow, Sovetsky pisatel', 1989).

ARKHANGELSKY, A. N., *U paradnogo pod"ezda: literaturnyye i kul'turnyye situatsii perioda glasnosti, 1987–1990* (Moscow: Sovetsky pisatel', 1991).

BASINSKY, P., 'O staroi i novoi literature', in *Literaturnaya gazeta*, 13 (1993).

BELAYA, GALINA, 'O prirode eksperimenta: k sporam o khudozhestvennykh poiskakh v sovremennoi literature', in *Literaturnoye obozreniye*, 7 (1985).

—— 'In the Name of Common Culture', in *Soviet Literature*, 9 (1988).

—— 'Ugrozhayushchaya real'nost'', in *Voprosy literatury*, 4 (1990).

BOCHAROV, ANATOLY, *Literatura i vremya* (Moscow: Khudozhestvennaya literatura, 1988).

—— and BELAYA, GALINA (eds.), *Sovremennaya russkaya sovetskaya literatura: v dvukh chastyakh* (Moscow: Prosveshcheniye, 1987).

BROWN, DEMING B., *Soviet Russian Literature since Stalin* (New York and Cambridge: Cambridge University Press, 1978).

—— *The Last Years of Soviet Russian Literature: Prose Fiction 1975–1991* (New York and Cambridge: Cambridge University Press, 1993).

BROWN, EDWARD J., *Russian Literature Since the Revolution* (rev. and enlarged edn.) (Cambridge, Mass.: Harvard University Press, 1982).

CHANCES, ELLEN, *Andrei Bitov: The Ecology of Inspiration* (Cambridge: Cambridge University Press, 1993).

CHUPRININ, S. I. (ed.), *Ottepel' 1953–1956: stranitsy russkoi sovetskoi literatury* (Moscow: Moskovsky rabochy, 1989).

—— 'Drugaya proza', in *Literaturnaya gazeta*, 6 (1989).

—— 'Situatsiya (bor'ba idei v sovremennoi literature)', in *Znamya*, 1 (1990).

—— 'Normal'ny khod. Russkaya literatura posle perestroiki', in *Znamya*, 10 (1991).

CLOWES, EDITH W., *Russian Experimental Fiction: Resisting Ideology after Utopia* (Princeton: Princeton University Press, 1993).

CORNWELL, NEIL, and CHRISTIAN, NICOLE (eds.), *Reference Guide to Russian Literature* (Chicago and London: Fitzroy Dearborn, 1998).

DANCHENKO V. T. *et al.*, *Literatura russkogo zarubezh'ya vozvrashchayetsya na rodinu: vyborochny ukazatel' publikatsii, 1986–1990* (Moscow: Rudomino, 1993–).

DARK, OLEG, 'Mir mozhet byt' lyuboi. Razmyshleniya o "novoi" proze', in *Druzhba narodov*, 6 (1990).

DEDKOV, IGOR', 'Khozhdeniye za pravdoi, ili vzyskuyushchiye novogo grada', in *Znamya*, 2 (1988).

—— 'Mezhdu proshlym i budushchim', in *Znamya*, 1 (1991).

EPSHTEIN, MIKHAIL, 'Pokoleniye, nashedsheye sebya: o molodoi poezii 80-kh godov', in *Voprosy literatury*, 5 (1986).

—— 'Posle budushchego. O novom soznanii v literature', in *Znamya*, 1 (1991).

ERMOLAYEV, HERMAN, *Censorship in Soviet Literature, 1917–1991* (Lanham, Md.: Rowman & Littlefield, 1997).

FRIEDBERG, MAURICE, *Russian Culture in the 1980s* (Washington: Georgetown University, 1992).

GARRARD, JOHN, and GARRARD, CAROL, *Inside the Soviet Writers' Union* (New York: Free Press; London: Collier Macmillan, 1990).

GLAD, JOHN (ed.), *Conversations in Exile: Russian Writers Abroad* (Durham, NC: Duke University Press, 1993).

HARRIS, JANE GARY (ed.), *Autobiographical Statements in Twentieth-Century Russian Literature* (Princeton: Princeton University Press, 1990).

HOSKING, GEOFFREY, *Beyond Socialist Realism: Soviet Fiction since Ivan Denisovich* (New York: Holmes & Meier and London: Elek, 1980).

IVANOV, VYACHESLAV, *Vzglyad na russky roman v 1992 godu* (Moscow: Rudomino, 1993).

IVANOVA, NATAL'YA, *Tochka zreniya: o proze poslednikh let* (Moscow: Sovetsky Pisatel', 1988).

—— 'Ispytaniye pravdoi' in *Znamya*, 1 (1987).

—— 'Namerennyye neschastlivtsy? (o proze "novoi volny")', in *Druzhba narodov*, 7 (1989).

—— 'Smena yazyka', in *Znamya*, 11 (1989).

—— *Smekh protiv strakha, ili Fazil' Iskander* (Moscow: Sovetsky pisatel', 1990).

KASACK, WOLFGANG, *Russian Literature 1945–1988* (Munich: O. Sagner, 1989).

—— *Entsiklopedichesky slovar' russkoi literatury s 1917 goda* (trans. from German by Elena Vargaftik and Igor Burikhin) (London: Overseas Publications Interchange, 1988).

—— (Kazak, Vol'fgang), *Leksikon russkoi literatury XX veka* (Moscow, RIK 'Kul'tura', 1996).

KURITSYN, VYACHESLAV, 'Postmodernizm: novaya pervobytnaya kul'tura', in *Novy mir*, 2 (1992).

LAHUSEN, THOMAS, and KUPERMAN, GENE (eds.), *Late Soviet Culture: From Perestroika to Novostroika* (Durham, NC: Duke University Press, 1993).

LANSHCHIKOV, ANATOLY, *Ishchu sobesednika: o proze 70–80-kh godov* (Moscow: Sovetsky pisatel', 1988).

LATYNINA, A., *Znaki vremeni: zametki o literaturnom protsesse, 1970–80-e gody* (Moscow: Sovetsky pisatel', 1987).

—— *Za okrytym shlagbaumom: literaturnaya situatsiya kontsa 80-kh* (Moscow: Sovetsky pisatel', 1991).

—— 'Ne meshaite konyu sbrosit' vsadnika', in *Literaturnaya gazeta*, 16 (1990).

LIPOVETSKY, M., *et al.*, 'Diskussii o postmodernizme', in *Voprosy literatury* (Nov.–Dec. 1991).

LOPUSOV, YU., *Put' k zrelosti: molodaya proza Rossii, 80-e gody* (Moscow: Molodaya gvardiya, 1991).

LOWE, DAVID, *Russian Writing since 1953: A Critical Survey* (New York: Ungar, 1987).

MARSH, ROSALIND J., *History and Literature in Contemporary Russia* (New York: New York University Press, 1995).

MATICH, OLGA, and HEIM, Michael (eds.), *The Third Wave: Russian Literature in Emigration* (Ann Arbor: Ardis, 1984).

'Na perelome? Krugly stol: proza—89', in *Literaturnoye obozreniye*, 1 (1990).

NEMZER, ANDREI, 'Net voprosov', in *Literaturnaya gazeta*, 8 (1991).

—— 'Oblachno s proyasneniyami', in *Literaturnoye obozreniye*, 2 (1991).

PANKEYEV, IVAN, *Besedy s literatorami* (Moscow: Znaniye, 1991).

PARTHE, KATHLEEN, *The Radiant Past: Russian Village Prose from Ovechkin to Rasputin* (Princeton: Princeton University Press, 1992).

PITTMAN, RIITA, 'Writers and Politics in the Gorbachev Era', in *Soviet Studies*, 4 (1992).

PORTER, R.C., *Four Contemporary Russian Writers* (Oxford and New York: Berg, 1989).

—— *Russia's Alternative Prose* (Oxford and Providence, RI: Berg, 1994).

POSTNIKOVA, T. V., 'Yesli ty nosish' nachalo vremyon v ushakh ...' (Avangardnaya poeziya 80-kh–nachala 90-kh godov) (Moscow: Rossiiskaya gosudarstvennaya biblioteka, 1995).

POTAPOV, VLADIMIR, 'Na vykhode iz "andergraunda"', in *Novy mir*, 10 (1989).

ROBIN, REGINE, *Socialist Realism: An Impossible Aesthetic*, trans. from the French Catherine Porter (Stanford, Calif: Stanford University Press, 1992).

RODNYANSKAYA, IRINA, *Khudozhnik v poiskakh istiny* (Moscow: Sovremennik, 1989).

RYAN-HAYES, KAREN L., *Contemporary Russian Satire: A Genre Study* (Cambridge and New York: Cambridge University Press, 1995).

S"ezd pisatelei SSSR 1986; Moscow, RSFSR: stenografichesky otchet (redaktsionnaya kollegiya, G. M. Markov *et al.*; sostaviteli S. P. Kolov, K. N. Selikhov, A. A. Tyurina) (Moscow: Sovetsky pisatel', 1988).

SHENTALINSKY, VITALY, *The KGB's Literary Archive: The Discovery of the Ultimate Fate of Russia's Suppressed Writers*, trans. John Crowfoot, with an Introduction by Robert Conquest (London: Harvill, 1995).

SHKLOVSKY, YEVGENY, *Proza molodykh: geroi, problemy, konflikty* (Moscow: Znaniye, 1986).

—— 'Neugasayushcheye plamya', in *Literaturnoye obozreniye*, 2 (1989).

—— 'Uskol'zayushchaya real'nost'', in *Literaturnoye obozreniye*, 2 (1991).

SHNEIDMANN, N. N., *Soviet Literature in the 1970s: Artistic Diversity and Ideological Conformity* (Toronto: University of Toronto Press, 1979).

—— *Soviet Literature in the 1980s: Decade of Transition* (Toronto: University of Toronto Press, 1989).

—— *Russian Literature 1988–1994: The End of an Era* (Toronto: University of Toronto Press, 1995).

SHTOKMAN, IGOR, *Zhizn' na miru: vremya i proza: shestidesyatyye-devyanostyye* (Moscow: Klyuch, 1996).

VAIL', PYOTR, and GENIS, ALEKSANDR, 'Novaya proza: ta zhe ili "drugaya"', in *Novy mir*, 10 (1989).

VOROBYOVA, N. N. (ed.), *Literaturnyye memuary XX veka: annotirovanny ukazatel' knig, publikatsii v sbornikakh i zhurnalakh na russkom yazyke, 1985–1989* (Moscow: Naslediye, 1995).

World Congress for Soviet and East European Studies 1990 (Harrogate, England). *New Directions in Soviet Literature: Selected Papers from the Fourth World Congress for Soviet and East European Studies, Harrogate, 1990*, ed. Sheelagh Duffin Graham (New York: St Martin's Press, 1992).

YEROFEYEV, VIKTOR, 'Pominki po sovetskoi literature', in *Literaturnaya gazeta*, 27 (1990). (Translated into English in *Glas: New Russian Literature*, 1 (1991).)

ZOLOTUSSKY, IGOR', *Ispoved' Zoila: stat'i, issledovaniya, pamflety* (Moscow: Sovetskaya Rossiya, 1989).

—— 'Krusheniye abstraktsii', in *Novy mir*, 1 (1989).

Anthologies of Recent Russian Prose in English Translation

AKSYONOV, VASILY *et al.* (eds.), *Metropol. Literary Almanac* (New York: Norton, 1982).

BROWN, CLARENCE (ed.), *The Portable Twentieth-Century Russian Reader* (New York: Penguin Books, 1993).

CHUKHONTSEV, OLEG (ed.), *Leopard 1: Dissonant Voices: The New Russian Fiction* (London: Harvill, 1991).

DECTER, JACQUELINE (ed.), *The New Soviet Fiction: Sixteen Short Stories*, compiled Sergei Zalygin (New York: Abbeville Press, 1989).

—— *Soviet Women Writing: Fifteen Short Stories* (New York: Abbeville Press, 1990).

EROFEYEV, VICTOR, and REYNOLDS, ANDREW (eds.), *The Penguin Book of New Russian Writing: Russia's Fleurs du Mal* (London and New York: Penguin Books, 1995).

Glas, a Tri-Quarterly magazine of Russian literature in English translation, ed. Natasha Perova and Arch Tait (Moscow: Glas Publishers).

GOSCILO, HELENA (ed.), *Balancing Acts: Contemporary Stories by Russian Women* (Blooming-ton, Ind.: Indiana University Press, 1989).

—— *Lives in Transit: A Collection of Recent Russian Women's Writing* (Ann Arbor: Ardis, 1995).

—— and LINDSEY, BYRON (eds.), *Glasnost: An Anthology of Literature Under Gorbachev* (Ann Arbor: Ardis, 1990).

—— *The Wild Beach: An Anthology of Contemporary Russian Short Stories* (Ann Arbor: Ardis, 1992).

FAZIL ISKANDER

WORKS IN RUSSIAN

Gornyye tropy. Stikhi (Sukhumi, 1957). [Mountain Paths: Poems]

Dobrota zemli. Stikhi (Sukhumi, 1959). [The Goodness of the Earth: Poems]

Zelyony dozhd'. Stikhi (Sukhumi, 1964). [Green Rain: Poems]

Molodost' morya (Moscow: Molodaya gvardiya, 1964). [The Sea's Youth]

'Dva rasskaza: Rasskaz o more; Petukh' in *Yunost'*, 10 (1962). [Two stories: Story about the Sea. The Cock]

'Tri rasskaza: Loshad' dyadi Kyaz'ma; Vremya schastlivykh nakhodok; Dom v pereulke', in *Yunost'*, 3 (1966). [Three stories: Uncle Kyazma's Horse; The Time of Happy Discoveries; The House in the Alley]

Sozvezdiye kozlotura, in *Novy mir*, 8 (1966). [The Goatibex Constellation]

Zapretny plod. Rasskazy (Moscow, 1966). [Forbidden Fruit: Stories]

Trinadtsaty podvig Geraklya. Korotkiye povesti i rasskazy (Moscow: Sovetskaya Rossiya, 1966). [The Thirteenth Labour of Hercules: Short Novellas and Stories]

'Tri rasskaza: Lov foreli v verkhov'yakh Kodora; Pis'mo; Letnim Dnyom, in *Novy mir*, 5 (1969). [Three stories: Trout-fishing in the Upper Kodor; The Letter; Summer Day]

Letny les. Stikhi (Moscow: Sovetsky pisatel', 1969). [Summer Forest: Poems]

Derevo detstva: rasskazy i povest' (Moscow: Sovetsky pisatel', 1970). [The Tree of Childhood: Stories and a Novella]

Pervoye delo: rasskazy i povest' (Moscow: Detskaya literatura, 1972). [First Task: Stories and a Novella]

Vremya schastlivykh nakhodok: rasskazy i povesti (Moscow: Molodaya gvardiya, 1973). [The Time of Happy Discoveries: Stories and Novellas]

Sandro iz Chegema. Roman, in *Novy mir*, 8–11 (1973). [Sandro of Chegem: A Novel; abridged version]

Sandro iz Chegema: Rasskazy, roman (Moscow: Sovetsky pisatel', 1977). [Sandro of Chegem: Stories, A Novel; abridged version]

Pod ten'yu gretskogo orekha: povesti (Moscow: Sovetsky pisatel', 1979). [Under the Shade of the Walnut Tree: Novellas]

Sandro iz Chegema (Ann Arbor: Ardis, 1979). [Sandro of Chegem; complete 1979 version]

Kroliki i udavy (Ann Arbor: Ardis, 1979), repr. (*Yunost'*, 9, 1987). [Rabbits and Boa Constrictors]

Novyye glavy: Sandro iz Chegema (Ann Arbor: Ardis, 1981). [New Chapters: Sandro of Chegem]

Zashchita Chika: rasskazy i povesti (Moscow: Sovetsky pisatel', 1983). [Chik's Defence: Stories and Novellas]

'Tabu: rasskaz', in *Novy mir*, 1 (1986). [Taboo: A Story]

Bol'shoi den' bol'shogo doma: rasskazy (Sukhumi: Alashara, 1986). [A Big Day in the Big House: Stories]

Prazdnik ozhidaniya prazdnika: rasskazy (Moscow: Molodaya gvardiya, 1986). [The Holiday of Waiting for the Holiday: Stories]

Put': stikhi (Moscow: Sovetsky pisatel', 1987). [The Journey: Poems]

Stary dom pod kiparisom: povest', in *Znamya*, 7 (1987). [The Old House under the Cypress Tree]

Izbrannoye: rasskazy, povest' (Moscow: Sovetsky pisatel', 1988). [Selected Works: Stories, a Novella]

Sandro iz Chegema: Glavy iz romana, in *Znamya*, 9, 10 (1988). [Sandro of Chegem: Chapters from a Novel]

Kroliki i udavy: proza poslednikh let. (Moscow: Knizhnaya palata, 1988). [Rabbits and Boa Constrictors. Prose of Recent Years]

Stoyanka cheloveka: povest', in *Znamya*, 7–9 (1989); repr. (Moscow: Molodaya gvardiya, 1990). [The Station of Man: A Novella]

Povesti, rasskazy (Moscow: Sovetskaya Rossiya, 1989). [Novellas, Stories]

Sandro iz Chegema: roman (Moscow: Moskovsky rabochy, 1989): repr. (Moscow: Sovetsky pisatel', 1991). [Sandro of Chegem: A Novel]

Sobraniye sochinenii v chetyryokh tomakh (Moscow: Molodaya gvardiya, 1991). [Collected Works in 4 vols.]

Kroliki i udavy: povesti (Moscow: Tekst, 1992). [Rabbits and Boa Constrictors: Novellas]

Chelovek i yego okrestnosti: roman, in *Znamya*, 2, 6, 11 (1992); repr. (Moscow: Olimp-PPP, 1993). [A Man and his Surroundings: A Novel]

Stikhotvoreniya (Moscow: Moskovsky rabochy, 1993). [Poems]

Pshada: povest', in *Znamya*, 8 (1993). [Pshada: A Novella]

Strashnaya mest' Chika, in *Znamya*, 2 (1994). [Chik's Terrible Revenge]

'Lastochkino gnezdo: rasskaz', in *Novy mir*, 1 (1994). [The Swallow's Nest: A Story]

Detstvo Chika: rasskazy (Moscow: Knizhny Sad, 1994). [Chik's Childhood: Stories]

Sofichka: povest', in *Znamya*, 11 (1995). [Sofichka: A Novella]

Stoyanka cheloveka: povesti i rasskazy (Moscow: SP Kvadrat, 1995). [The Station of Man: Novellas and Stories]

'Mimoza na severe. Rasskaz', in *Novy mir*, 3 (1996). [Mimosa in the North: A Story]

'Dva rasskaza: Chik chtit obychai; Zoloto Vil'gel'ma', in *Znamya*, 4 (1996). [Two Stories: Chik Respects Tradition; Vilhelm's Gold]

Sofichka: povesti i rasskazy (Moscow: Vagrius, 1997). [Sofichka: Novellas and Stories]

Sobraniye sochinenii v 6-ti tomakh (Khar'kov: Folio and Moscow: AST, 1997). [Collected Works in 6 vols.]

Poet. Povest', in *Novy mir*, 4 (1998). [The Poet: A Novella]

TRANSLATIONS INTO ENGLISH

Forbidden Fruit and Other Stories, trans. Robert Daglish (Moscow: Progress Publishers, 1972).

The Goatibex Constellation, trans. Helen Burlingame (Ann Arbor: Ardis, 1975).

The Thirteenth Labour of Hercules, trans. Robert Daglish (Moscow: Progress, 1978).

Sandro of Chegem, trans. Susan Brownsberger (New York: Vintage Books, 1983).

The Gospel According to Chegem: Being the Further Adventures of Sandro of Chegem, trans. Susan Brownsberger (New York: Vintage Books, 1984).

Chik and his Friends, trans. J. C. Butler (Moscow: Raduga Publishers, 1985).

Rabbits and Boa Constrictors, trans. Ronald E. Peterson (Ann Arbor: Ardis, 1989).

LYUDMILA PETRUSHEVSKAYA

WORKS IN RUSSIAN

'Dva rasskaza: Rasskazchitsa; Istoriya Klarissy', in *Avrora*, 7 (1972). [Two Stories: The Story-teller; Klarissa's Story]

'Rasskazy: Skripka; Manya', in *Druzhba narodov*, 10 (1973). [Stories: The Violin; Manya]

'Seti i lovushki', in *Avrora*, 4 (1974). [Nets and Snares]

Lyubov': odnoaktnaya p'esa, in *Teatr*, 3 (1979). [Love: A One-Act Play]

'Smotrovaya ploshchadka', in *Druzhba narodov*, 1 (1982). [The Lookout Point]

Tri devushki v golubom, in *Sovremennaya dramaturgiya*, 3 (1983); repr. (Moscow: Iskusstvo, 1989). [Three Girls in Blue]

'Cherez polya', in *Avrora*, 5 (1983). [Crossing the Field]

P'esy (Moscow: Sovetskaya Rossiya, 1983). [Plays by Viktor Slavkin and Lyudmila Petru-shevskaya]

'Slabyye kosti', in *Raduga*, 1 (1987). [Weak Bones]

'Elegiya', in *Chistyye prudy: Al'manakh* (Moscow: Moskovsky rabochy, 1987). [Elegy]

'Tri rasskaza: Yunost'; Udar groma; Milaya dama', in *Avrora*, 2 (1987). [Three Stories: Youth; A Clap of Thunder; That Delightful Young Lady]

'Svoi krug', in *Novy mir*, 1 (1988). [Our Circle]

Bessmertnaya lyubov': rasskazy (Moscow: Moskovsky rabochy, 1988). [Immortal Love: Stories]

Pesni XX veka: p'esy (Moscow: Soyuz teatral'nykh deyatelei RSFSR, 1988). [Songs of the Twentieth Century: Plays]

'Izolirovanny boks: Dialog', in *Novy mir*, 12 (1988). [The Isolation Box: A Dialogue]

'Novyye Robinzony (khronika kontsa XX veka)', in *Novy mir*, 8 (1989). [The New Robinsons: A Late Twentieth Century Chronicle]

'Pesni vostochnykh slavyan', in *Novy mir*, 8 (1990). [Songs of the Eastern Slavs]

Lecheniye Vasiliya i drugiye skazki (Moscow: Vsesoyuznoye tvorchesko-proizvodstvennoye ob"edineniye 'Kinotsentr', 1991). [Vasily's Treatment and Other Fairy Tales]

Vremya noch', in *Novy mir*, 2 (1992). [The Time: Night]

'V sadakh drugikh vozmozhnostei: rasskazy', in *Novy mir*, 2 (1993). [In the Gardens of Other Possibilities: Stories]

Po doroge boga Erosa: proza (Moscow: Olimp: PPP, 1993). [The Way of Eros: Prose]

'Nu, mama, nu: skazki, rasskazannyye detyam, in *Novy mir*, 2 (1993). [Go on, Mum, Go on: Fairy-Tales Told to Children]

'Skazki dlya vsei sem'i', in *Oktyabr'*, 1 (1993). [Fairy-Tales for the Whole Family]

'Karamzin: derevensky dnevnik', in *Novy mir*, 9 (1994). [Karamzin: A Country Diary]

Muzhskaya zona: kabare, in *Dramaturg*, 4 (1994). [The Male Zone: A Cabaret]

Taina doma: povesti i rasskazy (Moscow: SP Kvadrat, 1995). [The Secret of the House: Novellas and Stories]

Most Vaterloo: rasskazy, in *Novy mir*, 7 (1995). [Waterloo Bridge: Stories]

Malen'kaya volshebnitsa. Kukol'ny roman, in *Oktyabr'*, 8 (1995). [The Little Sorceress: A Puppet Romance]

'Prostyye i volshebnyye skazki', in *Oktyabr'*, 4 (1996). [Everyday and Magical Fairy-Tales]

Nepogibshaya zhizn'. Rasskazy' in *Oktyabr'*, 9 (1996). [Surviving Life: Stories]

'Dom devushek. Rasskazy iz tsikla "Rekviyema"', in *Znamya*, 11 (1996). [The Girls' House: Stories from the Cycle 'Requiem']

Bal poslednego cheloveka: povesti i rasskazy (Moscow: LOKID, 1996). [The Ball of the Last Man: Novellas and Stories]

Sobraniye sochinenii v pyati tomakh (Kharkov: Folio; Moscow: TKO AST, 1996). [Collected Works in 5 vols.]

Nastoyashchiye skazki (Moscow: Vagrius, 1997). [Real Fairy-Tales]

'Muzyka ada. Rasskaz', in *Znamya*, 3 (1997). [The Music of Hell: A Story]

'Priklyucheniya utyuga i sapoga. Skazochnaya povest'' in *Oktyabr'*, 1 (1998). [The Adventures of the Iron and the Boot: A Fairy-Tale Novella]

Malen'kaya Groznaya. Povest', in *Znamya*, 2 (1998). [Little Terrible: A Novella]

'Dva rasskaza: Nikogda; Nad'ka', in *Znamya*, 5 (1998). [Two Stories: Never; Nad'ka]

Dom devushek: Povesti i rasskazy (Moscow: Vagrius, 1998). [The Girls' House: Novellas and Stories]

TRANSLATIONS INTO ENGLISH

Cinzano: Eleven Plays, trans. Stephen Mulrine (London: Nick Hern, 1991).

The Time: Night, trans. Sally Laird (London: Virago; New York: Pantheon, 1994).

Immortal Love, trans. Sally Laird (London: Virago; New York: Pantheon, 1995).

VLADIMIR MAKANIN

WORKS IN RUSSIAN

Pryamaya liniya: roman, in *Moskva*, 8 (1965). [A Straight Line: A Novel]

Bezotsovshchina; Soldat i soldatka: povesti (Moscow: Sovetsky pisatel', 1971). [Orphanhood; A Soldier and a Soldier Woman: Novellas]

Povest' o starom poselke: povesti i rasskazy (Moscow: Sovetsky pisatel', 1974). [A Tale of the Old Settlement: Novellas and Stories]

Staryye knigi: povesti, rasskazy (Moscow: Sovetsky pisatel', 1976). [Old Books: Novellas, Stories]

Na pervom dykhanii (Moscow: Sovetsky pisatel', 1976). [At First Breath]

Portret i vokrug: roman (Moscow: Sovetsky pisatel', 1978). [A Portrait and its Surroundings: A Novel]

Klyucharyov i Alimushkin: roman, rasskazy (Moscow: Molodaya gvardiya, 1979). [Klyucharyov and Alimushkin: A Novel, Stories]

V bol'shom gorode: povesti (Moscow: Sovremennik, 1980). [In the Big City: Novellas]

Na zimnei doroge: povesti, rasskazy, roman (Moscow: Sovetsky pisatel', 1980). [On a Winter Road: Novellas, Stories]

'Chelovek "svity": rasskaz', in *Oktyabr'*, 3 (1982). [The 'Suite' Man: A Story]

Golosa: Povesti, rasskazy (Moscow: Sovetskaya Rossiya, 1982). [Voices: Novellas, Stories]

Predtecha: povest', in *Sever*, 3,4 (1982). [The Precursor: A Novella]

Predtecha: povesti (Moscow: Sovetsky pisatel', 1983). [The Precursor: Novellas]

Reka s bystrym techeniyem: povesti i rasskazy (Moscow: Moskovsky rabochy, 1983). [The Fast-Flowing River: Novellas and Stories]

Mesto pod solntsem: rasskazy (Moscow: Molodaya gvardiya, 1984). [A Place in the Sun: Stories]

Gde skhodilos' nebo s kholmami: povest', in *Novy mir*, 1 (1984). [Where the Sky Met the Hills]

Gde skhodilos' nebo s kholmami: povesti (Moscow: Sovremennik, 1984). [Where the Sky Met the Hills: Novellas]

Izbrannoye: rasskazy i povest' (Moscow: Sovetsky pisatel', 1987). [Selected Works: Stories and a Novella]

Utrata: povest', in *Novy mir*, 2 (1987). [Loss: A Novella]

Otstavshy: povest', in *Znamya*, 9 (1987). [The One Left Behind: A Novella]

Odin i odna: povest', in *Oktyabr'*, 2 (1988). [One and One: A Novella]

Otstavshy: povesti i rasskazy (Moscow: Khudozhestvennaya literatura, 1988). [The One Left Behind: Novellas and Stories]

Odin i odna: povesti (Moscow: Sovremennik: 1988). [One and One: Novellas]

Povesti (Moscow: Knizhnaya palata, 1988). [Novellas]

Predtecha: povesti (Moscow: Knizhnaya palata, 1988). [The Precursor: Novellas]

Utrata: povesti i rasskazy (Moscow: Molodaya gvardiya, 1989). [Loss: Novellas and Stories]

Rasskazy (Moscow: Sovremennik, 1990). [Stories]

Otdushina: povesti, roman (Moscow: Izvestiya, 1990). [The Safety Valve: Novellas, a Novel]

Dolog nash put': povest', in *Znamya,* 4 (1991). [Our Way is Long (also trans. as: The Long Road Ahead): A Novella]

Laz: povest', in *Novy mir,* 5 (1991). [The Manhole (also trans. as: The Escape Hatch): A Novella]

Laz: povesti i rasskazy (Moscow: SP IVO-SiD and Izdatel'stvo Renessans, 1991). [The Manhole: Novellas and Stories]

'Tam byla para ...: rasskaz', in *Novy mir,* 5 (1991). [There Was a Pair ...:A Story]

Syur v proletarskom raione: rasskazy, in *Novy mir,* 9 (1991). [A Surreal Incident in a Proletarian District: Stories]

Portret i vokrug; Odin i odna: romany (Moscow: Sovetsky pisatel', 1991). [A Portrait and its Surroundings; One and One: Novels]

'Syuzhet usredneniya', in *Znamya,* 1 (1992). [The Theme of Levelling]

Stol, pokryty suknom i s grafinom poseredine: povest', in *Znamya,* 1 (1993). [A Baize-Covered Table with a Decanter in the Middle: A Novella]

'Kvazi: rasskaz', in *Novy mir,* 7 (1993). [Quasi: A Story]

'Kavkazsky plenny: rasskaz', in *Novy mir,* 4 (1995). [A Captive of the Caucasus: A Story]

Kavkazsky plenny (Moscow: Panorama, 1997). [A Captive of the Caucasus]

Andergraund, ili Geroi nashego vremeni. Roman, in *Znamya,* 1–4 (1998). [Underground, or A Hero of Our Time: A Novel]

TRANSLATIONS INTO ENGLISH

'Klyucharyov and Alimushkin', trans. Arch Tait, in *Glas: New Russian Writing,* 4 (1993).

The Safety Valve, trans. Michael Falchikov, in *Glas: New Russian Writing,* 8 (1994).

'Those Who Did not Get Into the Choir' [Extract from *Voices*], trans. Michael Duncan, in Oleg Chukhontsev (ed.), *Leopard 1: Dissonant Voices: The New Russian Fiction* (London: Harvill, 1991).

'Captive of the Caucasus', trans. Arch Tait, in *Glas: New Russian Writing,* 11 (1996).

Escape Hatch and The Long Road Ahead: Two Novellas, trans. Mary Ann Szporluk (Ann Arbor: Ardis, 1996). [Alternative translation of titles: The Manhole and Our Way is Long]

Baize-Covered Table with Decanter, trans. Arch Tait (London: Readers International, 1995).

ANDREI BITOV

WORKS IN RUSSIAN

Bol'shoi shar (Moscow, 1963). [The Big Balloon]

Takoye dolgoye detstvo (Moscow and Leningrad: Sovetsky pisatel', 1965). [Such a Long Childhood]

Dachnaya mestnost': povesti (Moscow: Sovetskaya Rossiya, 1967). [Dacha District: Novellas]

Puteshestviye k drugu detstva (Leningrad, 1968). [Journey to a Childhood Friend]

Aptekarsky ostrov: rasskazy (Leningrad: Sovetsky pisatel', 1968). [Apothecary Island: Stories]

Obraz zhizni: povesti (Moscow: Molodaya gvardiya, 1972). [Way of Life: Novellas]

Tri puteshestviya (Moscow: 1974); repr. (New York: Orfei, 1986). [Three Journeys]

Dni cheloveka: povesti (Moscow: Molodaya gvardiya, 1976). [Days of Man: Novellas]

Sem' puteshestvii (Leningrad: Sovetsky pisatel', 1976). [Seven Journeys]

Pushkinsky dom (Ann Arbor: Ardis, 1978); repr. *Novy mir,* 10–12 (1987) and (Moscow: Sovremennik, 1989). [Pushkin House]

Uroki Armenii (Yerevan: Sovetakan grokh, 1978). [Lessons of Armenia]

Voskresny den': rasskazy, povesti, puteshestviya (Moscow: Sovetskaya Rossiya, 1980). [Sunday: Stories, Novellas, Journeys]

Gruzinsky al'bom (Tbilisi: Merani, 1985). [A Georgian Album]

Kniga puteshestvii (Moscow: Izvestiya, 1986). [The Book of Journeys]

Stat'i iz romana (Moscow: Sovetsky pisatel', 1986). [Articles from a Novel]

'Fotografiya Pushkina (1799–2099)', in *Znamya*, 1 (1987). [The Photograph of Pushkin (1799–2099)]

'Chelovek v peizazhe', in *Novy mir*, 3 (1987). [Man in a Landscape]

'Prepodavatel' simetrii. Vol'ny perevod s inostrannogo Andreya Bitova' [under the pseudonym E. Taird Boffin], in *Yunost'*, 4 (1987). [The Teacher of Symmetry: A Free Translation from the Foreign Andrei Bitov]

Chelovek v peizazhe: povesti i rasskazy (Moscow: Sovetsky pisatel', 1988). [Man in a Landscape: Novellas and Stories]

Povesti i rasskazy: izbrannoye (Moscow: Sovetskaya Rossiya, 1989). [Selected Novellas and Stories]

Uletayushchy Monakhov: roman-punktir (Moscow: Molodaya gvardiya, 1990). [Vanishing Monakhov: A Novel with Ellipses]

Zapiski iz-za ugla, in *Novy mir*, 2 (1990). [Notes from the Corner]

My prosnulis' v neznakomoi strane: publitsistika (Leningrad: Sovetsky pisatel', 1991). [We Have Awoken in an Unknown Country: Articles]

Zhizn' v vetrenuyu pogodu (Leningrad: Khudozhestvennaya literatura, 1991). [Life in Windy Weather]

Sobraniye sochinenii v tryokh tomakh (Moscow: Molodaya gvardiya, 1991–). [Collected Works in Three Volumes]

Na rannikh tsiklakh: rasskazy, kollazhi, in *Kontinent*, 73 (1992). [Early Cycles]

Vychitaniye zaitsa (Moscow: Olimp-PPP-Bagazh, 1993). [Subtracting the Hare]

'Ozhidaniye obez'yan', in *Novy Mir*, 10 (1993). [Waiting for the Monkeys]

Nachatki astrologii russkoi literatury (Moscow: Mezhdunarodnaya assotsiatsiya 'Mir kultury: Fortuna-Limited', 1994). [Elements of an Astrology of Russian Literature]

Oglashennyye: Roman-stranstviye (Moscow: Konsort 'Bagazh', 'Drugiye berega'; St Petersburg: Izdatel'stvo Ivana Limbakha, 1995). [The Possessed: A Travel Novel (also trans. as The Monkey Link)]

'Bez yazyka. Teksty, prislannyye iz Germanii', in *Zvezda*, 6 (1995). [Without Language: Texts sent from Germany]

Pervaya kniga avtora: Aptekarsky prospekt, 6 (St Petersburg: Izdatel'stvo Ivana Limbakha, 1996). [The Author's First Book: 6, Apothecary Avenue]

'Zhizn' bez nas. Stikhoproza', in *Novy mir*, 9 (1996). [Life without Us: Poetic Prose]

Imperiya v chetyryokh izmereniyakh (Kharkov: Folio; Moscow: TKO AST, 1996. [An Empire in Four Dimensions]

Zapiski novichka (Moscow: Lokid, 1997). [Notes of a Novice]

V chetverg posle dozhdya: Dnevnik prozaika (St Petersburg: Pushkinsky Fond, 1997). [On Thursday after the Rain: The Diary of a Prose Writer]

Derevo 1971–1997 (St Petersburg: Pushkinsky fond, 1998). [The Tree 1971–1997]

Obosnovannaya revnost': povesti (Moscow: Panorama, 1988). [Justified Jealousy: Novellas]

TRANSLATIONS INTO ENGLISH

Life in Windy Weather: Short Stories, ed. Priscilla Meyer (Ann Arbor: Ardis, 1986).

Pushkin House, trans. Susan Brownsberger (New York: Farrar, Straus & Giroux, 1992).

Ten Short Stories, ed. E. K. Nesterova (Moscow: Raduga Publishers, 1991).

A Captive of the Caucasus, trans. Susan Brownsberger (New York: Farrar, Straus & Giroux, 1992).

The Monkey Link, trans. Susan Brownsberger (New York: Farrar, Straus & Giroux, 1995). [Translation of Oglashennyye: roman-stranstviye]

TATYANA TOLSTAYA

WORKS IN RUSSIAN

' "Na zolotom kryl'tse sideli" ', in *Avrora*, 8 (1983). [On the Golden Porch]

'Svidaniye s ptitsei', in *Oktyabr'*, 12 (1983). [Meeting with a Bird]

'Sonya', in *Avrora*, 10 (1984). [Sonya]

'Chisty list', in *Neva*, 12 (1984). [A Clean Page]

'Milaya Shura', 'Okhota na mamonta', in *Oktyabr'*, 12 (1985). [Dear Shura; Hunting the Mammoth]

'Reka Okkervil'', in *Avrora*, 4 (1986). [Okkerville River]

'Peters', in *Novy mir*, 1 (1986). [Peters]

'Spi spokoino, synok', in *Avrora*, 4 (1986). [Sleep Tight, Little Son]

'Ogon' i pyl'', 'Samaya lyubimaya', in *Avrora*, 10 (1986). [Fire and Dust; Most Beloved]

'Poet i muza', 'Serafim', 'Fakir', in *Novy mir*, 12 (1986). [Poet and Muse; Serafim; Fakir]

'Lyubish'—ne lyubish'', 'Noch'', 'Krug', in *Oktyabr'*, 4 (1987). [Love Me, Love Me Not; Night; Circle]

'Vyshel mesyats iz tumana', in *Krest'yanka*, 4 (1987). [The Moon Came Out]

'Plamen' nebesny', in *Avrora*, 11 (1987). [Heavenly Flame]

'Na zolotom kryl'tse sideli': rasskazy (Moscow: Molodaya gvardiya, 1987). [On the Golden Porch: Stories]

'Somnambula v tumane', in *Novy mir*, 7 (1988). [Sleepwalker in a Fog]

'Limpopo', in *Znamya*, 11 (1991) and *Sintaksis*, 27, 1990. [Limpopo]

'Syuzhet', in *Sintaksis*, 31 (1991). [Subject]

Tri rasskaza (Three Stories), ed. with introduction, bibliography, notes, and vocabulary by S. Dalton Brown (Bristol Classical Press, 1996). [Texts in Russian]

Lyubish'—ne lyubish' (Moscow: OLMA Press, 1997). [Love Me, Love Me Not]

Sestry: sbornik (Moscow: Podkova, 1998). [Sisters: A Collection. Co-authored with Natal'ya Tolstaya]

TRANSLATIONS INTO ENGLISH

On the Golden Porch, trans. Antonina W. Bouis (New York: Knopf; London: Virago, 1989).

Sleepwalker in a Fog, trans. Jamey Gambrell (New York: Knopf; London: Virago, 1992).

YEVGENY POPOV

WORKS IN RUSSIAN

'Rasskazy', in *Novy mir*, 4 (1976). [Stories]

'Rasskazy', in *Druzhba narodov*, 3 (1977). [Stories]

'Chortova dyuzhina', in *Metropol'* (Ann Arbor, 1979). [A Devil's Dozen]

Veseliye Rusi (Ann Arbor: Ardis, 1981). [Merry-Making in Old Russia]

'Rasskazy', in *Znamya*, 5 (1987). [Stories]

'Rasskazy', in *Novy mir*, 10 (1987). [Stories]

'Rasskazy; p'esa *Avtovokzal'*, in *Volga*, 10 (1988). [Stories; Bus Station: A Play]

'Billi Bons: peizazh i zhanr', in *Vest'* (Moscow: Knizhnaya palata, 1989). [Billy Bones: Landscape and Genre Painting]

Zhdu lyubvi neverolomnoi: rasskazy (Moscow: Sovetsky pisatel', 1989). [I Await a Love That's True: Stories]

'Rasskazy', in *Novy mir*, 10 (1989). [Stories]

Prekrasnost' zhizni: glavy iz 'romana s gazetoi', kotory nikogda ne budet nachat i zakonchen (Moscow: Moskovsky rabochy, 1990). [The Splendour of Life: Chapters from a 'Romance with a Newspaper', Which Will Never Be Begun and Finished]

'Rasskazy', in *Volga*, 3 (1990). [Stories]

'Granatovy braslet', in *Kontinent*, 63 (1990). [The Garnet Bracelet]

'Shutsin-Putsin: rasskaz', in *Kontinent*, 66 (1991). [Shutsin-Putsin: A Story]

Restoran Beryozka: Poema i rasskazy o kommunistakh, in *Znamya*, 3 (1991). [The 'Beryozka' Restaurant: Poems and Stories about Communists]

'Kholoda', in *Volga*, 3 (1991). [The Cold]

Samolyot na Kyol'n: rasskazy (Moscow: Orbita, 1991). [Aeroplane to Cologne: Stories]

Nakanune nakanune, in *Volga*, 4 (1993); repr. (Moscow: Tekst, 1993). [On the Eve of On the Eve]

'Magazin 'Svet', ili Sumerki bogov. Rukopis', naidennaya v tret'em mikroraione', in *Druzhba narodov*, 4 (1993). [The 'Light' Shop, or The Twilight of the Gods. A Manuscript Found in the Third Mini-District]

Dusha patriota, ili, Razlichnyye poslaniya k Ferfichkinu: roman (Moscow: Tekst, 1994). [The Soul of a Patriot, or, Various Epistles to Ferfichkin: a Novel]

'Loskutnoye odeyalo. Rasskaz-entsiklopediya', in *Kontinent*, 83 (1995). [The Patchwork Quilt. A Story-Encyclopaedia]

TRANSLATIONS INTO ENGLISH

Merry-Making in Old Russia, trans. Robert Porter (London: Harvill, 1996).

The Soul of a Patriot, or, Various Epistles to Ferfichkin, trans. Robert Porter (Evanston, Ill: Northwestern University Press; London: Harvill, 1994).

VLADIMIR SOROKIN

WORKS IN RUSSIAN

Ochered': roman (Paris: Sintaksis, 1985). [The Queue: a Novel]

Vladimir Sorokin: sbornik rasskazov (Moscow: Russlit, 1992). [Vladimir Sorokin: A Collection of Stories]

Mesyats v Dakhau: Poema v proze (Germany: Igor Zakharov-Ross, 1992). [A Month in Dachau: a Poem in Prose]

Mesyats v Dakhau: Poema v proze, in *Segodnya* (22 Jan. 1994). [A Month in Dachau, shortened version]

Norma (Moscow: Obscuri viri: Izdatel'stvo Tri Kita, 1994). [Norma]

Roman (Moscow: Obscuri viri: Izdatel'stvo Tri Kita, 1994). [Roman]

Serdtsa chetyryokh, in *Konets veka*, 5 (1994). [The Hearts of the Four (also trans. as: Four Stout Hearts)]

Tridtsataya lyubov' Mariny (Moscow: Izdatel'stvo R. Elinina, 1995). [The Thirtieth Love of Marina]

Sobraniye sochinenii v 2-kh tomakh (Moscow: Ad marginem, 1998). [Collected Works in 2 vols.]

TRANSLATIONS INTO ENGLISH

The Queue, trans. Sally Laird (London/New York: Readers International, 1988).

'A Business Proposition' ['Delovoye predlozheniye'], and *Four Stout Hearts* [an excerpt from the novel *Serdtsa chetyryokh*], trans. Jamey Gambrell, in *Glas: New Russian Writing*, 2 (1991).

A Month in Dachau (trans. Jamey Gambrell), in *Grand Street*, 48 (1994).

ZUFAR GAREYEV

WORKS IN RUSSIAN

'Kogda krichat chuzhiye ptitsy: rasskaz', in *Novy mir*, 12 (1989). [When Other Birds Cry: A Story]

'Kanikuly: rasskaz', in *Novy mir*, 8 (1990). [Holidays: A Story]

Allergiya Aleksandra Petrovicha: povest', in *Volga*, 4 (1991). [The Allergy of Aleksandr Petrovich: a Novella]

Park, in *Kontinent*, 64 (1991). [Park]

Stereoskopicheskiye slavyane, in *Solo*, 4 (1991). [Stereoscopic Slavs]

'Podrazhaniye letu', in *Solo*, 4 (1991). [Facsimile Summer]

Multiproza, in *Solo*, 4 (1991). [Multiprose]

Multiproza: povesti (Moscow: Ob"edineniye 'Vsesoyuzny molodyozhny knizhny tsentr', redaktsiya 'Stil'', 1992). [Multiprose. Novellas]

Kholodnaya gost'ya serebristogo vetra: p'esa, in *Volga*, 9–10 (1992). [The Cold Guest of the Silvery Wind: A Play]

'Oznob: rasskaz', in *Znamya*, 8 (1993). [Fever: A Story]

'Osen' BE-U: rasskaz', in *Znamya*, 9 (1994). [Second-Hand Autumn: A Story]

TRANSLATIONS INTO ENGLISH

'When Other Birds Call' ('Kogda krichat chuzhiye ptitsy'), trans. Rachel Osorio, in *Glas: New Russian Writing*, 1 (1991).

'Facsimile Summer' ('Podrazhaniye letu'), trans. Arch Tait, in *Glas: New Russian Writing*, 4 (1993).

'Second-Hand Autumn' ('Osen' BE-U'), trans. Arch Tait, in *Index on Censorship*, 1 (1995).

VIKTOR PELEVIN

WORKS IN RUSSIAN

Siny fonar' (Moscow: Tekst, 1991). [The Blue Lantern]

Omon Ra: povest', in *Znamya*, 5 (1992); repr. (Moscow: Tekst, 1993). [Omon Ra]

'Buben verkhnego mira: rasskaz', in *Oktyabr'*, 2 (1993). [The Tambourine of the Upper World: A Story]

Zhizn' nasekomykh: roman, in *Znamya*, 4 (1993); repr. (Moscow: Vagrius, 1997). [The Life of Insects: A Novel]

Zholtaya strela: povest', in *Novy mir*, 7 (1993). [The Yellow Arrow]

Chapayev i Pustota: roman, in *Znamya*, 4,5 (1996); repr. (Moscow: Vagrius, 1996). [Chapayev and Emptiness: A Novel]

Zholtaya strela: Povesti i rasskazy (Moscow: Vagrius, 1998). [The Yellow Arrow: Novellas and Stories]

TRANSLATIONS INTO ENGLISH

'The Blue Lantern'; 'Mid-game'; 'The View from the Window', trans. Andrew Bromfield, in *Glas: New Russian Writing*, 4 (1993).

Omon Ra: with the novella The Yellow Arrow, trans. Andrew Bromfield (London: Harbord, 1994).

Omon Ra, trans. Andrew Bromfield (New York: Farrar, Straus & Giroux, 1996).

The Yellow Arrow, trans. Andrew Bromfield (New York: New Directions, 1996).

The Life of Insects, trans. Andrew Bromfield (London: Harbord, 1996; New York: Farrar, Straus & Giroux, 1998).

IGOR POMERANTSEV

WORKS IN RUSSIAN

Chitaya Folknera; 'Starik i drugiye', in *Sintaksis*, 5 (1979). [Reading Faulkner; The Old Man and Others]

'Oko i sleza', in *Sintaksis*, 4 (1979). [The Eye and the Tear]

'Monolog', in *Vremya i my*, 63 (1981). [Monologue]

Kratky razgovornik dlya priyezzhikh, in *Kovcheg*, 6 (1981). [Concise Phrasebook for New Arrivals]

'Ot avtora: stikhi', in *Dvadtsats' dva*, 36 (1984). [From the Author: Poems]

Vy menya slyshite?, in *Vremya i my*, 87 (1985). [Can You Hear Me?]

Al'by i serenady (London: R.R. Press, 1985). [Aubades and Serenades]

'Mit Blumen auch Schön', in *Sintaksis*, 15 (1986).

'Vskhlipy po uglam', in *Sintaksis*, 24 (1988). [Sobs in Corners]

'Chto yeshcho delat' s zhenshchinoi v lifte i drugiye rasskazy', in *Sintaksis*, 22 (1988). [What Else to Do with a Woman in a Lift and Other Stories]

'Pamyati Polyashchishki', in *Sintaksis*, 25 (1989). [Memories of a Little Pole]

'Russkiye zavetnyye skazki', in *Sintaksis*, 27 (1990). [Secret Russian Tales]

Otdykh na yuge, in *Sintaksis*, 28 (1990). [Holiday in the South]

Baskskaya sobaka, in *Sintaksis*, 31 (1991). [The Hound of the Basques]

'Ot avtora (iz yashchika 70-kh)', in *Znamya*, 5 (1991). [From the Author (from a Box from the Seventies)]

'Putevoditel' po formam i poverkhnostyam', in *Oktyabr'*, 4 (1993). [Guide to Forms and Surfaces]

Stikhi raznykh dnei (St Petersburg: Sovetsky pisatel', 1993). [Verses of Various Days]

'Muzei angliiskogo detstva, ili nenavizhu syna', in *Oktyabr'*, 2 (1994). [The Museum of English Childhood, or I Hate my Son]

'Dva stikhotvoreniya', in *Oktyabr'*, 11 (1994). [Two Poems]

'Opasnaya vstrecha s samim soboi', in *Oktyabr'*, 8 (1995). [A Dangerous Meeting with Myself]

Predmety roskoshi: belles-lettres: kniga prozy (St Petersburg: Inapress, 1995). [Luxury Items: Belles-Lettres: a Book of Prose]

'Bezzashchitnaya reaktsiya: stikhi', in *Druzhba narodov*, 8 (1996). [Non-Defence Mechanism: Poems]

Po shkale Boforta (St Petersburg: Izdatel'stvo Urbi, 1997). [On the Beaufort Scale]

News: stikhi, proza (Kiev: Fakt, 1998). [News: Poems, Prose]

TRANSLATIONS INTO ENGLISH

'With a Bouquet of Roses', trans. Frank Williams, in *Fiction Magazine*, 10 (1986).

'The Eye and the Tear', trans. Elizabeth Winter, in *Survey*, 3 (1979).

'Poems', trans. Sally Laird, in *Edinburgh Review*, 1 (1981).

'From a Diary', trans. Frank Williams, in *2+2: Collection of International Writing* (Lucerne: Mylabris Press, 1986).

'Aubades and Serenades', trans. Frank Williams, in *Stand* (Spring 1987).

'Lost in a Strange City', trans. Elizabeth Winter, in the *Times Literary Supplement* (26 June 1987). [Original title: 'Mezhdu pytkami']

'Poems', in *Skoob Review* (1989).

'My Motherland is Solitude', trans. Frank Williams, in *Stand* (Winter 1987/8).

'Sobs in Corners'; 'A Little about You, Yosip', trans. Frank Williams, in *Glas: New Russian Writing*, 6 (1993).

'Reading Faulkner', trans. Frank Williams, in the *Prague Revue* (Autumn/Winter 1996–7).

INDEX